Digital Transformation in Welfare Systems:

Data, Technologies, and Emerging Social Challenges

Gabriella Punziano
https://orcid.org/0000-0001-8783-2712
University of Naples Federico II, Italy

Domenico Trezza
https://orcid.org/0009-0003-0238-4458
University Pegaso, Italy

Giuseppe Luca De Luca Picione
University of Naples Federico II, Italy

IGI Global
Scientific Publishing
Publishing Tomorrow's Research Today

Vice President of Editorial Melissa Wagner
Director of Acquisitions Mikaela Felty
Director of Book Development Jocelynn Hessler
Production Manager Mike Brehm
Cover Design Jose Rosado

Published in the United States of America by
IGI Global Scientific Publishing
701 East Chocolate Avenue
Hershey, PA, 17033, USA
Tel: 717-533-8845 | Fax: 717-533-7115
Website: https://www.igi-global.com E-mail: cust@igi-global.com

Library of Congress Cataloging-in-Publication Data

Names: Punziano, Gabriella editor | Trezza, Domenico, 1986- editor | De Luca Picione, Giuseppe Luca editor
Title: Digital transformation in welfare systems : data, technologies, and emerging social challenges / edited by: Gabriella Punziano, Domenico Trezza, Giuseppe Luca De Luca Picione.
Description: Hershey PA : IGI Global Scientific Publishing, [2027] | Includes bibliographical references. | Summary: "By bridging perspectives from sociology, public policy, digital governance, and computational social science, this book unpacks the epistemic and ethical dilemmas of a welfare state that increasingly operates through platforms, algorithms, and data flows"-- Provided by publisher.
Identifiers: LCCN 2026005288 (print) | LCCN 2026005289 (ebook) | ISBN 9798337384238 hardcover | ISBN 9798337394350 paperback | ISBN 9798337394367 ebook
Subjects: LCSH: Public welfare--Data processing | Public administration--Data processing | Public administration--Automation
Classification: LCC HV29.2 .D54 2026 (print) | LCC HV29.2 (ebook)
LC record available at https://lccn.loc.gov/2026005288
LC ebook record available at https://lccn.loc.gov/2026005289
British Cataloguing in Publication Data
A Cataloguing in Publication record for this book is available from the British Library.

Table of Contents

Detailed Table of Contents

The present systematic review questions the digital transformation of Day to questions. The scope of the questionnaire focuses on artificial intelligence and data-driven technologies as a source of changes in the ways of welfare delivery, governance, and social equity of the welfare system. The results of the synthesis of 83 studies published during 2019 to 2025 have shown that digital technologies can increase efficiency and focus but have a high level of uneven maturity and few long-term evidences. Some of the recurrent issues include the gap in governance, computer biasness, the lack of cyberspace inclusiveness, and the lack of citizen participation. The research highlights the need to have inclusive, ethical, and humanistic governance of digital welfare.

This chapter looks at the ethics of automation in welfare governance, with reference to opportunities and risks posed by AI-based policy delivery. It discusses the ways in which the concept of algorithmic decision-making collides with the fundamental values of a modern system of public administration, including equality, procedural justice, and democratic responsibility. The chapter identifies the significance of transparent and human-oriented AI frameworks to secure trust in the population

explainability, and power imbalances. It argues that robust data governance frameworks are vital for public trust, social justice, and fairness in digital welfare systems.

With the increasing use of AI and data platforms to inform welfare systems, accountability, transparency, and inclusion have been brought to the forefront rather than the background. While data-supported welfare systems offer predictive capabilities and efficiencies through the use of algorithms, they run the risk of perpetuating societal inequities by failing to make clear how decisions are reached or how those decisions impact groups already disenfranchised within society through digital service delivery. This chapter offers a critical examination of the shift from algorithmic welfare—such as automated risk assessment and surveillance—towards participatory data justice. The chapter discusses how the digitization of complex organisations reshapes welfare governance, produces new forms of exclusion, and can also be mobilized to equip citizens with tools for meaningful engagement and ethical innovation.

This article examines the relationship between social participation and artificial intelligence within the context of welfare policies, highlighting how digital transformations have redefined the modalities of collective action. Starting from the classical concept of participation as active involvement in public life, the paper shows how the emergence of digital platforms and algorithmic systems has led to new forms of e-participation, characterized by an increasing hybridization between online and offline dimensions. In this scenario, artificial intelligence is not merely a supporting tool but an epistemic actor capable of influencing knowledge production, the construction of public opinion, and decision-making processes. The article also highlights the ambivalent nature of these dynamics: on the one hand, AI expands opportunities for inclusion and democratic participation; on the other, it introduces risks related to opacity, misinformation, and digital inequalities.

The chapter addresses the following research question: how do digital data infrastructures shape the evaluative capacities of social services? Drawing on a comparative document analysis of data infrastructures in Italy and Norway, the chapter investigates how different approaches to data digitalisation can shape the governance, integration, and use of social services information systems. By foregrounding infrastructural design and governance functions, the analysis contributes to the debate on digital welfare governance, evaluative capacity, and the conditions under which administrative data infrastructures can enable more reflexive, evidence-informed, and adaptive social service systems. The chapter provides an empirically grounded understanding of evaluation infrastructures as differentiated systems of data availability and use. The findings show how data infrastructures do not merely support evaluation but actively shape what becomes visible and evaluable in social services.

This chapter examines the integration of digital traces into welfare research from a methodological and epistemological perspective grounded in survey methodology. It argues that, although digitally generated data are analytically rich, they are insufficient for producing high-quality welfare evidence when detached from explicit research designs, as they lack defined reference populations, observable selection mechanisms, and contextual information. The chapter proposes Online Probability Panels as a methodological solution, conceptualised as research infrastructures that anchor digital traces within probability-based sampling and longitudinal designs. By linking digital data to inclusion probabilities, socio-demographic characteristics, and repeated observations, these infrastructures enable population inference, assessment of selection bias, and modelling of uncertainty. The chapter shows that high-quality data science for welfare governance depends on integrating digital traces within infrastructures that ensure interpretability, transparency, and methodological robustness.

Foreword

Digital transformation has become one of the most powerful forces reshaping welfare systems around the world. Public institutions increasingly rely on data infrastructures, platforms, artificial intelligence, automated procedures, and digital interfaces to organize access to services, allocate resources, monitor needs, and evaluate outcomes. These changes promise efficiency, integration, and responsiveness. Yet they also raise difficult questions about inequality, accountability, rights, trust, professional discretion, and democratic governance.

This volume, *Digital Transformation in Welfare Systems: Data, Technologies, and Emerging Social Challenges*, arrives at a crucial moment. It provides a timely and much-needed contribution to understanding how welfare systems are being reconfigured by digital technologies and data-driven governance. Its strength lies in the breadth of its perspectives and in its refusal to treat digital transformation as a purely technical process. Instead, the volume shows that digital welfare is a deeply social and political phenomenon, involving institutions, professionals, citizens, data infrastructures, ethical choices, and competing visions of social justice.

The chapters collected here cover a wide range of issues: artificial intelligence in welfare governance, digital health, administrative data infrastructures, digital exclusion, platform-mediated welfare communication, algorithmic inclusion, social services evaluation, gender-based violence, Third Sector data governance, homelessness, digital citizenship, and the transformation of public service delivery. This diversity is one of the volume's major strengths. It allows readers to understand digital welfare not as a narrow policy field but as a broad and evolving ecosystem in which technological innovation interacts with social inequalities, institutional arrangements, and democratic expectations.

Particularly valuable is the attention given to ambivalence. The book does not simply celebrate digital innovation, nor does it reject it. It asks under what conditions digital technologies can enhance welfare systems and under what conditions they may deepen exclusion, opacity, surveillance, or dependency. This balanced approach makes the volume relevant for scholars, policymakers, practitioners, and students interested in the future of welfare in datafied societies.

The volume also contributes to the development of a more mature language for discussing digital welfare. Concepts such as algorithmic inclusion, stacked exclusion, administrative entrapment, digital health citizenship, participatory data justice, data asymmetry, and epistemic visibility provide readers with analytical tools to interpret complex transformations that are already affecting social rights and public services.

For these reasons, this book represents an important contribution to contemporary debates on welfare, digital governance, and social justice. It will be of great interest to anyone seeking to understand how data and technologies are changing welfare systems and how these changes can be governed in more inclusive, accountable, and democratic ways.

Enrica Amaturo
University of Naples, Italy

Preface

INTRODUCTION

The digital transformation of welfare systems represents one of the most profound institutional shifts of the twenty-first century. Advances in artificial intelligence, big data analytics, digital platforms, and interoperable information infrastructures are reshaping how governments and public institutions design, deliver, evaluate, and govern welfare policies. These technologies offer unprecedented opportunities to improve administrative efficiency, strengthen evidence-based decision-making, personalize service delivery, and expand access to social protection. At the same time, they challenge long-standing assumptions about public accountability, democratic governance, privacy, transparency, and the protection of social rights. As welfare systems increasingly become data-intensive environments, understanding the implications of this transformation has become an urgent scholarly and policy priority.

As editors, we believe that digital innovation should not be understood merely as a technological process but as a social and institutional transformation that reshapes relationships among governments, citizens, communities, and civil society organizations. Digital welfare is ultimately about people: the ways in which technologies mediate access to rights, influence public participation, redefine administrative discretion, and produce new forms of visibility and exclusion. While algorithmic systems promise greater precision and responsiveness, they may also reproduce existing inequalities, reinforce biases, and marginalize vulnerable populations if they are not developed within robust ethical, legal, and democratic frameworks. Consequently, the future of digital welfare depends not only on technological sophistication but also on inclusive governance, participatory design, and sustained institutional accountability.

This volume brings together scholars from sociology, public administration, social policy, information science, law, governance studies, and digital research methodologies to explore the opportunities and complexities associated with the digital transformation of welfare systems. The contributions assembled in this book examine welfare governance from multiple perspectives, ranging from artificial intelligence and algorithmic decision-making to participatory data justice, digital infrastructures, methodological innovation, and public trust. Together, these chapters provide a comprehensive examination of how digital technologies are redefining welfare institutions while identifying pathways toward more equitable, transparent, and resilient systems capable of responding to emerging social challenges.

CHAPTER OVERVIEW

Chapter 1 establishes the conceptual foundation for the volume by examining the digital transformation of welfare systems through the lenses of data, artificial intelligence, and governance. Drawing upon a systematic review of recent scholarship, the chapter identifies both the opportunities and the structural challenges associated with digital welfare, emphasizing the importance of ethical governance, citizen participation, and social inclusion.

Chapter 2 explores the ethical dimensions of artificial intelligence in welfare governance and policy implementation. It discusses how algorithmic decision-making intersects with principles of procedural justice, democratic accountability, and public trust while proposing governance models that balance technological innovation with social responsibility.

Chapter 3 presents an institutional analysis of AI integration within the Italian welfare system. Through the examination of national initiatives and administrative reforms, the chapter argues that successful algorithmic integration depends upon institutional design, protected administrative discretion, meaningful transparency, and rights-based oversight rather than technological adoption alone.

Chapter 4 focuses on digital data governance as a cornerstone of contemporary welfare administration. The authors investigate issues of transparency, accountability, regulatory oversight, data privacy, and algorithmic explainability, demonstrating that effective governance frameworks are essential for maintaining public confidence and safeguarding social justice.

Chapter 5 critically examines the transition from algorithmic welfare toward participatory data justice. The chapter highlights how digital welfare systems can either reinforce structural inequalities or empower citizens through greater transparency, meaningful participation, and ethical approaches to data governance.

Chapter 6 investigates the evolving relationship between welfare policy, digital innovation, and civic participation. By positioning artificial intelligence as an epistemic actor within democratic processes, the chapter explores both the opportunities and the risks associated with digitally mediated public engagement and collective decision-making.

Chapter 7 offers a comparative analysis of digital data infrastructures supporting social service evaluation in Italy and Norway. The chapter demonstrates that data infrastructures do more than facilitate administrative functions; they actively shape evaluative capacity, evidence generation, and institutional learning within welfare systems.

Chapter 8 advances the methodological foundations of digital welfare research by examining Online Probability Panels as research infrastructures capable of integrating digital traces with rigorous survey methodologies. The chapter emphasizes methodological transparency, representativeness, and interpretability as essential conditions for producing reliable evidence in digital welfare governance.

Chapter 9 turns attention to the Third Sector and examines how fragmented and incomplete data infrastructures contribute to institutional invisibility and policy marginalization. The chapter proposes a conceptual framework for strengthening digital governance, interoperability, and evidence-based policymaking across nonprofit and civil society organizations.

Chapter 10 investigates homelessness and extreme poverty in metropolitan Rome through an integrated analytical framework combining administrative data, social network analysis, surveys, and qualitative research. The findings demonstrate how digital welfare infrastructures can strengthen multilevel governance, improve organizational coordination, and support more effective interventions for vulnerable populations.

Chapter 11 concludes the volume by examining public perceptions of artificial intelligence within European welfare systems. Drawing upon comparative survey data, the chapter analyzes how technological optimism, concerns about automation, institutional trust, and digital literacy shape the social legitimacy of AI-enabled welfare governance across different national contexts.

CONCLUSION

The contributions presented in this volume collectively demonstrate that the digital transformation of welfare systems is fundamentally reshaping the institutions responsible for promoting social protection, equity, and public well-being. While artificial intelligence, digital infrastructures, and data-driven governance offer remarkable opportunities to improve efficiency and responsiveness, they also redefine how social rights are administered, how citizens engage with public institutions, and how decisions affecting vulnerable populations are made. These transformations require careful attention not only to technological innovation but also to the broader institutional and democratic contexts within which digital welfare evolves.

A central message emerging throughout this collection is that trustworthy digital welfare depends upon the quality of governance rather than technology alone. Transparency, accountability, participatory approaches, methodological rigor, ethical oversight, and institutional capacity emerge repeatedly as the essential foundations upon which sustainable digital welfare systems must be built. Whether examining algorithmic decision-making, data infrastructures, public participation, or methodological innovation, the chapters collectively emphasize that digital transformation should strengthen rather than diminish social justice, democratic legitimacy, and citizens' trust in public institutions.

As editors, we hope that Digital Transformation in Welfare Systems: Data, Technologies, and Emerging Social Challenges contributes to ongoing international debates surrounding the future of welfare governance in increasingly digital societies. We further hope that this volume serves as a valuable resource for researchers, policymakers, practitioners, and students seeking to understand both the opportunities and the responsibilities associated with digital innovation in public welfare. By bringing together interdisciplinary perspectives and empirically grounded analyses, this collection aims to foster thoughtful dialogue and inspire future research that advances inclusive, transparent, and human-centered welfare systems for the digital age.

Editors

Gabriella Punziano
University of Naples Federico II, Italy

Domenico Trezza
University Pegaso, Italy

Giuseppe Luca De Luca Picione
University of Naples Federico II, Italy

Acknowledgment

The editors wish to express their sincere gratitude to all the authors who contributed to this volume. Their research, critical reflections, empirical analyses, and theoretical insights made it possible to build a rich and interdisciplinary discussion on the digital transformation of welfare systems.

We are also grateful to the reviewers and academic colleagues whose comments, suggestions, and expertise supported the development and refinement of the chapters. Their contribution was essential in strengthening the scientific quality, coherence, and relevance of the book. Specifically, in this volume we have employed a system of anonymous peer review amongst the authors in order to ensure a high level of consistency and coherence across all the submitted chapters. We would therefore like to express our double gratitude for the tremendous effort shown in maintaining critical consistency and for the spirit of teamwork.

Special thanks are due to IGI Global and to the editorial team for their professional guidance and support throughout the publication process. Their assistance was invaluable in coordinating the different phases of the project and bringing this collective work to completion.

Finally, we would like to acknowledge the broader scholarly and professional communities working on welfare, digital transformation, social policy, public administration, data governance, and social justice. This volume is part of an ongoing collective effort to understand how digital technologies are reshaping welfare systems and how such transformations can be oriented toward inclusion, accountability, and democratic responsibility.

Chapter 1
Welfare Systems, Data, and Analysis: Digital Transformation and Social Challenge

D. V. Lokeshwari
http://orcid.org/0000-0002-6112-3173
Dayanand Sagar College of Arts, Science, and Commerce, India

ABSTRACT

The present systematic review questions the digital transformation of Day to questions. The scope of the questionnaire focuses on artificial intelligence and data-driven technologies as a source of changes in the ways of welfare delivery, governance, and social equity of the welfare system. The results of the synthesis of 83 studies published during 2019 to 2025 have shown that digital technologies can increase efficiency and focus but have a high level of uneven maturity and few long-term evidences. Some of the recurrent issues include the gap in governance, computer biasness, the lack of cyberspace inclusiveness, and the lack of citizen participation. The research highlights the need to have inclusive, ethical, and humanistic governance of digital welfare.

INTRODUCTION

Digital transformation has gained relevance as a prominent feature of the new welfare system that essentially transforms how the social protection is managed, accessed, and governed. In recent years, administrative efficiency, targeting more precisely, and personalisation of service delivery have also become goals of incorporating artificial intelligence (AI), big data analytics, and automated decision-making

DOI: 10.4018/979-8-3373-8423-8.ch001

processes in welfare states in various institutional settings (Allhutter et al., 2024; Alexopoulou, 2025). All of these are signs that a structural change has taken place in the context of a traditional bureaucratic welfare administration to data-based and algorithmically mediated forms of governance (Kaun et al., 2023).

Widening sets of digital government agendas and further exacerbated by the COVID-19 pandemic, increased attention to digitally mediated provision of welfare has triggered the expansion of digital welfare infrastructures (Andreassen et al., 2021). The Datafied Welfare State, 2022). With millions of welfare recipients in the world, governments are turning to online platforms to process benefit payments, analyze eligibility, and detect fraud as well as administer services on the scale (Bielefeld, 2024). Although there are efficiency gains and modernization in the administration, the sudden implementation of these technologies has brought up other critical issues with respect to equity, accountability and democratic legitimacy.

Increasing literature pinpoints the concept that the digital transformation of welfare systems is not only a technical or administrative reorganization but a significant reorganization of the state citizen relations in a socio-technical way (Allhutter et al., 2024). Social rights become mediated with automated systems more often, which transforms the concept and example of vulnerability, risk, and deservingness (Zajko, 2023). In this regard, it has raised worries about the bias in algorithms, the lack of transparency in making decisions, the disappearance of human discretion, and the locking out of digitally marginalised groups (Dong et al., 2024; Saikkonen and Choroszewicz, 2025; Watson et al., 2024).

Nevertheless, the literature remains sparse and despite the growing amount of it, significant gaps remain in comprehending the interaction between the factors of AI and data-driven technologies with the structures of governance, social inclusion outcomes, and citizen engagement practices within the welfare regimes. Whereas certain officers report efficiency benefits and enhanced service targeting (Ejim -Eze, 2025; Gurumoorthy et al., 2025), others report such as a rise in the surveillance level, discriminatory profiling, and loss of agency among beneficiaries of welfare (Clarke et al., 2024; Toorn and Soldatic, 2024). Such contradictory outcomes represent unclarified conflicts between technology innovation and social justice in the context of digitalisation of welfare.

In this context, this study conducts a systematic review of the current body of research on the topic of digital transformation in welfare systems, specifically, data-driven technologies, governance structures, and developing social issues. The review aims to move the knowledge of the impact of digital welfare changes on service delivery, social equity, and institutional accountability by synthesising recently published empirical, theoretical, and policy-oriented literature between 2019 and 2025. The contribution of the review to the body of literature is that the technological dimension, the ethical dimension, and the social dimension are integrated to provide a comprehensive outlook of all three dimensions in order to make the digital welfare policies more inclusive and sustainable.

Research Questions

- RQ1: What are the dominant themes in digital transformation of welfare systems?
- RQ2: How do AI and data-driven technologies influence governance and social inclusion?
- RQ3: What gaps exist in current literature on digital welfare systems?

BACKGROUND AND CONCEPTUAL FRAMEWORK.

Digital Transformation In Welfare System

The term digital transformation in welfare systems refers to the application of digital technologies such as AI, machine learning, big data analytics, and interoperable information systems, to the management and provision of social protection programmes (Alexopoulou, 2025; Frey, 2024). In comparison to the previous stages of informatization that were associated with digitisation of records and processes, modern digital welfare implies algorithmic decision-making, predictive analytics, and automated service coordination thus changing the system of welfare governance fundamentally (Kaun et al., 2023).

Such changes are usually explained by the discourses of efficiency, accuracy, and financial sustainability. Automated systems are implemented to facilitate the assessment of eligibility, lessen the workload, and permit risk and need to be detected (Reinmund et al., 2024). Still, researchers warn that these systems are also characterized by normative assumptions regarding the recipients of welfare, in which the priority is given to managerial efficiency rather than relationship care and situational judgement (Lancker, 2020; Zakharova et al., 2024).

Datafication, automation and algorithms governance.

The major trend of digital welfare transformation is the process of datafication, when coded social facts are converted into measurable statistics and are used to make algorithmic decisions (Allhutter et al., 2024). The eligibility, compliance, and intervention criteria are being restructured around risk models based on data

(Haitsma, 2025), and welfare recipients are becoming categorised, profiled, and measured with risk models, rather than on their individual needs.

The algorithmic governance means new power and control in the welfare systems that are usually less transparent and contestable (Damen, 2025). Research reports about the ability of automated decision-making to blur accountability, reduce procedural fairness and harbor existing disparities, especially given highly biased or incomplete data utilized by these systems (Mugamba, 2025; Toorn & Carney, 2024). Such dynamics pose some basic questions regarding the issue of legality, due process, and protection of social rights in digitally mediated welfare systems (Enqvist, 2024).

Digital literacy, social sustainability and inclusion.

Social sustainability in digital welfare situations is inclusive and equal access as well as preservation of agency and dignity among the welfare recipients (Pasupuleti, 2025). Although digital tools may increase the access of certain groups of people, considerable data indicates that digital-by-default welfare regimes affect people with low digital literacy, flimsy online connections, impaired mobility, or widespread susceptibility disproportionately (Saikkonen et al., 2025; Watson et al., 2024).

Another issue is digital exclusion, which is especially noticeable in certain groups of people, such as the disabled, elderly, Indigenous and migrant groups (Bielefeld, 2024). The major focus of research is the fact that digital literacy is not only a technical skill, but a socio-cultural capability that is comprehensively supported by trust, institutional support, and design inclusiveness (Carras and Finken, 2022; Lopez-Pelaez et al., 2024). Digital welfare systems will increase social stratification and not reduce it when there are no alternative access channels and supportive infrastructures (Schou and Pors, 2019).

Social welfare emerging challenges in digital welfare.

Digital welfare systems give rise to various social issues, such as algorithmic discrimination, heightened surveillance, professional discretion, and corrosion of the relational care (Zajko, 2023). Data practices and automated systems tend to reproduce historical and structural forms of inequality, the problem of racism, ableism, and other forms of exclusion based on the socio-political basis of digital welfare (Toorn and Soldatic, 2024).

In addition, the institutions of governance are often at the backside of technological implementations and set up regulatory vulnerabilities and lack of accountability (Damen, 2025; Pasupuleti, 2025). Mechanism to increase legitimacy and responsiveness have been offered including participatory forms of governance and ethics-from-below approaches, but have not been properly institutionalised in welfare regimes (Sabater et al., 2025).

CONCEPTUAL INTEGRATION

This paper has based its conceptualization of digital welfare transformation using the reviewed literature as being a socio-technical process, influenced by the interplay of technological innovation, modes of governance and social situations. Digital technologies do not only affect welfare outcome alone, but as part of institutional structures, regulation, and capabilities of the citizens. The interdependencies help in the process of developing welfare systems which are not only technologically advanced but also socially just, inclusive and democratically answerable.

RESEARCH METHODOLOGY

The systematic literature review protocol discussed in this study is based on the PRISMA principles modified to adapt them to the interdisciplinary research in the social policy, digital governance, and welfare studies. Although the visual PRISMA flow diagram is not available, every step of the review process, i.e. identification, screening, eligibility assessment, and inclusion, is clearly recorded so that the methodological rigour, reproducibility, and readability were all made transparent and clear.

The research identifies relevant studies through various methods such as identifying respected and known authors, references, journals, books, and other sources that are pertinent to the topic and possess quality data regarding ERP and Boltzmann systems.

The identification step consisted of extensive search of peer-reviewed scholarly sources covering the topic of digital transformation in the welfare systems. Several academic databases and indexing systems were used in order to cover the research between social policy, public administration, information systems, and digital governance. The search strategy was based on the central theme of the research the digital transformation of the welfare systems, and increased with the help of systematic transformation of query.

To guarantee breadth and precision in concepts, the initial research question was operationalized into a few specific search strings consisting of the combination of major concepts, including artificial intelligence, data-driven welfare, algorithmic governance, social inclusion, digital literacy, and the ethical issues. This method allowed retrieving both classical works and the new entries representing different welfare regimes as well as applications of technology (Alexopoulou, 2025).

The first stage of identification gave 954 records, which indicates the interdisciplinary and fast-growing character of digital welfare studies.

Screening Process

At the screening phase, the titles and abstracts of the identified records were modified to determine the relevance of topicality and suitability in the study objectives. The screening was orientated to accepting publications, which discussed digitalization only in the framework of technical or engineering aspects without the discussion of welfare, social policy, the government, or social disparity.

At this point, the studies that showed no direct correlation with the welfare systems, social protection, or the delivery of services to people were excluded. Screening process included the studies which showed direct relevance in terms of AI adoption, data-driven decision making, governance structure, social inclusion, or citizen participation in the welfare setting.

After the abstract level screening process was conducted, 954 studies were carried forward to the eligibility assessment phase.

Eligibility Assessment

The eligibility stage consisted of a full-text test according to previously set inclusion and exclusion criteria. Surveys were incorporated on the basis of them:

- investigated digital transformation, AI, or data-based technologies in welfare system, social protection system or social services system;
- Targeted ethical, governance, social inclusion or citizen engagement;
- used empirical, conceptual, policy-based or systematic review methodology.
- Published since 2019 -2025 to see modern developments.

The studies were not included in case they:

- One-sided orientation on the development of technical systems without any social or policy consequences.
- Expressed an attitude to the digital transformation beyond the welfare or social protection spheres.
- Did not have enough methodological transparency or scholarly base.

Citation chaining was also done in the process of this stage to bolster coverage. Backward citation chaining identified the best works that were cited by core studies whereas forward citation chaining identified publications that were published recently and were based on those. Such a procedure led to the incorporation of 78 articles, which totalled the number of the candidate publications to 1,032.

Inclusion and final study selection.

Relevance scoring was applied to all the eligible studies according to the thematic correspondence with the review objectives, methodological rigor and in contribution to the knowledge on the digital welfare transformation. The outcome of this process was 1,030 relevant studies with 128 studies being found highly relevant.

Out of this subset 83 studies remained and were chosen to undergo a qualitative synthesis. The ultimate choice was done to have equal representation in:

- Geographical areas and welfare states;
- Technological maturity levels;
- Methodological (qualitative, quantitative, mixed-method);
- Welfare areas (social assistance, child welfare, unemployment services, disability support and social care).

DATA EXTRACTION AND SYNTHESIS

The researcher collected the data following observation and synthesized them to produce the existence of discrepancy or matches in the responses.

A structured review matrix was used to extract data in order to be consistent across research. The variables that were extracted were welfare domain, application of technology, governance and ethical frameworks, outcomes of social inclusion, mechanisms of citizen engagement and major findings.

Synthesis was done using thematic approach of analysis with aim of discovering common patterns, tension, and deviations inductively through the predetermined aim of reviewing objectives. Cross-hazardous study between contexts created the possibility of defining institutional, cultural and infrastructural forces that determine the consequences of digital welfare.

METHODOLOGICAL INTEGRITY AND LIMITATIONS.

According to the PRISMA-informed practices, methodological integrity has been ensured by clear recording of every step of the review. Nonetheless, some shortcomings have to be admitted. The review is also prone to publication bias since it has used peer-reviewed and institutional sources. Further, geographic concentration of some areas and no cause-and-effect longitudinal studies makes it difficult to infer and generalize.

In spite of these drawbacks, the systematic and structured approach makes the synthesis stronger and gives a viable basis to establish research gaps, theoretical contribution, and the policy implications.

Figure 1. PRISMA Flow Diagram of Study Selection Process

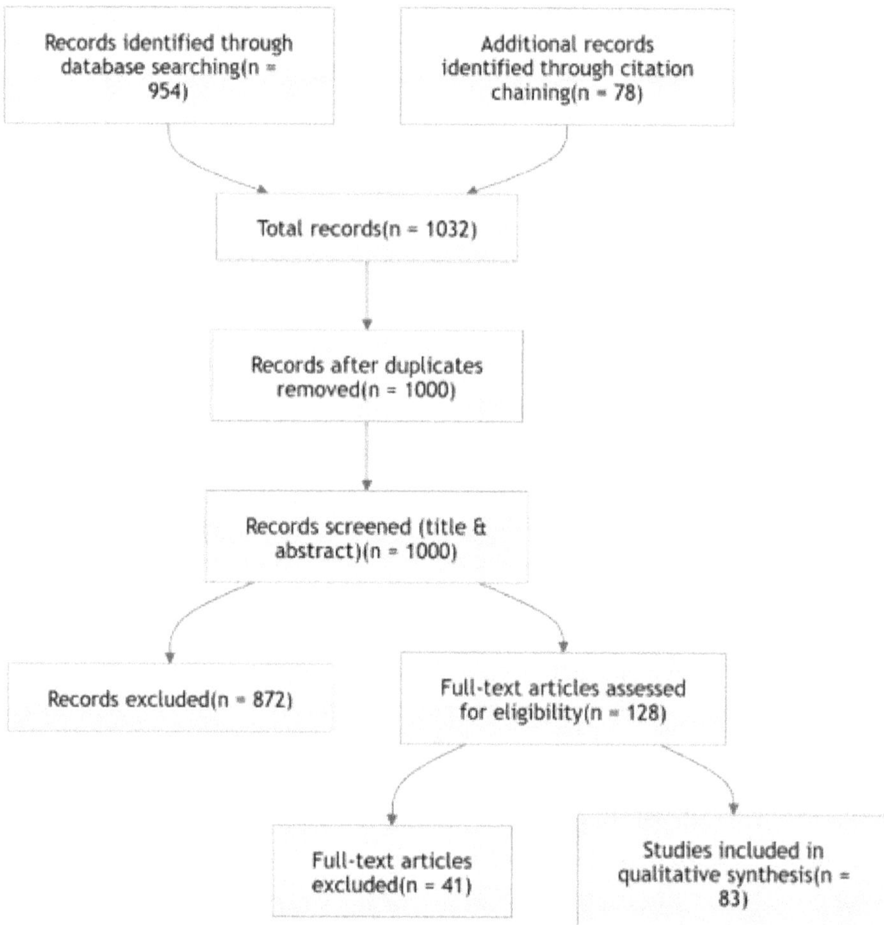

FINDINGS

This section shows the synthesized findings, which were obtained after conducting a systematic review on 83 selected studies on digital transformation in welfare systems. The results will be thematized to represent the main facets of analysis that formed within the literature, and which comprise technological integration, governance and ethics, social inclusion, citizen engagement and cross-national adoption patterns. Instead of repeating the results of particular studies, this section highlights general trends, intersections, and conflicts to be witnessed in different welfare settings.

Table 1. Summary of Key Themes in Digital Welfare Literature

Theme	Key Insights	Supporting Evidence
Technological Integration	Increasing use of AI, predictive analytics, and automation in welfare administration	Allhutter et al. (2024); Nicolas et al. (2024)
Governance & Ethics	Lack of transparency, accountability gaps, and weak regulatory frameworks	Damen (2025); Mugamba (2025)
Social Inclusion	Digital divide persists; vulnerable groups face exclusion	Watson et al. (2024); Saikkonen & Choroszewicz (2025)
Citizen Engagement	Limited participation in system design and governance	Dong et al. (2025); Gurumoorthy et al. (2025)
Cross-National Variation	Adoption varies based on institutional and regulatory context	Hwang (2024); Pertsas (2025)

Level Of Technological Integration

According to the review, there is a heterogeneous terrain of technological incorporation amid welfare systems. Eligibility determination, benefit distribution, predicting fraudsters and managing cases are some of the administrative processes that are becoming embedded on artificial intelligence (AI) and data-driven technologies. The high percentage of the researches state the progressive implementation of automated decision-making system or predictive analytics and the interoperable digital platform, indicating the transition to data-intensive welfare governance (Allhutter et al., 2024; Nicolas et al., 2024).

There are however wide differences in the level of technological maturity. Whereas certain welfare regimes are highly institutionalised in terms of the support of the AI in making decisions, other countries are still at the early phase of development, as they use prototypes and pilot projects (Laage-Thomsen et al., 2025; Reinmund et al., 2024). In a certain sense, there is also the tendency to continue to use automated systems and exercise discretion more or less in parallel with human judgment instead of complete replacement of professional judgment (Ranerup & Svensson, 2023; Stranz et al., 2024).

In the synthesis, it is shown that the priority of technological integration has commonly been placed on efficiency of administration and containment of costs at the cost of relational and contextual aspects of the welfare provision. It is still unclear whether it will prove to be effective in the long term, and many studies highlight that no longitudinal analysis has been conducted (Gurumoorthy et al., 2025).

Governance, and ethical structure.

The issue of governance and ethics are some of the primary issues that appear throughout the literature reviewed. Numerous investigations point to the formal governance policies that address the issues of transparency, accountability, and legal adherence, especially in the jurisdictions over which the data protection regulations, including the General Data Protection Regulation, are in effect (Damen, 2025; Enqvist, 2024). The ethical principles of AI like fairness, explainability, and auditability are often defined as normative principles in welfare digitalisation (Pasupuleti, 2025).

Regardless of these, the synthesis shows that there is a still a lag in governance as compared to the use of technology. These AI systems are deployed without a comprehensive institute of solid ethical protection, impact evaluation, or controls (Haitsma, 2025; Mugamba, 2025). The multi-level welfareism also makes the issue of accountability hard, especially in cases where the fragmentation of accountabilities is observed through the involvement of national, regional, and municipal governments (Petroons et al., 2025).

Models of multi, or participatory, governance are supported in the literature but are not even institutionalised. Whereas other studies record promising efforts on participatory practices, most systems of welfare remain based on top-down governance systems, implying that citizens cannot have an influence on the design and implementation of systems (Sabater et al., 2025).

Social Inclusion Outcomes

The results of social inclusion indicate contradictory and situation-specific results. Digital welfare systems show the potential of improving access, high in targeting, responsiveness of the service, especially when it is designed to suit the needs of different users (Ejim-Eze, 2025; Guder and BaltaOzkan, 2024). On the other hand, digital transformation often replicates the already existing social inequalities or enhances them.

By far, one of the issues evident through the studies is the continued persistence of digital exclusion, which is more often than not disproportionate towards participants with low digital literacy, limited access to the internet, disabilities, or other socio-economic weaknesses (Saikkonen and Choroszewicz, 2025; Watson et al., 2024). Digital-by-default models of services tend to marginalise such groups, and achieving less access, greater administrative workload, and greater reliance on informal support networks (Schou & Pors, 2019; Bielefeld, 2024).

Moreover, it has been discovered that algorithmic systems increase the risk of discrimination and stigmatization especially when profiling and risk-scoring tools receive a group of people that is already vulnerable (Dong et al., 2024; Toorn & Soldatic, 2024). Mitigating strategies have been suggested, inclusive design and community-based interventions, but there has not been a lot of empirical evidence on the prevalence of these solutions.

Citizen Engagement And Digital Literacy

Citizen participation and digital literacy are found to be key mediating variables that define the results of digital welfare change. According to the review, the meaningful engagement of welfare recipients and frontline workers is not yet developed, and the majority of systems have little to no opportunities to be involved in the design, evaluation, or even governance processes (Dong et al., 2025; Gurumoorthy et al., 2025).

It is always defined that digital literacy is the inherent condition to successfully have access to digital welfare services, which may be said to be transferred to users instead of provided by the institutions (Carras and Finken, 2022). Research points to gaps in the knowledge of automated decisions used by the user, lack of awareness of the processes of appeals, and the failure of trust in AI-mediated systems (Watson et al., 2024).

In instances where there is clear support in the form of training programmes, alternative access channels, and local intermediaries, it has been shown to have better experiences and fewer chances of exclusion (Adams, 2024; Crivellaro et al., 2020). However, these practices are still isolated and smaller in size in welfare systems.

Patterns of cross-national adoption.

Comparative analysis has shown that there is large variance in the way adoption is taking place with countries and welfare regimes. The institutional capacity, regulatory frameworks, digital infrastructure, and administrative traditions are the aspects of the digital welfare transformation that are different and affect the speed and mode (Hwang, 2024; Pertsas, 2025).

Trust-based governance and a relatively high level of data protection are also often presented as defining Nordic welfare systems, whereas they also face the problem of automation and professional discretion (Choroszewicz and Maihaniemi, 2020; Andreassen et al., 2021). On the other hand, welfare systems in other parts of the world tend to have disjointed execution, a looser regulatory framework, and increased liability to ethical and societal risks (Arkhipova and Borodkina, 2021; Kuoppamaki, 2021).

In all the contexts, the synthesis portrays that technological adoption is not linear and homogeneous and is strongly influenced by socio-political agendas, economic limitations, and cultural values. All these contextual factors can have a significant impact on welfare outcomes, risk governance, and the general trust of the population in the digital systems (Allhutter et al., 2024; Einhaus and Klenk, 2024).

DISCUSSION

This result of the systematic review reflects the multifaceted and contradictory nature of dynamics on which the digital revolutionization of welfare systems is built. Although the use of AI and data-driven technologies is thoroughly advocated as the tool of efficiency, precision, and modernity, cumulative evidence proves that their implications are highly dependent on the configuration of governance, institutional conditions, and citizen abilities. These findings are interpreted in the following discussion following the available literature, interacting with the relevant theoretical perspectives, and cogitating about how it impacts welfare governance and social policies.

Digital revolution and efficiency-equity tension.

The main conflict that was found in this review is between the efficiency of the administration and social fairness. In line with the existing literature, the data proves that artificial intelligence (AI) and automation have the potential to standardize the welfare procedure, decrease the number of administrative demands, and improve targeting accuracy (Alexopoulou, 2025). Nevertheless, the consequences of such efficient changes are often introduced with unwanted outcomes such as a lower benefit generosity level, higher denying rates, and a higher lack of human discretion in decision-making (Stranz et al., 2024; Germundsson and Stranz, 2024).

Such paradox cannot be disconnected with the criticism of technological solutionism in the sphere of welfare governance since sophisticated social issues are redefined as the problem of data-optimisation (Lancker, 2020; Zajko, 2023). Conventionally speaking, the findings dispute common sense amongst theorists of welfare-state that administrative rationalisation necessarily leads to equity improvements. In their turn, they favor the socio-technical descriptions in which welfare outcomes can be seen as co-produced with the help of interactions between technologies, institutions, human beings (Allhutter et al., 2024; Kaun et al., 2023).

Algorithms, power and accountability.

The findings of the review highlight the growing importance of the algorithmic governance in transforming the power relations in the welfare systems. Access to social rights is more and more mediated by automated decision-making systems that tend to lack any transparency and have few areas of challenge (Damen, 2025; Toorn and Carney, 2024). Even though governance systems that promote transparency and accountability are often proclaimed, there is an indication that such practices are usually trailing in the picture when it comes to the implementation of the technology (Haitsma, 2025; Mugamba, 2025).

The identified gap in governance is indicative of larger issues as determined in the literature on the public-administration and data-justice, wherein the accountability of algorithmic decisions is distributed among technical, organisational and political participants (Ranchordas and Schuurmans, 2020). Results support the idea that multi-level and participatory schemes of governance would raise the degree of legitimacy and reduce risks related to the concepts of the lack of openness and discrimination (Pasupuleti, 2025; Sabater et al., 2025). Despite that the unequal institutionalisation of such models shows the undamaged obstacles to the democratisation of digital welfare governance.

Data justice, social inclusion and digital divide.

It has been found that the results of digital welfare transformation are unevenly distributed in terms of achieving social inclusion, which supports the arguments of digital-divide and data-justice scholarship. Despite being digitally accessible and responsive to selected users, digital tools have a systematic negative impact on disadvantaging persons who have limitations in digital literacy, lack of connection, or concurring constraints (Saikkonen and Choroszewicz, 2025; Watson et al., 2024). Such trends indicate that digitalisation typically creates the same social stratifications and reproduces them on a broader scale instead of eliminating social stratification.

Considering the aspects of data-justice, the available evidence suggests that the practice of algorithmic profiling and datafication has a danger of reproducing the historical inequalities inherent in the welfare systems, especially based on the class, race, disability, and gender lines (Masieri and Das, 2019; Toorn and Soldatic, 2024). The continuation of digital-by-default service models indicates the move towards the responsibilities process, when one is supposed to traverse complicated digital systems lacking proper institutionalized assistance (Schou and Pors, 2019). This poses some fundamental questions on the dignity, autonomy, and right to social protection in digital welfare states.

The civic life and the citizen demobilization.

Even though citizen engagement is often promoted as a solution to ethical and inclusiveness issues, the results show that active participation is not yet introduced in reality. Welfare programs do not generally participate in the design, assessment, or management of AI systems and as such, there have been distortions between actual systems functionality and human experience (Dong et al., 2025).

The literature indicates that the concept of participatory can enhance the aspects of legitimacy and responsiveness using participatory approaches, including co-design, participatory action research, and ethics-from-below frameworks (Sabater et al., 2025). However, the facts testify that often such efforts are localised and they are not scaled to have systemic effects. This highlights why it is important to go beyond the figurehead practices towards institutionalised processes that incorporate the voice of citizens at each digital welfare lifecycle stage.

Cross-national variation and dependency.

The comparative results support the role played by contextual dependency in digital transformation of welfare. The welfare regime variations, regulatory, administrative, and digital infrastructures make significant differences in the trajectories and outcome of adoption (Hwang, 2024; Pertsas, 2025). Part of the risks could be reduced with trust-based governance models, including those found in Nordic countries, but tensions on automation and professional discretion are not eliminated (Choroszewicz and Maihaniemi, 2020).

These differences warn against the transfer of policy based on the technological best practices. Rather, the results confirm institutional and sociological theories of institutional adaptations of digital welfare reforms which, according to the capacity and cultural standards of a given area, as well as social contracts (Einhaus and Klenk, 2024). The lack of taking these contextual factors into consideration would pose a threat of increasing inequalities and losing people's trust.

Implications on policies and governance.

Combined, the conclusions reveal that there is nothing during the digital transition of welfare systems that can be made a value-neutral exercise but highly political and normative. One of the problems that policymakers have is to balance innovation and measures to protect social rights, initiate inclusion and provide accountability. There is an indication that effective governance systems, inclusion design, and long-term investment on digital literacy are all based on key premises of a just outcome of digital welfare (Adams, 2024; Pasupuleti, 2025).

Furthermore, the results are aiding the need to consider human-centered and hybrid governance systems, in which AI complements but does not replace human judgments and relationship care (Ranerup et al., 2023; Nuwasiima et al., 2024). Devoid of intentional policy tools, digital welfare systems may promote the infiltration of surveillance, exclusion, and distrust, which in turn will upset the principles of social safeguarding.

IMPLICATIONS

The contents of this systematic review have significant theoretical implications on the development, as well as the design and practical implementation of digital welfare systems. Through the integration of findings in the various welfare contexts, this paper makes visible the ways in which digital transformation alters the core premises regarding the ways in which welfare is provided, ruled, and the relationship between citizens and the state. It will be discussed below on the implications of this work in the context of theoretical contributions and practical/policy implications.

Theoretical Implications

By anticipating the presence of digital transformation as both a modernization of administration, and as a reorganization of the welfare state, the current synthesis extends the welfare state theory. Conventional welfare state approaches are based on bureaucratic discretion, institutional solidarity, and entitlements that are based on the rule. Concisely, the empirical data showcased in this paper reveals that data-driven and algorithmic systems mediate access to social rights more, thus altering the welfare provision to the predictive, actuarial, and automated logic (Lancker, 2020; Allhutter et al., 2024).

The results affirm new emerging views conceptualizing welfare as a social technical assemblage of the co-production of outcomes by technologies in interaction with institutions and human agents, as opposed to the transmission between linear policy mechanisms (Kaun et al., 2023). This questions the effectiveness of efficiency-driven reforms as part of promoting equity and demands welfare state theories with an explicit jurisdiction of digital infrastructures, data practices and algorithmic power.

Within the framework of digital governance, the review expands the existing literature on data justice and critical data studies, drawing an empirical example of how the process of datafication and algorithmic governance can recreate historical and structural inequalities embedded in the welfare systems (Masieri and Das, 2019; Toorn and Soldatic, 2024). Normative assumptions are frequently transformed into code in all types of algorithmic profiling, risk scoring and automated eligibility tests that bring up uncertainties about fairness, transparency and democratic accountability.

The research supports an argument that the governance systems should evolve beyond the procedural compliance to substantive data justice, under the focus of contestability, explainability, and marginalised voices involvement (Damen, 2025; Pasupuleti, 2025). This, in theory, highlights the need to incorporate welfare state analysis with the constructs of digital governance and data justice in order to understand the power disparities in digital mediation of social protection.

There is an artificial intelligence application in the field of human-AI interaction within the services.

The results also add to the theoretical discussion of human-AI interaction in the spheres of public service with the emphasis on automation limitations in the welfare areas. Instead of replacing the human judgment, AI systems are likely to transform the professional roles, discretion, and the practice of relationships (Ranerup & Svensson, 2023). These trends have suggested that human intervention is needed to maintain empathy, contextual sensitivity and moral judgment in the provision of welfare.

This cheers up the theoretical approaches to AI in the context of the application of AI to the field of administrating people and social work in general that propose human-centred AI, in which technology supplements professional knowledge instead of replacing it (Nuwasiima et al., 2024). The results actually confront techno-deterministic accounts, and highlight the relevance of relational as well as moral aspects of welfare work within the digitally transformed systems.

In the case of policymakers, the empirical evidence implies that digital welfare changes are to be considered as institutional and ethical rather than technological upgrades. It is necessary to make sure that welfare AI implementation is supported by the clear policy goals, evaluation of social impacts, and adherence to the principles of social protection. Constant checking and measurement systems are necessary to identify adverse side effects like exclusion, discrimination, or loss of reasonable benefit effectiveness (Gurumoorthy et al., 2025; Haitsma, 2025).

Another area of policy that should be in focus of policymakers is capacity building among welfare institutions, such as frontline workers, interdisciplinary teams, or regulators, so that they can effectively handle and supervise AI-enabled systems (Adams, 2024).

The review highlights the need to include design premises and incorporate digital exclusion taking an active part in the process. Welfare administration must not adopt the digital-by-default paradigm, and in its place, intergenerate access should be provided to people with lower digital literacy levels or limited access such as in-person, assisted, or offline opportunities (Saikkonen and Choroszewicz, 2025; Watson et al., 2024).

The usability, trust and legitimacy of the systems can be promoted using user-centred and participatory design frameworks, including co-design with the welfare recipients and frontline workers (Sabater et al., 2025). Institutional backing of digital literacy should not be unspoken passed onto the user since digital ability is not an individual lack and is a shared and structural burden (Carras and Finken, 2022).

The findings indicate the need to develop strong, multi-level regulation systems that ensure that they can stay in line with the implementation of technology, as regards governance. Policymaking tools and legal procedures must ensure algorithmic transparency, explainability, and redress, especially where there is a high stakes such as social rights determination (Enqvist, 2024).

To improve public trust and accountability, the institutions should be institutionalised with participatory governance structures (citizen panels, ethical review boards, independent auditing bodies, among others, Pasupuleti, 2025) to help the institutions become more accountable. Notably, the governance structures should also consider the fact that accountability of the algorithmic consequences belongs to the designers, administrators, policymakers, and political institutions, not to one person or one under-the-hood. (Ranchordas and Schuurmans, 2020).

LIMITATIONS OF THE STUDY

Although a systematic and rigorous method was embraced in this review, there are a number of limitations that should be recognised so that the findings can be put in context and interpretations made on them. These limitations need to be explicitly identified to promote the transparency of analysis and scholarly integrity.

Because numerous researchers convey their data through the lenses of a specific geography, it is necessary to discuss the concentration of the lenses to construct a comprehensive view of the literature field

Geographic Concentration Of The Literature

Since most of the researchers present their information through the prism of a particular geography, there is need to talk about the way the lenses are concentrated to create a more comprehensive picture of the literature sector.

The initial weakness of this review is the geographic concentration of the available literature. The proportion of the studies analysed dealing with welfare systems in Europe, especially that of Nordic and Western European countries, and some cases of the North American and Australian regions. Although these settings constitute useful information about advanced digital forms of welfare infrastructures, they might not set the full institutional, cultural, and infrastructural grounds of welfare systems of low- and middle-income countries or areas with emerging digital governance capabilities.

This geographical agglomeration limits the external validity of results in terms of wide welfare regimes, especially those that feature less developed digital infrastructure, informality of welfare systems or other socio-political settings. The synthesised outcomes, therefore, could be region-specific patterns of governance and technological directions as opposed to uniform rules and trends.

Methodological Constraints

The literature reviewed has a high degree of methodological heterogeneity and this has its positive and negative sides. Although the diversity and richness of qualitative case studies, ethnographic research, policy studies and mixed-method research provides context-sensitive information, numerous studies use small sample size, exploratory research, or single-case studies. This limits the process of drawing causal inferences or generalisation of findings across the welfare systems.

Moreover, standardisation of evaluation measures used in the studies makes their comparative synthesis difficult. Different conceptualisations of the same outcome (e.g. efficiency, fairness, inclusion and trust) and their different measurement reduce the comparability and consistency of the reported result.

Deficit Of Longitudinal Evidence

There was no longitudinal evidence or data on either study on the smoking reduction of the target group versus the control group.

Another weakness is associated with the relative lack of longitudinal studies, which would examine the long-term implications of artificial intelligence and data-driven technologies in the welfare systems. Most of the extant literature, mostly, is based on the initial level of implementation, pilot intervention or even a short term effect of such data, at least, of the sustaining, adjustability as well as the aggregate social impact of digital welfare reforms. Without longitudinal data it is tedious to determine how algorithmic systems evolve through time, how governance systems have become responsive to new hazards, or how the experience and belief of welfare recipients in the digital redesigned. As a result, the long-term consequences of digital change on the occurrence of social equity and welfare have not been well comprehended.

The given review is specifically focused on the digital transformation of welfare systems, in the future, anticipating artificial intelligence, data-oriented technologies, governance, and the social issues associated with them. As a result, allied but separate fields, including digitalisation in healthcare, education tools, or welfare technologies in the private sector are treated as such to the extent that they pass through the provision of welfare in the state. In addition, although the review addresses ethical, social, and governance aspects, it does not undertake a comprehensive technical evaluation of the subject matters like algorithmic buildings and system performance. Such a limited scope is a symptom of the socio-technical bias of the research but can hide the technical causes of system behaviour and results.

Lastly, the review can be prone to publication and linguistic bias, as it is based on peer-reviewed academic sources and institutional reports, which are in the English language. Research done in other languages or distributed via non-academic outlets is therefore limited and this may limit the breadth of the views that are getting captured.

FUTURE RESEARCH DIRECTIONS

On the basis of the results and the recognized weaknesses of this systematic review, it is possible to identify a series of crucial research areas in the future. These gaps need to be addressed to promote theoretical knowledge, better forms of policy design, and such that digital transformation leads to equitable and sustainable social protection through welfare systems.

longitudinal and impact-oriented research, the researcher is expecting possibly divergent effects in every period of measurements.

One of the most important areas of future research is that of coming up with longitudinal studies that will respond to the long-term effects of artificial intelligence and data-driven technologies in welfare systems. The current researches are mostly focused on pilot trials, initial implementations or initial results with little evidence of how this benefits welfare equity, adequacy of benefits, institutional trust, and social sustainability (Gurumoorthy et al., 2025; Reinmund et al., 2024). The future research attempts should incorporate longitudinal designs or quasi experimental designs or use panel data to determine the way the algorithmic systems develop over time, how the governance structures adjust to the new risks, and the way the experiences of welfare recipients would change due to the long-term exposure to digital systems. This kind of research would offer more empirical basis when it comes to testing the sustainability and validity of the digital welfare changes.

Comparative and cross- national research.

It is urgently necessary to conduct large-scale comparative and cross-national researches that consider the effect of the institutional, cultural, legal, and economic determinants of digital welfare adoption and results in a systematic manner. Although the literature in this field provides important country-specific results, they present Fortunato in terms of their transferability to other welfare regimes because there are no harmonised comparative frameworks (Hwang, 2024; Pertsas, 2025). Future studies need to incorporate mixed-method comparative research models that combine the policy research, institutional mapping and perspectives of stakeholders in many different welfare settings, such as under-represented areas such as the Global South. Such researches would promote the knowledge of mediation of risks and benefits of digital welfare transformation through various governance models.

Governance, accountability, and algorithmic fairness.

The creation of and empirical verification of powerful governance structures that can help overcome the algorithmic bias, lack of transparency, and even lack of accountability in welfare systems are further studies. Although there is a discussion on ethical AI principles, the practical application and implementation of these principles are not well explored (Haitsma, 2025; Mugamba, 2025). The efficiency of such mechanisms like algorithmic impact evaluations, independent audit, participant supervision institutions, and regulatory sandboxes should be investigated in future research to enhance transparency and fairness. The distribution of responsibility concerning the consequences of algorithms between the public agencies, those related to the sale of certain algorithms, and political bodies should also receive more attention (Ranchordas & Schuurmans, 2020).

Digital inclusion, literacy and lived experiences.

This research on digital exclusion and lived experience of welfare recipients is still urgent. In future literature, prioritisation must be laid on participatory as well as qualitative methods that place the voices of the marginalised groups, such as those with disabilities, the Indigenous populations, migrants and the elderly, in the spotlight, since they are the most disproportionately impacted by digital-by-default welfare regimes (Watson et al., 2024). The relationships among digital literacy interventions, community intermediaries, and other forms of access and the impact on user agency and trust are value-adding in such investigations and would be utilized practically in designing inclusive digital welfare services. Besides, studies ought to be conducted in the field of emotional, relational and experiential levels of AI-mediated rights to welfare, which are still under researched as per the existing body of literature.

Collaboration between humans and ai and the professional practice.

The models of human-AI cooperation in the welfare service provision should also be developed further in future studies to understand the way AI systems relate to professional discretion, moral judgment, and the relationship care. Although increasingly common models of hybrid decision-making are being observed, more empirical data has yet to be collected on optimal models that can balance automation with human supervision (Ranerup & Svensson, 2023; Nuwasiima et al., 2024). Research into workflow planning, training strategies and organisational cultures can help to highlight how AI can be used to complement, and not to impede, frontline welfare work. This type of research is especially significant when it comes to such a sensitive field as child protection, or disability services, and social care.

Supporting Structural And Historical Inequalities

Lastly, additional involvement of the historical and structural aspects of digital welfare change should be utilized in future research. Interdisciplinary research utilizing both social policy and sociology, history, and data science is critically required to reveal the connection of legacies of racism, ableism, and class-based discrimination to welfare data and algorithmic systems (Toorn & Soldatic, 2024; Zajko, 2023). It is crucial to tackle these problems in order to build justice-specific digital welfare structures that do not aim at alleviating the effects of technical bias but take down the structural inequalities that automation has recycled.

CONCLUSION

This review has explored digital transformation of welfare states, specifically, data-driven technologies, artificial intelligence, and the social issues that have accompanied the deployment of such technologies. The review, based on synthesis of evidence, which authors compiled based on 83 studies that were selected and involved different welfare contexts, provides an extensive account of how technological innovation is redefining welfare governance, service provision and citizen-state relationships.

The research indicates that the digital technologies have huge potential to supplement administrative effectiveness, personalization, and responsiveness in welfare systems. At the same time, the review shows that these advantages are disproportionately realized and often come with the risks that revolve around social marginalization, the bias of algorithms, the loss of the human judgment, and the vacuums in governance. The current existence of hybrid decision-making models stresses the timelessness of human judgment and relational care in the welfare provision, especially in the service areas where it is stakes and sensitive.

This research work adds to the literature as it will help further the socio-technical perspective of digital welfare transformation. It goes beyond technology-based stories to help clarify how welfare is co-produced by interaction in digital infrastructures, institutional formations, institutions of governance, and ability of citizens. The review suggests an inclusive approach to the regulation of welfare systems facilitated by AI and its data by combining knowledge about the welfare state theory, digital governance, and the data justice approach.

Most importantly, the review highlights that the process of digital transformation in welfare systems is not an issue of neutral value. Without the strong ethical governance, holistic design, and continued commitment to digital literacy, digital welfare reforms can still create or enhance the existing social inequalities. On the other hand, digital technologies in coordination with such postulates as transparency, accountability, participation, and human-focused design can promote more equitable and effective welfare provision.

To sum up, the evidence reviewed in this study emphasizes the necessity to combine technological innovation with governance inclusion and ethical protection. The policy makers, policy doers and policy analysts need to note that the effectiveness of digital welfare change will depend not only on its technological complexity but also on whether it is able to maintain social rights, encourage inclusiveness, and the ability to maintain public trust in the emerging socio-technical conditions.

REFERENCES

. Adams, D. (2024). Managing the challenges of leveraging technology and data advances to improve social protection. Modernising Access to Social Protection, 96.

Alexopoulou, S. (2025). Paradigm shift: Exploring the impact of digital technologies on the welfare state through a systematic literature review. *Social Policy & Administration*, *59*(1), 135–157. DOI: 10.1111/spol.13054

Allhutter, D., Alushi, A., Alcântara, R. C. D., Männiste, M., Pentzold, C., & Sosnowski, S. (2024). Public value in the making of automated and datafied welfare futures. *Internet Policy Review*, *13*(3). Advance online publication. DOI: 10.14763/2024.3.1803

Andreassen, R., Kaun, A., & Nikunen, K. (2021). Fostering the data welfare state: A Nordic perspective on datafication. *Nordicom Review*, *42*(2), 207–223. DOI: 10.2478/nor-2021-0051

Arkhipova, E. B., & Borodkina, O. (2021). The problems and contradictions of digital transformation of social services organizations in Russia. Sotsiologicheskie Issledovaniya, 4, 116–134. https://doi.org/DOI: 10.24412/2079-0910-2021-4-116-134

Bielefeld, S. (2024). Digitalisation and the welfare state–how first nations people experienced digitalised social security under the Cashless Debit Card. *Journal of Sociology (Melbourne, Vic.)*, *60*(3), 599–617. DOI: 10.1177/14407833241232636

Choroszewicz, M., & Mäihäniemi, B. (2020). Developing a digital welfare state: Data protection and the use of automated decision-making in the public sector across six EU countries. *Global Perspectives*, *1*(1), 12910. Advance online publication. DOI: 10.1525/gp.2020.12910

Clarke, R., Michael, K., & Abbas, R. (2024). Robodebt: A socio-technical case study of public sector information systems failure. *AJIS. Australasian Journal of Information Systems*, *28*, 28. DOI: 10.3127/ajis.v28.4681

Crivellaro, C., Coles-Kemp, L., & Wood, K. (2020). "Computer says no": Exploring social justice in digital services. In *Hope under neoliberal austerity: Responses from civil society and civic action* (pp. 89–104). Policy Press., DOI: 10.1332/policypress/9781447356820.003.0007

Damen, W. W. (2025). Exposed to the elements: How European data protection law facilitates welfare dystopias and how to improve its level of protection. *European Journal of Social Security*, *27*(2), 156–174. DOI: 10.1177/13882627251337402

Dong, M., Bonnefon, J. F., & Rahwan, I. (2024). False consensus biases AI against vulnerable stakeholders. arXiv. /arXiv.2407.12143 (Preprint.)DOI: 10.2139/ssrn.4876227

Dong, M., Bonnefon, J. F., & Rahwan, I. (2025). Heterogeneous preferences and asymmetric insights for AI use among welfare claimants and non-claimants. *Nature Communications*, *16*(1), 6973. Advance online publication. DOI: 10.1038/s41467-025-62440-3 PMID: 40730578

Einhaus, M., & Klenk, T. (2024). Towards a platformised welfare state? *Der Moderne Staat*, *17*(1), 13–34. DOI: 10.3224/dms.v17i1.02

Ejim-Eze, E. (2025). The role of AI in effective social protection delivery: A focus on national cash transfer programs. In *AI and public sector transformation*. Springer., DOI: 10.1007/978-3-031-71678-2_9

Enqvist, L. (2024). Rule-based versus AI-driven benefits allocation: GDPR and AIA legal implications and challenges for automation in public social security administration. *Information & Communications Technology Law*, *33*(2), 222–246. DOI: 10.1080/13600834.2024.2349835

. Frey, V. (2024). 1 Modernising access to social protection for the challenges ahead. Modernising Access to Social Protection, 11.

Germundsson, N., & Stranz, H. (2024). Automating social assistance: Exploring the use of robotic process automation in the Swedish personal social services. *International Journal of Social Welfare*, *33*(3), 647–658. DOI: 10.1111/ijsw.12633

Gurumoorthy, R., Rees, D., Miller, E. S., & Thomas, R. (2025). Data-driven AI in social care Wales: Identifying gaps and opportunities. *Proceedings of the European Conference on Innovation and Entrepreneurship*, 20(1), 285–294. https://doi.org/ DOI: 10.34190/ecie.20.1.4200

Haitsma, L. M. (2025). Addressing discrimination in algorithmic profiling: Examining risk governance in Dutch public social security agencies. *European Journal of Social Security*, *27*(2), 191–212. DOI: 10.1177/13882627251351093

Hwang, J. (2024). Navigating digital transformations: Innovation strategies in European social services. *Open Access Research Journal of Multidisciplinary Studies*, *8*(1), 189–203. DOI: 10.53022/oarjms.2024.8.1.0040

Kaun, A., Lomborg, S., Pentzold, C., Allhutter, D., & Sztandar-Sztanderska, K. (2023). Crosscurrents: Welfare. *Media Culture & Society*, *45*(5), 877–883. DOI: 10.1177/01634437231154777

Lancker, W. V. (2020). Automating the welfare state: Consequences and challenges for the organisation of solidarity. In *The digital welfare state* (pp. 149–168). Springer., DOI: 10.1007/978-3-030-44062-6_8

. Mugamba, E. (2025). Predictive Protection or Profiling? A Legal-Ethical Framework for Algorithmic Risk Tools in Child Welfare Systems in Spain.

Nuwasiima, M., Ahonon, M. P., & Kadiri, C. (2024). The role of artificial intelligence and machine learning in social work practice. *World Journal of Advanced Research and Reviews, 24*(1), 80–97. DOI: 10.30574/wjarr.2024.24.1.2998

Pasupuleti, M. (2025). Governance frameworks for ethical AI deployment in public sector services. [IJAIRI]. *International Journal of Academic and Industrial Research Innovations, 5*(5), 561–573. DOI: 10.62311/nesx/rphcr17

Pertsas, G. (2025). Interoperability for welfare: Digitalization and state transformation in Greece. In *AI and welfare governance*. Springer., DOI: 10.4337/9781035338153.00011

Ranerup, A., & Svensson, L. (2023). Automated decision-making, discretion and public values: A case study of two municipalities and their case management of social assistance. *European Journal of Social Work, 26*(5), 948–962. DOI: 10.1080/13691457.2023.2185875

Sabater, A., López, B., Campdepadrós, R., & Sánchez, C. (2025). Participatory action research for AI in social services. In *AI and public sector innovation*. Springer., DOI: 10.1007/978-3-031-71678-2_4

Saikkonen, P., & Choroszewicz, M. (2025). Fostering socially and ecologically sustainable digitalisation of welfare states. *Social Inclusion (Lisboa), 13*, 10937. Advance online publication. DOI: 10.17645/si.10937

Schou, J., & Pors, A. S. (2019). Digital by default? A qualitative study of exclusion in digitalised welfare. *Social Policy & Administration, 53*(3), 464–477. DOI: 10.1111/spol.12470

Stranz, H., Germundsson, N., Hussénius, K., & Bergmark, Å. (2024). Automatisering av ekonomiskt bistånd. *Socialvetenskaplig Tidskrift, 31*(1), 7–27. DOI: 10.3384/SVT.2024.31.1.4869

van Toorn, G., & Carney, T. (2025). Decoding the algorithmic operations of Australia's National Disability Insurance Scheme. *The Australian Journal of Social Issues, 60*(1), 21–39. DOI: 10.1002/ajs4.342

Van Toorn, G., & Soldatić, K. (2024). Disablism, racism and the spectre of eugenics in digital welfare. *Journal of Sociology (Melbourne, Vic.)*, *60*(3), 523–539. DOI: 10.1177/14407833241244828

Watson, C., Crivellaro, C., Parnaby, A. W., & Kharrufa, A. (2024, May). Hostile Systems: A Taxonomy of Harms Articulated by Citizens Living with Socio-Economic Deprivation. In *Proceedings of the 2024 CHI Conference on Human Factors in Computing Systems* (pp. 1-17). DOI: 10.1145/3613904.3642562

Zajko, M. (2023). Automated government benefits and welfare surveillance. *Surveillance & Society*, *21*(3), 246–258. Advance online publication. DOI: 10.24908/ss.v21i3.16107

Zakharova, I., Jarke, J., & Kaun, A. (2024). Tensions in digital welfare states: Three perspectives on care and control. *Journal of Sociology (Melbourne, Vic.)*, *60*(3), 540–559. DOI: 10.1177/14407833241238312

Chapter 2
Artificial Intelligence and Ethical Automation in Welfare Governance and Policy Delivery

Nikhil Kumar Goyal
http://orcid.org/0009-0007-4532-8033
Noida International University, Greater Noida, India

Prince Kumar Choudhary
http://orcid.org/0009-0000-3306-8026
Poornima University, Jaipur, India

Yash Agarwal
http://orcid.org/0009-0001-9184-5249
Poornima University, Jaipur, India

Ayan Rehman
http://orcid.org/0009-0007-9391-4600
Poornima University, Jaipur, India

ABSTRACT

This chapter looks at the ethics of automation in welfare governance, with reference to opportunities and risks posed by AI-based policy delivery. It discusses the ways in which the concept of algorithmic decision-making collides with the fundamental values of a modern system of public administration, including equality, procedural justice, and democratic responsibility. The chapter identifies the significance of transparent and human-oriented AI frameworks to secure trust in the population by evaluating the ethical frameworks, the governance models, and new regulatory

DOI: 10.4018/979-8-3373-8423-8.ch002

strategies. Finally, the chapter concludes that to be responsible in integrating artificial intelligence in the governance of welfare, it would be necessary to have strong ethical principles, a policy designed to be inclusive and the institution open to constant monitoring to attain a balance between innovation and social responsibility.

1. INTRODUCTION

1.1 Emergence of AI in Welfare Governance Systems

The adoption of an artificial intelligence in welfare governance has been necessitated by the rising administrative complexity, the rising demand of the public services, and the pressure on the governments to become more efficient and cost effective. Welfare systems are charged with the responsibility of handling masses of people, varying eligibility requirements and scarce national resources and are frequently operating within a context of financial constraint and media scrutiny. Machine learning and predictive analytics as well as automated decision-support systems AI technologies are becoming more popular in the stream of processes like benefit allocation, eligibility determination, fraud detection, and service personalization (Calo, 2017).

In ancient times, the system of welfare administration was dependent on rule-based and bureaucratic practices, which were characterized by the focus on standardization and human discretion. Though these systems guaranteed consistency in the procedures, they were frequently criticized to be inefficient, time consuming as well as prone to human error or prejudice. The automation provided by AI is expected to eliminate these deficiencies since it will help to make decisions faster, decongest administration, and use big data to make informed policy delivery. One of the strengths of AI is that it is perceived to be objective, it is scalable, and it can run all night and all day without exhaustion.

Nevertheless, the introduction of AI in the welfare regulation is not just a matter of technical improvements, but it is an important shift in the mode of exercising the authority by the state. The connection between the state and citizens is becoming more and more mediated by automated systems, which affects those to which it is provided, in what circumstances, and with what implications. This change should be seriously considered in terms of ethical, social and institutional consequences of placing the welfare choices under the algorithmic mechanisms (Kumari & Goyal, 2026).

1.2 From Administrative Automation to Ethical Automation

The history of AI in the welfare governance could be explained as a movement toward the questions of the automation of the administrative procedures to the ethical automation. The initial types of automation were mainly aimed at digitizing records, electronic processing of the applications and the implementation of predetermined rules with little human intervention. These systems maximized efficiency, but were not very flexible and did not radically transform the decision-making reason. Modern AI systems, on the contrary, can study and analyze data, draw conclusions, and provide probabilistic judgments that have a policy impact (Eubanks, 2018).

Ethical automation does not only consider operational efficiency, but also takes into consideration the normative values of fairness, transparency, accountability and respect towards human dignity. Ethical considerations are especially relevant in the sphere of welfare, where any choice has a direct impact on the access to medical services, residential facilities, unemployment checks, and social welfare. Depending on how automated decisions are made, the marginalized groups can be disproportionately affected by them, so it is crucial to ensure that AI systems comply with the principles of social justice and democratic principles.

Ethical automation concept underlines that AI systems are not supposed to be the replicas of the current administrative practices, but they are expected to be developed in order to contribute to equity and inclusiveness. This involves the incorporation of ethical values in the system design, data governance and institutional control. Instead of considering ethics as a second thought or a compliance activity, ethical automation makes moral responsibility one of the fundamental elements of technological innovation in welfare governance (European Commission, 2016).

1.3 Data, Algorithms, and Power in Welfare Policy Delivery

The welfare systems that are operated by AI are extremely dependent on data. Administrative data, socioeconomic, behavior data, and past welfare outcomes are combined in order to train algorithms and guide decision-making. Although data-driven methods may enhance targeting and help in cutting down fraud, it also leads to the issues of data quality, representativeness, and surveillance. The incomplete or partial datasets may result in erroneous forecasts and unfair results, which will strengthen the social injustices.

Welfare governance algorithms are not considered to work in a clean-slate fashion; they contain assumptions, priorities, and policy goals dictated by those who design them and institutional settings. Value judgments exist in choices of which variables to include, the definition of risks and the maximization of outcome. Consequently, AI systems are able to change the balance of power in the welfare governance since it clouds decision-making procedures and restricts the possibility of human will and redress (Goyal et al., 2026).

The monopoly of decision making powers in the opaque algorithmic systems questions the concept of accountability. The automated decisions can confuse citizens in their attempts to comprehend the method of reaching the outcomes or the way of appealing against such decisions. It is this imbalance between information and power that highlights the necessity to have clear and explainable AI systems and effective procedural protection. To be responsible with automating welfare, it is important to understand that the automation process has political and ethical aspects of data and algorithms (OECD, 2019).

1.4 Ethical Stakes of AI-Driven Welfare Decision-Making

There are especially high ethical stakes involved in the implementation of AI in welfare governance, as beneficiary populations are vulnerable. The timely and correct decision-making is crucial to satisfy the basic needs of welfare recipients, mistakes, or delays can be disastrous to them. Misplaced denial of benefits, wrongly labeling people as high-risk, or having them investigated by an automated system can contribute to social exclusion and the lack of trust in official institutions.

Figure 1. Integrated Framework of AI-Driven Ethical Automation in Welfare Governance and Policy Delivery

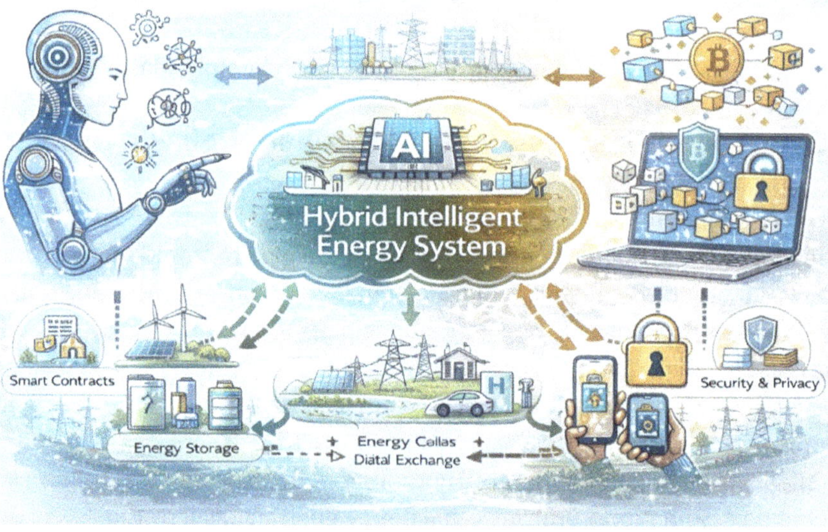

The ethical issues regarding AI in welfare systems are mostly preoccupied with the problem of bias and discrimination. The machine learning models trained on historical data are likely to reproduce past discrimination based on race, gender, disability, or socioeconomic status. Even in cases where the design of algorithms follows the principle of fairness, unwanted disparities may arise since there are complicated interactions among data, models, and institutional practices. These risks need to be handled through constant monitoring, auditing, and modification of AI systems during their lifecycle (Pasquale, 2019).

2. EVOLUTION OF AUTOMATED DECISION-MAKING IN WELFARE POLICY DELIVERY

2.1 Early Digitization and Rule-Based Welfare Administration

The development of the automated decision-making process of the welfare policy delivery started with the computerization of the administrative processes instead of the application of the intelligent systems. Initial welfare automation was concerned with changing the paper records to electronic databases that would allow storage and retrieval of data faster and intended basic processing. Information systems that are rule-based were adopted to normalize the eligibility checks, determining the amount of benefits, and adherence to predetermined policy regulations. Those systems were based on clear legal and administrative standards that have a direct coded representation in software, with hardly chances of interpretation or contextual validation.

As the efficiency of administration and minimal clerical errors increased with the rule-based automation, it turned out to be a manifestation of structural limits, as well. These systems were highly inflexible and could not respond to dynamic or changed social circumstances, and in most cases did not reflect the subtlety of the lives of welfare recipients. There were welfare cases which were hard to process accurate according to strictly result-oriented rules of an irregular employment, informal caregiving duties, or overlapping weaknesses. Thus, initial automation occasionally contributed to bureaucratic rigidity instead of making people more responsive and fair (Farooqi et al., 2026).

Although these shortcomings can be seen, rule-based systems formed the basis of superior types of automation. They non only introduced welfare institutions to digital governance, but also standardized data collection practices, as well as, generated massive administrative datasets. The developments made it possible to adopt machine learning and predictive analytics at a later stage by establishing the data structure required to make decisions on an algorithmic basis (European Commission High-Level Group on Artificial Intelligence, 2019).

2.2 Transition to Data-Driven and Predictive Welfare Systems

The following stage of the welfare automation development was the occurrence of data-driven and predictive technologies. The developments in the field of computational capability and the availability of data enabled the governments to leave the deterministic rules behind and incorporate probabilistic evaluations. Machine learning techniques started to be applied in risk scoring, fraud detection and prioritization of resources. Such systems use the past information to forecast the future outcome and predict the future and provide the policymakers with the tools to manage the welfare programs proactive (Veale & Brass, 2019).

Predictive systems were a major deviation in welfare governance since they played a part in decision-making even before the events happened. Instead of reacting to the applications or the changes reported in the circumstance, the welfare agencies could proact to identify the risk of long-term dependency, overpayment of the benefits, or non-compliance. This change was in line with the trends of general move towards preventive governance and evidence-based policymaking, with early intervention and efficiency.

Nevertheless, the new ethical and policy issues were also associated with predictive welfare systems. The risk scores and predictive classifications usually happen as black boxes, and therefore, an administrator and recipients may not be able to comprehend the method of decision-making. Besides, the structural inequalities can be imposed and increased due to predictions based on past events, with marginalized populations being disproportionately impacted. This increased dependence on predictive technologies therefore brought up the issue of equity, accountability, and due boundaries of algorithmic power in welfare policy (Kumari et al., 2026).

2.3 Algorithmic Decision-Making and Policy Discretion

With the development of welfare automation, the algorithms performed more advisory tasks than the functions of decisions. In other systems, the results of the ran algorithms directly dictate the eligibility, benefit rates/sanctions with little or no human intervention. Such a change has a powerful impact on the policy discretion, which has always been conducted by front range workers in the welfare system, through personal circumstances and professional discretion. Such decision makers as act upon algorithms are more likely to homogenize what comes out, being less prone to McClellan bias but, equally, more deprived of flexibility and empathy (Friedman & Nissenbaum, 1994).

This shift in public administration with efficiency and consistency privileged over the personal evaluation inherent in the delegation of decision-making power to algorithms is more indicative of a broader change in the operation of the contemporary state. Advocates believe that, with the help of algorithmic systems, arbitrariness and corruption will decrease, and there will be uniform enforcement of rules of policy. Opponents, though, argue that eliminating human judgment has the propensity of dehumanizing welfare administration and holds lineages of accountability in case of mistakes.

This conflict brings out a fundamental conflict in automated welfare systems between standardization and responsiveness. Algorithms are very efficient in that processing a large amount of cases at once but fail to process contextual elements like sudden health crises, domestic instability, or unofficial support system. The death of human discretion may then result in means of that which is technically right and socially wrong, and this then highlights the importance of adopting hybrid models, which combine algorithmic effectiveness with the element of human judgment (Johns, 2017).

2.4 Institutionalization of Automation in Welfare Governance

With the passing of time, automated decision-making institutionalization has become a part of the welfare governance structures. Algorithms have ceased to be experimental systems, but they are part of systems of policy delivery. An automated platform is becoming a daily activity of welfare agencies, which determines the organizational routine, staff functions, and interactions with citizens. Not only does this institutionalization change the process of decision making but also changes the conceptualization of welfare systems of its beneficiaries, risks and policy success (Goyal et al., 2026).

The incorporation of AI into welfare organizations tends to redistribute power in the administrative pyramids. Technical workers, data scientists and vendors of technologies are becoming more influential in system design and implementation, often at the cost of frontline workers and beneficiaries. The change provokes the doubts about the accountability of democracy and the policy process transparency, especially through proprietary algorithms.

The dependency on automated systems institutionalized can also be path dependencies which are hard to overcome. After implanting the system, alternative ways of collecting data are not as visible or even feasible, as algorithmic systems influence data collection habits and policy expectations. It is important to understand this dynamic in order to ethically automate since it also focuses on the significance of governance systems that support continual review, modification, and in some instances discontinuation of automated systems. In order to assure the ongoing trust and policy legitimacy, it is critical that the welfare automation will be flexible and responsible (Selbst et al., 2019).

3. ETHICAL FOUNDATIONS OF AI-DRIVEN WELFARE SYSTEMS

3.1 Normative Principles Guiding Ethical Welfare Automation

The ethical bases of AI-powered welfare systems design and implementation are among the focal points since the presented systems are the ones that directly influence or affect the access to the important social guarantees of people. These normative principles have been historically in the foundation of governance of welfare, which include equity, justice, solidarity and respect to human dignity. The implementation of artificial intelligence to this field requires a review of the operations of these principles, in the context of the automated decision-making processes. Automation of ethics means that the ethically appropriate systems addressing computer-assisted and robotic ethics must ensure that they establish not technical accuracy but moral legitimacy in the service delivery to the population.

One of the ethical principles that govern welfare is fairness in which like cases should be treated equally taking into consideration any pertinent differences in need and circumstances. The systems of AI should therefore be established to prevent misplaced differences within demographic categories and social classes. Vitality is also needed in transparency because welfare recipients have a moral and democratic value to know how their lives are influenced in decision making. Devoid of meaningful transparency, the automated systems can diminish procedural justice and terminate the faith in the social institutions (Government of Canada, 2019).

The second fundamental pillar of ethics is accountability where welfare judgment should be distinctly left to the human actors and institutions. Although it is possible that AI systems are used to support or automate the process of making decisions, they do not have just a moral or legal responsibility. Ethical theories thereby emphasize on the need to uphold transparent lines of accountability whereby the government of crucial decisions and the results of AI-programmed welfare systems are accountable.

Figure 2. Ethical Governance and Human Oversight Loop in AI-Enabled Welfare Policy Delivery

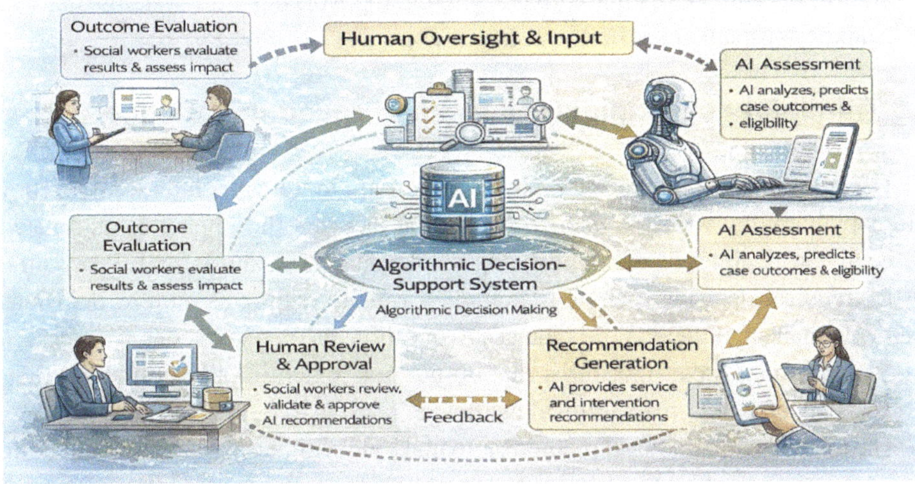

3.2 Fairness, Equity, and Social Justice in Algorithmic Welfare Decisions

The desire to achieve fairness of AI-inspired welfare systems is made complex owing to social realities as noted within administrative data. Historical disparities on race, sex, disability, employment level, and geographic position are usually encoded in welfare datasets. Machine learning models that are trained on this type of data will replicate or amplify patterns of disadvantage. Automation of ethical welfare thus necessitates the need to change the technical key terms that define fairness into the broader social justice terms (Dandotiya et al., 2026).

Equity-oriented strategies have been found to acknowledge that treating someone equally will not always lead to fair results. Populations should be taken into consideration in terms of their structural disadvantages and different vulnerabilities in AI systems that are used in welfare governance. As an illustration, the subjective predictive models that can be implemented to evaluate compliance risk or benefit dependency can focus on marginalized groups in an unequal manner in case social circumstances are not put into focus. Ethical design should then be sensitive to context and need to have mechanisms that reduces disparate effects.

Social justice is another aspect applied to the allocation of benefits and costs related to automation of welfare. As much as governments can experience more efficiency as well as cut costs, the welfare recipients can experience the dangers of inaccuracy, misclassification, or omission. The moral theories indicate that it is important to consider the welfare of the vulnerable groups, so automation should not hurt the social inclusion. This demands the constant scrutiny of the alerts of the algorithms and the readiness to reassess or stop working with systems that will have unfair consequences (Lodge & Mennicken, 2017).

3.3 Transparency, Explainability, and Procedural Justice

The key ethical guidelines of AI-driven welfare systems include transparency and explainability, which is needed due to the fact that the impact of automated decisions on livelihoods and well-being of people can be substantial. Procedural justice requires decision making to enlighten welfare recipients on how decisions are being made and meaningful chances to question any negative consequences. In this respect, black-box algorithms that do not give much information about their internals become a dramatic ethical challenge.

The goal of explainable AI methods is to make algorithm-based decision-making easier to understand by the administrator and citizens. Explainability facilitates a caseworker in a welfare setting to interpret systems recommendation and make informed judgment instead of blindly taking the outputs of the algorithm. To recipients, explanations explain the due process of the right by giving the reasons as to why they were granted benefits, not granted, or had their benefits adjusted. Devoid of such explications, the automated systems of welfare can be viewed as the arbitrary or esoteric performances of state authority (OECD, 2019).

Experiential justice must also have effective and available appeal procedures. Ethical automation systems emphasize that people should have the capability of appealing automated decisions and facilitating human authority to review such decisions. This makes it possible to rectify errors and also to take into account situational factors, which algorithms have not taken into account. Transparency and entitlement to appeal should be incorporated into welfare automation thus not a moral task but a democratic requirement.

3.4 Human Dignity and the Limits of Automation

Due respect to human dignity is one of the basic moral values that puts boundaries on the degree to which the welfare governance can be automated. The welfare systems are not just administrative structures, but social obligations to take care of a person if he or she is at disadvantage. Automatic decision-making will lead to removing all human elements in decision-making, removing the individual to a data point and the lived circumstances and personal situations of the individual.

There are ethical theories that suggest that AI is supposed only to provide supplements to human judgment when governing welfare. The human-in-the-loop models do not exclude the ability to empathize, make decisions, and think morally, which is something algorithms are unable to do. The caseworkers are important in clarification of complex situations, responsiveness to unique requirements, and the facilitation of relationship support that is beyond the technical eligibility guidelines. Preservation of human elements prevents the welfare systems to be inhumane.

The boundaries of automation also indicate the general interest in the issues of moral agency and responsibility. Giving the AI systems full responsibility in making decisions in the field of welfare might blur the lines when some damage happens, and thus ethical responsibility will be compromised. Ethical automation therefore involves one having an established limit beyond which some decisions cannot be automated but instead they should be carried out by humans. Respect toward human dignity is a key factor that allows waiving AI by making the use of technology innovation advantageous, as well as keeping its moral foundations intact through the welfare government (Kumari et al., 2026).

4. ALGORITHMIC TRANSPARENCY, ACCOUNTABILITY, AND FAIRNESS IN WELFARE AUTOMATION

4.1 Transparency as a Democratic Requirement in Welfare Algorithms

One of the principles that underpin ethical application of artificial intelligence in welfare governance is transparency since artificial systems exert a great influence on the citizens to access public benefits and services. It is anticipated in the democratic societies that the process of making decisions by the populace is transparent, comprehensible, and examinable. Transparency is needed to make welfare decisions held by algorithm systems, and along this, the legitimacy and trustworthiness of the system. In the absence of transparency, the automated welfare systems may be viewed as obscure devices of state authority and not as instruments of state responsibility.

transparency Algorithms The logic, data sources and decision criteria hidden in AI systems can be brought to light in algorithmic transparency. This, in welfare setting, would involve clarifying how eligibility limits go, risk scores are computed, and what various data characteristics have an effect on. Nevertheless, it is not an easy task to gain transparency because machine learning models are commonly rather technical, and they often are engaged with the technologies owned by private producers. The dilemma between transparency and intellectual property issues and system security is a lasting violence on welfare automation (Zuboff, 2015).

Transparency should be meaningful and should not just be technical disclosure, but rather such that it can be interpreted by the non-experts. The explanations are needed in such a manner that can be comprehensible to welfare recipients, caseworkers, and policymakers in their specific jobs. Openness of algorithmic processes creates the opportunity to have informed oversight, conduct a discussion which citizens have the right to know and challenge the choices made on their social and economic lives (Pew Research Center, 2018).

4.2 Accountability Mechanisms in AI-Driven Welfare Systems

One of the values of ethical governance is accountability, which means that the decision-makers are subjected to responsibility of their actions and consequences. Welfare systems that are operated by artificial intelligence make accountability complicated because the process of algorithmic decision-making is distributed across the software developers, data providers, policymakers, and frontline administrators. Welfare automation based on ethics needs to have clear institutional set ups which make it clear that who will design the system, and implement, monitor and correct them.

Algorithms are not used to override the decisions in welfare made by the public authorities, even in case these decisions are supported or automated. This principle relates the fact that governance structures that bar transfer of responsibility to technical systems are critical. In case of failures or injuries, the welfare institutions should be in a position to find the causes of failure and offer solutions. Audit, impact assessment and independent oversight bodies are examples of accountability that can assist in making sure that AI systems do not cross the ethical or legal boundary (Sharma et al., 2026).

Procedural safeguards are also needed in the integration of accountability in the automation of welfare. Since decision processes are clearly documented, algorithms are version-controlled, and the inputs to the data can be traced, the institutions may access and defend the outcomes in a hindsight manner. The mechanisms play a critical role in solving grievances and rectifying institutional biases and learning. AI-friendly welfare systems can be used to substitute the principles of citizen responsibility but not without a strong accountability framework which will steer these systems towards their doom.

4.3 Fairness Metrics and Bias Mitigation Strategies

Neutrality in algorithmic welfare systems is a complex phenomenon, which is not limited to formulating technical precision, but also includes social and distributive justice. The outcome of analytics services created by AI systems might be biased due to the historical data that could communicate the inequalities that are enshrined in history or a discriminatory behavior. Such prejudices may lead to the unequal distribution of benefits, inequalities in the scrutiny of particular groups or unfair exclusion by vital services in a case of welfare governance.

In order to deal with such risks, scholars and policy makers have come up with fairness measurements and bias reduction methods which aim at detecting and alleviating discriminatory results. These methods involve statistical measures of parity, demographic-based error comparison and algorithmic changes that give preference to equity goals. But fairness measurements are generally trade-offs in that once results of one group are better then the results of another would be impacted. These trade-offs have to be taken into serious consideration in terms of ethical welfare automation through the wider normative lenses (Panoptykon Foundation, 2015).

Mitigation of bias should also be perceived as a continuous process since it cannot be a one-time technical solution. The welfare systems are dynamic social environments and algorithmic performance may vary with changes in policies, population and economic conditions. Constant supervision, involvement of stakeholders, and continuous enhancement are thus good in ensuring that the meaning of fairness is maintained in the long run. Making both institutional culture and technical interventions more aware of bias is as significant in fulfilling fair welfare results.

4.4 Institutional Trust and the Role of Public Oversight

Ethical welfare automation requires as well as results in institutional trust. When the citizens feel that systems are transparent, just and responsible, they will tend to accept AI-driven decision making. On the other hand, the sense of transparency or unfairness might destroy trust and bring up opposition, especially in those who are either already disadvantaged by an existing system of welfare or who are those who feel that fair treatment is unjustified. To sustain trust, much technical competence is necessary as well as ethical sensitivity and practice of inclusion in governance (White House, 2016).

The inclusion of the public in the oversight approaches is instrumental in building trust since it guarantees that AI systems are made compliant with social values and legal regulations. External scrutiny of welfare algorithms is done by independent review bodies, civil society organizations, and academics of research. They also play a greater role by maximizing legitimacy by showing that automated systems are not above criticism but it is open to democratic checks and balances.

Finally, accountability, fairness and transparency are also mutually supporting concepts that ought to be combined as a whole in welfare automation. The danger of focusing on these values as individual technical demands is that adhering will be superficial instead of ethical governance. Welfare systems can use artificial intelligence in a more responsible way by incorporating them into the institutional processes and the policy design, as well as the engagement of people, without compromising democracy responsibility and social justice (Misuraca et al., 2012).

5. BIAS, DISCRIMINATION, AND SOCIAL EQUITY IN WELFARE AUTOMATION

5.1 Sources of Algorithmic Bias in Welfare Systems

The factors that cause algorithmic bias in the automation of welfare tend to be the data, design decisions, and institutional conditions under which artificial intelligence applications are created and executed. Algorithms of welfare are generally based on past administrative records, which possibly incorporate old social disparities concerning salary, color, gender, disability or physical geographical location. In case of using such data without critical analysis, such systems may follow a similar path that once the disparities exist, they only repeat and increase them. Consequently, in spite of the lack of discriminatory intention, automated decisions in welfare may work against some groups of people systematically.

The process of creating a design that is used in the model development further affects the development of bias. Distributional impacts can be considerably influenced by the choices regarding the type of variables to incorporate, definitions of outcomes and priorities of the objectives. In this regard, cost-minimizing or fraud detection algorithms might have a higher likelihood of focusing on marginalized groups that are already under an inflated level of attention. Most of such biases are usually entrenched deep in the structure of the system, they can be hard to spot unless critical and ethical studies are conducted (Kumari et al., 2026).

There are also the institutional pressures that lead to biased outcome of the welfare automation. The use of AI systems by the public agencies will be imposed by the efficiency constraints, budgetary issues, or political requirements, which will leave no significant room to reflect and consult with the stakeholders ethically. Within this kind of setting, bias is not a technical vice but a structural problem between the technology and governance set-ups occurring through the interaction of the two. This means that bias will have to be dealt with both technically and institutionally (Oxford Insights, 2019).

5.2 Discriminatory Impacts on Vulnerable Populations

Welfare systems affect the impact of algorithmic bias especially when the vulnerable population that relies on the state to secure their basic needs are involved. The automated decision-making systems may influence the eligibility decisions, level of benefits, observation of compliance, and sanctioning. In case such systems give unfair results, they might deny people their warranted benefits, add administrative loads, or become more monitored, which enhances social exclusion and economic insecurity.

The ability of marginalized populations to challenge automated decisions is usually undermined by factors like the digital illiteracy or language barriers or the absence of legal support. Consequently, discriminatory effects can go uncontested, which paves the way to disadvantage cycles. This is also complicated by the fact that most AI systems are opaque, which means that the affected individuals might not even comprehend why and how they made their decisions to pursue redress. The disempowering and mistrust can be further increased because of the presence of power asymmetries in the framework of welfare where the algorithmic discrimination is particularly acute (Zittrain, 2018).

In addition to personal injustices, discriminatory automation of welfare can have a wider ramification in the society. The instructional grouping and exclusion of specific groups of people are detrimental to the redistributive ambitions of the welfare policy and diminish societal integration. Perceived unfairness or punishments by AI systems can undermine the political trust of welfare institutions, which may result in a decrease in the number of people being drawn to the program, and the polarization of society. It is hence paramount to ensure equity in automation of welfare to ensure justice to individuals as well as stability in society (Government of Canada, 2019).

5.3 Equity-Oriented Design and Inclusive Policy Frameworks

To overcome the lack of social equity in AI-inspired welfare systems, it is necessary to redirect the focus of the welfare systems toward a range of narrow efficiency-focused goals to the principles of well-rounded and justice-based design. Equity-based strategies indicate the necessity to evaluate the impact of the automated decision on various social groups and actively reduce the unproportional harms. This is by ensuring that fairness is factored in all levels of AI lifecycle, data collection and models development, deployment and evaluation.

The comprehensive policy frameworks are important in the operationalization of equity objectives. Policy makers should develop some parameters that will ensure that the welfare algorithms would meet the principles of non-discrimination, proportionality, and social protection. Early identification of risks and informative corrective actions can be achieved through impact assessments that are done to measure the potential distributional impacts prior to deployment. Such evaluations ought to be dynamic and responsive to the evolving social circumstances in that equity is dynamic but not a fixed goal (Veale et al., 2018).

The other vital ingredient of equity-based welfare automation is stakeholder involvement. Inclusion of welfare recipients, advocacy groups and frontline workers in the system design and evaluation can be a good source of information about the lived experiences and unintended outcomes of the system. This type of participatory strategies questions the tendency to make decisions technocratically and make sure the AI systems represent various opinions and values. Inclusivity can be integrated into the governance processes, and the welfare institutions will be able to shift to the direction of the fair and legitimate application of artificial intelligence.

5.4 Toward Socially Just Welfare Automation

To reach social justice in welfare automation, it is necessary to have a holistic view of bias and discrimination as a socio-technical phenomenon and not a technical mistake. The ethical automation should be aware that AI systems are functioning in more extended systems of inequality, power relations, and policy priorities. The problem of bias, by definition, thus requires institutional consequences, the interdisciplinary collaboration and the reflection on normative aspirations (ePanstwo Foundation, 2019).

Going forward welfare governance ought to focus on dynamic systems that will enable the AI systems to be updated and recalibrated in regard to perceived inequities. These are frequent audit checks, transparency programs, and accountability mechanisms enabling the impacted members of the society in question to question decisions. The human touch can never be eliminated when it comes to making the automated systems a means of social support and not a means of marginalizing the members of society.

Finally, there is a great potential to make welfare automation more fair, and even more efficient, provided that it is directed by ethical principles and governance that are equitable. Governments can use artificial intelligence to enhance and not erode the very principles of welfare systems by directly challenging the existence of prejudice and making social justice the main priority in the development of their policies (Russell & Norvig, 2013).

6. HUMAN-IN-THE-LOOP MODELS AND RESPONSIBLE AI GOVERNANCE

6.1 Conceptual Foundations of Human-in-the-Loop Welfare Systems

HITL models are a suburb of approach that is a critical element of governance in the implementation of artificial intelligence in welfare systems. Taking the place of complete automation of decisions-making, HITL models incorporate human decision-making in vital steps of the algorithm functioning, including system development, decision justification, exception management and complaint resolution. This methodology recognizes the shortcomings of artificial intelligence to reflect the contextual finesses, ethical issues, and moral argument which are the fundamental aspects of welfare governance (Jobin et al., 2019).

In welfare procedures, the choice usually entails complicated measures of need, weakness, and social conditions which cannot be entirely validated to information-driven regulations. HITL models will also provide that the automated outputs are vetted and put into perspective by trained practitioners who will be capable of discretion and empathy. Such a hybrid form of decision-making can be used to retain the human component of the welfare policy and maintain the positive aspects of AI technologies at the same time.

Notably, HITL governance is no more than professional protection but a normative obligation to accountability by democratic means. The welfare institutions reconstruct their ethical accountability to citizens by keeping up human responsibility on the final decisions. This strategy is a counter mechanism against the risk of moral disengagement that might come up in case the decision authority would be completely given to the automated systems.

6.2 Operationalizing Human Oversight in Welfare Automation

To achieve effective human oversight, there should be a keen institutional design and well-defined procedure. Welfare agencies should establish the criteria of when and how the human intervention is necessary with thresholds of the cases to be reviewed and escalated. Automated systems can be applied as an illustration of cases being flagged to be assessed further instead of being definitively granted the eligibility. These organized intervention sites allow not to be blindly dependent on the output of an algorithm and make decisions more balanced (Frey & Osborne, 2013).

Capacity building and training are the key elements of the HITL models that are operational. Caseworkers and administrators should be aware of the functionality of AI systems, their limitations, and possible prejudice of the system. In the absence of proper training, the human control will turn more of a symbolic one than a substantive one, as employees are expected to act blindly and follow it through the algorithmic advice. Institutional resilience and ethical governance are enhanced by it because welfare professionals are able to critically interact with AI outputs.

The issue of resource constraints becomes a major problem to the implementation of HITL frameworks. The human supervision is time-consuming, knowledgeable and needs to be supported by an organization, which is not always evident within under-resourced welfare networks. Nevertheless, it is necessary to consider HITL as an investment and not as a cost. Human oversight helps to promote the sustainability and legitimacy of the welfare automation initiatives in the long-term by minimizing the number of errors, deterring unfair results and fostering human trust (Gasser & Schmitt, 2019).

6.3 Responsible AI Governance Frameworks in the Public Sector

Responsible AI governance is not only limited to a particular system but includes institutional norms, policies, and regulation processes that would govern the ethical application of the artificial intelligence in the welfare governance framework. Common features of such frameworks focus on such principles as transparency, accountability, fairness, human autonomy, and social well-being. The application of these principles in the automation of welfare needs coordination both in the technical as well as legal and administrative spheres (University of Toronto – Citizen Lab, 2018).

The public-sector AI governance models are usually provided with the instruments of algorithmic impact assessment, independent audit, and ethical review boards. These processes will allow addressing the risks before they happen and allowing regular tracking of the system performance. Governance structures need to also be aware of power disparities between the state and the citizens in the welfare context so that automation does not further expose the vulnerable, moving them toward the situation of being unable to obtain the necessary services.

The key to the responsible AI governance is interdisciplinary cooperation. Ethical system design and implementation draws the critical views of legal experts, social scientists, technologists, and even welfare practitioners. Through the engagement of discussions across sector and joint accountability, welfare institutions will be able to formulate governance models that are resilient, adaptive and consistent with the values of the people (OECD, 2019).

6.4 Balancing Automation and Human Judgment for Sustainable Welfare Systems

The future of welfare governance is not decided on either human decision-making or artificial intelligence, rather it is in the compromise of both. Robots have the potential to strengthen efficiency and consistency, statistical knowledge, and analytical awareness, whereas biases give the context, ethical sensitivity, and moral responsibility. HITL models provide a realistic way of incorporating these complementary capabilities.

To put this balance into place, continuous review and learning in an institution would be required. The systems of welfare should be adaptable so that the system of governance will change according to the changes in technology and social response. The continuous contact with the affected communities would play the crucial role of pinpointing the arising issues and making sure that automation keeps up to date with the demand (Government of Canada, 2018).

Finally, the concept of human-in-the-loop governance will strengthen the idea that AI must be used as a means of decision support but not as an independent agent in the welfare systems. Through the provision of human controls and the responsible governance practices, the welfare institution could be able to utilize AI innovation by keeping the moral principles behind the social protection and democratic responsibility intact.

7. FUTURE DIRECTIONS AND POLICY IMPLICATIONS FOR ETHICAL WELFARE AUTOMATION

7.1 Emerging Trends in AI-Enabled Welfare Governance

The future of the governance of welfare is becoming more and more defined by the accelerated development of the field of artificial intelligence, data analysis, and online government infrastructure. Current trends show that the move is no longer rule based automation to adaptive, learning based systems that have the capability to combine various sources of data and dynamically react to policy targets. Probability to make more use of predictive analytics, natural language processing, and agent-based systems are likely to assist in the needs assessment, service personalization, and policy assessment.

Although these developments promise opportunities in every aspect of becoming more efficient and responsive, they bring new governance issues. Thc greater the autonomy and complexity of the AI systems, the harder it is to make sure that they are transparent and explainable. The policymakers should therefore expect the technological pathways and design governance mechanisms that can keep up with innovations as opposed to respond to the emergencies once implemented.

There is also another important trend which is the growing unification of welfare systems in diverse sectors such as healthcare, employment, education, and housing. Interoperability is enhanced by AI, which may enhance holistic service delivery, however, there are concerns on data sharing, monitoring, and consent. The governance of future welfare will have to strike a balance between the positives of combined intelligence and significant provisions against privacy, self-determination, and democratic self-control.

7.2 Policy Design for Ethical and Inclusive Automation

Ethical welfare automation needs the policy frameworks that clearly emphasise the social inclusion, equity, and human dignity. The design of future policies should not be based on the technical efficiency measures, but it should integrate the ethical performance measures, such as fairness results, rates of errors fixing, and citizens satisfaction. Incorporation of ethical goals in policy requirements is a method that would make automation process consistent with generic objectives of welfare governance.

The design of the inclusive policy is also inclusive and requires the participatory forms of policy decision making, which involve frontline workers, beneficiaries, and the civil society organizations in the process. Such engagement aids in the identification of the contextual risks, solving of the community-specific issues, and development of the legitimacy. Welfare automation will not produce the beneficial outcomes without meaningful engagement, thus it recreates top-down governments that discriminate against the vulnerable groups.

In addition, the policies should target structural disparities, which determine the quality of the data and the results of algorithms. Data governance, standardization, and representativeness should be adequately invested in to minimize the systemic bias. Accessibility must also be added as an ethical policy design and, hopefully, the digital welfare systems can provide other people who have little to no digital literacy, disabilities, or access to technology.

7.3 Regulatory Adaptation and Institutional Capacity Building

With the development of AI technologies, regulatory frameworks should be changed so that they should be resilient to new risks but allow responsible innovation to occur. Expected traditional methods of regulation such as rules and enforcement ex post might not be adequate to control dynamic AI systems. In the future, there is a high probability that regulation mechanisms will focus on the use of principles, dynamic regulation, and ongoing surveillance.

Effective regulation is essential in institutional capacity building. The welfare agencies need to establish internal AI governance, ethics, and information custodian skills. This involves educating administrators and policymakers on the knowledge of algorithmic systems, interpretation of technical audit, and interaction with experts of other disciplines. Absent such power, regulatory systems will end up being symbolic and not operational.

The cross-jurisdictional cooperation will also be quite relevant in the future regulatory settings. The artificial intelligence means of implementing the welfare systems are often based on the providers of global technologies or the common digital platforms. Regulatory fragmentation that occurs due to differences in the standards across the jurisdictions can be reduced through harmonization and best practice sharing to enhance the ethical consistency of welfare automation (Sheikh et al., 2026).

7.4 Long-Term Implications for Trust and Democratic Governance

Public trust is a key to the success of the AI-enabled welfare systems in the long-term. Transparency problems, unethical behavior, or the feeling of unfairness may decrease the confidence towards technology and society institutions. The governance strategies that should be adopted in the future should therefore focus on the measures of trust building and these should entail transparency, accountability and provision of proper redress mechanisms.

The growing importance of automation in the process of making decisions by the population is also changing the concept of democratic government. Otherwise, the AI can, with a lack of careful management, concentrate power, decrease the possibility of discretionary space among the personnel, and diminish agency among citizens. On the other hand, an AI that is regulated and maturely used can promote democratic potential due to its ability to assist in policymaking based on evidence and make services more responsive.

In future prospective, it is important to perceive ethical automation, in using welfare governance as a process and not the end. Hardly any opportunities assess the situation, discuss it on the mass scale, and learn within an institution, which are the key to overcoming the unpredictability and complexity. With technological innovation aligned with the principles of democracy and social justice, the welfare systems will have an opportunity to use AI not as a replacement of the government, but as the instrument of enhancing ethical and inclusive policies.

CONCLUSION

Ethical automation and artificial intelligence are radically transforming the welfare governance and policy delivery by bringing new skills of efficiency, personalization, and predictable decision-making. In this chapter, it has been revealed that though AI-driven systems can bring major prospects to enhance access and efficacy of welfare services, they also lead to complicated ethical, legal, and governance issues and risks. The problems related to the supposition of algorithms, the lack of transparency in automated decision-making processes, threats to data privacy, and the loss of human discretion provoke the necessity of its careful and value-oriented implementation. Ethical automation in welfare systems can then only be perceived not just as a technical increase, but as a change that has a direct implication in social justice, equity as well as public trust.

The discussion also shows that welfare automation should be a multidimensional governance strategy in order to be responsible. It should have a high level of regulation, clear algorithm design, human-in-the-loop, and participatory policy to enhance accountability and fairness. The other critical aspect is that the welfare agencies should have the capacity to comprehend, supervise and regulate AI systems. The automated welfare systems will only contribute to the existing inequalities and will toxify the democratic values without sufficient knowledge, control mechanisms and ethics. It is therefore important to align AI use with social values and ethical principles to remain legitimate and inclusive in delivering services to the masses.

To sum it up, the future of the welfare governance is associated with the balance between the technological innovation and the aspect of moral accountability and democracy. AI ought to be a facilitative tool, which enhances human sense, increases policy responsiveness, and builds the trust between citizens and the state. Such a balance requires an ongoing assessment, dynamic control, as well as transparency and inclusivity. It is possible to use AI to disrupt the existing welfare systems and government administration, preserving the principal principles of governance by integrating ethical concerns throughout the design, implementation, and governance processes.

REFERENCES

Calo, R. (2017). Artificial intelligence policy: A primer and roadmap. *SSRN*, *51*(2), 399–436. DOI: 10.2139/ssrn.3015350

Dandotiya, M., Goyal, N. K., Yadav, P., Sankhla, K., & Kumari, M. (2026). GEN-ALYTICS: A Deep Dive Into Real-Time Insights via Generative AI. In *Generative AI-Powered Data Architectures* (pp. 105–134). IGI Global Scientific Publishing. https://doi.org/DOI: 10.4018/979-8-3373-5616-7.ch005

ePanstwo Foundation. (2019). *alGOVrithms: Are citizens governed by computer programmes?*

Eubanks, V. (2018). *Automating inequality: How high-tech tools profile, police, and punish the poor*. St. Martin's Press.

European Commission. (2016). Regulation (EU) 2016/679 of the European Parliament and of the Council of 27 April 2016 on the protection of natural persons with regard to the processing of personal data and on the free movement of such data, and repealing Directive 95/46/EC (General Data Protection Regulation). *Official Journal of the European Union, L,* •••, 119.

European Commission High-Level Group on Artificial Intelligence. (2019). *Ethics guidelines for trustworthy artificial intelligence*. European Commission. https://digital-strategy.ec.europa.eu/en/library/ethics-guidelines-trustworthy-ai

Farooqi, A., Das, D., Tripathi, M., Dutta, R., Goyal, N. K., & Sheikh, M. F. (2026). Navigating Ethical Frontiers in AI-Driven Geriatric Care. In Stolakis, K., & Efthymiou, I. (Eds.), *AI for Geriatric Care in an Aging Society* (pp. 243–266). IGI Global Scientific Publishing., DOI: 10.4018/979-8-3373-5462-0.ch009

Frey, C. B., & Osborne, M. A. (2013). *The future of employment: How susceptible are jobs to computerisation?* Oxford Martin School.

Friedman, B., & Nissenbaum, H. (1994). *Bias in computer systems*. Stanford University.

Gasser, U., & Schmitt, C. (2019). Professional norms in AI governance. In *Oxford handbook of ethics of AI*. Oxford University Press.

. Government of Canada. (2018). *Responsible artificial intelligence in the Government of Canada*.

Government of Canada. (2019). Directive on automated decision-making. Treasury Board of Canada Secretariat. https://www.tbs-sct.canada.ca/pol/doc-eng.aspx?id=32592

Government of Canada. (2019). *Algorithmic impact assessment*. Treasury Board of Canada Secretariat.

Goyal, N. K., Gulati, K., Avasthi, A., Kapoor, S. K., Keswani, B., & Gupta, S. (2026). Securing the Imagination: Security and Privacy Challenges in Generative AI Systems. In Elbaghazaoui, B. (Eds.), *Generative AI-Powered Data Architectures* (pp. 239–266). IGI Global Scientific Publishing., DOI: 10.4018/979-8-3373-5616-7.ch010

Goyal, N. K., Kumar, S., Dutta, R., Kothari, V., & Sinha, S. K. (2026). Empowering Elderly Care Through Artificial Intelligence. In Stolakis, K., & Efthymiou, I. (Eds.), *AI for Geriatric Care in an Aging Society* (pp. 1–28). IGI Global Scientific Publishing., DOI: 10.4018/979-8-3373-5462-0.ch001

Jobin, A., Ienca, M., & Vayena, E. (2019). *Global landscape of AI ethics guidelines*. AlgorithmWatch. DOI: 10.1038/s42256-019-0088-2

Johns, F. (2017). Data mining as global governance. In *Oxford Handbook of Law, Regulation and Technology*. Oxford University Press.

Kumari, M., & Goyal, N. K. (2026). Artificial Intelligence in the Cryptocurrency Ecosystem: Crime Mechanisms, Detection Strategies, and Legal Perspectives. In Lin, L. (Ed.), *Innovations in Cryptocrime and Financial Fraud* (pp. 245–282). IGI Global Scientific Publishing., DOI: 10.4018/979-8-3373-0675-9.ch007

Kumari, M., Khan, S. T., Gulati, K., Sharma, P., Goyal, N. K., & Sheikh, M. F. (2026). Procedural Content Generation Using Generative AI. In *Reshaping the Video Game Landscape With AI* (pp. 205–232). IGI Global Scientific Publishing., DOI: 10.4018/979-8-3373-4637-3.ch007

Kumari, M., Kumawat, R., Dutta, R., Khan, S. T., Goyal, N. K., & Sheikh, M. F. (2026). Wireless Communication and IoT Integration in Smart Clothing. In *Smart Wearables* (pp. 195–232). IGI Global Scientific Publishing., DOI: 10.4018/979-8-3373-4287-0.ch008

Kumari, M., Kumawat, R., Tripathi, M., Suganthi, K., Goyal, N. K., & Sheikh, M. F. (2026). Blockchain for Transparency and Traceability in Supply Chains. In Khan, M. (Eds.), *Maximizing Operational Efficiency* (pp. 35–64). IGI Global Scientific Publishing., DOI: 10.4018/979-8-3373-3109-6.ch002

Lodge, M., & Mennicken, A. (2017). Regulation of and by algorithm. *Regulation & Governance*.

Misuraca, G., Broster, D., & Centeno, C. (2012). Digital Europe 2030. *Government Information Quarterly, 29*(S1), S121–S131. DOI: 10.1016/j.giq.2011.08.006

OECD. (2019). *Artificial intelligence in society*. OECD Publishing.

OECD. (2019). *Oslo manual 2018: Guidelines for collecting, reporting and using data on innovation* (4th ed.). OECD Publishing.

OECD. (2019). *Artificial intelligence in society*. OECD Publishing.

. Oxford Insights. (2019). *Government AI Readiness Index.*

Panoptykon Foundation. (2015). *Profiling the unemployed in Poland.*

Pasquale, F. (2019). *The second wave of algorithmic accountability*. Law and Political Economy.

Pew Research Center. (2018). *Public attitudes toward computer algorithms*. https://www.pewresearch.org/

Russell, S., & Norvig, P. (2013). *Artificial intelligence: A modern approach* (3rd ed.). Pearson.

. Selbst, A. D., Boyd, D., Friedler, S. A., Venkatasubramanian, S., & Vertesi, J. (2019). Fairness and abstraction in sociotechnical systems. *FAT*'19 Proceedings*.

Sharma, P., Kumawat, R., Jain, G., Keswani, G., Goyal, N. K., & Sheikh, M. F. (2026). ML-Based IDS for Healthcare IoT. In *Resilient HIoT Systems* (pp. 185–214). IGI Global Scientific Publishing., DOI: 10.4018/979-8-3373-7610-3.ch007

Sheikh, M. F. A., Kapoor, S. K., Goyal, N. K., Tuba, E., & Rao, A. (2026). Enhancing Healthcare Security with Fog Computing and Blockchain Technology. In *Recent Advancements in Artificial Intelligence*. Springer., DOI: 10.1007/978-981-96-7760-3_38

. University of Toronto Citizen Lab. (2018). Bots at the gate: A citizen's rights approach to automated decision-making in Canada.

Veale, M., & Brass, I. (2019). Administration by algorithm? In *Algorithmic Regulation*. Oxford University Press. DOI: 10.1093/oso/9780198838494.003.0006

Veale, M., Van Kleek, M., & Binns, R. (2018). Algorithmic fairness in high-stakes public decisions. In *Proceedings of the 2018 CHI Conference on Human Factors in Computing Systems*. DOI: 10.1145/3173574.3174014

White House. (2016). *Artificial intelligence, automation, and the economy*. Executive Office of the President.

Zittrain, J. (2018). How to exercise the power you didn't ask for. *Harvard Business Review*.

Zuboff, S. (2015). Big other: Surveillance capitalism and the prospects of an information civilization. *Journal of Information Technology*, *30*(1), 75–89. DOI: 10.1057/jit.2015.5

Chapter 3
Artificial Intelligence in Welfare Governance:
Institutional Change and Algorithmic Integration in the Italian Case

Francesco Amato
http://orcid.org/0000-0003-4384-1646
University of Naples "Federico II", Italy

Vincenzo Laezza
http://orcid.org/0009-0001-4564-0066
University of Naples "Federico II", Italy

ABSTRACT

This chapter examines the integration of AI into Italian welfare governance, arguing that it is best understood as an infrastructural intensification rather than a technological rupture. Drawing on analysis of three institutional cases: the SIISL affinity index, INPS Directive No. 8/2024, and the Welfare as a Service strategy, the chapter traces how interoperability infrastructures, algorithmic design, and organisational embedding are interconnected. The analysis centres on two claims: that algorithmic systems reorganise administrative attention by stabilising new regimes of visibility and classificatory relevance, and that public administrations face a structural double bind between governing algorithms and governing through them. The chapter argues that the evaluation of AI in welfare governance is a question of institutional design. Useful transparency, meaningful contestability, protected discretion, and rights-based audit are not ancillary correctives but the conditions under which algorithmic integration can remain compatible with legality, accountability, and social rights.

DOI: 10.4018/979-8-3373-8423-8.ch003

1. INTRODUCTION: WORKING DEFINITION AND ANALYTICAL PERIMETER: WHAT IS AI IN WELFARE GOVERNANCE?

In this chapter, we refer to AI in welfare governance to the situated use of predictive modelling, recommendation, and automation within welfare-related administrative processes. Studies on this hybrid field converge around three intersecting research threads: studies of the digital welfare state document the growing reliance on data warehouses, dashboards, and predictive analytics in the design, implementation, and management of social policy (van Zoonen, 2020); analyses of public-sector algorithmic systems show that such tools increasingly underpin core government functions, including benefits provision (Levy et al., 2021; Madan & Ashok, 2023); and empirical investigations of welfare dashboards reveal that even ostensibly supportive data infrastructures can reorder caseloads, priorities, and frontline roles in practice (Kersing et al., 2022). Taken together, this literature suggests that the analysed concept denotes neither a generic technological trend nor an autonomous decision-maker, but rather a set of computational techniques that become socially and institutionally consequential when embedded in the policy delivery chain (van Zoonen, 2020; Levy et al., 2021; Kersing et al., 2022; Madan & Ashok, 2023), the sequence through which data are collected, integrated, interpreted, and translated into administrative action. Analytically, AI is therefore relevant not in the abstract, but insofar as it enters procedures that shape access to services, care pathways, resource allocation, monitoring and recovery, labour market intermediation, and citizen–institution interactions (Bowker & Star, 1999; Kuziemski & Misuraca, 2020).

This definition assumes a sociotechnical understanding of welfare governance. What matters is not the model alone, but the assemblage within which it operates, composed of databases and registers, interoperability arrangements, platforms, interfaces, integration rules, and the outputs, scores, rankings, alerts, recommendations, through which algorithmic processing becomes actionable in everyday administration (Kitchin, 2014). AI, in this sense, is not treated as an external layer added to welfare institutions, but as an operative component of institutional work (Cordella & Tempini, 2015; Kuziemski & Misuraca, 2020). Its effects become visible when computational outputs are incorporated into routines of classification, prioritisation, routing, verification, or follow-up, thereby beginning to influence how administrations see, sort, and intervene in cases (Bowker & Star, 1999; Bovens & Zouridis, 2002; Kuziemski & Misuraca, 2020).

The analytical perimeter adopted here follows a criterion of administrative translation. An AI system falls within the scope of the chapter when its output is incorporated into a welfare-related process that shapes how cases are handled, even if formal decision-making authority remains with a human operator. This criterion is crucial because the institutional effects of AI do not depend only on whether a decision is formally automated. They also depend on whether outputs enter workflows as guides for action and justification. Rankings, similarity scores, and risk indicators may not issue binding determinations, yet they can still orient behaviour by structuring what appears relevant, urgent, or administratively defensible (Amato, 2025). In welfare settings, where action is often exercised under time pressure, resource constraints, and procedural complexity, tools presented as "support" may nonetheless reorganise discretion through ordering mechanisms that shape practical judgement (Lipsky, 1980; Kuziemski & Misuraca, 2020).

This perimeter is empirically tractable because the sociotechnical assemblage leaves followable traces across documents, systems, and practices. These traces include the construction and linkage of databases, data-sharing agreements, interoperability standards, interface designs, and the procedural junctures at which outputs trigger scrutiny, accelerate routing, or support refusals, recoveries, and prioritisation (Kitchin, 2014; Seaver, 2017). Emphasising observability does not imply full transparency (Ananny & Crawford, 2018; Burrell, 2016). Rather, it identifies a methodological commitment to investigating the points at which algorithmic outputs acquire administrative force and begin to affect recipients' lived conditions. In welfare governance, these points are often located in routine operations, eligibility screening, case prioritisation, fraud detection, compliance monitoring, matching, and referral, where efficiency imperatives can be translated into differentiated distributions of attention and burden (Eubanks, 2018; Bowker & Star, 1999).

At the same time, conceptual clarity requires explicit exclusions. The chapter does not treat all forms of digitisation as AI. Conventional digital workflows or rule-based automation remain outside the scope unless they involve algorithmic inference or recommendation that enters welfare procedures in consequential ways. Nor does the analysis include internal analytics that do not feed into classification, prioritisation, routing, or enforcement. This distinction matters because conflating digitisation, automation, and AI would blur the specific governance issues raised by probabilistic outputs and ranking logics. Conversely, systems are included even when officially described as decision support rather than automated decision-making, because the relevant threshold is not formal automation, but procedural uptake. Once outputs become part of how eligibility, deservingness, compliance, or risk are institutionally produced, they belong to the field of AI in welfare governance.

This working definition serves a mapping function. It delimits the object of inquiry to the socio-organisational embedding of algorithmic outputs within welfare administration, thereby allowing the chapter to remain anchored in a concrete and observable domain rather than a diffuse technology label. It also anticipates a key evaluative implication. When scores, rankings, or recommendations influence welfare trajectories, explainability and contestability are no longer optional normative add-ons; they become conditions of procedural accountability, especially where individuals must be able to understand and challenge how administrative treatment has been shaped by algorithmic mediation (Wachter et al., 2017). On this basis, AI in welfare governance can be defined, more precisely, as the set of sociotechnical arrangements through which algorithmic outputs acquire administrative relevance within welfare processes.

2. FROM INNOVATION AS A "LEAP" TO INNOVATION AS INFRASTRUCTURAL INTENSIFICATION

Understanding how AI enters Italian welfare governance requires situating it within a longer trajectory of administrative digital transformation, rather than treating it as a technological leap. In this chapter, the idea of a leap refers to a view of innovation as a discontinuous, largely self-standing break, such as the moment in which a new technology appears to transform welfare administration on its own, independent of the data architectures, interoperability arrangements, and organisational routines that precede it (Laezza et al., 2025). Recent research shows that this interpretation is analytically misleading (Madan & Ashok, 2023). Algorithmic systems do not arrive in an institutional vacuum, nor do they replace earlier forms of administration (Cordella & Tempini, 2015; Kersing et al., 2022). They become operationally relevant only where databases, platform environments, data-sharing arrangements, and organisational programmes have already created the conditions for their uptake (Cordella & Tempini, 2015; Dunleavy et al., 2006; Margetts & Dunleavy, 2013).

From this perspective, AI is better understood as a process of infrastructural intensification, a distinction that is not simply terminological but carries significant analytical implications. On this reading, AI does not enter welfare governance as an exogenous rupture. It emerges from, and acts upon, infrastructures already undergoing consolidation. This also means that innovation is unlikely to suspend pre-existing institutional asymmetries. More plausibly, it reworks them through new forms of coordination, standardisation, and data-based intervention, often reinforcing differences in analytical capacity, access to data, and agenda-setting power across administrative actors and territorial levels (Janssen & van der Voort, 2016; Kuziemski & Misuraca, 2020).

Recent literature on AI in public administration and welfare has engaged with questions concerning the predictive performance, bias, and fairness of individual systems (Levy et al., 2021; Madan & Ashok, 2023). While a growing but still developing strand of work has begun to examine the institutional processes through which algorithmic outputs are gradually incorporated into welfare procedures, classifications, and routines (Kersing et al., 2022; Sztandar-Sztanderska & Mazur, 2025). Within this latter strand, country-specific contributions on the Italian case appear comparatively limited, particularly in relation to the PNRR-driven investment in interoperable data infrastructures (Sacchi & Scarano, 2024). Where the institutional dimension is addressed, contributions often concentrate on one analytical level at a time, whether on infrastructural enablers, on the design of specific algorithmic artefacts, or on patterns of organisational uptake, with the result that the connection between infrastructural consolidation, system design, and incorporation into administrative routines tends to be presupposed rather than reconstructed in an integrated manner. The contribution of this chapter is to address this gap by treating these levels as connected moments of a single institutional process, observable in Italian documentary materials.

From this starting point, the chapter pursues three connected objectives.

The first is to reconstruct the trajectory of digital transformation in the Italian welfare system and to place AI adoption within that trajectory rather than outside it. The analytical purpose is to show that interoperability and data integration are not secondary technical details, but practical preconditions for the deployment of algorithmic systems in public administration. Official documents that link welfare innovation to shared data infrastructures and inter-institutional coordination are therefore read as indicators of an infrastructural phase in which algorithmic techniques become both thinkable and administratively actionable. In this sense, initiatives such as Welfare as a Service, the use of shared data hubs, and the broader emphasis on interoperability do not merely provide contextual background. They reveal the organisational and infrastructural environment that makes AI deployable in welfare governance, while also making visible the risk that these same developments deepen existing stratifications rather than displace them.

The second objective is to examine how algorithmic integration reorganises administrative attention. The central claim here is that the significance of AI in welfare does not lie only in prediction or efficiency gains, but in its capacity to alter what becomes visible, urgent, traceable, and therefore actionable within institutional routines. Once rankings, scores, recommendations, or alerts are incorporated into welfare processes, they reshape the practical economy of administration, whereby some cases are surfaced earlier, some trajectories are accelerated, some populations become more intensely monitored, while others recede from institutional visibility. In this sense, AI does not simply add an informational layer to pre-existing procedures. It can modify temporalities of intervention, hierarchies of relevance, and the operational thresholds through which welfare institutions distinguish priority from non-priority, risk from normality, and responsiveness from delay (Bowker & Star, 1999; Eubanks, 2018; Alston, 2019). This objective prepares the ground for the empirical analysis by clarifying why apparently heterogeneous materials, including a matching system, an internal directive, and a sustainability report, can be read within the same analytical frame, insofar as each captures a different point at which algorithmic rationalities are translated into administrative ordering.

The third objective is to develop an institutional analysis of how algorithmic outputs are embedded in organisational routines, discretionary practices, and accountability arrangements. The chapter therefore moves beyond evaluations centred exclusively on bias, fairness, or predictive accuracy. These dimensions remain important, but they are not sufficient to explain how welfare effects are actually produced. Even when formal decision-making authority remains with human actors, the incorporation of outputs into workflows can structure how discretion is exercised, how justifications are formulated, and how responsibility is distributed across the organisation. In digitised welfare settings, judgement does not disappear; rather, it is mediated by systems, interfaces, classifications, and documentation procedures that redefine the informational environment of administrative action (Lipsky, 1980; Bovens & Zouridis, 2002). For this reason, accountability is treated here as a property of institutional design rather than as an intrinsic feature of models. What matters is not only whether an output can be technically explained, but whether its use is documented, contestable, and situated within a recognisable chain of administrative responsibility (Wachter et al., 2017; Kuziemski & Misuraca, 2020).

These three objectives converge in the chapter's main argument: the evaluation of AI in welfare governance is, before anything else, a question of institutional design. This claim guides the structure of the analysis and explains the logic of the empirical section that follows. Rather than attempting a comprehensive survey of the Italian welfare system, the chapter adopts an exploratory selection of three cases that together make it possible to reconstruct a specific chain: from infrastructural consolidation to algorithmic design, to organisational uptake. The empirical materials are therefore chosen not because they are exhaustive, but because they illuminate analytically distinct yet connected moments in this process. The SIISL case makes visible how algorithmic recommendation enters service delivery through the ordering of opportunities; Directive No. 8/2024 shows how AI is formalised as an internal governance programme through mapping, classification, and procedural oversight; and the Sustainability Report, together with Welfare as a Service, reveals the broader institutional rationality through which data integration, proactivity, and personalisation are framed as strategic assets (INPS, 2024a; INPS, 2024b; INPS, 2024c).

This is also why the chapter relies on documentary analysis of official sources. Press releases, directives, sustainability reporting, and PNRR-related materials are treated as institutional artefacts that do more than describe innovation. They define problems, stabilise solution frames, and encode implicit hierarchies of value concerning efficiency, coordination, responsiveness, and control (Margetts & Dunleavy,

2013; Cordella & Tempini, 2015). The aim is not to infer measurable outcomes from these documents, nor to claim that institutional discourse fully captures implementation in practice. The ambition is more delimited and methodologically cautious. It is to reconstruct how AI is positioned, justified, and rendered governable within the Italian welfare field, and to show why the connection between infrastructural consolidation, design choices, and organisational embedding is the key analytical pathway for understanding its sociological significance.

3. ITALIAN CONTEXT: DIGITAL TRANSFORMATION OF PUBLIC ADMINISTRATION, INTEROPERABILITY, AND WELFARE STRATIFICATION

The integration of AI within Italian welfare governance must be situated within this broader trajectory. Over the past decade, Italy has pursued an extensive programme of administrative digitalisation, increasingly shaped by European policy frameworks and accelerated by the implementation of the National Recovery and Resilience Plan (PNRR) (European Commission, 2021; Presidenza del Consiglio dei Ministri, 2021). In this light, the current incorporation of AI systems can be understood as part of an ongoing process of administrative reorganisation centred on interoperability, data integration, and platform-based service provision.

In the literature on digital-era governance, administrative digitalisation is rarely interpreted as mere technological modernisation. Instead, it is understood as a form of institutional reconfiguration that transforms coordination mechanisms, redistributes informational resources, and reshapes organisational capabilities within the public sector (Dunleavy et al., 2006; Margetts & Dunleavy, 2013; Cordella & Tempini, 2015). From this perspective, the relevance of interoperability becomes evident. Algorithmic systems depend on structured, accessible data environments. Without interoperable infrastructure, recommendation tools and automated classification cannot operate effectively, especially within administrative routines. Interoperability thus functions as the pragmatic condition of possibility for algorithmic governance (Janssen & Estevez, 2013; Zuiderwijk & Janssen, 2014).

This infrastructural dimension acquires particular significance in the Italian welfare system, historically characterised by a highly stratified institutional architecture. Responsibilities for welfare provision are distributed across multiple levels of government, central administrations, regions, municipalities, and semi-autonomous agencies, within a framework marked by regulatory complexity and significant territorial variation in administrative capacity (Ferrera, 2005; Ascoli & Pavolini, 2015). Institutional fragmentation and differentiated digital maturity mean that efforts to integrate data and coordinate infrastructures do not unfold within a neutral organisational landscape. They interact with pre-existing asymmetries of resources, expertise, and authority.

Within this trajectory, the PNRR identifies digital transformation and interoperability as enabling conditions for both administrative efficiency and policy innovation (European Commission, 2021; Presidenza del Consiglio dei Ministri, 2021). A central component of this strategy is the development of the Piattaforma Digitale Nazionale Dati (PDND; in English, National Digital Data Platform), conceived as a national infrastructure for secure data exchange among public administrations (Dipartimento per la Trasformazione Digitale, 2022). By standardising protocols and facilitating real-time information flows among institutional actors, the PDND aims to mitigate long-standing fragmentation in administrative data ecosystems.

In the welfare domain, these infrastructural efforts are accompanied by initiatives to foster inter-institutional collaboration through shared data environments. Projects such as Welfare as a Service (WaaS) illustrate this orientation. Developed within the broader digital transformation agenda, WaaS promotes the creation of a shared data hub designed to support policy analysis and service development through cooperation among INPS, municipalities, the Ministry of Labour, and ANCI (INPS, 2024a). In relation to the chapter's first objective, initiatives of this kind are analytically relevant not simply because they mention innovation, but because they make visible the infrastructural environment in which algorithmic techniques can be operationalised within welfare governance.

These developments suggest that the adoption of AI should not be interpreted as an isolated technological innovation. Algorithmic systems are instead layered onto infrastructures that are themselves undergoing consolidation. This layering dynamic produces ambivalent institutional consequences. On the one hand, interoperable infrastructures may reduce informational fragmentation, enable more coordinated interventions across agencies, and support more responsive forms of service delivery. Comparative research on digital governance indicates that integrated data environments can improve cross-agency coordination and facilitate more tailored policy responses (Janssen & Estevez, 2013; Margetts & Dunleavy, 2013).

On the other hand, infrastructural integration can also intensify existing disparities within the welfare system. When algorithmic tools rely on centrally consolidated datasets, the actors responsible for designing infrastructures and governing data flows may acquire enhanced agenda-setting power. Control over standards, classifications, and data architectures becomes a source of institutional influence, shaping which forms of knowledge are operationalised within welfare administration and which forms of intervention become technically feasible (Kitchin, 2014; Van Dijck et al., 2018).

Moreover, the benefits of data-driven administration are unevenly distributed across territories. Regions and municipalities differ substantially in terms of digital readiness, technical expertise, and organisational resources (OECD, 2020). In such circumstances, the introduction of data-intensive infrastructures may advantage administrations already equipped with stronger analytical capacity, while placing additional adaptation pressures on less resourced actors. Digital transformation thus risks reinforcing what Bovens and Zouridis (2002) describe as a transition toward system-level bureaucracy, in which administrative discretion becomes increasingly mediated by centrally designed information systems.

These developments unfold against the backdrop of broader sustainability pressures affecting welfare governance. Demographic ageing, fiscal constraints, and labour market volatility have intensified demands for efficiency, monitoring, and fraud prevention within welfare administration (Ferrera, 2005; Bonoli & Natali, 2012). Interoperable data infrastructures promise to support these objectives by enabling more extensive forms of data linkage, real-time monitoring, and predictive analysis. However, the same capabilities also expand the scope of administrative visibility. Data integration alters what becomes measurable, traceable, and administratively actionable within welfare governance (Kitchin, 2014).

From a sociological perspective, the significance of this transformation lies not only in improved coordination but also in the classificatory power of data infrastructures. As Bowker and Star (1999) emphasise, systems of classification shape how institutions perceive and organise social reality. Similarly, research in the sociology of data has shown that data linkage and algorithmic categorisation actively structure opportunities, constraints, and forms of institutional attention (Fourcade & Healy, 2017). Integrated data environments, therefore, do not simply reflect welfare populations; they participate in producing the categories and priorities through which those populations are governed.

4. THEORETICAL FRAMEWORK FOR GOVERNING THROUGH ALGORITHMS, ADMINISTRATIVE ATTENTION, AND CLASSIFICATORY POWER

Today's algorithmic integration in welfare administration is most commonly evaluated in terms of prediction accuracy (Aarab et al., 2025) and operational efficiency (Madan & Ashok, 2023). These are not irrelevant criteria; however, they are insufficient. What such integration reorganises, more fundamentally, is the structure of administrative attention, the conditions under which certain cases, needs, and claimants become visible, urgent, and actionable within institutional routines, and others do not (Bowker & Star, 1999; Kersing et al., 2022). Engaging with this transformation requires a theoretical posture that is neither uncritically enthusiastic about innovation nor dismissive of it. Drawing on Amaturo and Aragona (2021), this chapter adopts a stance of critical optimism: an analytically vigilant yet constructively oriented engagement with digital systems, which treats algorithmic tools as arrangements whose effects are contingent upon the institutional, organisational, and professional contexts in which they operate.

Within this orientation, the core theoretical tension can be articulated as a double bind dilemma faced by public administrations (Røhnebæk & Breit, 2022). On the one hand, administrations are required to govern algorithms, to regulate, scrutinise, and constrain their operation in order to prevent harms, discrimination, opacity, and infringements of rights. On the other hand, they are increasingly expected to govern through algorithms, deploying data-driven systems to enhance efficiency, responsiveness, and coordination in public service delivery (Yeung, 2018; Kuziemski & Misuraca, 2020). These imperatives are structurally intertwined. The term double bind is used here in an institutional and analytical sense, rather than in Bateson et al.'s (1956) original clinical formulation, specifically to designate a situation in which public administrations face two simultaneous and partially contradictory imperatives that cannot simply be chosen between.

The double bind acquires specific salience in welfare contexts because efficiency is not a neutral administrative value (Alston, 2019; Considine et al., 2022). In welfare administration, efficiency materialises as operational rules, thresholds, categories, prioritisation criteria, and temporal benchmarks (Kersing et al., 2022; Gallagher & Griffin, 2023). It shapes which cases are processed first, which beneficiaries are flagged for scrutiny, and how quickly interventions are triggered (Alston, 2019; Kersing et al., 2022; Gallagher & Griffin, 2023). When algorithmic systems are introduced to optimise matching, detect anomalies, or prioritise cases, they do not merely accelerate existing procedures but stabilise new regimes of visibility and urgency in which certain needs become more readily detectable and particular behaviours become traceable and governable, while others recede from administrative attention.

This dynamic finds a precise theoretical anchorage in the sociology of classification, since Bowker and Star (1999) demonstrate that standards and classificatory systems are not neutral technical devices but infrastructures in which political choices and social consequences are sedimented. In welfare governance, algorithmic scoring systems, recommendation models, and risk classifications operate as classificatory infrastructures (Bowker & Star, 1999; Sztandar-Sztanderska & Mazur, 2025). They organise populations into categories of eligibility, employability, compliance, or vulnerability (Eubanks, 2018; Desiere et al., 2019; Sztandar-Sztanderska & Mazur, 2025). Once embedded in data architectures and interfaces, these categories orient action, justify decisions, and shape accountability practices (Bowker & Star, 1999; Bovens & Zouridis, 2002; Kersing et al., 2022).

From this perspective, classification operates as an infrastructure of power. It stabilises distinctions that become consequential for access to services, monitoring intensity, and resource allocation. It defines what is administratively legible and what remains peripheral. In welfare systems facing fiscal pressure and organisational fragmentation, these infrastructural choices can intensify stratifications rather than neutralise them (Kuziemski & Misuraca, 2020). The institutional effects of classificatory logics are therefore irreducibly context-dependent, since the same scoring system may reinforce stratification in one administrative setting and reduce it in another, depending on how thresholds, overrides, and accountability arrangements are designed.

The same infrastructures that enable coordination, proactivity, and service responsiveness (Kuziemski & Misuraca, 2020; Mergel et al., 2024) are those that generate opacity, data fragility, and explanatory difficulty, and it is precisely this co-production that makes the tension between governing algorithms and governing through them structurally irresolvable rather than merely practical (Røhnebæk & Breit, 2022).

Opacity may derive from model complexity or proprietary constraints (Burrell, 2016; Busuioc, 2021). Practical inscrutability arises when frontline operators lack the interpretive resources to situate outputs within their professional judgement. Data fragility refers to the dependence of algorithmic systems on heterogeneous and evolving infrastructures, whose incompleteness or inconsistencies may propagate through predictive processes (Pellegrino et al., 2019; Kuziemski & Misuraca, 2020). At the same time, the very process that makes welfare cases legible to algorithmic systems may also make them thinner in social and interpretive terms. To be processed computationally, heterogeneous life situations must be translated into standardised variables, comparable categories, and machine-readable proxies.

These forms of added complexity do not negate the potential of AI systems for welfare governance, but they underscore that introducing AI thickens rather than simplifies institutional arrangements. Governance must therefore address not only risks of discrimination or error, but also the infrastructural and classificatory transformations that accompany algorithmic integration. The theoretical framework adopted here holds these dimensions together, affirming the possibility of service enhancement while foregrounding the structural tension between governing algorithms and governing through them.

5. FROM DATA TO ADMINISTRATIVE DECISION IN WELFARE GOVERNANCE

The analytical bridge between the theoretical framework and the empirical reconstruction lies in identifying the concrete points at which algorithmic output enters administrative processes and becomes consequential for action. The object is therefore not the model in isolation, but the moment of translation through which rankings, scores, similarity indices, or risk classifications are incorporated into case management systems, dashboards, matching platforms, and monitoring tools. At these junctures, output ceases to be a technical artefact and becomes an operational input within welfare governance.

The theoretical framework elaborated above establishes the conditions under which algorithmic outputs become consequential for discretion, justification, and accountability. The analytical task of this section is to identify the concrete organisational junctures at which this mediation occurs and to specify the mechanisms through which it shapes administrative conduct. The passage from data to decision unfolds along identifiable segments of the policy delivery chain. Outputs may shape the ordering of job offers, the prioritisation of beneficiaries, the triggering of verification procedures, or the allocation of appointments. Incorporation can occur through interface design, automated alerts, colour-coded indicators, or default sorting criteria. Each of these mechanisms structures the field of visible possibilities. What becomes salient, urgent, or administratively actionable is filtered through the system's classificatory logic. A distinction is then required between systems formally described as decision support and systems that produce de facto binding effects (Amato, 2026). Many welfare applications are presented as advisory instruments that leave final authority to human officials. They generate ordered lists or probabilistic assessments without issuing formal determinations. However, ordering mechanisms are not neutral. Rankings establish hierarchies of relevance. Scores compress complex situations into comparable metrics. Thresholds activate procedural consequences. Even without formal decisional status, these devices orient behaviour by delimiting the range of plausible or institutionally defensible options (Yeung, 2018).

The decision remains formally human, but the conditions under which it is taken are reconfigured. Street-level bureaucrats operate within constrained environments shaped by time pressure, organisational targets, and available information (Lipsky, 1980). When algorithmic outputs become embedded in workflows, they modify that informational environment. A high-risk score may automatically prompt additional scrutiny. A high-affinity ranking may be interpreted as an indicator of appropriateness. Ignoring a system-generated alert may require explicit justification. Discretion persists, yet it becomes exercised in dialogue with, or in response to, the output (Amato, 2026).

This mediation affects practices of justification and responsibility throughout the organisation. Decisions may increasingly be explained by reference to system indicators rather than exclusively through narrative assessment. Conversely, departures from algorithmic recommendations may need to be documented to remain auditable. Interaction logs, timestamps, and decision histories generate new forms of visibility for oversight bodies and internal control mechanisms. Accountability is thereby recalibrated. It is no longer solely a matter of individual judgment but of the interplay between human action, procedural design, and system-generated classification (Bovens & Zouridis, 2002).

Studying AI in welfare governance, therefore, requires attention to the micro-junctures of incorporation through which outputs enter routines and begin to influence conduct. This includes how outputs are displayed, which thresholds trigger procedural consequences, whether alerts are optional or mandatory, who is authorised to override them, and how such overrides are recorded. These design choices determine whether a system operates as a weak advisory cue or as a strong orienting device that structures administrative conduct.

6. THREE ITALIAN CASES AS AN INFRASTRUCTURE–DESIGN–ORGANISATIONAL USE CHAIN

The empirical analysis presented in this section is based on the qualitative documentary analysis of institutional sources produced by INPS, the Ministry of Labour and Social Policies, and the Department for Digital Transformation, supplemented by the regulatory and programmatic materials that frame them (PNRR documentation, the legal acts that reformed the Italian activation regime, and the European AI Act). The aim is neither to provide an exhaustive account of AI adoption in Italian welfare governance nor to evaluate outcomes comprehensively. The ambition is more delimited and methodologically cautious. Here we reconstruct how AI is framed, institutionalised, and rendered operational within welfare administration, and make visible how institutional discourse positions algorithmic systems within ongoing infrastructural and organisational transformations.

The case selection followed a logic of theoretically informed purposive sampling (Patton, 2002) that is coherent with the analytical chain articulated in Section 2. Building on our argument that AI in welfare governance is best understood as the result of a chain connecting infrastructural consolidation, algorithmic design, and organisational uptake, each case was chosen to occupy a distinct, non-substitutable position along that chain. The 2023 Sustainability Report, read alongside the Welfare as a Service initiative, captures the macro-level rationale for framing data integration and infrastructural consolidation as strategic assets of the Institute. The SIISL platform, and specifically the "affinity index", captures the level of algorithmic design, where a specific artefact is built upon the data infrastructures and made to act on labour-market matching. Directive No. 8 of 2024 captures the meso-level of organisational uptake, since it formalises the conditions under which AI systems are mapped, classified, and rendered governable inside INPS as an organisation. Three additional criteria reinforce this selection. First, all three sources refer to the same institutional ecosystem, namely the INPS perimeter and its inter-institutional partners (the Ministry of Labour, municipalities, ANCI, the Department for Digital Transformation), thereby reconstructing the analytical chain within a coherent organisational field rather than across heterogeneous administrations. Second, the documents are recent and clustered in 2023–2024, which corresponds to the implementation phase of the PNRR and to the period in which AI has begun to be explicitly thematised within INPS as an object of internal governance. Third, the three documents have different communicative functions: a press release, an internal directive, and a sustainability report, which makes it possible to address how the same institutional rationality is articulated for different audiences and through different discursive registers. The cases are therefore not selected as representative of all AI applications in Italian Welfare, but as "information-rich" cases (Patton, 2002) that maximise variation along the analytical dimensions relevant to the chain.

The analytical procedure follows established conventions of qualitative document analysis as developed in the sociology of documents and in interpretive policy research (Prior, 2003; Atkinson & Coffey, 2004; Bowen, 2009). In line with this tradition, the documents were not approached as transparent records of organisational practice, nor were they processed through formal thematic coding aimed at achieving categorical saturation. Saturation-driven coding presupposes a corpus large enough to support cross-document categorial inference. In contrast, the analysis carried out here works with a small, carefully selected set of institutional artefacts whose interest lies precisely in their specific position within the chain. The reading of each document was therefore organised in three sequential movements. The first was descriptive: it mapped the document's structure, its declared purposes, the institutional actors mobilised, and the technical-administrative vocabulary employed. The second was contextual: it situated the document within the regulatory and infrastructural environment described in Sections 3 and 5, in particular the PNRR, the PDND, the post-2023 reform of activation policies, and the European AI Act. The third was interpretive: it identified the institutional rationality articulated by the document, that is, how problems are defined, which solutions are stabilised, which actors are made responsible, and which value hierarchies (efficiency, coordination, responsiveness, control) are encoded. The same three-movement procedure was applied uniformly to all three cases. A consistent set of analytical questions guided the procedure: how the AI system or governance device is named and bounded; which problems it is presented as solving; which infrastructures, actors, and procedures it presupposes or mobilises; how its expected effects on administrative routines are described; how accountability, oversight, and discretion are addressed (or left implicit); and which value hierarchies underpin the document's justificatory work.

We jointly analysed these documents, which rest on the analytical understanding of documents as institutional artefacts rather than as neutral descriptions of innovation (Atkinson & Coffey, 2004; Prior, 2008; Bowen, 2009). On this view, these documents are social products that are made, circulated, and consumed in institutionally organised ways; they exercise agency in defining problems, stabilising solution frames, and constructing legitimate audiences (Yanow, 2000; Prior, 2008). What allows the three documents to be read alongside one another is therefore not their genre or their evidentiary status, but their common function as discursive operations through which an institution makes AI thinkable, governable, and presentable within welfare administration. The press release performs the public framing of the system for citizens and the labour market; the directive performs the internal codification of governance responsibilities and procedural safeguards; the sustainability report performs the strategic narration of digital transformation for institutional stakeholders. Read together, these three discursive operations make visible the same institutional rationality at three different levels of articulation, which is precisely what the chain infrastructure–design–organisational uptake requires.

The three cases illuminate analytically distinct yet connected dimensions of the broader argument, each operationalising a specific node of the theoretical framework developed in Sections 4 and 5. SIISL provides an empirical instance of algorithmic recommendation as a mechanism of administrative attention: it makes visible how ordering logics restructure which possibilities appear salient and actionable at the point of interaction between citizens and welfare services. Directive No. 8/2024 instantiates the double bind dilemma at the meso-level of organisational governance, showing how the same administration simultaneously attempts to govern algorithms and govern through them by formalising oversight structures, risk classifications, and procedural checkpoints. The 2023 Sustainability Report and Welfare as a Service, finally, operate at the level of classificatory infrastructure and strategic datafication: they reveal the macro-rationality through which interoperability and data integration are framed as enabling conditions for anticipatory and personalised welfare provision.

6.1 SIISL and the "Affinity Index": Recommendation and Matching as the Ordering of Possibilities

The introduction of the "affinity index" within the Sistema Informativo per l'Inclusione Sociale e Lavorativa (SIISL; in English, Information System for Social and Work Inclusion) platform marks a significant step in the integration of

AI-based recommendation systems into Italian welfare governance. According to official INPS communication, the index employs machine learning techniques and natural language processing to estimate semantic similarity between textual fields contained in curricula vitae and job vacancies (INPS, 2024a). The stated objective is to facilitate user interaction with the database and to offer beneficiaries employment opportunities deemed "more suitable" within the broader framework of labour-market activation policies.

Analytically, the affinity index can be understood as an instance of administrative translation. It converts a complex and contested construct, "employability", into a semantic similarity metric that becomes operational through interface ranking. This translation is not merely descriptive. Once implemented as a default ordering of vacancies, semantic proximity begins to function as a proxy for suitability, thereby influencing what is rendered visible, plausible, and institutionally defensible within activation pathways (Bowker & Star, 1999; Lipsky, 1980). The system does not simply retrieve information; it organises possibilities.

From an institutional perspective, the system is not formally presented as an automated decision-making system in the strict sense (Amato, 2025). It does not determine eligibility, nor does it impose legally binding outcomes. Rather, it is framed as a support tool to help users and operators navigate a large, complex set of employment opportunities. However, research on algorithmic governance has shown that the distinction between "support" and "decision" is often analytically insufficient (Yeung, 2018; Amato, 2025). Recommendation systems do not need to issue final determinations in order to exercise institutional effects. By producing rankings, filters, and prioritised lists, they structure the field of visible options and thereby orient trajectories of action.

The affinity index performs this ordering by ranking potential matches based on calculated semantic proximity. In doing so, it introduces an implicit metric of appropriateness grounded in the representational choices embedded in the model's training data, feature-extraction logic, and textual-reduction processes. Natural language processing techniques necessarily transform complex occupational biographies and job descriptions into structured representations. This operation is never neutral. It privileges certain attributes, keywords, and semantic associations while marginalising others. As Bowker and Star (1999) argue, every classificatory system embeds assumptions about what counts as relevant, comparable, and similar.

A second analytical dimension concerns temporality. Welfare-to-work policies have traditionally depended on iterative interactions among beneficiaries, caseworkers, and service providers, involving assessment, counselling, and contextual evaluation of available opportunities. By accelerating the preliminary matching phase, the affinity index compresses the temporal interval between profile registration and job proposal. This acceleration may enhance responsiveness and align with digital-era governance narratives centred on immediacy, personalisation, and service efficiency (Margetts & Dunleavy, 2013). At the same time, temporal compression modifies the rhythm within which discretion is exercised.

The system must also be understood within the broader reconfiguration of Italian activation policies following the replacement of the Citizenship Income (Reddito di Cittadinanza) with instruments such as the Support for Training and Work (Supporto per la Formazione e il Lavoro) and the Inclusion Allowance (Assegno di Inclusione) (Decreto-legge 4 maggio 2023, n. 48). In this policy environment, job matching is not merely informational. It is embedded within conditionality regimes linking benefit access and continuity to participation in activation pathways.

At this point, a methodological distinction is required to specify the evidentiary status of the analysis presented in this subsection. The press release and the related INPS communications support directly only one of the three levels at which the affinity index can be discussed. They document what the institution declares about the system, namely its technical principles (machine learning and natural language processing), its stated function (semantic similarity between curricula and vacancies), and the policy purposes it is meant to serve within the activation regime. A second level is analytically inferable from this documentary evidence in combination with the conceptual frame developed in Sections 4 and 5: that an interface-level ranking operates as a classificatory infrastructure, that semantic proximity functions as a proxy for suitability, and that the recommendation reorganises the field of visible options. A third level concerns the actual consequences of the system for caseworkers' discretion, user trajectories, and the redistribution of administrative attention within activation services. Statements about this third level, including the effect of temporal compression on professional judgement, are plausible in light of the existing literature on street-level discretion and digital welfare (Lipsky, 1980; Bovens & Zouridis, 2002; Kersing et al., 2022), but they cannot be directly established based on press releases or technical descriptions.

In analytical terms, SIISL displays how AI enters welfare governance through recommendation infrastructures that reorder possibilities rather than directly impose outcomes. The affinity index shows that even non-binding systems can reconfigure visibility, accelerate administrative temporalities, and embed normative assumptions within apparently neutral matching processes. The crucial point is not to treat the system as inherently problematic or inherently beneficial, but to recognise that its institutional effects depend on how algorithmic ordering interacts with activation rules, organisational discretion, interface design, and user interpretation.

6.2 Directive No. 8/2024 of the INPS Director General: The Institutionalisation of Internal AI Governance

If the SIISL case shows how algorithmic ordering enters welfare delivery at the operational interface, Directive No. 8 of 8 April 2024 issued by the INPS Director General makes visible the meso-level at which AI becomes governable as an organisational programme (INPS, 2024b). Unlike the affinity index, which operates at the point of interaction between the user and the platform, the Directive acts on the internal architecture of governance. It defines responsibilities, establishes classification criteria, and introduces procedural safeguards for the adoption and management of AI systems within the Institute.

The Directive functions as a mechanism of administrative translation, transforming the open-ended, potentially indeterminate problem of AI governance into a structured set of typologies, risk classes, responsibilities, and procedural checkpoints. It converts sociotechnical uncertainty into an organisational grammar that can be documented, allocated, and monitored, thereby shaping how accountability is produced in practice (Bovens, 2007; Kuziemski & Misuraca, 2020). What this reveals is that AI enters welfare institutions not simply through technical systems, but also through governance devices that stabilise its acceptability and define the conditions for its legitimate use.

Structurally, the Directive situates AI adoption within a framework comprising the mapping of existing systems, risk classification, and the construction of a working governance architecture. It also clarifies the range of AI typologies under consideration, including recommendation systems, scoring tools, and decision-support applications (INPS, 2024b), and makes explicit that AI is not conceived narrowly as automated decision-making but as a broader family of data-driven instruments with varying degrees of influence over administrative processes.

From this perspective, the Directive treats AI not as a discrete technological acquisition but as an organisational transformation requiring intervention across multiple dimensions, encompassing people, processes, governance structures, technological choices, and the management of data sources. The importance of this formulation lies in its breadth, since it recognises that the implications of AI extend beyond model performance or software procurement to affect staff training, the allocation of responsibilities, the organisation of workflows, the design of documentation requirements, and the governance of the data infrastructures upon which algorithmic systems depend.

A central analytical issue concerns accountability. In conventional bureaucratic settings, accountability chains are typically linked to hierarchical structures and clearly defined roles. The introduction of AI complicates these arrangements because responsibility may be distributed across developers, data providers, internal

IT units, policy designers, procurement actors, and frontline staff. The Directive addresses this problem by formalising oversight responsibilities and procedural checkpoints designed to contain the diffusion of responsibility. This is especially relevant in light of what Bovens (2007) describes as "many hands" problems, in which the multiplication of actors involved in a decision environment obscures who may ultimately be held answerable.

By imposing system mapping and governance oversight, the Directive attempts to stabilise this complexity. Accountability is not treated as an intrinsic attribute of a model but as a property of organisational design. This distinction is crucial for the chapter's argument. It reinforces the claim that AI governance in welfare administration is fundamentally an issue of institutional architecture rather than merely one of technical calibration.

The Directive constructs a framework of intentional governance defining responsibilities, classification criteria, and procedural checkpoints for the adoption and management of AI systems within INPS. It does not, however, document a system that is already fully operating. The analysis of the Directive therefore supports conclusions about the formal institutionalisation of AI governance within the Institute, that is, about the discursive and regulatory establishment of a governance architecture, but not about the effective implementation of that architecture in everyday administrative practice. Whether the mapping of existing systems, the risk classes, and the oversight procedures actually shape decisions, workflows, and accountability practices once operationalised remains an empirical question beyond the scope of our analysis. The contribution of this subsection is therefore confined to showing how AI is rendered governable as an organisational programme, while the question of how this governance programme is enacted in everyday administration remains open and would require organisational ethnography, interviews with the actors charged with its implementation, and analysis of the documentation produced by the procedural checkpoints the Directive establishes.

At the same time, the institutionalisation of governance frameworks may generate new forms of bureaucratic layering. The introduction of risk registers, compliance procedures, inventories, and documentation obligations does not eliminate proceduralism; rather, it reconfigures it. As Cordella and Tempini (2015) suggest, digital transformation frequently produces new bureaucratic forms rather than displacing bureaucracy altogether. Directive No. 8/2024, therefore, exemplifies the entry of AI into welfare governance as an organisational programme. It shows that algorithmic systems are embedded within formalised structures of risk management, procedural control, and institutional oversight.

6.3 2023 Sustainability Report and Datafication Projects: Personalisation, Proactivity, Digital Assistance, and Welfare as a Service as an Infrastructural Asset

Where the previous two cases illuminate AI at the operational interface and internal governance, the 2023 Sustainability Report opens a third analytical window onto the broader strategic rationality through which datafication is framed within INPS (INPS, 2024c). Unlike technical documentation or internal regulatory acts, the report articulates the organisational narrative by which AI, interoperability, and data integration are presented as drivers of service enhancement, efficiency, and institutional modernisation.

The report foregrounds a set of interconnected initiatives, including the development of personalised services, the move toward proactive welfare provision, the expansion of digital assistance tools and cognitive systems, and the positioning of Welfare as a Service (WaaS) as a strategic asset (INPS, 2024c). These initiatives are part of the broader digital transformation agenda promoted by the PNRR and enabled by the PDND, which supports structured data exchange across public administrations.

The evidentiary status of this material requires explicit specification before proceeding to its analytical reading. The 2023 Sustainability Report belongs to the genre of strategic institutional narration. The report is produced for external stakeholders and articulates how the Institute wishes to position its digital transformation agenda within the broader ecosystem of Italian welfare governance. It is therefore not a record of verified implementation, but an act of institutional self-presentation. References to "personalisation", "proactivity", "digital assistance", and the framing of Welfare as a Service as a strategic asset must be read accordingly. They constitute institutional frames through which datafication is rendered desirable, coherent, and legitimate, rather than measured outcomes of administrative performance. The analysis that follows treats these frames as objects of inquiry, asking what kind of welfare rationality they articulate and which institutional asymmetries they presuppose or stabilise, while remaining agnostic about the extent to which they correspond to operational realities. Documenting the actual scope, uptake, and effects of the initiatives narrated in the report would require sources beyond institutional self-reporting.

From an analytical perspective, this discourse can be read through the concept of datafication, understood as the transformation of social and administrative processes into quantifiable and interoperable data flows that can be analysed, recombined, and rendered actionable (Kitchin, 2014). In this framing, data are not merely collected for archival purposes but are positioned as infrastructural resources that make possible anticipatory and personalised forms of intervention. Within welfare governance, this implies a shift from reactive administration, in which the institution responds to claims, demands, or applications, to proactive administration, in which needs are inferred and intervention is imagined as preceding formal request.

The Sustainability Report frames this shift in explicitly positive terms, emphasising better targeting, enhanced user experience, improved efficiency, and optimised resource use. This language resonates with broader narratives of digital-era governance, in which platform integration, user-centricity, and real-time responsiveness are treated as hallmarks of administrative modernisation (Margetts & Dunleavy, 2013). The presentation of WaaS as a shared data hub is particularly revealing in this respect, signalling a move toward infrastructural coordination in which data integration across municipalities, the Ministry of Labour, and other actors is framed as a condition for overcoming the longstanding fragmentation of Italian welfare governance (INPS, 2024c).

However, the analytical significance of this development lies not only in the promise of coordination but also in the transformation of administrative visibility that it entails. As Fourcade and Healy (2017) argue, data integration does not simply improve access to information but redefines what becomes knowable, comparable, and actionable within institutional settings. Once datasets concerning employment trajectories, benefit receipt, demographic characteristics, and service interactions are rendered interoperable, new forms of cross-referencing and profiling become technically possible.

This shift toward anticipatory governance carries both coordinating potential and stratifying effects. While integrated data environments may support more coherent policy design and cross-agency coordination, centralised data hubs may simultaneously accentuate asymmetries in analytical capacity and agenda-setting power, reproducing at the level of strategic datafication the infrastructural stratifications already described in Section 3.

The report's emphasis on data sharing as a lever for resource optimisation also needs to be situated against the wider fiscal and demographic pressures affecting the Italian welfare state. Efficiency is not presented as an isolated technical aim but is tied to sustainability. In a context marked by demographic ageing, budgetary constraint, and pressure to improve monitoring and fraud control, the capacity to identify overlaps, unmet needs, or anomalous patterns through integrated data becomes politically salient.

In sum, the 2023 Sustainability Report situates AI within a broader infrastructural vision of welfare transformation. Welfare as a Service is not presented merely as a technical platform but as an enabling asset for policy coordination, proactive intervention, and more efficient resource allocation. This case makes visible the macro-level rationality through which algorithmic systems are framed as instruments of personalisation and administrative anticipation.

7. EXPECTED BENEFITS AND ENABLING CONDITIONS

The preceding analysis has argued that AI in Italian welfare governance is best understood as a process of infrastructural intensification rather than technological leap. Any discussion of the potential benefits associated with AI must therefore remain attentive to the structural tension running through the cases examined, since the same systems that promise greater responsiveness, coordination, and proactivity also raise questions of legitimacy, mediation, and institutional control.

One of the recurrent risks of data-driven governance is that probabilistic inference comes to function as administrative judgment. Predictive analytics identify patterns, associations, and potential mismatches across integrated datasets, enabling earlier detection and potentially more anticipatory intervention. In welfare administration, this analytical capacity may support a more proactive approach, for instance by identifying individuals exposed to labour-market exclusion, detecting service gaps before formal demand is expressed, or surfacing cases that might otherwise remain institutionally invisible.

At the same time, the argument developed in the chapter requires that these analytical capacities not be confused with legitimate grounds for decision. As the broader literature on algorithmic regulation has repeatedly stressed, predictive signals do not amount to normative determinations (Yeung, 2018; Citron & Pasquale, 2014). Correlation is not culpability, risk indication is not suspicion, and scoring is not entitlement. Once inference is operationalised without sufficient institutional mediation, analytical outputs may begin to function as quasi-deterministic judgements.

A second dimension concerns the possible reduction of friction in citizen–institution interactions. In the Italian welfare system, marked by institutional fragmentation, procedural density, and a high degree of regulatory stratification, digital assistance tools, personalised interfaces, and recommendation systems may offer tangible benefits by simplifying access pathways, reducing search costs, and making available options more intelligible. However, reduced friction does not necessarily produce greater equity. One of the persistent findings of digital transformation research is that access, skills, and trust remain unevenly distributed across populations (van Dijk, 2005; Helsper, 2021).

A third plausible benefit concerns automating repetitive administrative tasks. Routine activities such as document classification, data verification, and cross-referencing procedures absorb considerable organisational time and resources. Under favourable conditions, AI-supported automation may reduce standardised errors, accelerate routine processing, and allow staff to redirect effort toward relational, interpretative, and evaluative tasks. In principle, such a shift could strengthen rather than diminish the meaningful exercise of discretion, especially in welfare settings where contextual judgement remains indispensable.

However, the realisation of such gains depends on organisational conditions that cannot be taken for granted. Technology does not generate efficiency on its own. Research on e-government and administrative reform has consistently shown that process redesign, staff training, skill development, and incentive alignment are critical to the effective uptake of digital systems (Cordella & Tempini, 2015; Fountain, 2001). Without these supporting conditions, automation may fail to simplify administrative work and instead create additional layers of compliance, verification, and technical dependence.

A further plausible advantage lies in the coordinating potential created by infrastructural consolidation, which may allow administrations to identify duplications, trace unmet needs, and detect forms of fragmentation that remain obscured when information is dispersed across institutional boundaries (Gil-Garcia et al., 2010). Nevertheless, as the preceding analysis has shown, interoperability simultaneously enlarges the field of administrative visibility and potential control.

Taken together, these considerations suggest that the benefits associated with AI integration in welfare governance are neither demonstrable from the documentary record nor self-executing. They are claimed and, under specific institutional conditions, plausible. The distinction between epistemic function and operational deployment therefore remains analytically indispensable. AI systems generate knowledge in the form of rankings, scores, classifications, and correlations. However, institutions decide how those outputs are taken up, how much weight they are given, how they are documented, and whether they become actionable within administrative routines.

8. CONCLUSIONS

The analysis developed across this chapter supports an equilibrium thesis for the Italian case. AI can contribute to service strengthening, coordination, and administrative responsiveness in welfare governance, and the three empirical cases examined here offer concrete evidence of this potential. SIISL demonstrates how recommendation infrastructures can reduce search costs and accelerate labour-market activation. Directive No. 8/2024 shows that internal governance frameworks can institutionalise anticipatory risk management. The datafication strategy embedded in Welfare as a Service points toward more coordinated, evidence-informed forms of policy planning across institutional levels. Nevertheless, these gains remain conditional upon explicit governance of the institutional trade-offs they entail, and this is why interpreting AI as infrastructural intensification rather than technological rupture is not merely a descriptive refinement but a policy-relevant choice. The key question is not whether AI works in the abstract, but how algorithmic outputs are translated into administrative routines, how classifications and thresholds are stabilised, and how responsibility, visibility, and discretion are redistributed across interoperable infrastructures.

From this perspective, the dilemmas raised by AI in welfare governance cannot be treated as a secondary ethical layer to be added after implementation. They are internal to the very conditions under which algorithmic systems become administratively consequential. When algorithmic systems influence access to services, prioritisation, monitoring, or the maintenance of entitlements, they intervene directly in conditions of social protection. In such contexts, explainability is not a purely communicative add-on, nor a matter of formal compliance alone. It becomes a condition of contestability and institutional trust.

A first policy implication concerns useful transparency. Transparency must be operational rather than declarative. It should provide intelligible accounts of how rankings, scores, and recommendations are produced, how they are meant to be used, which thresholds activate procedural consequences, and under what conditions outputs may be overridden. The point is not exhaustive technical disclosure, but practical comprehensibility. In welfare settings, transparency is useful only insofar as it supports contestability, enables accessible appeal, and allows affected individuals to understand how algorithmic outputs contributed to their treatment.

The rise of interoperability and data integration, as illustrated by both Directive No. 8/2024 and the Welfare as a Service strategy, complicates the chain of responsibility across the welfare system. Algorithmic systems are rarely self-contained administrative devices. They rely on data from multiple public bodies, software supplied by external vendors, infrastructure designed elsewhere, and implementation decisions made by internal organisational units. A second policy implication follows: accountability under interoperability cannot be delegated to technical artefacts or reduced to model properties. It must be institutionalised through role allocation, documentation practices, risk classification, and governance procedures that trace how outputs are used.

At the level of day-to-day welfare practice, the decisive issue is discretion. Even where no formally automated decision is made, rankings, alerts, and scores can exert de facto binding force, structuring what appears relevant, urgent, or defensible within organisational routines. A third policy implication follows: discretion must be protected as a substantive institutional capacity. Organisational design must ensure that algorithmic outputs do not become de facto mandates without explicit authorisation, clear override procedures, and documented safeguards.

These concerns become particularly acute when one considers the risks of indirect discrimination and intensified administrative surveillance. Systems introduced to support fraud detection, recover improper payments, or prioritise intervention may slide into pre-emptive selection practices that concentrate scrutiny on populations already exposed to vulnerability. Models trained on historical data may reproduce prior patterns of exclusion even in the absence of explicit discriminatory intent (Eubanks, 2018).

The interpretive scope of this contribution is shaped by three methodological limits that should be explicitly acknowledged before concluding. First, the analysis is based exclusively on official institutional sources, which are particularly informative about how AI is framed and institutionalised, but they articulate intended uses and authoritative narratives, not the contested, situated, and often invisible work of implementation. Second, the documentary corpus has not been triangulated with primary empirical materials, such as interviews with caseworkers and managers, observations of administrative routines, or analyses of operational data. Claims about the actual effects of algorithmic systems on discretion, attention, and accountability, therefore, remain plausible inferences grounded in the existing literature, rather than direct empirical findings. Third, the chapter examines three cases within a single institutional ecosystem in a specific policy phase, so its analytical reach is limited to the reconstruction of an institutional process and does not support generalisations about Italian welfare administration as a whole. These limits define the boundaries within which the conclusions of this chapter should be read, and they also identify the most pressing directions for the empirical work that should follow.

The overall conclusion is consistent with the definitional, theoretical, and empirical choices that have structured the chapter. In Italian welfare governance, AI adoption is a matter of institutional design before it is a matter of technology. Useful transparency, meaningful contestability, co-design oriented to upstream choices, and rights-based forms of impact assessment and audit are not ancillary correctives to this assemblage. They are the institutional conditions under which AI can be integrated into welfare governance in ways that remain compatible with legality, accountability, and the substantive protection of social rights.

REFERENCES

Aarab, A., El Marzouki, A., Boubker, O., & El Moutaqi, B. (2025). Integrating AI in public governance: A systematic review. *Digital*, *5*(4), 59. Advance online publication. DOI: 10.3390/digital5040059

Amato, F. (2025). *Assessing the Social Implications of Automated Decision Making Systems: A Case Study*. PhD Dissertation, University of Naples "Federico II".

Amato, F. (2026). Sistemi di Decisione Automatizzata. In Amaturo, E., Aragona, B., Acampa, S., & Amato, F. (Eds.), *Tecnologie emergenti e ricerca sociale. Prospettive teoriche e pratiche empiriche* (pp. 50–60). FrancoAngeli.

Amaturo, E., & Aragona, B. (2021). Critical optimism: A methodological posture to shape the future of digital social research. *Italian Sociological Review*, 11(4S), 167. DOI: 10.13136/isr.v11i4S.429

Ananny, M., & Crawford, K. (2018). Seeing without knowing: Limitations of the transparency ideal and its application to algorithmic accountability. *New Media & Society*, *20*(3), 973–989. DOI: 10.1177/1461444816676645

Ascoli, U., & Pavolini, E. (Eds.). (2015). *The Italian welfare state in a European perspective: A comparative analysis*. Policy Press., DOI: 10.1332/policypress/9781447316886.001.0001

Atkinson, P., & Coffey, A. (2004). Analysing documentary realities. In D. Silverman (Ed.), Qualitative research: Theory, method and practice (2nd ed., pp. 56–75). Sage.
Bateson, G., Jackson, D. D., Haley, J., & Weakland, J. (1956). Toward a theory of schizophrenia. *Behavioral science*, 1(4), 251-264

Bonoli, G., & Natali, D. (Eds.). (2012). *The politics of the new welfare state*. Oxford University Press. DOI: 10.1093/acprof:oso/9780199645244.001.0001

Bovens, M. (2007). Analysing and assessing accountability: A conceptual framework. *European Law Journal*, *13*(4), 447–468. DOI: 10.1111/j.1468-0386.2007.00378.x

Bovens, M., & Zouridis, S. (2002). From street-level to system-level bureaucracies: How information and communication technology is transforming administrative discretion and constitutional control. *Public Administration Review*, *62*(2), 174–184. DOI: 10.1111/0033-3352.00168

Bowen, G. A. (2009). Document analysis as a qualitative research method. *Qualitative Research Journal*, *9*(2), 27–40. DOI: 10.3316/QRJ0902027

Bowker, G. C., & Star, S. L. (1999). *Sorting things out: Classification and its consequences*. MIT Press. DOI: 10.7551/mitpress/6352.001.0001

Burrell, J. (2016). How the machine "thinks": Understanding opacity in machine learning algorithms. *Big Data & Society*, *3*(1), 2053951715622512. Advance online publication. DOI: 10.1177/2053951715622512

Busuioc, M. (2021). Accountable artificial intelligence: Holding algorithms to account. *Public Administration Review*, *81*(5), 825–836. DOI: 10.1111/puar.13293 PMID: 34690372

Citron, D. K., & Pasquale, F. (2014). The scored society: Due process for automated predictions. *Washington Law Review (Seattle, Wash.)*, *89*(1), 1–33.

Considine, M., McGann, M., Ball, S., & Nguyen, P. (2022). Can robots understand welfare? Exploring machine bureaucracies in welfare-to-work. *Journal of Social Policy*, *51*(3), 519–534. DOI: 10.1017/S0047279422000174

Cordella, A., & Tempini, N. (2015). E-government and organizational change: Reappraising the role of ICT and bureaucracy in public service delivery. *Government Information Quarterly*, *32*(3), 279–286. DOI: 10.1016/j.giq.2015.03.005

Decreto-legge 4 maggio 2023, n. 48. (2023). *Misure urgenti per l'inclusione sociale e l'accesso al mondo del lavoro*. Gazzetta Ufficiale della Repubblica Italiana.

Desiere, S., Langenbucher, K., & Struyven, L. (2019). *Statistical profiling in public employment services: An international comparison*. OECD Social, Employment and Migration Working Papers.

Dipartimento per la Trasformazione Digitale. (2022). *Piattaforma Digitale Nazionale Dati (PDND)*. Presidenza del Consiglio dei Ministri.

Dunleavy, P., Margetts, H., Bastow, S., & Tinkler, J. (2006). New public management is dead—Long live digital-era governance. *Journal of Public Administration: Research and Theory*, *16*(3), 467–494. DOI: 10.1093/jopart/mui057

Eubanks, V. (2018). *Automating inequality: How high-tech tools profile, police, and punish the poor*. St. Martin's Press.

European Commission. (2021). *Italy's recovery and resilience plan*. European Commission.

European Union. (2024). *Regulation (EU) 2024/1689 laying down harmonised rules on artificial intelligence (AI Act)*.

Ferrera, M. (2005). *The boundaries of welfare: European integration and the new spatial politics of social protection*. Oxford University Press. DOI: 10.1093/0199284660.001.0001

Fountain, J. E. (2001). *Building the virtual state: Information technology and institutional change*. Brookings Institution Press.

Fourcade, M., & Healy, K. (2017). Seeing like a market. *Socio-economic Review*, *15*(1), 9–29.

Gallagher, P., & Griffin, R. (2023). (In)accuracy in algorithmic profiling of the unemployed: An exploratory review of reporting standards. *Social Policy and Society*, 1–14.

Gil-Garcia, J. R., Pardo, T. A., & Burke, G. B. (2010). Conceptualizing information integration in government. In Scholl, H. J. (Ed.), *E-government: Information, technology, and transformation* (pp. 179–202). M.E. Sharpe.

Helsper, E. J. (2021). The digital disconnect: The social causes and consequences of digital inequalities. *Sage (Atlanta, Ga.)*. Advance online publication. DOI: 10.4135/9781526492982

INPS. (2024a). *Arriva l'Intelligenza Artificiale per l'incrocio tra domanda e offerta di lavoro* [Comunicato stampa, 5 aprile 2024].

INPS. (2024b). *Messaggio n. 1384 del 08-04-2024. Linee guida per l'implementazione di sistemi di Intelligenza Artificiale – Direttiva n. 8.*

INPS. (2024c). *Bilancio di Sostenibilità 2023.*

INPS. (2024d). *Welfare as a Service (WaaS): Piattaforma dati per la cooperazione nel welfare territoriale.*

Janssen, M., & Estevez, E. (2013). Lean government and platform-based governance—Doing more with less. *Government Information Quarterly*, *30*, S1–S8. DOI: 10.1016/j.giq.2012.11.003

Janssen, M., & Van Der Voort, H. (2016). Adaptive governance: Towards a stable, accountable and responsive government. *Government Information Quarterly*, *33*(1), 1–5. DOI: 10.1016/j.giq.2016.02.003

Kersing, M., van Zoonen, L., Putters, K., & Oldenhof, L. (2022). The changing roles of frontline bureaucrats in the digital welfare state: The case of a data dashboard in Rotterdam's Work and Income department. *Data & Policy*, *4*, e24. DOI: 10.1017/dap.2022.16

Kitchin, R. (2014). The data revolution: Big data, open data, data infrastructures and their consequences. *Sage (Atlanta, Ga.)*. Advance online publication. DOI: 10.4135/9781473909472

Kuziemski, M., & Misuraca, G. (2020). AI governance in the public sector: Three tales from the frontiers of automated decision-making in democratic settings. *Telecommunications Policy*, *44*(6), 101976. DOI: 10.1016/j.telpol.2020.101976 PMID: 32313360

Laezza, V., Petrosino, A., & Luise, V. (2025). ChatGPT and the social appropriation of AI on Discord. *Fuori Luogo Journal of Sociology of Territory, Tourism. Technology*, *22*(1), 49–64. DOI: 10.6093/2723-9608/11111

Levy, K., Chasalow, K. E., & Riley, S. (2021). Algorithms and decision-making in the public sector. *Annual Review of Law and Social Science*, *17*(1), 309–334. DOI: 10.1146/annurev-lawsocsci-041221-023808

Lipsky, M. (1980). *Street-level bureaucracy: Dilemmas of the individual in public services*. Russell Sage Foundation.

Madan, R., & Ashok, M. (2023). AI adoption and diffusion in public administration: A systematic literature review and future research agenda. *Government Information Quarterly*, *40*(1), 101774. DOI: 10.1016/j.giq.2022.101774

Margetts, H., & Dunleavy, P. (2013). The second wave of digital-era governance: A quasi-paradigm for government on the Web. *Philosophical Transactions of the Royal Society A*, 371(1987).

Mergel, I., Dickinson, H., Stenvall, J., & Gasco, M. (2024). Implementing AI in the public sector. *Public Management Review*, 1–14.

OECD. (2020). *Digital Government Index: 2019 results*. OECD Publishing.

Patton, M. Q. (2002). *Qualitative research and evaluation methods* (3rd ed.). Sage.

Pellegrino, G., Söderberg, J., & Milan, S. (2019). Datafication from below: Epistemology, ambivalences, challenges. *Tecnoscienza – Italian Journal of Science &. Technology Studies*, *10*(1), 89–113.

Presidenza del Consiglio dei Ministri. (2021). *Piano Nazionale di Ripresa e Resilienza*. PNRR.

Prior, L. (2003). Using documents in social research. *Sage (Atlanta, Ga.)*.

Prior, L. (2008). Repositioning documents in social research. *Sociology*, *42*(5), 821–836. DOI: 10.1177/0038038508094564

Røhnebæk, M. T., & Breit, E. (2022). 'Damned if you do and damned if you don't': A framework for examining double binds in public service organizations. *Public Management Review, 24*(7), 1001–1023. DOI: 10.1080/14719037.2021.1882542

Sacchi, S., & Scarano, G. (2024). Digital transformation of public employment services in the post-pandemic era: Evidence from Italy as a latecomer country. *The Australian Journal of Social Issues*. Advance online publication. DOI: 10.1002/ajs4.385

Seaver, N. (2017). Algorithms as culture: Some tactics for the ethnography of algorithmic systems. *Big Data & Society*, *4*(2). Advance online publication. DOI: 10.1177/2053951717738104

Sztandar-Sztanderska, K., & Mazur, J. (2025). Politics and algorithmic articulation of law: Tracing the discrepancies and backstage decision-making in the development of the profiling algorithm in Polish labour market policies. *International Journal of Law in Context*, *21*(4), 1–20. DOI: 10.1017/S1744552325100141

Van Dijck, J., Poell, T., & De Waal, M. (2018). *The platform society: Public values in a connective world*. Oxford University Press. DOI: 10.1093/oso/9780190889760.001.0001

van Dijk, J. A. G. M. (2005). The deepening divide: Inequality in the information society. *Sage (Atlanta, Ga.)*. Advance online publication. DOI: 10.4135/9781452229812

van Zoonen, L. (2020). Data governance and citizen participation in the digital welfare state. *Data & Policy*, *2*, e10. DOI: 10.1017/dap.2020.10

Wachter, S., Mittelstadt, B., & Floridi, L. (2017). Why a right to explanation of automated decision-making does not exist in the General Data Protection Regulation. *International Data Privacy Law*, *7*(2), 76–99. DOI: 10.1093/idpl/ipx005

Yanow, D. (2000). Conducting interpretive policy analysis. *Sage (Atlanta, Ga.)*.

Yeung, K. (2018). Algorithmic regulation: A critical interrogation. *Regulation & Governance*, *12*(4), 505–523. DOI: 10.1111/rego.12158

Zuiderwijk, A., & Janssen, M. (2014). Open data policies, their implementation and impact: A framework for comparison. *Government Information Quarterly*, *31*(1), 17–29. DOI: 10.1016/j.giq.2013.04.003

ADDITIONAL READING

Alston, P. (2019). *Report of the Special Rapporteur on extreme poverty and human rights*. United Nations.

Bowker, G. C., & Star, S. L. (1999). *Sorting things out: Classification and its consequences*. MIT Press. DOI: 10.7551/mitpress/6352.001.0001

Eubanks, V. (2018). *Automating inequality: How high-tech tools profile, police, and punish the poor*. St. Martin's Press.

Fourcade, M., & Healy, K. (2017). Seeing like a market. *Socio-economic Review, 15*(1), 9–29.

Janssen, M., & van den Hoven, J. (2015). Big and open linked data (BOLD) in government: A challenge to transparency and privacy? *Government Information Quarterly, 32*(4), 363–368. DOI: 10.1016/j.giq.2015.11.007

Kuziemski, M., & Misuraca, G. (2020). AI governance in the public sector: Three tales from the frontiers of automated decision-making in democratic settings. *Telecommunications Policy, 44*(6), 101976. DOI: 10.1016/j.telpol.2020.101976 PMID: 32313360

Lipsky, M. (1980). *Street-level bureaucracy: Dilemmas of the individual in public services*. Russell Sage Foundation.

Margetts, H., & Dunleavy, P. (2013). The second wave of digital-era governance: A quasi-paradigm for government on the Web. *Philosophical Transactions of the Royal Society A*, 371(1987).

van Zoonen, L. (2020). Data governance and citizen participation in the digital welfare state. *Data & Policy, 2*, e10. DOI: 10.1017/dap.2020.10

Wachter, S., Mittelstadt, B., & Floridi, L. (2017). Why a right to explanation of automated decision-making does not exist in the General Data Protection Regulation. *International Data Privacy Law, 7*(2), 76–99. DOI: 10.1093/idpl/ipx005

Yeung, K. (2018). Algorithmic regulation: A critical interrogation. *Regulation & Governance, 12*(4), 505–523. DOI: 10.1111/rego.12158

KEY TERMS AND DEFINITIONS

Administrative Attention: The practical economy of relevance within welfare institutions, the conditions under which certain cases, claimants, or needs become visible, urgent, and actionable within organisational routines, and others do not. Administrative attention in the context of algorithmic systems recalibrates this economy by stabilising new hierarchies of salience through rankings, scores, and alerts.

Algorithmic Governance: The use of computational systems, including recommendation engines, scoring tools, and risk classifiers, to orient, structure, or mediate administrative decision-making in the public sector. Distinguished from full automation by the persistence of formal human authority alongside system-generated outputs that nonetheless shape institutional conduct.

Classificatory Power: The capacity of classification systems, including algorithmic ones, to shape institutional perception and organise social reality. Following Bowker and Star (1999), classificatory infrastructures in welfare governance sort populations into administrative categories of eligibility, risk, or compliance, with consequential effects on access, monitoring, and resource allocation.

Datafication: The transformation of social and administrative processes into quantifiable, interoperable data flows that can be analysed, recombined, and rendered actionable. In welfare governance, datafication enables anticipatory forms of intervention by making patterns, needs, and anomalies detectable before formal claims are submitted.

Double Bind: An institutional condition in which public administrations face two simultaneous and partially contradictory imperatives that cannot simply be chosen between: the obligation to govern algorithms (through oversight, contestability, and rights protection) and the pressure to govern through algorithms (for efficiency, responsiveness, and coordination). Used here in an institutional and analytical sense, not in the original clinical formulation.

Infrastructural Intensification: An analytical frame for understanding AI adoption in welfare governance as an emergent layer grafted onto pre-existing data architectures, interoperability arrangements, and organisational routines, rather than as a discontinuous technological leap. This framing highlights continuities, path dependencies, and the conditional character of algorithmic deployment.

Interoperability: The capacity of information systems, databases, and digital platforms operated by distinct public authorities to exchange, integrate, and render mutually usable data. In welfare governance, interoperability functions as the practical precondition for algorithmic operation, enabling recommendation systems, risk classifiers, and proactive service tools to draw on integrated, cross-institutional data flows.

Street-Level Bureaucracy: A concept developed by Lipsky (1980) referring to front-line public servants whose exercise of discretion directly shapes the lived experience of policy for citizens. In digitised welfare settings, street-level discretion is not eliminated but increasingly mediated by algorithmic outputs, interface designs, and documentation requirements that reconfigure the informational environment in which professional judgement is exercised.

Welfare as a Service (WaaS): An INPS-led initiative promoting the creation of a shared data hub for cross-institutional cooperation in welfare governance, involving municipalities, the Ministry of Labour, and ANCI. Analytically significant as an instance of infrastructural coordination that positions data integration as a strategic enabler of proactive, personalised, and evidence-informed welfare provision.

Chapter 4
Governance of Digital Data in Welfare:
Transparency, Accountability, and Regulation in Data-Driven Decision-Making

Noorjahan Siddiqui
http://orcid.org/0009-0009-8252-0053
Lovely Professional University, Punjab, India

Manzoor Ahmad Ahmad Khanday
http://orcid.org/0000-0002-0053-098X
Lovely Professional University, Punjab, India

ABSTRACT

The growing use of digital technologies, artificial intelligence (AI), and data analytics has transformed modern welfare systems, enabling data-driven policy design, eligibility assessment, and benefit distribution. While these technologies improve efficiency and accuracy, they raise significant challenges related to digital data governance. This chapter examines transparency, accountability, and regulation in data-driven welfare systems. Transparency ensures citizens understand how their data is collected and used, while accountability mechanisms enable oversight and redress for errors or discriminatory outcomes. Regulation is essential to protect data rights and ensure ethical AI use. Drawing on theoretical and empirical examples, the chapter highlights challenges such as data bias, privacy risks, limited algorithmic explainability, and power imbalances. It argues that robust data governance frameworks are vital for public trust, social justice, and fairness in digital welfare systems.

DOI: 10.4018/979-8-3373-8423-8.ch004

INTRODUCTION

Digital Transformation of Welfare Governance

Over the past few decades, digital technologies have significantly transformed the way governments design and administer welfare systems. Traditionally, welfare administration was largely manual, paper-based, and dependent on human decision-making processes. However, the rapid advancement of digital technologies—such as big data, cloud computing, and artificial intelligence—has fundamentally altered the structure and functioning of welfare governance (Dunleavy & Margetts, 2010; Fountain, 2004). Today, governments collect and manage large volumes of digital data related to citizens, including social benefits, employment records, and demographic characteristics. This transformation has enabled public institutions to improve administrative efficiency and expand the reach and effectiveness of welfare programs. Digital welfare governance can therefore be understood as the application of digital tools and data infrastructures in the planning, implementation, and monitoring of social welfare programs. Through digital platforms, governments are able to identify eligible beneficiaries, monitor service delivery, and evaluate policy outcomes in real time. Many countries have adopted integrated systems that combine multiple welfare databases, such as social security records, employment data, and healthcare information. These systems allow governments to process large datasets efficiently and support evidence-based policymaking (Mayer-Schönberger & Cukier, 2013).

The adoption of digital systems has also improved transparency and coordination across government departments. Digital databases help policymakers better understand social needs, leading to more efficient resource allocation. For instance, digital identification systems and centralized databases enable governments to verify beneficiaries and reduce duplication or fraud in welfare programs. Additionally, online platforms have increased accessibility to welfare services, minimizing the need for physical visits to government offices (Noveck, 2021).

Despite these advantages, the digital transformation of welfare governance also introduces several challenges. Increasing reliance on digital systems raises concerns related to data privacy, cybersecurity, and technological inequality. Digitally disadvantaged populations may face barriers in accessing welfare services, which can lead to exclusion.

Growth of Data-Driven Public Policy

A major development in contemporary governance is the increasing reliance on data-driven policymaking. Governments are progressively using data analytics and statistical models to inform policy decisions. Instead of relying solely on traditional evaluation methods, digital datasets are now used to analyze social patterns, assess policy outcomes, and predict future needs. Large administrative datasets collected through welfare systems provide valuable insights into the socio-economic conditions of citizens. These datasets include information on employment, income, health, education, and demographics. Such data enables policymakers to identify vulnerable groups and design targeted welfare programs. Furthermore, data analytics helps governments evaluate policy effectiveness and improve program implementation. Digital data has also strengthened accountability and monitoring in governance. Governments can track welfare distribution, identify inefficiencies, and detect irregularities in service delivery. For example, real-time monitoring systems allow administrators to oversee welfare payments and program enrollment, thereby reducing corruption and mismanagement. However, the growing dependence on data-driven decision-making also raises important governance concerns. Government datasets often contain sensitive personal information, creating significant privacy risks. Additionally, data analytics models may introduce bias, potentially leading to unfair policy outcomes. If datasets are incomplete or unrepresentative, decision-making processes may disadvantage certain groups in society (O'Neil, 2017). This shift alters traditional administrative discretion, introducing new variables in how organizational networks navigate algorithmic outputs and power dynamics (Goldsmith & Yang, 2025; Kawakami et al., 2024).

Role of Artificial Intelligence in Welfare Systems

Artificial intelligence (AI) has become an increasingly important component of modern welfare administration. AI technologies enable governments to process large volumes of data and perform complex decision-making tasks with minimal human intervention. These systems are used to determine eligibility for benefits, detect fraud, predict social trends, and enhance service delivery (Ahn & Chen, 2022). AI systems can analyze multiple variables simultaneously and identify patterns that may not be easily detectable by human decision-makers. For instance, machine learning algorithms can assess risk factors related to unemployment or poverty, supporting the development of preventive social policies. Additionally, automation of routine administrative tasks allows government officials to focus on more complex policy issues. Another key advantage of AI is its ability to improve accuracy and efficiency in decision-making. Automated systems can process large numbers of applications quickly and consistently, reducing administrative delays and enhancing program performance. Predictive analytics further enables governments to anticipate social needs and allocate resources more effectively. Nevertheless, the use of AI in welfare governance raises significant ethical and regulatory concerns. Algorithmic systems often function as "black boxes," making it difficult for citizens to understand how decisions are made. This lack of transparency can reduce public trust in welfare institutions. Moreover, if AI systems are trained on biased data, they may produce discriminatory outcomes that disproportionately affect vulnerable populations (Eubanks, 2018).

Objectives of the Chapter

The primary objective of this chapter is to examine how digital data is governed in modern welfare systems. As governments increasingly adopt digital technologies and artificial intelligence, it is essential to understand how data is managed, regulated, and utilized in policymaking processes.

Specifically, the chapter aims to fulfill the following objectives:

- **Analyze Key Governance Principles:** Evaluate transparency, accountability, and regulatory practices within the context of data-driven welfare frameworks.
- **Assess Infrastructure and Algorithmic Impact:** Explore the role of digital data infrastructures in policy implementation and understand how algorithmic decision-making alters access to essential welfare services.
- **Address Systemic Risks and Challenges:** Investigate critical bottlenecks in digital welfare governance, including data privacy vulnerabilities, algorithmic bias, and digital exclusion.
- **Ground Theory in Empirical Reality:** Bridge the gap between high-level conceptual frameworks and concrete administrative realities by grounding the analysis in Digital Public Infrastructures (DPI). The text focuses specifically on India's biometric Aadhaar system and its structural integration with the Public Distribution System (PDS) and Direct Benefit Transfer (DBT) networks.
- **Evaluate Global Empirical Trends:** Analyze patterns related to AI policy alignment, algorithmic accountability, and global digital equity through the visualization of secondary datasets to illustrate how structured data workflows operationalize transparency.

Overall, this chapter contributes to ongoing academic and policy debates on responsible digital governance. It emphasizes the importance of effective regulatory frameworks and inclusive data governance practices to ensure fairness, protect citizens' rights, and maintain public trust in digital welfare systems.

BACKGROUND

Digital Governance and Welfare State

Digital governance is a concept that has received considerable attention over the past few years, as governments increasingly adopt digital technologies to enhance administrative processes and service delivery to citizens. Digital governance can be defined as the incorporation of information and communication technologies (ICTs) in the operation of government to achieve efficiency, transparency, and engagement with citizens. Digital governance plays a significant role within the context of the welfare state in managing social welfare programs and allocating state resources. The traditional welfare state was dependent on bureaucracies and manual systems of administration. These systems were usually slow, ineffective, and prone to administrative mistakes. As new digital technologies continue to develop, governments have gradually transitioned to digital forms of governance that are based on electronic records, computer databases, and automation. Helen Margetts and Patrick Dunleavy argue that digital governance allows governments to transform administrative structures through integrated digital infrastructures while also reshaping citizen–state interactions. Digital welfare governance is the operation of social programs using digital platforms to administer these programs, including unemployment benefits, social security payments, health assistance, and poverty alleviation programs. Through these platforms, governments are able to gather substantial amounts of information on citizens and use it as a policy instrument. As an illustration, electronic identification systems and centralized welfare databases allow authorities to verify the identity of beneficiaries and curb fraud in social programs.

It has also been established that digital governance is capable of enhancing policy coordination among government agencies. Digital systems enable various departments to share information and work more efficiently. Christopher Hood believes that digital technologies can reinforce accountability systems by rendering administrative processes more transparent and traceable, thereby strengthening institutional trust. Nevertheless, other researchers also outline some of the risks of digital governance in welfare systems. The increased concentration of information in government institutions is one of the key issues. Extensive digital databases contain sensitive personal data, which raises concerns regarding privacy protection as well as data security. Additionally, digital systems can inadvertently exclude citizens who are not technologically or digitally literate. Because of this, the shift toward digital technologies in welfare governance needs to be closely regulated and supported by well-developed data governance systems. Governments should ensure that digital systems are developed in a manner that guarantees citizens' rights while also enhancing administrative efficiency.

Data-driven Policy Making in Public Administration

Evidence-based policymaking is now a necessary element of contemporary government. Digital data and statistical analysis are becoming increasingly important in government decision-making and in measuring program effectiveness. Data-driven governance can be defined as the application of empirical evidence, predictive analytics, and algorithmic instruments in policymaking. The rise of data-driven policymaking is directly connected to the expansion of digital government infrastructure. Indeed, administrative data on employment, education, healthcare, tax, and social welfare programs are now collected in large amounts by public institutions. These datasets are useful in providing information about social conditions and enable policymakers to determine trends that affect policy outcomes. Viktor Mayer-Schönberger and Kenneth Cukier argue that the emergence of big data has fundamentally changed how governments interpret and respond to social challenges by enabling large-scale pattern recognition and predictive insights. Through the analysis of large datasets, policymakers are able to identify trends in poverty, unemployment, and demographic changes. This allows governments to formulate specific welfare policies that meet the needs of vulnerable groups.

Another notable benefit of data-driven policymaking is improved policy assessment. Digital systems are able to collect real-time data that can be used by governments to monitor policy outcomes. For instance, welfare administrators can monitor benefit distribution and determine whether programs are reaching the targeted beneficiaries. This enhances accountability and transparency in government institutions. Along with such benefits, data-driven governance also brings a number of challenges. Policy analysis is highly dependent on data quality and reliability. Incorrect or incomplete datasets may result in poor policymaking. Besides, big data analysis sometimes requires advanced technical skills that may not be present in government organizations. Another issue highlighted by scholars is the need for ethical considerations in data-driven policymaking. Government institutions should ensure that data collection processes respect citizens' privacy and adhere to legal standards. In the absence of proper governance systems, data-driven approaches can create power imbalances between citizens and the government. Thus, although data-driven policymaking has the potential to enhance the quality of public administration, it should be supported by effective governance structures that promote transparency, accountability, and responsible use of data.

Artificial Intelligence in Government Decision-Making

The application of artificial intelligence in the decision-making process in the public sector is increasing. AI technologies enable governments to process big data, automate government functions, and generate predictive insights that can inform policymaking. Applications of AI in welfare systems include determining eligibility for benefits, detecting fraud, and optimizing the distribution of social resources. Virginia Eubanks argues that automated decision-making systems are gaining significance in welfare administration in many countries, particularly in determining eligibility and monitoring welfare distribution. Machine learning algorithms are used by governments to process data about citizens and provide recommendations regarding eligibility for welfare benefits. These systems have the potential to significantly reduce administrative workloads and enhance decision-making processes. AI technologies are particularly useful in analyzing complex social data. Machine learning models can detect patterns in large datasets and provide forecasts regarding future trends. For instance, AI systems can analyze labor market data to predict unemployment trends and inform employment assistance programs.

Another benefit of AI in governance is improved administrative efficiency. Automated systems can process large numbers of welfare applications quickly and consistently. This helps minimize delays in service delivery and enhances the performance of welfare programs. Nevertheless, the application of AI in public administration is also associated with significant ethical and governance challenges. Algorithmic decision-making systems may lack transparency, and citizens may find it difficult to understand how decisions are made. Frank Pasquale argues that many AI systems function as "black boxes," meaning that their internal logic is not easily understandable or accessible to the public. Another challenge is algorithmic bias. When AI models are trained on biased data, they may produce discriminatory outcomes that disproportionately affect marginalized groups. This is especially concerning in welfare systems where decisions directly affect access to essential services. Consequently, researchers emphasize the need for regulatory frameworks that ensure fairness and accountability in AI governance. Governments need to develop policies that promote algorithmic transparency, ethical data use, and citizen-centric control mechanisms.

Computerized Services in Welfare Services

Digital data infrastructure forms the foundation of contemporary welfare governance. It includes technological systems that collect, store, and process data related to welfare programs. These systems include digital identity systems, central databases, cloud computing platforms, and data analytics tools. Many governments have adopted unified online platforms that integrate different social service schemes. Through these platforms, administrators can access beneficiary information, track program participation, and evaluate policy outcomes. For example, digital welfare systems often integrate data from employment agencies, healthcare providers, and social security institutions. The development of digital data infrastructure has significantly improved the efficiency of welfare administration. Digital systems enable governments to process large volumes of data quickly and reduce administrative errors. Beth Simone Noveck states that data-driven infrastructures can help governments make more informed policy decisions and deliver services more efficiently. Moreover, computerized data systems enhance transparency in welfare management. Electronic records make it easier to audit government activities and monitor the distribution of public funds. This reduces corruption and increases public trust in government institutions.

A prime contemporary manifestation of such an integrated architectural network is India's Digital Public Infrastructure (DPI) framework, anchored by the Aadhaar biometric identity ecosystem. As conceptualized in Figure 1 of this manuscript, the technological infrastructure transitions systematically from foundational data acquisition (biometric enrollment via the Aadhaar framework) to inter-agency processing for targeted service delivery mechanisms, specifically the Public Distribution System (PDS) and Direct Benefit Transfer (DBT) networks. Historically evolving from fragmented, manual cash and commodity transfers prone to leakages, the incorporation of automated verification has minimized structural intermediaries and optimized fiscal outlays. This alignment demonstrates how national digital building blocks re-engineer systemic financial inclusion, structural transparency, and public accounting across the entire administrative ecosystem (Kanu, 2025).

Nevertheless, the expansion of digital data infrastructure also introduces new challenges. Large-scale data systems require strong cybersecurity measures to prevent data breaches and unauthorized access. The information stored in welfare databases is often highly sensitive, including health records, income data, and demographic details. Another challenge is interoperability across government systems. Welfare programs are often managed by different departments, making data integration complex. Effective digital governance requires coordination among institutions and standardization in data management practices. Thus, digital welfare systems require not only technological infrastructure but also strong governance mechanisms to regulate data use and ensure accountability.

The Data Governance challenges: Privacy, Bias, and Exclusion

The growing dependence on digital data in welfare governance has raised important issues related to privacy, bias, and social exclusion, highlighting the need for effective data governance mechanisms that balance citizens' rights with efficient policy implementation. One of the most critical concerns in digital welfare systems is the protection of privacy, given that governments collect large amounts of personal data, including income levels, employment records, medical history, and demographic information. Without adequate safeguards, such data may be misused or become vulnerable to cybersecurity threats. Another critical issue is algorithmic bias. Data-driven decision-making systems rely on historical datasets that may reflect existing social inequalities. If biased data is utilized, AI systems may replicate and reinforce these systemic biases in policymaking, producing unfair outcomes if not carefully monitored and managed (O'Neil, 2017).

Digital exclusion remains another major concern, as not all citizens have equal access to digital technologies or stable internet infrastructure. Individuals with limited digital literacy face distinct difficulties in accessing online welfare services or completing digital applications, creating barriers for the very vulnerable populations who rely most heavily on government support. Furthermore, the increasing use of digital surveillance systems in welfare governance raises ethical concerns. Automated monitoring systems used to detect fraud or assess eligibility may lead to intrusive surveillance practices, potentially harming citizens' privacy. To address these multi-dimensional challenges, a comprehensive approach to data governance is essential. Governments need to develop legal frameworks, ethical guidelines, and institutional regulations that promote responsible data use, ensuring that the governance of digital welfare systems heavily emphasizes transparency, accountability, and active citizen participation.

RESEARCH METHODOLOGY

Research Design

The chapter adopts an analytical and exploratory research design to investigate how digital data **is** governed in modern welfare systems. The aim of the research is to understand the impact of digital technologies, data analytics, and artificial intelligence on welfare governance and the policy decision-making process. The study is concerned with the core concepts of transparency, accountability, and regulation in data-driven welfare systems. The relationship between welfare program management and digital data governance is analyzed through an analytical research strategy, allowing a structured examination of governance mechanisms. Under this strategy, the study investigates critical issues such as algorithmic decision-making, data privacy risks, digital exclusion, and regulatory challenges in digital welfare systems. The study represents a synthesis of both conceptual discourse and empirical research, supported by datasets and graphical presentation. At the same time, the study is exploratory in nature, which is useful in identifying emerging trends in digital governance. As digital welfare systems are rapidly evolving across countries, the exploratory analysis provides insights into how governments are adapting to these transformations.

The research therefore integrates theoretical insights from digital governance literature with empirical evidence derived from data analysis, thereby strengthening both the conceptual and analytical dimensions of the chapter.

Data Sources

The research in this chapter is grounded in secondary data related to governance indicators, digitization trends, and socio-economic characteristics. Secondary data is a widely accepted method in policy research, as it enables the analysis of large-scale datasets collected by governmental agencies and international organizations. The datasets used in this chapter comprise information on socio-economic indicators, digital governance variables, and demographic characteristics. These datasets are used to analyze trends related to welfare coverage, digital access, and the outcomes of algorithmic decision-making.

To enhance transparency and replicability, publicly available datasets reflecting global AI readiness indexes, international open data barometers, and institutional metrics on digital public infrastructure deployments were selected. The variables included in the datasets consist of income levels, education, employment, digital infrastructure indicators, and policy governance measures. These variables are relevant to the study of digital welfare governance as they reflect the socio-economic conditions that influence access to welfare services. The analysis of the datasets was conducted through systematic data cleaning and organization to ensure consistency and reliability. Basic data preprocessing techniques were applied to address missing values and irregular observations. Statistical visualizations were then generated using the processed datasets, which support and strengthen the analytical discussion presented in the chapter.

Data Analysis Techniques

The study employs descriptive data analysis and visual data interpretation methods to investigate trends in digital governance and welfare systems. Data visualization plays a crucial role in interpreting relationships between governance variables and welfare outcomes.

The datasets were analyzed using multiple graphical techniques, including line charts, bar charts, scatter plots, histograms, pie charts, and box plots. Each visualization method provides a different perspective on the data and helps in identifying key governance patterns. Line charts are used to observe trends and comparisons over time, while bar charts facilitate comparison across categories or governance risk levels. Scatter plots are applied to examine relationships between variables such as transparency and accountability. Histograms illustrate the distribution of values related to governance indicators or privacy risks, and pie charts represent proportional relationships among different categories of risks. Box plots are used to analyze variation and detect potential biases across groups.

These graphical methods enable the research to present complex data patterns in a simplified and interpretable manner. Visual analytics therefore reinforces the analytical depth of the chapter and enhances the reader's understanding of the findings.

Graphical Analysis Framework

Graphical analysis is a key component of this research, as it supports the demonstration of relationships between digital governance variables and welfare system outcomes. Visual representation of data enables researchers to identify trends, relationships, and governance risks more intuitively and effectively. This chapter includes eight graphical visualizations that support the analytical discussion. These figures focus on key themes such as AI governance, transparency, accountability, privacy risks, and digital welfare coverage. For instance, the accuracy of artificial intelligence systems is compared with traditional human decision-making using a line chart, illustrating the role of automation in welfare policy. A bar chart is used to analyze different levels of governance risks associated with AI technologies. Scatter plots highlight relationships between governance indicators such as transparency and accountability, helping to identify how governance quality influences policy outcomes.

Further, privacy risks and data protection concerns in digital welfare systems are analyzed using histograms and pie charts. Variations in algorithmic outcomes across different groups are examined through box plots, which help in identifying potential biases in AI-driven decision-making. Another scatter plot explores the relationship between digitalization and welfare coverage, providing insights into how technological infrastructure influences access to social programs.

Collectively, these graphical analyses provide empirical support for the arguments developed in this chapter. They illustrate the interaction between digital data, AI technologies, governance structures, and welfare policy outcomes.

Figure 1. Integrated Digital Welfare Governance and Analysis Framework

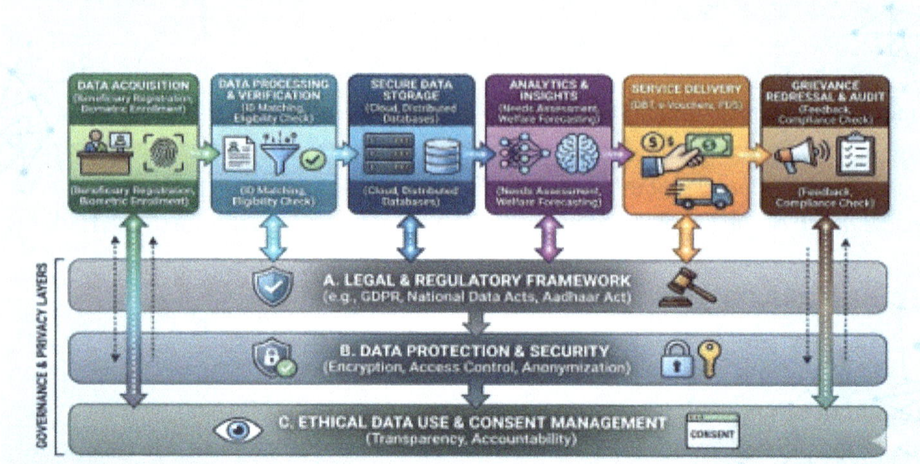

As Figure 1 demonstrates, this framework highlights how the analytics and insights phase is operationalized through the graphical methods presented in this section. For example, correlations between transparency and accountability are **analyzed** using scatter plots, while box plots are used to reveal potential algorithmic bias, thereby linking empirical analysis with governance concepts. By mapping foundational layers like the Aadhaar identity architecture directly to transactional execution (PDS and DBT), this framework visually establishes the operational pipeline analyzed throughout the subsequent subsections.

MAIN FOCUS OF THE CHAPTER

Issues, Controversies, and Problems in Data-Driven Welfare Governance

The growing adoption of digital technologies and artificial intelligence in welfare systems has created both opportunities and challenges for public administration. While digital systems enhance efficiency and accuracy in decision-making, they also raise critical concerns related to transparency, accountability, and ethical governance. Since welfare systems rely heavily on sensitive personal data, the governance of digital data becomes a central policy issue.

One of the most significant concerns in digital welfare governance is the increasing reliance on automated decision-making systems. Governments use algorithms to determine eligibility for welfare benefits, detect fraud, and monitor program participation. These systems process large volumes of data and generate patterns that inform policy implementation. Although automated systems ensure speed and consistency, they may also introduce governance risks if not properly regulated. Algorithmic decision-making processes are often non-transparent, making it difficult for citizens to understand how decisions are made. In many cases, individuals who are denied benefits are not provided with clear explanations, raising concerns about fairness and accountability.

The second issue is the possibility of algorithmic bias. Data-driven systems depend on historical datasets that may reflect existing social inequalities. If such biases are embedded in training data, AI systems may unintentionally produce discriminatory outcomes. This presents serious ethical and governance challenges, particularly in welfare programs that serve vulnerable populations. Another major concern in digital welfare systems is privacy protection. Governments collect large volumes of personal data, including income records, employment history, health data, and demographic information. Without adequate safeguards, such data may be exposed to misuse, unauthorized access, or cyber threats. In addition to privacy risks, digital welfare systems may also contribute to social exclusion. As welfare services increasingly shift to online platforms, access becomes dependent on digital literacy and internet availability. Individuals lacking these resources may face difficulties in accessing essential services, thereby widening existing inequalities.

These challenges are further examined in the following subsections through graphical analysis based on selected datasets. The visualizations help illustrate patterns related to AI governance, transparency, privacy risks, and digital welfare coverage, thereby strengthening the analytical discussion.

Artificial Intelligence is accurate in Welfare Decision-Making

Artificial intelligence has emerged as a central tool in processing welfare applications and identifying eligible beneficiaries. Automated decision-making systems are capable of analyzing large volumes of data and identifying patterns that may not be easily detectable through traditional methods. This enhances the efficiency and consistency of welfare administration.

Figure 2. AI vs. Human Accuracy

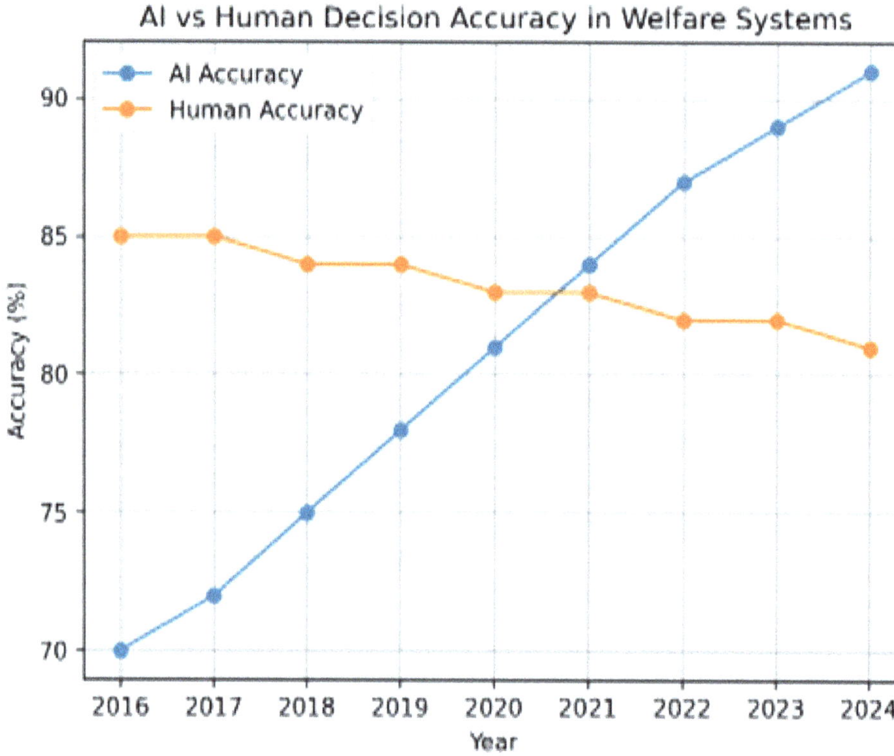

This graph 2 presents the comparative levels of accuracy of AI-based decision systems against the conventional process of human evaluation. As shown in the figure, AI systems tend to be more consistent when dealing with large amounts of data. Several variables can be analyzed by automated algorithms, which enhances efficient administrative decision-making. Nevertheless, the quality of AI systems depends on the quality of the data used in their training. Decisions may become inaccurate if there are errors or biases within the training datasets. This computational variance highlights how automated scaling reduces baseline human processing friction, yet fundamentally shifts the administrative landscape toward subtle technical and systemic dependencies that require continuous organizational calibration (Tiwari, Kostenko, & Yekhanurov, 2025).

Governance Risk of Artificial Intelligence

With the introduction of AI technologies in welfare systems, several governance risks emerge. These include algorithmic bias, lack of transparency, data misuse, and weak regulatory controls.

Figure 3. AI Governance Risk Levels

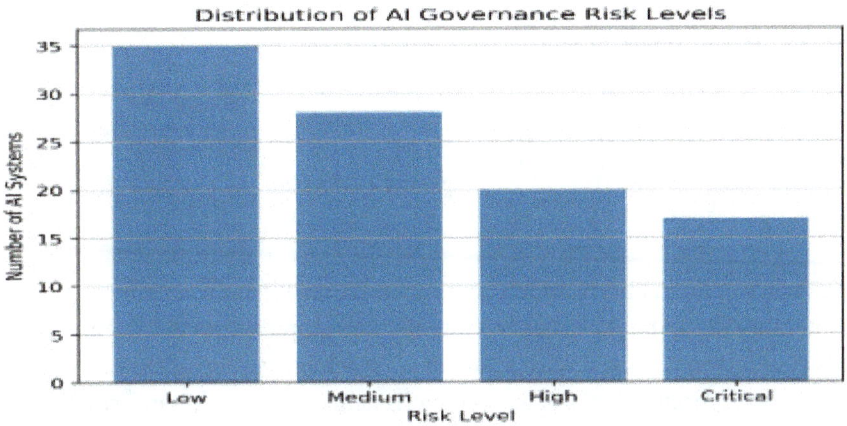

This bar chart shows various types of governance risks associated with AI technologies. The illustration indicates that major challenges include algorithmic bias and lack of transparency. Data privacy is also a significant risk factor. Figure 3 highlights that technological innovation in welfare systems must be supported by appropriate regulatory measures. The systemic severity of these localized systemic points outlines how unmonitored digital deployments can inadvertently institutionalize organizational gaps rather than resolving structural vulnerabilities.

Correlation of Transparency and Accountability

Transparency and accountability are fundamental principles of democratic governance. In digital welfare systems, transparency refers to the ability of citizens to understand how decisions are made and how their data is used. Accountability refers to the responsibility of institutions for policy outcomes.

Figure 4. Transparency vs Accountability

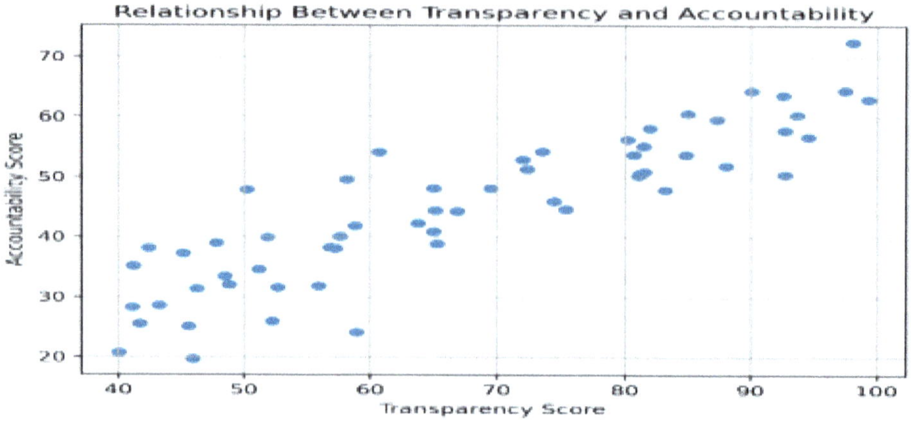

This scatter plot in Figure 4 represents the relationship between transparency and accountability in digital governance systems. The graph shows that higher transparency is generally associated with stronger accountability mechanisms. Public trust in welfare institutions increases when governments openly share information about data practices and decision-making processes.

However, many AI-based systems lack transparency due to their complex algorithmic structures. Citizens may face challenges in questioning unfair decisions without clear explanations of how algorithms operate. The positive correlation observed in this visual matrix confirms that digital tracking mechanisms directly institutionalize bureaucratic oversight, mirroring broader international structural shifts in data survey standards aimed at sustainable public monitoring (Misuraca, Medaglia, & Aquaro, 2021).

Privacy Risks in Digital Welfare Systems

Digital welfare systems rely heavily on large datasets containing personal information. While these datasets improve service delivery and policy analysis, they also introduce privacy risks.

Figure 5. Privacy Risk Distribution

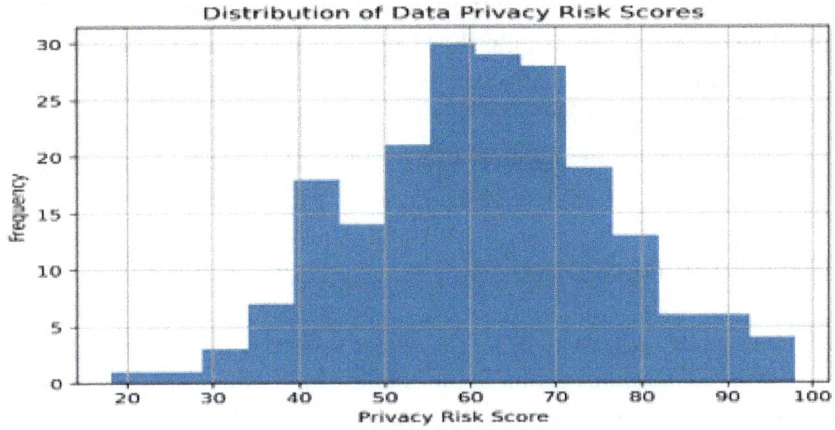

The histogram in Figure 5 shows the distribution of privacy risks in digital welfare data systems. It indicates that moderate to high privacy risks are common in large databases. These risks may arise due to weak data protection, unauthorized access, or cyberattacks. This concentration within higher statistical intervals suggests that structural data aggregation creates centralized vectors of vulnerability, making traditional perimeter-based security measures increasingly insufficient to safeguard distributed benefit records.

Data Privacy Concerns Categories

Privacy risks in digital governance arise from multiple sources, including data collection, data sharing between institutions, and surveillance technologies.

Figure 6. Privacy Risk Categories

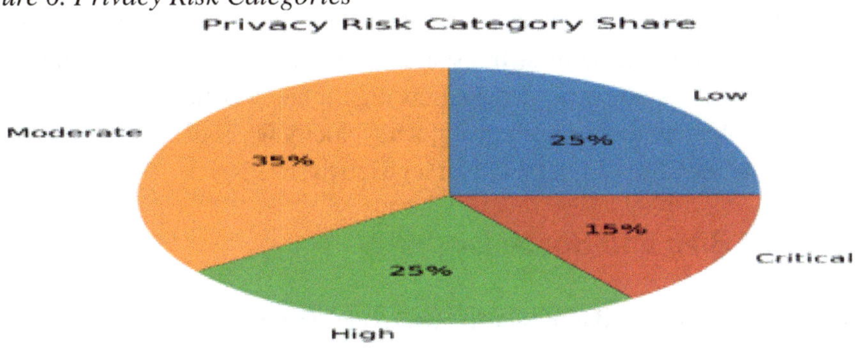

The pie chart in Figure 6 illustrates the proportion of different types of privacy risks. Major concerns include unauthorized data access, data breaches, and excessive surveillance. This visualization shows that privacy risks are not only technical issues but also institutional challenges related to data management practices. The proportional dominance of organizational and structural failures over purely technical exploits reinforces the argument that administrative data custody mandates definitive governance parameters rather than standard software patches.

Comparison of AI Regulation

Different countries have adopted varying regulatory approaches to govern the use of AI in public administration. Some countries have developed comprehensive frameworks, while others rely on general data protection laws.

Figure 7. Artificial Intelligence Regulations by Nation

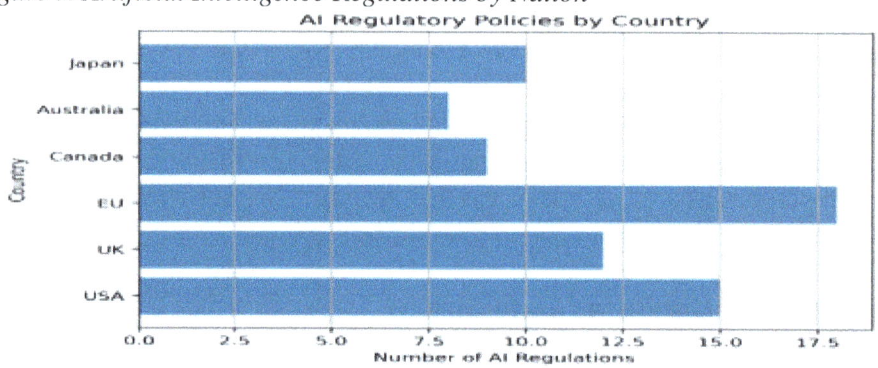

This chart in Figure 7 compares the extent of AI regulation across countries. It shows significant differences in regulatory approaches based on legal systems and institutional capacity. Countries with stronger regulatory frameworks tend to emphasize ethical AI principles, transparency requirements, and accountability mechanisms. This asymmetric distribution highlights a critical governance lag, wherein technological tools deploy at a global velocity while accountability mechanisms remain bound to distinct national legislative speeds.

Automated Bias and Social Disparity

One of the most debated issues in AI governance is algorithmic bias. Algorithms trained on historical data may reproduce existing patterns of discrimination.

Figure 8. Box Plot: Algorithms Bias by Group

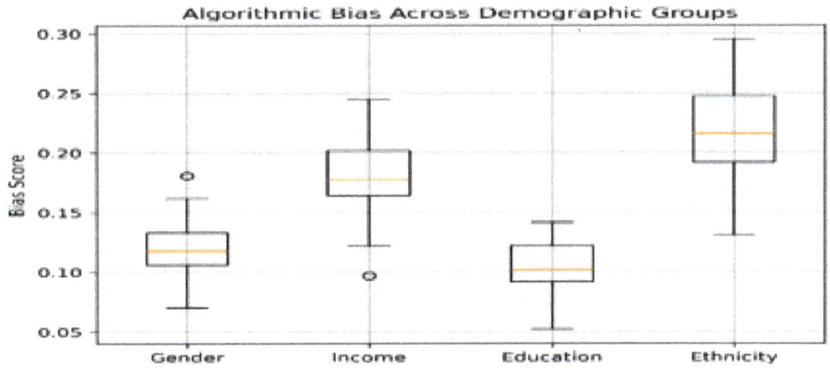

The box plot in Figure 8 shows variations in algorithmic outcomes across different population groups. The visualization suggests that certain groups may be more negatively affected by automated decision-making systems. This raises concerns about fairness and equality in welfare governance.When biometric datasets or historical resource allocation workflows carry fundamental data imbalances—such as those encountered in large-scale targeted commodity or transfer infrastructures—machine learning architectures tend to multiply these discrepancies across marginal groups rather than smoothing them out.

Welfare Coverage and Digitalization

Digital technologies can improve the accessibility and efficiency of welfare programs. Countries with advanced digital infrastructure often achieve better welfare administration.

Figure 9. Digitalization vs Welfare Coverage

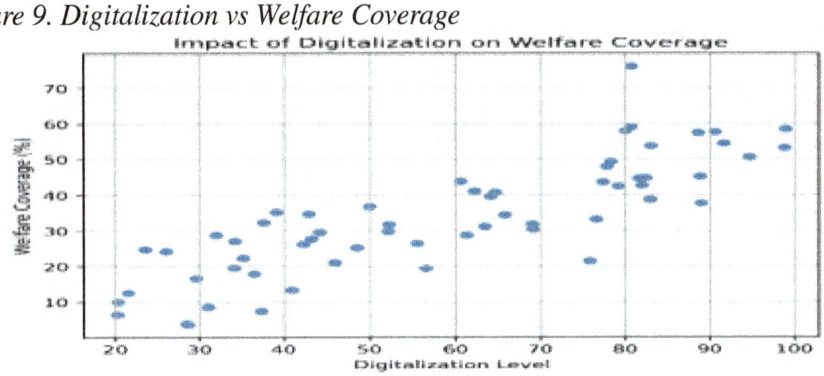

This scatter plot in Figure 9 examines the relationship between digitalization and welfare coverage. It suggests a positive correlation between technological development and access to welfare services. Digital systems can enhance administrative efficiency and expand program reach.However, this relationship is not always straightforward. Rapid digitalization may create operational and access barriers for individuals lacking basic digital literacy or robust local internet infrastructure, turning a tool meant for universal financial and resource inclusion into a new vector of social stratification.

Analytical Insights Concisely

The graphical analysis highlights several key trends in digital welfare governance. First, AI technologies improve administrative efficiency but also introduce governance risks related to transparency and bias. Second, privacy protection remains a major concern in large digital data systems. Third, accountability in data-driven decision-making requires strong governance mechanisms that balance technological innovation with the protection of citizens' rights to ensure institutional legitimacy and public trust.

Overall, the findings suggest that digital transformation in welfare systems must be supported by robust regulatory frameworks and ethical governance principles. Governments need to balance technological innovation with the protection of citizens' rights to ensure fairness and legitimacy.

SOLUTIONS AND RECOMMENDATIONS

The dynamic growth in digital technologies and artificial intelligence in welfare governance has provided new opportunities to enhance government service delivery. Simultaneously, it has also brought about several governance challenges such as transparency, accountability, privacy protection, and algorithmic fairness. To ensure that digital welfare systems are both effective and equitable, governments must adopt a holistic governance approach that addresses these issues. This section outlines policy recommendations to strengthen digital data governance in welfare systems. These recommendations focus on developing regulatory frameworks, improving transparency in automated decision-making, and promoting inclusive digital welfare programs.

Enhancing Digital Data Governance Frameworks

The establishment of robust data governance frameworks is one of the key steps toward responsible digital welfare governance. Governments should establish clear policies governing the collection, storage, processing, and sharing of data within welfare systems. These frameworks must ensure the secure and ethical handling of personal data.

To begin with, governments need to enact strong data protection laws to safeguard citizens' personal information. Welfare databases contain sensitive information, including financial details, employment records, and demographic data. Without proper legal safeguards, such information is vulnerable to misuse or unauthorized access. Well-developed data protection laws help ensure that personal data is used only for legitimate policy purposes.

Second, governments should establish clear guidelines for data management and inter-agency data sharing. Many welfare programs require coordination among multiple government departments. Therefore, data-sharing practices must be governed by strict protocols that ensure privacy protection and data security.

Another important element is the establishment of independent oversight mechanisms. Regulatory bodies or data protection authorities should monitor government data practices to ensure compliance with legal and ethical standards. These institutions can also investigate cases of data misuse and provide remedies to affected citizens.

Lastly, governments must invest in secure digital infrastructure to protect welfare databases from cybersecurity threats. The integrity of digital welfare systems should be maintained through strong encryption, access control systems, and regular security audits.

Assuring AI Systems Transparency and Accountability

The governance of artificial intelligence systems in welfare administration requires transparency and accountability as fundamental principles. When automated systems are used to determine eligibility for welfare benefits, citizens must be able to understand how such decisions are made.

One key recommendation is the adoption of explainable AI technologies. Explainable AI refers to systems that provide clear and understandable explanations for their decisions. By making algorithmic processes more transparent, governments can help citizens understand the factors influencing automated decisions.

Moreover, governments should establish accountability mechanisms that allow individuals to appeal automated decisions. Citizens who believe they have been unfairly denied benefits should have access to appeal procedures and human review processes. Human oversight is essential to ensure fairness in automated decision-making systems.

Another important governance tool is algorithm auditing. AI systems used in welfare administration should be regularly evaluated by independent experts to identify potential biases or errors. Routine audits help ensure that algorithms operate fairly and do not discriminate against specific social groups.

Public transparency initiatives can further enhance accountability. Governments should disclose information about the algorithms used in administration, including their objectives, decision criteria, and risk management strategies. Such transparency can significantly improve public trust in digital welfare systems.

Advancing Digital Welfare Systems of Inclusion

While digital technologies improve efficiency, they can also create barriers for individuals lacking access to digital resources. Governments must ensure that digital welfare systems remain inclusive and accessible to all citizens.

One effective strategy is the development of hybrid service delivery models. In addition to online platforms, governments should maintain traditional service channels such as physical offices and telephone services. This ensures that individuals without digital access are not excluded from welfare programs.

Promoting digital literacy is another crucial policy measure. Many citizens face difficulties accessing online welfare services due to limited digital skills. Governments should provide training programs to help individuals effectively use digital platforms.

Inclusive welfare governance also requires strengthening digital infrastructure. In many regions, limited internet connectivity restricts access to online services. Governments must invest in expanding broadband networks and ensuring affordable internet access for all communities.

Furthermore, policymakers should consider the needs of vulnerable populations when designing digital systems. Interfaces should be user-friendly and accessible to persons with disabilities, elderly citizens, and individuals with lower levels of education. Applying inclusive design principles ensures that digital systems cater to diverse user needs.

Creating AI Governance Ethical and Regulatory Frameworks

Ethical and regulatory frameworks are essential for the responsible use of artificial intelligence in welfare systems. Governments should establish clear policies guiding the development and deployment of AI technologies in public administration.

One important approach is the adoption of ethical AI guidelines that emphasize fairness, transparency, and accountability. These principles ensure that AI systems do not violate fundamental rights or produce discriminatory outcomes. Ethical frameworks also help policymakers balance technological innovation with social responsibility.

Governments should also implement risk assessment procedures before deploying AI systems in welfare administration. Potential risks such as privacy concerns, algorithmic bias, and social exclusion must be carefully evaluated. These assessments help identify and mitigate risks before they impact citizens.

International cooperation is another critical component of AI governance. Since digital technologies often transcend national boundaries, governments should collaborate with international organizations to develop shared regulatory standards. Such cooperation promotes responsible innovation while protecting citizens' rights.

Lastly, governments should encourage interdisciplinary collaboration among policymakers, technologists, and social scientists. Effective governance of digital welfare systems requires expertise from data science, law, public administration, and ethics. Collaborative policymaking leads to more balanced and sustainable governance solutions.

Summary of Policy Recommendations

The recommendations outlined in this section highlight the importance of responsible governance in digital welfare systems. Governments must develop strong data governance frameworks to protect personal data and ensure ethical data use. AI-driven decision-making processes should be supported by transparency and accountability mechanisms.

At the same time, policymakers must ensure that digital welfare systems remain inclusive and accessible to all citizens. Investments in digital infrastructure, digital literacy, and inclusive system design can reduce digital inequalities.

Ultimately, the governance of digital welfare systems requires a balanced approach that integrates technological innovation with strong ethical and regulatory safeguards. By implementing these policy measures, governments can build public trust and ensure that digital transformation contributes to fair and sustainable welfare governance.

FUTURE RESEARCH DIRECTIONS

The increasing use of digital technologies and artificial intelligence in welfare governance has opened numerous opportunities to enhance policy effectiveness. However, this transformation also raises several important research questions that require further academic investigation. Future studies can help policymakers better understand the impact of digital systems on welfare governance and identify strategies to mitigate associated risks.

One of the key areas for future research is the regulation of artificial intelligence in public administration. The growing use of automated systems in policy decision-making necessitates the development of clearer and more comprehensive regulatory frameworks for responsible AI use (Radu, 2021; Castilla Barraza & Romero-Rubio, 2024). Researchers can examine how different countries design and implement such frameworks to govern algorithmic decision-making in social welfare systems. Comparative studies in this area can provide valuable insights into best practices for managing AI-related risks while still promoting innovation.

Another important research direction involves the development of ethical data governance models. Digitized welfare systems collect and process large volumes of personal data, raising serious concerns related to privacy, consent, and surveillance (Mayer-Schönberger & Cukier, 2013). Future research should focus on how ethical principles can be effectively integrated into data management practices. Scholars may also explore new governance models that balance the benefits of data-driven policymaking with the protection of individual rights.

Additionally, the long-term effects of digital welfare infrastructures require further investigation. While digital technologies can improve administrative efficiency, their broader social implications are not yet fully understood. Future studies can analyze how digital systems influence access to welfare programs, particularly for vulnerable groups such as low-income households, older adults, and individuals with limited digital literacy (Eubanks, 2018).

Another promising area of research is the application of emerging technologies in welfare governance. Innovations such as blockchain, advanced data analytics, and predictive modeling have the potential to improve transparency and reduce fraud in welfare programs. However, their effectiveness and associated risks should be carefully evaluated through empirical research (Panda et al., 2025).

Finally, interdisciplinary research will play a crucial role in shaping the future of digital welfare governance. Collaboration among experts in public administration, data science, law, and ethics can lead to more comprehensive and balanced solutions for managing digital transformation in government processes. Such collaborative efforts can contribute to the development of welfare systems that are technologically advanced, socially responsible, and inclusive.

Overall, future research will be essential in guiding policymakers toward the responsible use of digital technologies in welfare governance. By addressing issues related to regulation, ethics, and social inclusion, scholars can contribute to the development of more sustainable and equitable digital welfare systems.

CONCLUSION

The digitalization of governance has significantly transformed the way welfare programs are designed and delivered. Digital data infrastructures, data analytics, and artificial intelligence have become essential tools for governments worldwide to improve efficiency and effectiveness in public service delivery (Dunleavy & Margetts, 2010). These technological advancements enable better policy implementation, reduce administrative costs, and expand access to welfare services. However, the growing reliance on digital technologies also introduces several critical governance challenges. Issues such as digital exclusion, algorithmic bias, privacy risks, and limited transparency in automated decision-making have become major concerns for policymakers, scholars, and civil society organizations (O'Neil, 2017; Eubanks, 2018). Without appropriate safeguards, digital welfare systems may reinforce existing inequalities or create new forms of social exclusion.

This chapter has examined how digital data and artificial intelligence are transforming welfare governance. The analysis demonstrates that data-driven policymaking is reshaping public administration and influencing decision-making processes in welfare programs. At the same time, the study highlights significant risks associated with large-scale digital welfare infrastructures, particularly in relation to data governance, accountability, and fairness.

The findings emphasize the importance of establishing strong governance frameworks to manage the digital transformation of welfare systems. Enhancing data protection laws, promoting transparency in AI-driven decision-making, and ensuring inclusive access to digital welfare services are critical policy priorities (Noveck, 2021; Radu, 2021). Governments must also invest in digital infrastructure and digital literacy programs to reduce inequalities in access to public services. Furthermore, the future of digital governance will depend on the development of robust ethical and regulatory frameworks for artificial intelligence. Policymakers must ensure that technological innovation is guided by principles of equity, accountability, and respect for fundamental rights. In conclusion, digital technologies have the potential to significantly enhance welfare governance. However, their successful implementation requires careful policy design and responsible governance practices. By integrating technological innovation with ethical safeguards and inclusive approaches, governments can develop digital welfare systems that promote both efficiency and social justice.

ACKNOWLEDGMENT

The author would like to express sincere gratitude to colleagues, mentors, and academic peers for their valuable insights and constructive feedback, which significantly contributed to the clarity and depth of this chapter.

Special appreciation is extended to academic institutions and research communities that continue to advance interdisciplinary research in digital governance, public policy, and artificial intelligence. Their contributions have played a vital role in enhancing understanding of the opportunities and challenges associated with digital welfare systems.

The author also acknowledges the work of scholars and policymakers whose research on digital governance, data-driven policymaking, and artificial intelligence in public administration has provided the conceptual foundation for this study.

REFERENCES

Ahn, M. J., & Chen, Y. C. (2022). Digital transformation toward AI-augmented public administration: The perception of government employees and the willingness to use AI in government. *Government Information Quarterly*, *39*(2), 101664. DOI: 10.1016/j.giq.2021.101664

Castilla Barraza, J. G., & Romero-Rubio, S. A. (2024). The use of artificial intelligence in governance: A systematic review. In *International Conference on Advanced Research in Technologies, Information, Innovation and Sustainability* (pp. 110–125). Springer.

Dunleavy, P. (2006). *Digital era governance: IT corporations, the state, and e-government*. Oxford University Press. DOI: 10.1093/acprof:oso/9780199296194.001.0001

Dunleavy, P., & Margetts, H. Z. (2010). The second wave of digital era governance. *APSA 2010 Annual Meeting Paper*.

Fountain, J. E. (2004). *Building the virtual state: Information technology and institutional change*. Rowman & Littlefield.

Goldsmith, S., & Yang, J. (2025). AI and the transformation of accountability and discretion in urban governance. *arXiv preprint arXiv:2502.13101*.

Kanu, D. H. (2025). Digital public infrastructure: The building blocks for digital financial inclusion and taxation of the digital economy in Liberia. *SSRN*. DOI: 10.2139/ssrn.5738263

Kawakami, A., Coston, A., Heidari, H., Holstein, K., & Zhu, H. (2024). Studying up public sector AI: How networks of power relations shape agency decisions around AI design and use. *Proceedings of the ACM on Human-Computer Interaction, 8*(CSCW2), 1–24. DOI: 10.1145/3686989

Mayer-Schönberger, V., & Cukier, K. (2013). *Big data: A revolution that will transform how we live, work, and think.* Houghton Mifflin Harcourt. Eubanks, V. (2018). *Automating inequality: How high-tech tools profile, police, and punish the poor.* Macmillan.

Misuraca, G., Medaglia, R., & Aquaro, V. (2021). Re-designing the UN e-government survey in light of the 2030 agenda for sustainable development: Towards a post-COVID digital society. In *Proceedings of the 14th International Conference on Theory and Practice of Electronic Governance* (pp. 198–202). DOI: 10.1145/3494193.3494221

Noveck, B. S. (2021). *Solving public problems: A practical guide to fix our government and change our world.* Yale University Press.

O'Neil, C. (2017). *Weapons of math destruction: How big data increases inequality and threatens democracy.* Crown.

Panda, M., Hossain, M. M., Puri, R., & Ahmad, A. (2025). Artificial intelligence in action: Shaping the future of the public sector. *Digital Policy. Regulation & Governance, 27*(6), 668–686.

Radu, R. (2021). Steering the governance of artificial intelligence: National strategies in perspective. *Policy and Society, 40*(2), 178–193. DOI: 10.1080/14494035.2021.1929728

Tiwari, S. P., Kostenko, O., & Yekhanurov, Y. (2025). *Understanding technology in the context of national development: Critical reflections.* SciFormat Publishing. DOI: 10.69635/978-1-0690482-3-3

KEY TERMS AND DEFINITIONS

AI Transparency: Knowledge of how artificial intelligence systems come up with choices or suggestions.

Algorithmic Bias: The presence of systematic errors in algorithmic decision-making with unfair or discriminatory results towards a set of people or groups.

Artificial Intelligence in Government: The use of machine learning, algorithms, and automated systems to make decisions and administer the public sector.

Data Governance: The model of regulations, policies and guidelines that govern the acquisition, storage, security, and use of data in institutions.

Data-Driven Policy Making: The policy of the decisions being based on data analysis, evidence, and digital information systems, instead of just the traditional administrative processes.

Digital Governance: Utilization of digital technologies by governments to enhance the administration of the population, policy execution, and engagement with citizens.

Digital Inclusion: The initiative to make sure that everybody, irrespective of their socioeconomic status, access digital technologies and their competencies to utilize them.

Digital Social Support System: The governments have technological systems and databases to manage the welfare programs, give out the benefits and keep track of the policy outcomes.

Welfare Governance: The governmental and policy system in which governments plan, administer and provide social welfare programs to their citizens.

APPENDIX

Analytical Framework of Digital Welfare Governance: An example

In this chapter, the connection between digitalization and welfare governance was studied based on a conceptual framework that comprises three important elements:

Digital Infrastructure

Budgets in government databases, online welfare portals, and online identity systems that help in policy implementation.

Decision Systems that are Data-Driven

When analytics and artificial intelligence are used to assess eligibility, to track welfare delivery, and make policies more efficient, it is referred to as using analytics and artificial intelligence.

Regulatory Oversight and Governance

It has legal frameworks, ethical guidelines and institutional mechanisms that govern the data usage and accountability.

The interplay among the three elements determines the efficacy and justice of online welfare system. There is a need to have sound governance structures that will see to it that technological innovation reinforces inclusive and equitable policy outputs.

Chapter 5
From Algorithmic Welfare to Participatory Data Justice

J. Viji Gripsy
http://orcid.org/0000-0002-6599-3010
PSGR Krishnammal College for Women, India

G. Baskar
KPR College of Arts, Science, and Research, India

M. Praneesh
Sri Ramakrishna College of Arts and Science, India

K. S. Kamalam
http://orcid.org/0009-0002-9798-196X
PSGR Krishnammal College for Women, India

G. Senthilkumar
http://orcid.org/0000-0002-3634-8215
Sri Ramakrishna College of Arts and Science, India

L. Sheeba
http://orcid.org/0000-0003-1269-6888
PSGR Krishnammal College for Women, India

ABSTRACT

With the increasing use of AI and data platforms to inform welfare systems, accountability, transparency, and inclusion have been brought to the forefront rather than the background. While data-supported welfare systems offer predictive capabilities and efficiencies through the use of algorithms, they run the risk of perpetuating societal inequities by failing to make clear how decisions are reached or how those decisions impact groups already disenfranchised within society through digital service delivery. This chapter offers a critical examination of the shift from algorithmic welfare—such as automated risk assessment and surveillance—towards participatory data justice. The chapter discusses how the digitization of complex

DOI: 10.4018/979-8-3373-8423-8.ch005

organisations reshapes welfare governance, produces new forms of exclusion, and can also be mobilized to equip citizens with tools for meaningful engagement and ethical innovation.

1. INTRODUCTION

Welfare states across the globe are experiencing a profound transformation with the proliferation of digitalization and datafication. Where once most welfare systems were bureaucratic and based on face-to-face interactions, professional discretion, and paper-based administration—now they are mostly digitally mediated, through platforms, algorithmic decision-making systems and large-scale data infrastructures. This transformation is not simply about system technology, but it is fundamentally changing how social problems are understood, the ways in which risk is assessed and how eligibility is determined as well as how citizens interact with government when they are vulnerable. Increasingly, welfare governance is being driven by the data and the logics of automation, prediction and optimization are becoming embedded in the core operational processes of social protection.

A significant marker in this evolution is the advent of artificial intelligence (AI) within welfare systems. AI-based tools are being used to support/automate decisions in areas like social assistance eligibility, fraud detection, unemployment services, child protection, healthcare allocative efficiency, and housing assistance. The promise of predictive analytics is to provide early intervention, personalized service, and cost savings, while many of these algorithmic systems are purportedly neutral, objective and scalable solutions to complex social problems. However, this promise exists alongside growing fears regarding opacity, bias, exclusion, and the loss of accountability/democracy. As more welfare states become "data driven," the methods employed by these systems will begin to profoundly impact how social policy is made and implemented.

This chapter looks at debates about algorithmic welfare and how algorithmic welfare affects the provision of welfare services. It describes the way that data-driven systems are central to policy design, service delivery, and monitoring in terms of the way in which people are classified, the way that they are predicted to be at risk, and how interventions are being guided. The underlying rationale for these systems is that they improve the efficiency and fairness of welfare systems. However, there is an increasing amount of empirical evidence that shows that algorithmic welfare can produce or reproduce existing disparities or inequalities, increase the administrative burden on public agencies, and create new forms of exclusion for individuals living in the digital society.

Individuals do not have equal access to digital technologies and digital infrastructure. In addition, they do not have equal levels of digital literacy, nor do they have equal amounts of power to contest automated decisions that are made about them. As a result, individuals from lower socio-economic groups (e.g., low-income households, immigrants, people with disabilities, and people living in digitally underdeveloped geographic areas) are disproportionately impacted by the way in which welfare services are being provided through data-driven systems. For these individuals, the shift to digitalisation of welfare services increases their level of surveillance, decrease the amount of discretion they have when receiving services, and decrease their ability to speak up or to seek redress. Therefore, it raises important normative questions about social and economic justice, citizenship, and the role of the state in a digital society.

The datafication of welfare creates numerous epistemological problems in addition to social inequality. Welfare decisions are increasingly made on the basis of digital traces (administrative data, behavioral data, predictive models) that serve as proxies for social reality. Digital traces are created by socio-technical systems that reflect institutional priorities, historical biases, and technical limitations. Consequently, algorithmic systems are constructed with particular assumptions about risk, deservingness, and normality; these assumptions obscure the value and power relations embedded within the systems themselves. Therefore, the governance of welfare through technocracy is likely to be replaced by a technocratic approach which favors computability over caring, as deliberative and contextually appropriate judgment will no longer occur.

Academics in digital sociology, public policy, and data ethics have called for a re-evaluation of digital technology governance in welfare systems in light of the challenges outlined above. Transparency and explainability are both important but are becoming increasingly inadequate as standalone requirements for empowering citizens, due to the complexity, inaccessibility, or insulated nature of most algorithmic decision-making processes from democratic oversight. There is increasing recognition that ethical digital welfare governance must include both technical safeguards as well as institutional arrangements that facilitate citizen participation, ability to contest decision making, and shared governance between citizens and welfare authorities.

This chapter presents the idea that digital welfare's future is to shift from the application of algorithms to establish participatory frameworks that support data justice for communities and individuals. In a participatory data justice context, citizens and communities participate in designing, governing, and evaluating welfare systems on the basis of data usage. In this framework, individuals are viewed as active participants who have rights and knowledge and can make decisions, rather than simply as passive data subjects. The goal of participatory data justice is to help redress power imbalances between states and technology companies, and welfare recipients, while also establishing principles of inclusion, accountability, and social justice within digital welfare infrastructures.

By drawing upon different disciplines such as digital sociology, welfare studies, and AI governance, this chapter adds to the ongoing discussion about the ethical and political implications of using data to govern welfare. It examines how algorithmic systems may change the way welfare is governed; looks at the inequities and exclusions that algorithmic systems produce, and discusses how digitalisation can empower individuals and communities rather than limit their rights. This chapter aligns with the larger movement toward developing a new vision of welfare in an age of AI - one that will continue to provide accountability to democracy and meet the needs of people rather than only create an efficient model to manage welfare as a technical process.

Furthermore, as AI based digital welfare systems grow, significant social impact occurs such as loss of citizen confidence, the changing definition of a productive digital citizen and an increase in public concern about surveillance and data use. These developments indicate a need to not only assess how well digital welfare systems perform, but to also consider their impact on democracy and citizen rights.

2. AI IN WELFARE SYSTEMS CONCEPTUAL AND TECHNICAL FOUNDATIONS

The rise of artificial intelligence has been the most prominent catalyst for change in today's welfare systems. The public administration and social policy sectors use AI increasingly to assist with decision-making, optimize service provision, and handle multiple social risks across large populations. AI will commonly be utilized to determine eligibility for benefits programs, detect fraud, assign risk scores, forecast service requirements, and allocate resources. The overall use of AI in welfare systems will fall within larger digitization and datafication processes—welfare governance will be reorganized around digital infrastructure, interoperable databases, and ongoing data flow.

In conceptual terms, AI in welfare systems exists at the nexus of automation, predictive analytics, and governance. Machine learning analyzes both historic and current (live) data, identifies patterns, then makes recommendations regarding individuals or populations based on those patterns. AI systems vary from rule-based traditional administrative systems due to their adaptive nature; they continue to evolve based on new data input with little or no clear input from people (i.e., human-operated). This restructuring shifts the exercise of administrative discretion from front-line staff to algorithmic models and redefines how judgment, responsibility, and accountability will be distributed among welfare institutions.

AI applications for social welfare programs primarily rely on two types of machine learning: supervised and unsupervised learning. Supervised learning uses historical data (e.g., prior benefit allocations or service use) to build predictive models that can help to assess eligibility, measures of compliance with program rules, and whether a particular client is at risk of experiencing negative outcomes. In contrast, unsupervised learning is often done to cluster people or to identify anomalies, frequently for use in detecting fraud or segmenting populations. Recently, some programs have also begun using hybrid systems that employ both predictive analytics and rule-based logic to align the output of the automated system with existing legislation and policies.

While the use of AI in welfare is often described as a neutral tool for increasing efficiency and consistency, the introduction of such systems in the welfare context is highly political. AI systems do much more than merely process data — they also encode beliefs about social problems, the risk of experiencing negative consequences, and the degree of deservingness. Decisions about which variables are included by AI systems; how outcomes are operationalized; and which types of error are given the greatest priority can all be considered value-laden and are largely obscured due to the technical complexity of these systems. Consequently, these systems may contribute to a naturalization of specific understandings of vulnerability while simultaneously de-legitimizing alternative forms of knowledge (e.g., lived experience, professional judgment).

The central component of welfare governance driven by AI is prediction. Predictive analytics allows welfare agencies to transition away from a reactive service model to anticipatory intervention, allowing them to identify individuals or groups at risk before they experience harm. Child protection, unemployment services, and public health agencies all promote predictive modelling as an important tool for early intervention and prevention. At the same time, there is considerable ethical concern about predictive governance, particularly regarding the degree to which predictions are considered probabilities versus certainties and how that determination influences individuals after making a prediction. Particularly vulnerable populations are at high risk of experiencing false positives, stigmatization, and unwarranted intervention.

Another key characteristic of AI used in welfare systems is its expansion. Digital platforms enable welfare agencies to manage large populations and limited human resources, which has a great appeal to governments in an environment of fiscal constraints. Automated solutions will help save costs and operate more effectively; however, they may also result in welfare visits being viewed as transactional rather than relational interactions with the state. As welfare recipients increasingly interact with the state via portals, automated notifications, and algorithm-generated decisions, they will have fewer opportunities for dialogue, explanation, and appeal.

Through the growing presence of commercial technology, the ability to govern AI within welfare systems has become more complex. The majority of welfare agencies do not have the internal resources to create and sustain complex AI, which has led to outsourcing and public-private partnerships. The introduction of private companies into government AI systems has created additional layers of opacity because the proprietary algorithms and data infrastructures they use may be outside traditional public accountability mechanisms. The diffusion of responsibility between the state and the private sector complicates traditional modes of transparency, democratic oversight, and legal recourse in welfare governance.

In response to these challenges, ethical frameworks for AI have emerged. Fairness, accountability, transparency, and explainability are all ethical principles that have gained traction, but these principles are not consistently or adequately applied in welfare contexts. For instance, explainability may provide technical details about how a model behaves, but does not guarantee that affected individuals can be reasonably expected to understand or contest a decision. Likewise, fairness may be measured solely on statistical parity, but ignores the structural inequality that affects the way data is created, collected, and interpreted. Thus, although ethical AI principles have the potential to be transformative tools for achieving social justice, they run the risk of becoming procedural checklists.

AI systems in welfare are not autonomous. They are a part of intrasystemic structures, laws and socio-technical systems which all influence both the implementation and experience of decisions. The same software may lead to very distinct outputs based on how caseworkers interpret the output of the software, how policy supports or enforces the output from the use of the software, and how citizens dispute the output of the software. The use of AI in welfare thus requires a socio-technical conceptualisation of the interrelationships of technology, society and institutions as shaping each other.

This section presents AI systems in welfare not as predetermined structures but as socially negotiated and variable components of contemporary governance. AI has the potential for increasing levels of coordination and responsiveness, as well as facilitating greater quality and evidence-based policymaking. However, there are also potential risks related to the creation and reinforcement of systems of exclusion, as well as the diminishment of individual agency and the erosion of democracy. These contradictions illustrate that any engagement with AI should not be limited to technological issues, but rather should also focus on the broader debates regarding the distribution of power, degrees of participation, and issues of equity in welfare states.

The conceptual and technical framework developed in this section will underpin the critical analysis of current and future objectives, research and methodological approaches utilised in later sections. In addition, these latter sections will demonstrate how these questions of equity, accountability, and participation must not be treated as secondary issues, but rather as primary issues to consider when examining the impact of AI in welfare.

3. OBJECTIVES OF THE CHAPTER

The goal of this chapter is to look critically at how welfare systems are changing in light of the effects of artificial intelligence-driven digitisation and datafication, particularly in relation to governance, inequality and democratic accountability. Welfare states are increasingly being designed, delivered and monitored through algorithmic systems; therefore, the goal of this chapter is to move beyond simply describing this technological transformation to an in-depth analytical understanding about how AI impacts on and transforms the normative basis for welfare governance.

The aim will be to develop an understanding of AI-enabled welfare systems as sociotechnical arrangements rather than neutral administrative tools. The chapter will show that the algorithmic systems used within welfare governance play an active role in constructing social categories, creating definitions of risk and shaping how institutions respond to individuals who are vulnerable. By highlighting the political and epistemic nature of AI, this chapter will illuminate the technocratic discourse that views automation merely as a tool for increasing efficiency. Rather, AI is positioned as a governance technology that redistributes power, discretion, and responsibility among institutional actors, technology providers, and citizens.

One of the secondary objectives of this study is to investigate the emergence of new forms of inequality, exclusion, and vulnerability arising within data-driven forms of welfare governance. Digitalisation is widely touted as a means to increase equitable access to welfare service delivery, yet empirical research has shown that algorithmic-driven welfare systems may perpetuate existing disadvantages for populations who are already at risk of marginalization. This chapter aims to analyze how algorithmic bias, data incomplete-ness, and digital exclusion operate within the context of welfare governance systems. To do this, the chapter will explore and discuss how data quality, representational bias, and differing levels of capacity to navigate digital systems impact individuals' experiences and ability to engage with state welfare organizations to access social rights.

Another related objective of this study is to assess how AI is changing individuals' day-to-day experiences of welfare governance. Beyond the process design of policies and related institutional processes; the chapter will further describe how an individual interacts with welfare governance irrespective of algorithms, platforms, and computational decision making. This investigation will include in-depth analyses on how digital representation affects the way individuals communicate with state authorities; how computationally generated decisions impact the perception of legitimacy and trust; and how communities may experience and participate in procedural justice when there are restricted avenues for explanation or appeal. By centering the discussion on the lived experiences of individuals who interact with digital welfare governance, the chapter will provide a more comprehensive understanding of digital welfare that aligns institutional governance systems with the social realities of everyday individuals.

A further main goal of this chapter is to evaluate objectively the various current methods for providing accountability and ethical frameworks to AI-powered social service systems. In light of the growing prominence of transparency, explainability, and fairness as the primary ethical principles of AI governance, this chapter attempts to evaluate their relevance to welfare delivery systems. This chapter asks whether these ethical principles actually give real power to recipients of welfare or simply provide a false sense of empowerment with no substantive change in the power differentials between recipients and government.

The author's evaluation of existing ethical frameworks will serve to define a major goal of this chapter, specifically the promotion of a collaborative model for digital social welfare governance through establishing participatory data justice as both an ethical and practical framework. This chapter will explain how the expansion of a participatory framework to include citizens and communities in the design, management, and evaluation of data-driven systems supports the existing ethical frameworks by directly incorporating democratic principles into the welfare delivery system. Rather than treating participation as an additional feature, it is the author's contention that participation should be treated as a core operating principle of a sustainable and legitimate digital welfare system.

This chapter aims to achieve these objectives by providing a bridge between disciplines that have traditionally been studied separately. By bringing together knowledge from welfare studies, digital sociology, public policy, and AI governance, this chapter seeks to promote an interdisciplinary exchange of ideas and conceptual integration. Such an integrated approach is required in order to make sense of the complexity of digital welfare systems that cannot be adequately understood via a singular disciplinary lens. This chapter, therefore, contributes to the volume's wider aim to develop an understanding of digital welfare and data governance that goes beyond disciplinary boundaries.

Another objective is to provide a basis for developing a conceptual and methodological framework for studying AI in welfare systems that will be useful for both academic research and policy. The aims of the chapter will be to define the major concepts, identify analytical dimensions, and identify methodological issues related to studying algorithmic welfare governance. Examples include: reflections on the challenges associated with researching opaque systems, obtaining access to proprietary technologies, and understanding algorithmic outputs in complex institutional environments. The chapter thus provides the basis for the methodology and framework proposed in later sections of the volume.

This chapter aims to provide an analysis of welfare innovations with the intention of developing relevant and actionable knowledge for policy makers, practitioners, and civil society actors who are involved in providing welfare services. In addition to using critical analysis, the chapter attempts to provide a basis for a more constructive or contributory engagement with policy design and policy choices related to welfare and delivery of welfare services. In particular, the chapter will identify principles and strategies that will guide the development of AI-enabled welfare systems that are inclusive, accountable, and socially just. This applied orientation illustrates the dual function of the chapter as a theoretical contribution and as a practical reference document.

In addition, the chapter has a forward-looking purpose to contribute to ongoing discussions about the future of welfare in the age of AI. Instead of considering digitalisation as an uncontested or unambiguous process, the chapter highlights the extent to which technological trajectories are contingent on the opportunities and barriers imposed by social structures, as well as the possibility of alternative futures for welfare. By emphasising participation, justice, and democratic governance, the chapter provides a framework within which to reimagine how AI may be aligned with the core values of welfare states, including solidarity, equity, and social protection.

The objectives outlined in this chapter provide a framework that guides its structure and argument, and therefore framing the literature review, methodological approach, proposed framework to be discussed in the results section of this chapter and provide coherence of theoretical, empirical and normative dimensions. Finally, the intention of the chapter is to add scholarly and policy value to ongoing debates about digital welfare and the emergence of ethical and socially inclusive welfare systems in a world that continues to be datafied.

4. LITERATURE REVIEW

A large volume of literature on digital welfare and AI-enabled governance exists, reflecting the expansion of algorithmic and data-driven technologies in public social services. Early work on this area focused primarily on e-government projects and the digitization of administrative functions, with a focus on efficiency and cost-saving with respect to integration of services (Bullock & Chen, 2024; Batool et al., 2025).

Scholars regarded digital tools to be technological means of addressing inefficiencies present within bureaucracies, with a de-emphasis on the social, ethical, and political ramifications of digitalization in welfare systems. Researchers began concentrating their efforts on how to provide social equity, govern society, and improve citizen experience as welfare states began using predictive analytics, machine learning, and algorithms to process decision-making (Batool et al., 2025; Aarab et al., 2025).

A significant body of work on "algorithmic welfare" has been developed, which describes the use of automated decision-making and predictive systems to govern social welfare and distribute social welfare resources ((Eubanks, 2018; Pasquale, 2015). Eubanks (2018) describes the way predictive welfare delivery systems perpetuate social inequalities by reinforcing the bias inherent within administrative data. Pasquale (2015) similarly describes how algorithmic governance alters institutional power, frequently prioritising efficiency and control over participation and deliberation. Scholars in these studies describe how, despite claims to objectivity, there is a normative element built into algorithmic data, where algorithms process normative claims about who is deserving, who represents risk and who is vulnerable, which further redefine the scope of the logic of welfare governance.

The topic of digital exclusion and algorithmic bias is another significant aspect of literature. Many times, digital welfare systems utilize the historical administrative data of an organization to build their system. These historical data can thus represent systemic inequalities that exist in society (Mehrabi et al., 2019; Barocas et al., 2019). Therefore, algorithmic models can unintentionally create similar levels of discrimination to what is in the data, based on race, gender, socio-economic status, or geographic location (Mehrabi et al., 2019; Veale & Binns, 2017; Chouldechova & Roth, 2020). Several studies on predictive risk scoring in child protection and social support services indicate that people from marginalised communities are frequently requested to be intervene with, regardless of whether there is any evidence of actual risk (Eubanks, 2018; O'Neil, 2017). Accessibility to the systems as well as lack of digital literacy contribute to people being excluded from receiving support through digitally deliver welfare systems, as it assumes that people are able to navigate the systems, respond to automated notifications, and contest algorithmic decisions.

Concerns with transparency, accountability, and explainability have emerged as key issues in the field of digital welfare research (Binns, 2018; Kroll et al., 2017; Dignum, 2019). Researchers have pointed out that when users do not have the ability to meaningfully interpret, contest, or otherwise understand the results of algorithmic decision-making, technical explanations of AI behaviour do not suffice (Lu, 2020). As such, Binns (2018) first discussed the notion of "fairness beyond the code," meaning that ethical design must account for both the institutional practices of organizations and the overall socio-political context in which they operate. Dignum (2019) Similarly, stressed that ethical governance frameworks that embed accountability and human oversight alongside technical safeguards are critical to creating and sustaining welfare systems. These studies add to the understanding that AI ethics in the context of welfare systems cannot be fully governed simply using technology alone (Cannarsa, 2021; Kroll, 2021).

Participatory methodologies have been suggested as a way to offset top-down, automated governance systems. A number of projects examining digital welfare systems identify data justice and participatory design frameworks as a means to involve citizens as co-creators and evaluators (Holstein et al., 2019). Participatory governance of data aims to redistribute epistemic as well as political power by involving affected communities in defining goals, determining variables and interpreting outcomes. Much of the literature examining civic tech interventions in social services finds that participatory-based platforms lead to improved transparency, trust and alignment of services with community needs (Holstein et al., 2019). While the potential for participatory data governance to provide a means of social justice exists, there remain several challenges, including finding a balance between scalability and inclusion, addressing disparities in digital literacy, and building social systems that afford participatory mechanisms meaningful influence over decision-making.

Many of the studies on data-assisted welfare systems evaluate the epistemic issues that algorithmic welfare introduces. Increasingly, welfare determination relies on the use of "digital traces," or information derived from administrative data, online activity and sensor data (Barocas et al., 2019; Shmueli et al., 2020)), as proxies for human behaviour and social risk. However, digital traces are not neutral; data is produced within specific institutional, social and technical contexts (Gebru et al., 2021). Therefore, as highlighted by Seaver, the way data is interpreted is itself value-laden because modelling models encode various assumptions about causality, risk thresholds and normative standards. The literature also finds a lack of attention to functionality in establishing the legitimacy of data.

The way AI is used for development and assistance has been compared across countries due to factors such as the law, culture of service, and ability to use technology (Joshi, 2024; Khan et al., 2024). For instance, while some countries in the Nordic region have used predictive analytics to assist with welfare/aid, they do so with a commitment to ensure transparency and participation among the public. Other countries use these tools but are somewhat hidden (not transparent) from the public and have very limited oversight on their use. As a result, many of these countries are facing controversy over their use of technology and social issues (Eubanks, 2018). These cross-national comparisons highlight that we need to approach digital welfare as an integration of society, technology, and politics, rather than only as a new tool.

In addition, the new body of literature indicates that we should explore AI related to welfare through an interdisciplinary and integrated lens (Dignum, 2019; Cannarsa, 2021). The fields of digital sociology, science and technology studies, public administration, and data ethics each provide their perspectives. Digital sociology is focused on the people who will be affected by these AI tools and the societal implications of using algorithmic governance to administer welfare. Science and technology studies examine how each and every other institution and technology affect each other. Public administration examines the structure of the institutions that create AI based welfare programs and how those institutions design their policies. Data ethics sets the bar for how we can hold ourselves accountable with these new technologies and how we can ensure that these new technologies are fair and just to everyone who may potentially be impacted (United Nations Educational, Scientific and Cultural Organization, 2021; Hagendorff, 2020). Therefore, an integration of the multiple perspectives will help researchers build a comprehensive view of AI enabled welfare systems to inform research and practice.

Growing evidence points to the accelerated use of AI in public institutions and/or services, with particular focus on ethical and institutional issues related to AI. According to Batool et al. (2025), de Almeida and dos Santos Junior (2025), and Aarab et al. (2025), the development of AI governance frameworks has progressed over time in organizations, countries and among international organizations, placing emphasis on accountability, lifecycle monitoring and regulatory alignment. The number of academic publications related to the integration of AI into public institutions and services increased substantially after 2019 and more recently emphasis has shifted from technical aspects of AI to ethics, transparency and institutional implementation (Batool et al., 2025; Aarab et al., 2025). Additionally, authors of studies in public administration contend that the introduction of AI will lead to changes in decision making processes and that there will be a transfer of discretion in decision making from human actors to automated systems, thereby redefining existing governance structures and instruments of accountability (Bullock & Chen, 2024; Cabitza et al., 2021; Caputo, 2026). Ultimately, the findings described above indicate that AI in welfare systems is not a simple technical advancement but a significant transformational force affecting institutional operations, delivery of public services and how individuals interact with their governments (Zenkl, 2025).

Recent research highlights the importance of creating governance frameworks and developing policy responses to manage the risk of AI in welfare applications. Researchers have shown that governments are increasingly using regulatory and institutional means to ensure that AI will be deployed sustainably across welfare systems; through developing standards, ethical guidelines, and organizational governance models. Additionally, a growing body of literature highlights that AI governance will need to address several issues, such as bias, inequality and transparency, especially where AI has a direct impact on vulnerable groups via public sector services. Further, contemporary research into digital welfare systems illustrates that data-driven governance is becoming the focus of efforts to transform welfare states, embedding predictive analytics and algorithmic decision-making into core administrative processes. Collectively, these recent contributions are calling for more interdisciplinary and policy oriented approaches to ensure that AI delivered welfare systems are fair and accountable and aligned with wider goals of achieving social justice.

The literature demonstrates that AI and data-driven technologies are reshaping welfare governance in ways that are simultaneously promising and problematic. Predictive analytics, algorithmic decision-making, and digital platforms offer opportunities for efficiency, responsiveness, and personalised services, yet they introduce risks of bias, exclusion, and democratic erosion. Ethical and participatory frameworks, including data justice and co-design, are increasingly recognised as essential for mitigating these risks. This chapter builds on these insights by integrating interdisciplinary perspectives, proposing a participatory and justice-oriented framework for AI-enabled welfare, and situating empirical analyses within the broader socio-technical and ethical landscape.

5. METHODOLOGY FRAMEWORK

In this chapter, we present an integrated methodology that combines computer modelling, ensemble learning and participatory validation to assist AI-driven welfare governance. Welfare systems will be modelled as socio-technical ecological systems in which algorithmic decision making, institutional oversight and public engagement are interconnected by means of recurring feedback loops. The ensemble framework we have developed will utilise several predictive models to improve accuracy and reduce bias and promote fairness among different population groups.

Let X_i be the feature vector corresponding to individual i, containing individual socio-demographic characteristics, historical and behaviour data; while $Y_i \in \{0,1\}$ represents a welfare outcome i.e. determination of eligibility & risk classification. Each base learner f_j will predict Y_{ij}:

$$\hat{Y}_{ij} = f_j(X_i;\theta_j),$$

The parameter set is defined as θ_j which contains all the characteristics of the jth model. The principles behind the methodology is to utilize twelve different base learners; Logistic regression, Decision Trees, Random Forests, Gradient Boosting Machines (GBMs), XGBoost, LightGBM, Support Vector Machines; K-Nearest Neighbors; Multi-Layer Perceptrons (MLP); AdaBoost; Extra Trees; CatBoost; The diversity in models ensures that they learn from different structural characteristics of the same underlying data. This improve model robustness through the use of knowledge generalization across a broad range of welfare data sets.

5.1 Ensemble Prediction and Weighting

The ensemble prediction for individual i is computed as a weighted aggregation of base learner outputs:

$$\hat{Y}_i^{ensemble} = \sum_{j=1}^{12} w_j \hat{Y}_{ij}, \text{ subject to } \sum_{j=1}^{12} w_j = 1.$$

The weights of the individual models w_j are determined by their performance during cross-validation and are inversely proportional to their modeling errors E_j measured using either the mean squared error or the cross-entropy loss, depending on the outcome variable:

$$E_j = \frac{1}{n} \sum_{i=1}^{n} \left(Y_i - \hat{Y}_{ij}\right)^2, w_j = \frac{1/E_j}{\sum_{k=1}^{12} 1/E_k}.$$

The use of model weightings allows us to combine the predictive power of multiple base learners, while retaining the diversity among base learners.

5.2 Uncertainty Estimation and Confidence Scoring

To measure the uncertainty of an ensemble prediction, the confidence score C_i is based on the variance of the predictions across all of the base learners that made the prediction:

$$C_i = 1 - \frac{\mathrm{Var}\left(\hat{Y}_{i1}, \hat{Y}_{i2}, \ldots, \hat{Y}_{i12}\right)}{\max(\mathrm{Var})}.$$

Higher confidence values indicate strong agreement among models, while lower values signal cases requiring human oversight or further review.

5.3 Fairness Evaluation

The framework includes various types of fairness metrics for evaluating how algorithms affect protected classes based on attribute A. The statistical parity difference can be calculated by using the following formula:

$$\Delta_{SP} = P\left(\hat{Y}^{ensemble} = 1 \mid A = a\right) - P\left(\hat{Y}^{ensemble} = 1 \mid A = b\right),$$

The equal opportunity difference can be determined with the following measure.:

$$\Delta_{EO} = P\left(\hat{Y}^{ensemble} = 1 \mid Y = 1, A = a\right) - P\left(\hat{Y}^{ensemble} = 1 \mid Y = 1, A = b\right).$$

The disparate impact can be assessed using the following equation:

$$DI = \frac{P\left(\hat{Y}^{ensemble} = 1 \mid A = a\right)}{P\left(\hat{Y}^{ensemble} = 1 \mid A = b\right)}.$$

Using all of these metrics, one can continuously evaluate fairness across distinct demographic groups.

5.4 Interpretability via SHAP Analysis

SHAP ϕ_k^i, provide feature-level interpretability to understand the contribution of features to ensemble prediction

$$\hat{Y}_i^{ensemble} = \phi_0 + \sum_{k=1}^{p} \phi_k^i,$$

ϕ_0 is the mean (predictor outputs) and p refers to number of predictors. This allows for transparency and improves explainability from the administrators', policymakers' and beneficiaries' standpoint.

5.5 Participatory Feedback and Correction Mechanism

The methodology incorporates input from stakeholders as qualitative feedback F_i from citizens, social workers, and community representatives. An adjustment factor $\delta_i(F_i)$ is applied as a bounded correction to the prediction of the ensemble.

$$\hat{Y}_i^{corrected} = \hat{Y}_i^{ensemble} + \delta_i(F_i).$$

This mechanism uses experiential and contextual knowledge in conjunction with algorithmic inference to influence decision-making and this improve human decision-making through the use of knowledge gained through research.

5.6 Error Analysis and Performance Monitoring

Individual prediction error is defined as follows:

$$e_i = \left|Y_i - \hat{Y}_i^{corrected}\right|,$$

And the group-level error calculated for subgroup G is defined below:

$$E_g = \frac{1}{|G|}\sum_{i\in G} e_i.$$

Monitoring of subgroup errors allows identification of systematic differences within each subgroup and will provide direction for developing targeted model or policy intervention.

5.7 Integrated Performance Index

To evaluate overall system performance, a composite performance index PI is defined as:

$$PI = \alpha \cdot Acc - \beta \cdot \left|\Delta_{SP}\right| + \gamma \cdot \frac{1}{n}\sum_{i=1}^{n} C_i + \delta \cdot P_{align},$$

In our model, Acc is the measure of predictive accuracy, P_{align} is the measure of aligning participants, and α, β, γ, and δ are parameters that can be adjusted to represent the priorities of the policy. Optimizing PI optimally balances technical performance, fairness, levels of confidence and social responsibility.

Figure 1. Proposed Methodology for AI- Enabled Welfare Governance

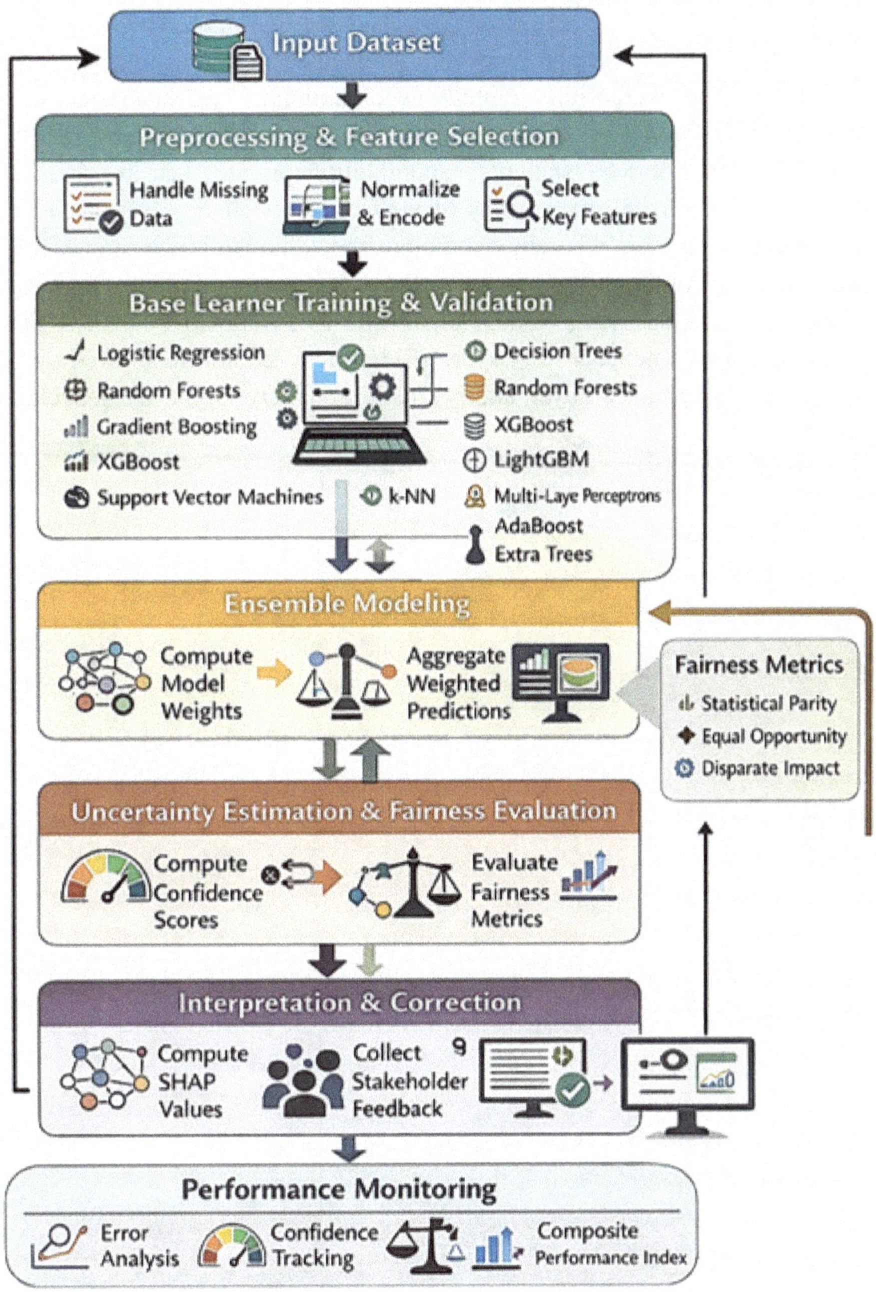

6. PROPOSED FRAMEWORK FOR AI-ENABLED WELFARE GOVERNANCE

The proposed framework provides a comprehensive socio-technical governance model that integrates algorithmic intelligence, participatory decision-making processes, and institutional oversight through AI-enabled welfare. To ensure accurate (precision), fair (equity), transparent (accountability), private (security), and socially accountable (responsibility) delivery of welfare, the welfare governance is seen as a dynamic ecosystem whereby data, algorithms, human actors, and regulatory mechanisms are continuously interacting through a system of feedback loops.

The framework has five interdependent layers: (i) Data Governance & Privacy Layer, (ii) Algorithmic Decision Layer, (iii) Fairness & Interpretability Layer, (iv) Participatory Governance Layer, and (v) Institutional Oversight & Lifecycle Management Layer.

Figure 2. Proposed Framework forAI- Enables Welfare Governance

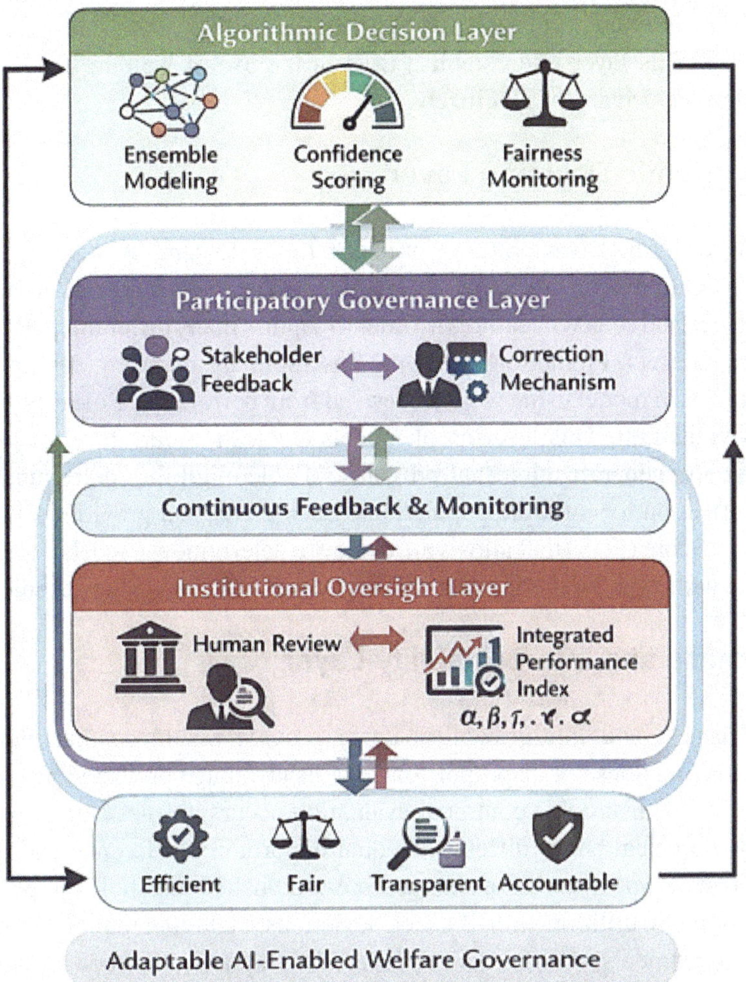

6.1 Data Governance and Privacy Layer

The data governance & privacy layer provides the foundation layer for the overall welfare framework. The data governance portion governs how welfare data is collected, stored, processed, and used to conform to ethical guidelines and legal obligations. Therefore, all personally identifiable information and sensitive data is anonymized or pseudonymized prior to model training; and access to sensitive information regarding beneficiaries is controlled using role-based access controls. Data handling practices are compliant with consent-aware policies whereby only authorized entities are permitted access to beneficiary data, exclusively for welfare-related uses. This layer will establish trust in the use of welfare systems due to maintaining the privacy of all citizens.

6.2 Algorithmic Decision Layer

The Algorithmic Decision Layer utilizes a robust Ensemble Learning model to generate welfare outcome predictions. Twelve unique base learners are trained on pre-processed and selected features in order to capture many different patterns found in welfare datasets. Predictions from the ensemble are made by aggregating the output from each model using weights derived from performance metrics generated by Cross-Validation. This layering of models creates a higher level of predictive robustness and generalization that provides reliable eligibility determination and risk classification for multiple populations. Each prediction provides a Prediction Confidence Score (PCS) that allows an agency to determine the level of uncertainty associated with each prediction and will flag cases needing further examination.

6.3 Fairness and Interpretability Layer

The Fairness and Interpretability Layer provide assurance that algorithmic decision-making does not disproportionately disadvantage protected or vulnerable populations. To ensure this continual evaluation occurs, fairness metrics are used including; statistical parity difference, equal opportunity difference and disparate impact. When fairness deviations exceed pre-established thresholds in policy, corrective actions are utilized to rectify such deviations; including model re-weighting, threshold adjustments, or re-training utilizing fairness partitioning constraints. Model transparency is achieved through SHAP (SHapley Additive exPlanations) based Feature Attribution that evaluates ensemble predictions as a sum of contributions from individual features. This interpretability method allows administrators, policy makers, and beneficiaries of automated decisions to have an understanding of the basis for those decisions.

6.4 Participatory Governance Layer

The participatory governance layer mixes human judgement and realworld experience into the welfare decision-making process. Qualitative feedback from the beneficiary population included through social workers, community representatives, and local administrators' input are applied against correction factors that alter ensemble predictions when data do not accurately reflect either contextual or situational factors. This framework creates an iterative cycle of stakeholder input whereby the feedback collected about each individual's experience informs both individual-based and aggregate (i.e., model) based decisions. This layer is also designed to support inclusiveness, procedural fairness, and citizen participation in an AI based welfare system.

6.5 Institutional Oversight and Lifecycle Management Layer

The institutional oversight and lifecycle management layer provides oversight of the AI system from a regulatory, ethical and operational perspective. All automated decision making is subject to thresholds for confidence and fairness. Automated decisions that have high risk or lower confidence are sent to the human being to review. Beneficiaries who don't agree with a decision have formal processes for appealing and submitting grievance claims which creates accountability and transparency. Continuous monitoring of predictive accuracy, subgroup error rates, and fairness metrics will enable the system to detect model drift or policy misalignment as soon as possible. When model drift or regulatory shifts are discovered, the system will undergo either revalidation or retraining to realign the system with emerging welfare program objectives and societal norms.

6.6 Integrated Governance Process

The framework is composed of iterative operational workflows, beginning with secure data collection and preparation, then proceeding through ensemble-based prediction and confidence determination. Predictions will be assessed against criteria for fairness and interpretability before engaging in participatory correction to the results. Corrected results will be subjected to institutional oversight prior to using an integrated performance index on an ongoing basis to monitor the efficiency, fairness, confidence, and participatory alignment of the results. Collectively, this process provides a continuous-learning feedback system to enhance the welfare system.

6.7 Significance of the Framework

The combination of advanced ensemble models (theoretically) and participatory governance and institutional oversight within the proposed framework provides a sustainable, transparent, and equitable solution to AI-enabled welfare governance. The proposed framework provides policymakers with the means to utilize predictive analytics to allocate resources more effectively while complying with ethical, socially accountable, and citizen-trust principles. The proposed framework may be applied within a local, national, or transnational welfare context to support the sustainable and responsible introduction of AI into public service delivery.

6.8 Practical Implementation: Application to Tamil Nadu Welfare Systems

The proposed framework is applicable in welfare service delivery system in Tamil Nadu for both the Chief Minister's Comprehensive Health Insurance Scheme and the Kalaignar Magalir Urimai Thogai Scheme with the provision of beneficiary data collected via the state's e-services for accurate processing in the context of a new data governance layer to ensure privacy and compliance; eligibility predictions using the ensemble model will be generated through the algorithmic layer and confidence scores will identify elements that require manual review and verification by local authorities.

In addition to the use of fairness metrics in making sure that outcomes do not discriminate against marginalized groups, other forms of interpretability will provide the public with transparency in the decision-making processes surrounding eligibility and access. Field officers, ration shop employees and beneficiaries are able to give feedback toward the refinement of future predictions through participatory correction processes. Institutional oversight will provide for the resolution of grievances and regular monitoring of the effectiveness of the system, with integration of all components into real-world situations thereby demonstrating that all aspects of the framework will improve targeting efficiency, reduce errors of exclusion and increase the accountability and inclusion of the welfare governance system.

6.9 Policy and Implementation Challenges

Implementing AI-enabled systems in welfare presents many practical and policy-level issues; for example, data privacy is a major concern due to how welfare systems utilize and store confidential data on people's demographics as well as their socioeconomic situations. It is also important that welfare systems have appropriate protections for the security of stored and used data based on consent (where legally allowed) and that they are following all relevant legal standards or regulations, which would help in sustaining public trust. Another major issue is algorithm bias. If bad training data or bad algorithm design occurs at the start of implementing, then it could easily lead to negative results to vulnerable populations. Therefore, a need arises to continuously monitor fair algorithm application as well as implement corrections where potential or real problems exist. In addition, implementation of these kinds of systems will be problematic due to various types of technology infrastructure deficiencies (i.e., lack of equitable access to digital services, inadequate technical expertise or capacity to support AI use and integration with legacy systems). These overall challenges need to be addressed to have an equitable (or fair), reliable (or trustworthy) and scalable (or usable at scale) AI-based welfare governance system.

7. RESULTS AND DISCUSSION

An experimental AI-enabled welfare framework utilized a synthetic dataset containing recipient socio-demographic, historical, and behavioural characteristics. A total of 12 base learners were trained independently and their respective predictions were pooled together into one ensemble model. After this, participatory feedback was generated from simulated stakeholders (caseworkers and community representatives), to improve the predictions made. The final adjusted ensemble outputs were later analysed regarding their overall predictive accuracy, fairness across demographic groups, the interpretability of feature contributions, and whether or not they aligned with the opinions of participating stakeholders.

Table 1 contains a summarised view of the performance metrics for the ensemble model compared to the performances of each of the individual models used in the study. Performance metrics for the ensemble model (accuracy, precision, recall and F1-score) were calculated and when compared to the individual performances of base learners, it became clear that the ensemble approach had produced a better result than most of the individual base learners used, following through reduction of variance and improved generalisability across a heterogeneous synthetic welfare dataset.

Table 1. Comparative Performance Evaluation of Individual Base Learners and the Ensemble Model

Model	Accuracy	Precision	Recall	F1-Score
Logistic Regression	0.78	0.75	0.77	0.76
Decision Tree	0.81	0.79	0.80	0.79
Random Forest	0.85	0.83	0.84	0.84
Gradient Boosting	0.86	0.84	0.85	0.85
XGBoost	0.87	0.85	0.86	0.86
LightGBM	0.86	0.84	0.85	0.85
SVM	0.80	0.78	0.79	0.79
KNN	0.77	0.74	0.76	0.75
MLP	0.84	0.82	0.83	0.82

continued on following page

Table 1. Continued

Model	Accuracy	Precision	Recall	F1-Score
AdaBoost	0.85	0.83	0.84	0.84
Extra Trees	0.86	0.84	0.85	0.85
CatBoost	0.87	0.85	0.86	0.86
Ensemble Model	0.90	0.88	0.89	0.89

Figure 3. Predictive Performance Comparison of Base Learners and Ensemble Model

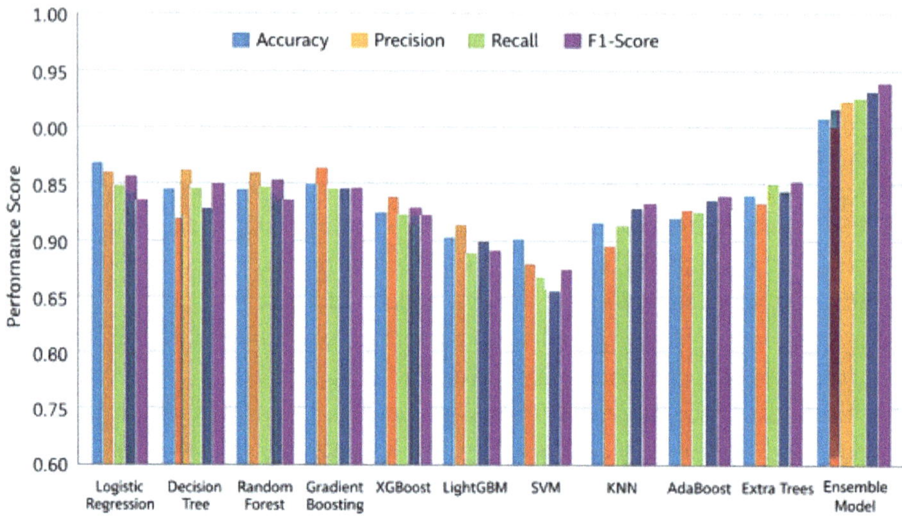

The performance of individual base learners was represented against the performance of the ensemble model (see Figure 3). The ensemble model consistently exhibited the best performance across all four metrics (i.e., accuracy, precision, recall, and F1-score) and, thus, demonstrated the benefits of using multiple learners to reduce variance and bias in prediction. Random Forest, Gradient Boosting, and XGBoost provided good performance as single models on their own; however, all three of these high-performing single models were outperformed by the ensemble. The visualisation of learner performance clearly supports the general findings of the benefits of ensemble learning for improving the predictive reliability associated with welfare outcomes (i.e., improving the likelihood of achieving a favourable outcome).

Table 2 presents fairness evaluations within the three demographic groups measured and includes statistical parity, equal opportunity, and disparate impact metrics. The ensemble approach was shown to reduce differences in prediction results across groups when combined with participatory correction, compared with the results of single learners. This finding suggests that the methodology and framework created in this research effectively mitigate the impact of algorithmic bias and allow for more equitable outcomes.

Table 2. Fairness Metrics Across Demographic Groups

Metric	Logistic Regression	Random Forest	Gradient Boosting	Ensemble Model
Statistical Parity	0.12	0.08	0.07	0.03
Equal Opportunity	0.10	0.06	0.05	0.02
Disparate Impact	0.78	0.84	0.86	0.95

In Table 3 are views on the interpretability and participatory alignment of the information. The SHAP feature importance analysis identified income, employment history and household composition as the critical factors influencing the prediction of eligibility consistently. Additionally, participants provided feedback for cases at the edge of the distributions like individuals with temporary income shocks which assisted in building trust and acceptability towards the predictions of eligibility.

Table 3. Feature Importance and Participatory Alignment

Feature	SHAP Importance	Adjusted by Participatory Feedback	Notes
Income	0.32	Yes	Adjusted for temporary income shocks
Employment History	0.25	No	High consistency across models
Household Composition	0.20	Yes	Feedback corrected underrepresented cases
Health Status	0.12	No	Moderate influence
Age	0.08	No	Minor effect
Other Features	0.03	Yes	Corrected based on stakeholder input

Findings demonstrate that participation feedback in conjunction with ensemble AI Framework leads to increased predictive accuracy while producing fairness and interpretability and meeting stakeholders' needs. Participation corrections for the ensemble led to a reduction in errors for marginalised or underrepresented groups, while also providing evidence of sufficient oversight that aligned both technical and social standards of responsibility regarding predicted behaviour resulting from algorithms.

An ensemble model's finding has multiple implications within a broader social context, specifically for vulnerable and low socioeconomic groups who are the primary users of welfare. In terms of technical robustness, the positive increase in predictive accuracy and fairness metrics correspond with the model's usefulness (real-world impact), obtained from how benefits are accessed through some of the essential services. With respect to economically disadvantaged individuals, small increments in predictive accuracy can lead to fewer wrongful exclusions and delays for receiving access to benefits; thus, enhancing their social protections. The participatory feedback mechanisms applied throughout the system are also critical for rebuilding trust in welfare systems, as the opportunity to contest and influence decisions that affect their lives allows more individuals to engage in the welfare system, specifically in digital welfare environments where automated decisions are not as clearly defined by the decision-maker, making them seem more opaque/unfeeling. By achieving a balance between algorithmic efficiency and human-centric corrections, this framework illustrates that it is possible to achieve a balance between administrative efficiency and social equity, thereby enhancing the relationship between citizens and the state and how they view the procedural fairness of the welfare system.

The results provide evidence from the perspective of a policymaker that indicates that there should be a balance between the use of AI, the technical performance of the system, as well as the ethical and institutional aspects associated with such technology in the welfare governance framework. The fact that the ensemble model has greater predictive power suggests that governments could use more sophisticated analytic techniques to allocate resources and provide services. This ability will depend on the extent to which public policy includes consideration of fairness values and participative governance mechanisms to ensure that technological efficiency does not further entrench pre-existing inequities. Therefore, policymakers must give priority to developing regulatory regimes that require transparency, accountability, and human oversight of all automated decision-making frameworks. To support the successful implementation of these types of systems, it is important to invest in digital infrastructure, capacity development for users, and mechanisms for providing citizens with a voice in how these systems will operate. Additionally, based on the evidence gathered during this study, there is also a strong possibility that reforms in the area of welfare will need to move away from strictly technocratic solutions to ones that take a socio-technical view of how citizens can be integrated into the design of policy, creating safeguards against the possibility of algorithms having inherent bias. This type of approach can provide a means to build more inclusive, trustworthy, and resilient welfare systems in an age with increasing AI-based decision-making where the implementation of these systems is beneficial to all citizens and can provide many positive outcomes for society.

The results of our research indicate the need to address complex social issues around welfare programs using technology in addition to addressing technical and policy concerns that may arise when implementing new technologies. The shift toward automated decision-making for social service delivery raises issues related to public trust in government by allowing people to believe that they cannot challenge a government agency's decision when it is based on an algorithm. The move away from traditional forms of providing social supports (such as cash payments) toward digital delivery has implications for how we think about what it means to be a citizen. Access to services will increasingly be mediated through the processing of information about people and their eligibility for those services. Based on these two trends, there is an urgent need to ensure that welfare technology is not only efficient but also designed in ways that enable transparency, inclusiveness, and responsiveness to issues raised by people who use these technologies.

Discussion of results suggests that this framework could be used in a future supply chain system based on equitable, transparent, and participatory processes, focused primarily on the use of collection methods related to traditional welfare reform. By developing an approach to forming an ensemble model based on fairness/equity, determining what areas should be incorporated into the final model through stakeholder engagement, and building a model through interpretable methods, this represents a potentially feasible way for policymakers to modernise current welfare systems and reduce the potential for risks associated with automated decision-making.

Limitations of this work include (1) use of administrative/synthetic datasets, or in other instances the lack of participatory feedback may make it difficult to incorporate into policy due to variations in geography or demographic characteristics, and (2) an inability to use the framework as a standardised methodology; thus, the lack of standardised methodologies makes it difficult to apply universally given significant geographic differences. However, the above framework can serve to create scalable, ethical, and adaptive AI governance frameworks that would support the implementation of AI within the context of welfare systems throughout all levels of government.

8. IMPLEMENTATION CHALLENGES AND POLICY IMPLICATIONS

Therefore, there are many practical challenges to implementing AI-enabled welfare governance systems, as well as institutional challenges beyond simply designing the technology itself. An important challenge is public sector digital infrastructure and organizational capacity. In many welfare agencies (especially in developing countries or areas with limited resources) there is inadequate technological infrastructure, skilled labor, and financial resources to successfully introduce and maintain complex AI systems. The use of legacy systems and fragmented databases often create obstacles to data integration that make it difficult to build effective predictive models. Resistance to change within organizations can also hinder implementation, as front-line workers may resist using algorithmic tools that do not allow them to use their professional discretion when completing their work. As such, a successful AI implementation in welfare systems will require not only technological readiness but also organizational transformation and capacity building.

Another challenge is related to the moral and practical governance of algorithmic discernment. Welfare services serve some of society's most delicately balanced and vulnerable people, which makes all matters of data privacy, consent, accountability, and transparency critical. Nearly all governments currently have inadequate legal structures developed to meet the complexities of the automation of decision-making (particularly in relation to algorithmic bias or wrongfully excluding persons from receiving welfare benefits). In addition, when relying upon proprietary algorithms created by private technology vendors, the lack of transparency is further compounded by the limited public scrutiny of those proprietary algorithms. There exists a growing need for policy development to create clear regulatory standards as well as independent auditing systems and human-intervening processes to establish accountability from a policy perspective. Additionally, when developing solutions, ethical trade-offs between efficiency and the application of social justice must be integrated into the implementation of a solution so that optimizing costs does not undermine fairness and inclusion nor violate citizen rights. Therefore, addressing these issues will require a multifaceted, comprehensive approach, to integrate technological innovation with institutional reform, legal protections, and participatory governance.

9. CONCLUSION AND FUTURE RESEARCH

The chapter has developed a general framework for AI-enabled welfare governance using an integrated framework of ensemble machine learning and participatory feedback that occurs within an environment of institutional oversight. Empirical analysis shows that combining multiple base learners into an ensemble has resulted in increased accuracy and reliability, as well as decreased model-based bias, when making predictions. Participatory feedback allows predictions to be socially accountable, interpretable and contextually aligned with the needs of the citizens of the jurisdiction being served. The multi-layer approach of the framework (algorithmic decision-making, stakeholder involvement and ethical oversight) provides a replicable approach to implementing AI-based welfare systems while promoting fairness, transparency and social inclusion.

Additional conclusions from the empirical analysis include: As well as ensemble modelling producing lower prediction errors and higher levels of confidence across all cases when compared to all other individual base models, at least three conclusions can be drawn about the impact of the use of participatory feedback in reducing inequalities in prediction accuracy across all demographic groups; the use of SHAP based interpretability and stakeholder validation to enhance trust in algorithmic decisions in edge cases where historical data may be the only way to determine how to allocate resources; and that the integration of technical performance and participatory and ethical considerations must be done in conjunction with AI governance to ensure fair and equitable decisions are made by the systems that are being developed.

Several new research directions will need further clarification and the expansion of applied frameworks to the context of physical world application of real-time datasets across multiple welfare system contexts and the incorporation of dynamic return function mechanisms (learning through continuous stakeholder interaction) can help to improve both the amount of immediate response and fairness. In addition to conducting comparative studies among various ensembles and participatory models, further research will examine what individual ensemble configurations and participatory model configurations produce the most effective accuracy/interpretability/social equity trade-off combinations.

In addition to analyses of policy outcomes as a result of deployed frameworks, citizen satisfaction surveys and administrative efficiency studies will also provide important, practical understanding of the effectiveness of AI in welfare governance models. Future research has both ethical and legal implications (data privacy, accountability, automated decision-making) which will require additional research in order to develop standards regarding AI-enabled governance systems that conform to social values and regulatory compliance.

Overall, the chapter presents an integrated approach to AI enabled welfare systems, providing an evaluation of the potential for improving governance; demonstrating collective strengths/participation while providing traditional machine learning, fairness evaluation and participatory engagement mechanisms. The development of the AI frameworks proposed in this chapter will provide a foundation for the generation of additional AI enabled strategies for promoting social justice through the use of increasingly efficient digital welfare systems around the world.

REFERENCES

Aarab, A., El Marzouki, A., Boubker, O., & El Moutaqi, B. (2025). Integrating AI in public governance: A systematic review. *Digital*, *5*(4), 59. DOI: 10.3390/digital5040059

Barocas, S., Hardt, M., & Narayanan, A. (2019). *Fairness and machine learning: Limitations and opportunities*. MIT Press.

Batool, A., Zowghi, D., & Bano, M. (2025). AI governance: A systematic literature review. *AI and Ethics*, *5*(3), 3265–3279. DOI: 10.1007/s43681-024-00653-w

Binns, R. (2018). Fairness in machine learning: Lessons from political philosophy. *Proceedings of the 2018 Conference on Fairness, Accountability, and Transparency*, 149–159. https://doi.org/DOI: 10.1145/3287560.3287598

Bullock, J. B., & Chen, Y. C. (2024). The brave new world of AI: Implications for public sector agents, organisations, and governance. *Asia Pacific Journal of Public Administration*, *46*(4), 321–325. DOI: 10.1080/23276665.2024.2356540

Cabitza, F., Campagner, A., & Balsano, C. (2021). Humans in the loop: Investigating the integration of machine learning predictions into decision-making. *Artificial Intelligence in Medicine*, *115*, 102055. DOI: 10.1016/j.artmed.2021.102055

Cannarsa, M. (2021). Ethics guidelines for trustworthy AI. *The Cambridge handbook of lawyering in the digital age, 30*, 97-283.

Caputo, N. (2026). Administrative Law's Fourth Settlement: AI and the Capability-Accountability Trap. *arXiv preprint arXiv:2602.09678.*

Chouldechova, A., & Roth, A. (2020). A snapshot of the frontiers of fairness in machine learning. *Communications of the ACM*, *63*(5), 82–89. DOI: 10.1145/3376898

de Almeida, P. G. R., & dos Santos, C. D.Junior. (2025). Artificial intelligence governance: Understanding how public organizations implement it. *Government Information Quarterly*, *42*(1), 102003. DOI: 10.1016/j.giq.2024.102003

Dignum, V. (2019). *Responsible artificial intelligence: How to develop and use AI in a responsible way* (Vol. 2156). Springer. DOI: 10.1007/978-3-030-30371-6

Eubanks, V. (2018). *Automating inequality: How high-tech tools profile, police, and punish the poor.* St. Martin's Press.

Gebru, T., Morgenstern, J., Vecchione, B., Vaughan, J. W., Wallach, H., Iii, H. D., & Crawford, K. (2021). Datasheets for datasets. *Communications of the ACM*, *64*(12), 86–92. DOI: 10.1145/3458723

Hagendorff, T. (2020). The ethics of AI ethics: An evaluation of guidelines. *Minds and Machines*, *30*(1), 99–120. DOI: 10.1007/s11023-020-09517-8

Holstein, K., Wortman Vaughan, J., Daumé, H.III, Dudik, M., & Wallach, H. (2019). Improving fairness in machine learning systems: What do industry practitioners need? *Proceedings of the 2019 CHI Conference on Human Factors in Computing Systems*, 1–16. DOI: 10.1145/3290605.3300830

Joshi, D. (2024). AI governance in India–law, policy and political economy. *Communication Research and Practice*, *10*(3), 328–339. DOI: 10.1080/22041451.2024.2346428

Khan, M. S., Umer, H., & Faruqe, F. (2024). Artificial intelligence for low-income countries. *Humanities & Social Sciences Communications*, *11*(1), 1–13. DOI: 10.1057/s41599-024-03947-w

Kroll, J. A. (2021, March). Outlining traceability: A principle for operationalizing accountability in computing systems. In *Proceedings of the 2021 ACM Conference on fairness, accountability, and transparency* (pp. 758-771). DOI: 10.1145/3442188.3445937

Kroll, J. A., Huey, J., Barocas, S., Felten, E. W., Reidenberg, J. R., Robinson, D. G., & Yu, H. (2017). Accountable algorithms. *University of Pennsylvania Law Review*, *165*(3), 633–705. DOI: 10.2139/ssrn.2765268

Lu, S. (2020). Algorithmic opacity, private accountability, and corporate social disclosure in the age of artificial intelligence. *Vand. J. Ent. & Tech. L.*, *23*, 99.

Mehrabi, N., Morstatter, F., Saxena, N., Lerman, K., & Galstyan, A. (2019). A survey on bias and fairness in machine learning. *ACM Computing Surveys*, *54*(6), 1–35. DOI: 10.1145/3457607

O'neil, C. (2017). *Weapons of math destruction: How big data increases inequality and threatens democracy*. Crown.

Pasquale, F. (2015). *The black box society: The secret algorithms that control money and information*. Harvard University Press. DOI: 10.4159/harvard.9780674736061

Shmueli, G., Bruce, P. C., Gedeck, P., & Patel, N. R. (2020). *Data mining for business analytics: Concepts, techniques, and applications in Python* (3rd ed.). Wiley.

United Nations Educational, Scientific and Cultural Organization. (2021). Recommendation on the ethics of artificial intelligence.

Veale, M., & Binns, R. (2017). Fairer machine learning in the real world: Mitigating discrimination without collecting sensitive data. *Big Data & Society*, *4*(2), 1–17. DOI: 10.1177/2053951717743530

Veale, M., & Binns, R. (2017). Fairer machine learning in the real world: Mitigating discrimination without collecting sensitive data. *Big Data & Society*, *4*(2), 2053951717743530. DOI: 10.1177/2053951717743530

Zenkl, T. (2025). The taming of sociodigital anticipations: AI in the digital welfare state. *Frontiers in Sociology*, *10*, 1556675. DOI: 10.3389/fsoc.2025.1556675 PMID: 40438260

Chapter 6
Welfare Policies and Digital Innovation:
Is There Scope for Action Between Social Participation and AI?

Beba Molinari
http://orcid.org/0009-0003-1108-860X
University of Rome Tor Vergata, Italy

ABSTRACT

This article examines the relationship between social participation and artificial intelligence within the context of welfare policies, highlighting how digital transformations have redefined the modalities of collective action. Starting from the classical concept of participation as active involvement in public life, the paper shows how the emergence of digital platforms and algorithmic systems has led to new forms of e-participation, characterized by an increasing hybridization between online and offline dimensions. In this scenario, artificial intelligence is not merely a supporting tool but an epistemic actor capable of influencing knowledge production, the construction of public opinion, and decision-making processes. The article also highlights the ambivalent nature of these dynamics: on the one hand, AI expands opportunities for inclusion and democratic participation; on the other, it introduces risks related to opacity, misinformation, and digital inequalities.

INTRODUCTION

Our understanding of how we use Artificial Intelligence (AI) has changed considerably in recent years. Initially, it was seen as a tool that replaced humans in mainly repetitive tasks, where no form of reasoning was required. Today, however,

DOI: 10.4018/979-8-3373-8423-8.ch006

the relationship between humans and machines is becoming ever closer (Benanti & Maffettone, 2024) since AI began utilising generative models; it is therefore increasingly necessary to rethink this relationship, recognising that continuous renegotiation is essential (Kissinger et al., 2023). The requests we make of AI are not only an integral part of daily life, but are also increasingly becoming part of our working practices. Numerous studies support the view that, particularly in the workplace, AI is perceived and used as a colleague; among these, according to the findings of the research "*The Cybernetic Teammate*" (Hardman et al, 2024), AI is used as if it were a cognitive partner capable of enhancing work performance. Another study conducted in an educational setting, entitled "Backwards Planning with Generative AI: Case Study Evidence from UA K12 Teachers" (Keppler et al, 2024), highlights that in instructional design, teachers who achieved higher student performance used AI to generate ideas, whereas their colleagues used AI for requests related to simple tasks. We must increasingly ask ourselves how the divergent thinking generated by AI is becoming ever more similar to human thinking, even though it is generated by a series of inscrutable algorithms (Mittelstadt et al. 2016). It is now well established that language models produced by the latest generation of bots are capable of formulating a greater number of possible solutions, both in the form of alternatives and hypotheses.

In practice, the use of AI has been an integral part of many tools installed on our devices for at least 10 years (Sanjeev & Barak, 2009), and its use is often implicit and not fully recognised (Airoldi, 2022). Many users, whilst making constant use of systems based on machine learning, do not recognise their presence; one need only think of weather services, interactive maps or recommendation systems. We could describe this as a sort of 'invisible integration' of AI. In this regard, contemporary social participation is increasingly taking the form of 'datafied' participation, in which everyday practices produce data that feeds algorithmic systems. From this perspective, it is interesting to explore the concept of social participation and how AI can actively intervene in the very concept of participation.

The aim of this chapter is to understand the contribution that AI makes to social participation, whether this is considered 'strong' or 'weak' participation (Gallino 2014), that is, as the direct consequence of a real and significant change in collective action, to a greater or lesser extent, on the part of the individual and/or the group, or linked to different contexts, such as political, trade union, educational, religious, etc. In this regard, it is necessary to ask ourselves the following questions: how do we participate, with whom, and through which means. Answering this last aspect is straightforward: alongside the mass media of the past, we must include not only Web 2.0, but in particular AI. Particular attention will be paid to AI-related automation, the semantic web, the geospatial web, chatbots, deep learning (Abadi, Chu, Goodfellow, et al., 2016) and the platforms associated with it. The introduction of new AI tools shapes new scenarios for action by developing a social reference whose feedback generates forms of self-organisation and the formation of new communities. It is easy to see how such a developmental path leads towards greater bottom-up social participation within the sphere of social policies.

These topics will be addressed in order to understand what opportunities for action may emerge through the use of AI, where the latter can become a new tool capable of identifying, from the grassroots level, emerging needs to which local governance has not provided a response. Ample space for discussion will be given to the various areas in which social participation makes a concrete contribution to welfare policies, from the employment of people with disabilities to educational inclusion, to name but a few examples, with a critical eye aimed at understanding how AI fits into the policy inquiry model, which highlights not only the decision-making process but, above all, the actors involved in this process through an understanding of the mechanisms that guide choices.

The first section will examine the relationship between social participation and AI, highlighting how digital technologies have transformed the spaces of collective action. Starting from the concept of social participation in its various facets, the discussion will focus on the different forms of the agora as a space for shared debate, where participation is now mediated by platforms and algorithms that influence information, interactions and public opinion.

The second section analyses the transformation of social participation in the digital age, highlighting the gradual blurring of the distinction between online and offline, with particular attention to the platform society, where new forms of integration between AI and grassroots participation in digital environments are emerging.

The third section explores the relationship between the role of AI and digital arenas, highlighting the impact on social and political participation. Using concrete examples, we will discuss how generative models and algorithmic systems contribute to the co-production of dialogue and the definition of participation in grassroots movements, highlighting both the opportunities and threats involved.

1. FROM PARTICIPATION TO ARTIFICIAL INTELLIGENCE: A COMPARISON OF TWO WORLDS.

The concept of participation brings to mind, first and foremost, the Greek agora – the quintessential venue for debate, where the voices of many people intermingle. At the same time, albeit at different times, social media has become one of many such agoras; though it has its strengths and weaknesses, it remains a place where everyone can freely express their views, and where forms of information control risk becoming increasingly lax. Consequently, social participation is increasingly mediated by digital platforms and algorithmic infrastructures (Kyriakidis, De Winter, Stanton, et al., 2019). AI does not merely support decision-making processes, but helps to redefine the ways in which individuals participate in social life, influencing forms of interaction, access to information and the formation of public opinion.

The concept of participation is inherently multifaceted. Indeed, its various manifestations span a wide range of spheres – political, religious, trade union, community, healthcare and educational – highlighting its cross-cutting nature and semantic complexity. Within this framework, the notion of social participation takes on particular significance, understood as the set of practices through which individuals and groups actively take part in collective life, contributing to the construction, reproduction and transformation of social relations and institutions (Gallino, 2007). Social participation is not limited solely to the political-institutional sphere, but extends to the everyday dynamics of interaction, cooperation and the production of shared meaning.

Furthermore, the very etymology of the term lends itself to different interpretations: on the one hand, it refers to an identity-based dimension, namely being part of an institution; on the other, it implies taking an active and proactive part in the institution itself. From this perspective, it is clear that active participation presupposes prior membership of some form of association and/or group, just as membership is substantiated through forms of participation. Social participation is situated precisely at this intersection between belonging and action, taking the form of a relational and process-oriented practice. It is therefore necessary to understand whether AI makes a real contribution in terms of action; it can be situated in the space between the sense of belonging and the action itself, acting as a sort of megaphone and amplifier of one's own thoughts.

In an attempt to identify a definition that is as appropriate as possible for exploring the dynamics at play in AI, whilst also spanning various theoretical and ideological perspectives, it can be argued that participation represents the process through which individuals and groups seek to improve their position within the social structure by redefining modes of action, norms and rules (Ceri, 2007). In this sense, social participation takes on a transformative function, as it enables actors to intervene actively in the production of social order, both through processes of integration and through forms of conflict.

Regardless of its origin, participation is primarily characterised as action. As Ceri emphasises, 'participation takes the form of taking part in collective action; it manifests itself neither as fulfilment nor as influence (in the technical sense), but as involvement in the action itself' (Ceri, 1996, p. 8). Therefore, involvement represents the core of social participation, understood as a lived experience of interaction and co-construction.

Such involvement takes place within institutions understood as centres of governance for a community – groups, associations, organisations, local communities or states – in which forms of participatory action are situated along a continuum that distinguishes between 'strong' and 'weak' participation (Gallino, 2014). In the former case, participation implies the concrete possibility of contributing, under conditions of relative equality, to the definition of collective objectives, the distribution of resources and the construction of models of coexistence. In the latter case, however, social participation is limited to a more or less intense involvement in the group's activities, without any guarantee of a real influence on decision-making processes. [1]

The hope is that AI can play a proactive role in both 'strong' and 'weak' forms of participation. It is undisputed that AI facilitates a range of actions, redefines the boundaries of the audiences within which discussions take place, suggests new modes of action, reshapes group activities, supports the associative context, and so on.

However, the debate on AI (McCarthy et al., 1955) is frequently characterised by a certain conceptual confusion, which tends to place profoundly different tools on the same level. This critical issue also emerges in the academic sphere, where reflection often focuses on a general level, neglecting the technical and functional specificities of the various systems. In particular, it is essential to distinguish between predictive tools and cognitive tools (Bostrom, 2024), but a further distinction is necessary as AI falls into two main macro-areas: software and embedded intelligence. The former includes everyday tools such as virtual assistants, search engines and recognition systems – those we most commonly use in daily life and which are fully relevant to the discussion in this article; whilst embedded intelligence encompasses technologies such as robots, autonomous vehicles, drones and connected devices within the Internet of Things. Whilst software represents the most widespread and invisible form of AI, embedded intelligence is the most immediately recognisable, yet one we rarely encounter in our daily lives.

There are many definitions of AI, but three in particular are worth discussing as they are most relevant to the topics covered in this chapter: a first, encyclopaedic definition, defines AI as the "discipline that studies whether and in what way the most complex mental processes can be reproduced through the use of a computer. This research follows two complementary paths: on the one hand, AI seeks to bring the functioning of computers closer to the capabilities of human intelligence; on the other, it uses computer simulations to formulate hypotheses about the mechanisms employed by the human mind" (Treccani Encyclopaedia).

The second is one of many definitions adopted in the scientific field and it focuses on the procedural aspect of the data analysis phase, namely: "The computer receives data (already prepared or collected via sensors, or derived from big data, or alternatively provided directly by the researcher), analyses it and provides a response (Rediet, Barocas, Kleinberg et al, 2020).

Finally, the third definition is a regulatory one from the European Union, the first institution to have been involved in regulating the digital world for many years. According to the EU Artificial Intelligence Act (Regulation (EU) 2024/1689), an artificial intelligence system is: "a machine-based system designed to operate with varying levels of autonomy and which may demonstrate adaptability following deployment. Such a system, through explicit or implicit objectives, processes inputs to generate outputs such as predictions, content, recommendations or decisions that may affect physical or virtual environments".

In general terms, AI can therefore be defined as the ability of machines to exhibit typically human functions, such as learning, reasoning, planning and creativity. It enables systems to interpret their surroundings, process information and act in accordance with specific objectives. The most advanced systems are also capable of learning from the effects of previous actions, progressively improving their performance.

Between 'strong' and 'weak' participation, we explore how AI intervenes in spheres of action and what path has led to the integration of such diverse public spheres.

2. FROM TRADITIONAL PARTICIPATION TO WEB 3.0 PARTICIPATION AND BACK AGAIN.

The continuous transition between the real and virtual worlds has radically transformed forms of social participation, particularly over the last 20 years (Preece, 2000; Shirky, 2011). The hyper-connectivity of the 2000s, driven by mobile applications and wireless connections, has now given way to the introduction of pervasive artificial intelligence, not only in mobile applications but also through the emergence of digital platforms (Thottoli, 2024).

In this context, the separation between online and offline is gradually dissolving, giving rise to a hybrid reality in which connective action and collective action (Bennett & Segerberg, 2012) can no longer be interpreted as distinct spheres. According to Shirky (2011), as early as the first decade of the 2000s, 'the experience of the average 25-year-old is one of a substantial overlap between online and offline friends and colleagues [...] The Internet enhances real-world social life rather than offering an alternative world' (Shirky, 2011, p. 146).

If the distinction between online and offline is becoming increasingly blurred, the actions taken by social actors in engaging with public policy are also becoming increasingly fluid and linked to contexts that originated online. In this case, it is necessary to rethink democratic participation (Habermas, 2006) and how communicative processes are now more oriented towards rational debate and discursive construction. Digital platforms no longer represent mere spaces for interaction, but genuine socio-technical environments that structure the modes of access, visibility and circulation of content.

The context is increasingly dominated by the *platform society* (van Dijck et al., 2018), where platforms are regarded as key infrastructures that mediate social, economic and political relations. Virtual arenas do not merely facilitate interaction between social actors; they actively shape them through algorithmic logic, selection criteria and engagement dynamics, thereby influencing the very forms of participation.

The integration of AI represents a further step in the unchecked development of technology, fitting into an ecosystem where social media are already recognised as mediating devices between individual demands and collective dynamics. In fact, we are witnessing a reversal of traditional communication processes: whereas in the past the dissemination of information took place predominantly from the real world towards the media, today organisational forms originating in digital environments are emerging with increasing frequency. Groups of individuals united by personal and/or professional interests meet online, giving rise to relational networks that can subsequently develop into associations or structured organisations, capable of transferring the strength of the weak ties formed online into the offline context.

In this context, for over a decade, traditional participation and e-participation have taken on an increasingly interconnected and circular nature.

Defining the context within which the dynamics of social participation unfold is therefore becoming increasingly complex, given the range of actions linked to decision-making processes mediated or automated by algorithmic systems. Through algorithms for recommendation, filtering and content definition, platforms intervene directly in the construction of the public agenda. This results in a tension between the promises of media democratisation (Markham and Baym, 2009) and the risk of new forms of information asymmetry, which are often too difficult and invisible to identify because they are linked to the algorithmic context. From this perspective, social participation can no longer be understood solely as a relational practice, but must be analysed as a socio-technical phenomenon, in which communicative, technological and political dimensions are deeply interdependent.

There is therefore a fundamental ambivalence, which is difficult to demonstrate and equally complex to analyse. On the one hand, we see a landscape dominated by virtual arenas; on the other, there are individual social actors expressing themselves on a multitude of topics mediated by the algorithms of discussion platforms, in which the social actor contributes to the discussion of 'public affairs' through the construction of their own digital identity (Golder and Macy, 2014), which does not necessarily coincide with their offline personal identity.

The proliferation of spaces for interaction allows individuals to express themselves on a variety of topics using different languages and within multiple online communities. From this perspective, the social actor's identity is continually fragmented and reconstituted, giving rise to a process of constant deconstruction and renegotiation between the real and digital dimensions (Lastrico, 2013).

With the introduction of AI (Xu, 2019) into virtual platforms, the content accessed by users is not neutral, but mediated by the AI itself, filtered and prioritised through systems whose algorithms are based on user profiling, thereby significantly influencing the processes of identity construction and redefinition.

In fact, digital platforms do not merely facilitate interaction between users, but exercise an implicit governance function, determining the visibility of content, the relevance of information and opportunities for participation.

Whilst the scenario is, to some extent, oriented and defined by the 'machine', it is equally true that participation is increasingly an action undertaken by social actors on the basis of individual motivation, aimed at building relationships and sharing common interests. In this process, different types of social ties emerge: on the one hand, *bridging* ties, which connect similar but distant social actors; on the other, *linking* ties, which connect individuals with different resources and social positions (Pais, 2012). The distinction between these relational forms further highlights the recursive nature of contemporary participation: bonds formed online can transform into offline participatory practices and vice versa, giving rise to hybrid dynamics that continually traverse both spheres.

When discussing social participation, the focus centres on the purpose of the action on the one hand and on ties of ascription on the other (Ceri, 2007); whether one is in the context of digital and/or traditional arenas, there is no difference. On the one hand, participation may be oriented towards utilitarian ends or objectives that transcend individual interest; on the other, the constraints of ascription may be partially redefined through digital practices. However, the introduction of digital platforms and the integration of AI into them can still reproduce and sometimes even amplify pre-existing inequalities resulting from categorisation processes and so-called 'lucid hallucinations' (Bellamy et al., 2019).

It is therefore necessary to clarify that citizenship in the digital age must be conceived in an equitable manner, accessible to anyone and everywhere (Mossberger, Tolbert and McNeal 2008) as a process of active participation and civic literacy; yet at this juncture we face a significant problem linked to the concept of 'new media literacies' (Jenkins, 2007), understood as the social actor's ability to navigate digital environments consciously with specific skills, enabling them to evaluate sources and build spaces for online public discussion through the collaboration of multiple users. The greater the capacity for understanding and conscious action, the lower the risk of encountering unfounded, uninformed arenas; lucid hallucinations are reduced, as are the digital divide and the spread of disinformation. It is also necessary to emphasise that with *deep learning*, we are increasingly entering the realm of *Emotional AI*, through which we inevitably risk being strongly influenced by destabilising videos and/or information that can significantly affect participatory dynamics, fundamentally undermining the concept of democratisation.

3. SPACES FOR ACTION BETWEEN THE REAL WORLD AND THE VIRTUAL WORLD.

As we have seen so far, the digital world is highly complex, but above all diverse, and it is therefore necessary to take a brief look at the various forms in which AI manifests itself.

The real 'Copernican turn' in the field of AI occurred with the introduction of systems based on generative models that produce actual language, rather than merely a response to a specific task. This initial phase was followed by many others, each increasingly sophisticated, as we moved from neural networks to Large Language Models, which have enabled the proliferation of chatbots capable of delivering increasingly advanced performance that closely mimics human thought. However, a training period is necessary, along with continuous human support for the machine; without this, errors and misinformation take over.

Algorithms, in fact, do not merely organise information, but actively shape the construction of social reality, influencing what is perceived as relevant, credible or worthy of attention. In this sense, AI becomes an epistemic actor participating in the co-production of knowledge.

This gives rise to a structural tension: on the one hand, digital technologies and AI expand opportunities for access to information and political participation; on the other, they introduce new forms of inequality, opacity and concentration of power, linked to control over algorithms and digital infrastructure. Political participation, therefore, cannot be understood without considering the role of platforms and AI systems as devices for mediating and, at the same time, regulating social practices.

Virtual arenas become an uncontrolled stage for information of all kinds, which often takes the form of deepfakes, with increasingly dangerous implications in terms of the negative impact they can have on a discussion centred on public policy. This is a fundamental issue that must not be underestimated, as every democratic system must ensure that public debate is in no way mediated and/or manipulated. If, therefore, AI is used to generate false but all-too-plausible content, the very foundation of participation is undermined. However, it is not fair to highlight only the negative aspects; AI can still support the use of applications that facilitate democratic dialogue between social actors online.

Among the tools that utilise AI models internally, the first to be developed – and equally significant in the public debate – is the application for the simultaneous translation of comments and video content, which has now achieved ever-higher standards of quality. This effectively reduces the barriers caused by the language divide and brings a much wider range of people into the discussion of 'public affairs'. Such high levels of performance have only been possible thanks to AI and deep learning (Thompson, Greenewald, Lee, et al. 2020). On the other hand, it is mistakenly believed that content filtering is an overly coercive form of control dictated by unknown algorithms. Whilst a negative view of content filtering was justified up to a decade ago, the situation today is very different. With AI, comment filtering makes use of content analysis and becomes a highly effective tool for sifting through thousands of insignificant comments; it goes without saying that errors may occur when thousands of comments need to be analysed simultaneously. Finally, the third ally is represented by all the tools that create videos and/or text for increasingly high-performing content to be posted directly on social media. There is a wide divergence of opinion on the latter; indeed, misuse can lead to deepfakes, as discussed earlier, but at the same time it can facilitate public debate through videos and text with a strong emotional impact.

What sets these new tools apart is the creativity they inject into the content itself, and this is what distinguishes them from previous applications. Of course, the concept of creativity generated by AI cannot, obviously, be compared to that of humans, but it is nonetheless the result of deep learning – that is, trial and error and the machine's continuous progress towards a mode of thinking similar to that of humans. According to Chomsky (1980), we are in the realm of 'rule-governed creativity', where a system of rules instructs the algorithm on which information to use according to the logic of statistical inference. It is in these cases that the gap between humans and machines is reduced to a minimum; having an agent that supports you in creating content that we might consider 'authentic' and which can subsequently become a topic of debate in a public arena is a reality that was unimaginable just 10 years ago.

The graphical interface with which AI is usually mistakenly equated is that of BOTS, which often fully enter the public debate with the risk of influencing the discussion itself without actually being genuine stakeholders. On the other hand, it is practically impossible to control bots through concrete action, despite numerous and varied attempts, given how pervasive they are across many platforms, such as X, where political discussions take place on micro, meso and macro dynamics. This makes it difficult to control content, whether of a violent nature or entirely unfounded, leading to the proliferation of fake news.

There is also another aspect to consider regarding deplatforming, whereby certain individuals and/or groups are excluded from digital platforms for reasons relating to content moderation. In this case, it is AI that determines who can discuss what, thereby indirectly influencing the ongoing discussion. It is a tool that was in fact created to limit disinformation, but which over the years has become so automated that it excludes, according to parameters it imposes on itself, certain categories of users.

It is possible to summarise the various tools – though by no means exhaustively – in a broad overview that brings together different types of tools within the broad field of *Information Retrieval*. Each tool obviously has its own strengths and weaknesses, but this is even more evident when discussing grassroots social participation in Web 3.0 environments.

Figure 1. Information Retrieval Tools in AI

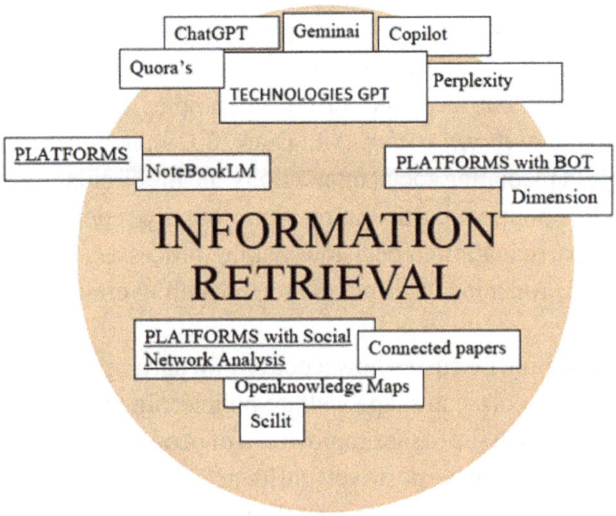

It must be recognised that the field of Information Retrieval is founded on machine learning techniques (Burrel, 2016) designed to represent, store, organise and provide access to various types of information objects, ranging from documents and web pages to online catalogues and multimedia content. The main objective of Information Retrieval is to provide users with information relevant to their interests and queries. In this context, GPT technologies represent the driving force behind widespread public adoption; amongst these, ChatGPT is by far the most downloaded (Spennemann, 2023), though others include Quora's, Gemini, Copilot, Perplexitu, and so on. Among the best-known tools are Google AI Studio, NotebookLM, Nano Banana and Veo3, to name but a few, which allow users not only to access information, but also to produce, rework and adapt it to specific communicative contexts. There are also interactive tools combining bots and platforms where, to access the platform's content, you can interact directly with the bot itself; others allow you to convert any text into a real voice (the *ElenLabs* app); others, such as *HeyGen*, let you create a virtual avatar with your own face and voice that speaks in any language; or produce a video based on certain parameters of interest to the user (for example, the *Veo3* app).

To give some concrete examples, it is possible to create new content to post on discussion platforms using NotebookLM, even summarising a book or a newspaper article,

create a press release, create an image that uses Social Network Analysis to represent the group's interest in a specific topic with *Connected Papers* or *Opeknowledge Maps*, create a video with a pre-determined text using *NotebookLM* featuring an avatar that speaks a language unknown to the video creator, and so on.

It is obvious that in these circumstances it is difficult to gauge the extent to which AI influences the dynamics of digital social participation, so we might say that in the contemporary digital context, this space is no longer organised exclusively around traditional institutions, but takes the form of a complex hybrid, best summarised by the concept of the *platform society* (van Dijck, 2020), in which digital platforms play a central role in mediating social interactions and the circulation of information.

In this scenario, political participation is profoundly redefined: it is no longer limited to formal participation in decision-making processes, but extends to widespread practices of producing, sharing and reinterpreting content within platforms (Gillespie, 2014).

The following section discusses how a bottom-up participatory process, through the use of specific AI tools, can shape welfare policies. In this regard, we cite as an example the emblematic issue of the employment of people with disabilities and how an associative context may have positively influenced future integration policies. As the public administration was unable to meet the full employment demand of disabled people registered with the association, the latter decided to change its approach to job seeking and opened several social media pages to promote the employability of disabled people through motivational videos created by AI. This sparked a major media debate across social media groups, which fostered greater awareness within the media sphere but also increased the number of the association's supporters. Some videos went viral and sparked a response within the business community. This 'model' has been used on several occasions not only by the association for people with disabilities, but also by various other voluntary organisations, resulting in a significant increase in the response to the need 'publicised' online. In this case, the informed use of AI to create videos and content has met a real local need that would otherwise not have received such a swift and appropriate response to the specific requirement.

This approach has prompted the designated public body to pay greater attention to the recruitment stages; it has provided for the expansion of the range of recognised disability categories in subsequent job vacancies aimed at employment, and has also included dedicated social media campaigns featuring motivational videos on workplace inclusion to raise awareness of the true capabilities of people with disabilities.

The next step, expected over the next two years, is the integration of AI into welfare policies, not merely to facilitate e-democracy (Lindner, Aichholzer, Hennen, 2016) and e-participation (Medaglia, 2012), but to formalise an intervention model that goes beyond the physical realm and also considers the possibility of incorporating digital technology, used in a conscious and structured manner, into the performance of one's work activities, with the aim of achieving greater productivity by expanding the scope of vulnerable individuals.

CONCLUSION

This chapter has addressed various aspects of social participation in the age of AI, linking classical theoretical frameworks with the aim of exploring the emerging dynamics associated with digitalisation. Participation has been discussed in its traditional sense as associated with a space for public debate: from the concept of the Roman agora (Manti, 2014) to a more innovative vision linked to digital environments such as social media and online platforms (Molinari, 2025). In this context, social participation takes the form of a relational practice that connects belonging and action, enabling individuals and groups to contribute to the transformation of the 'public sphere'.

AI fits into this scenario not only as a support tool, but as an active element in redefining participatory methods. AI acts as an amplifier of social practices, influencing access to information, the formation of public opinion and the forms of interaction between social actors, thereby redefining the spaces, languages and dynamics of collective action. The transition from Web 1.0 to Web 3.0 has led to a growing hybridisation between the online and offline worlds, to the point where the distinction between the two is becoming increasingly blurred. In this reality, connective action and collective action intertwine, whilst digital platforms are rewriting participatory dynamics through algorithmic logics that regulate the visibility and circulation of content, directly affecting opportunities for participation.

This significant shift is exemplified by the transition from generative models to Large Language Models, in which algorithms do not merely organise information but participate in the co-production of knowledge, emerging as genuine epistemic actors. This entails a structural tension: on the one hand, AI expands possibilities for access, inclusion and democratic participation; on the other, it introduces risks linked to opacity (Zerilli et al., 2019), disinformation and deepfakes.

We must not forget that platforms also exercise a form of implicit governance through recommendation, ranking and personalisation mechanisms, influencing what can be viewed, discussed and shared; in this way, the conditions for access to the digital public sphere are further redefined, and a new scenario emerges in which a sort of social identity is constructed, one that is increasingly fragmented and negotiated between the real and virtual dimensions.

A complex picture is emerging within which it is necessary to have ‘antibodies’ that allow the social actor to navigate consciously in environments that are ‘other’ than what takes place in the real world. It is within this scenario that the social actor can and must adopt new forms of digital literacy, the so-called *new media literacies*, which are fundamental for navigating complex environments with awareness and for countering disinformation and direct and indirect manipulation. In the absence of such skills, there is a risk of amplifying pre-existing inequalities and fuelling forms of unwitting participation.

Concrete examples help us understand the ambivalence within which the social actor operates: whilst, on the one hand, tools such as machine translation, content filtering and creative generation can foster public debate and inclusion, on the other, practices such as deplatforming, the presence of bots and the dissemination of manipulated content via tools for creating multilingual avatars, video production, etc. raise constant questions regarding the quality and authenticity of content, risking undermining genuine, informed democratic participation (Dahlberg, 2011; Coleman & Shane 2012).

It is therefore important to understand which tools are best suited to effectively facilitate grassroots social participation in digital contexts. Two key areas can be identified, which can be summarised in two words: digital regulation and digital education.

In the contemporary European context, the governance of digital technologies is characterised by increasing regulatory intensity, reflecting a broader tension between technological innovation, the protection of rights and democratic governance. This trend is part of a trajectory which, over the last decade, has seen the European Union systematically strengthen its regulatory intervention in key technological areas, from digital platforms to artificial intelligence, culminating in the adoption of the Artificial Intelligence Act (2024). This process can be understood in the light of the transformation of the public sphere outlined by Habermas (1989), according to whom the conditions of democratic deliberation are profoundly redefined by technological intermediation. From this perspective, the issue concerns not merely the degree of regulation, but rather its capacity to have an effective impact within a highly asymmetrical transnational digital context. Large technology firms tend to comply formally with European regulations, but continue to operate within a global framework that is rather complex because it is fragmented. The social actor is not fully aware of the protections, let alone the limitations, that this entails; nor does he or she realise that they are embedded within algorithmic governance (Kitchin,

2017; Gillespie, 2014), that is, the set of practices through which social decisions and processes are mediated by algorithmic systems; instead, they believe they can put forward their own ideas and thoughts without censorship and contribute to policy-making.

The situation is further complicated by the fact that social actors often navigate the digital realm by applying analogue practices within digital environments; this does not automatically simplify matters, but often replicates the existing complexity (Bovens & Zouridis, 2002). Furthermore, the variability in digital skills highlights how participation in the digital public sphere is heavily influenced by structural inequalities linked to the digital divide (van Dijk, 2020), which persist today regardless of age group. In this context, digital education plays a strategic role in fostering greater awareness, to be implemented through tailored policies. In this regard, it is important to remember that the quality of public deliberation depends on individuals' ability to participate in communicative spaces in an informed and critical manner (Habermas, 2006). However, this objective is hampered by the rapid obsolescence of skills in a digital world that moves too fast and by the heterogeneity of training needs, making an approach based on lifelong learning necessary (Selwyn, 2016).

It is therefore worth asking whether deliberative autonomy (Van Dijck et al., 2018; Gillespie, 2014) is diminished by the introduction of AI tools, or whether it makes a concrete contribution. Among the main critical issues are phenomena of decision-making disempowerment; in this context, the concept of e-civility highlights the need to incorporate behavioural norms and ethical responsibility into online participation (Benanti & Maffettone, 2024), whilst the digital divide continues to be a factor leading to exclusion (Arnold, Bellamy, Hind et al., 2015) that is difficult to address.The opacity of AI systems contributes to the creation of a decision-making system that is difficult to challenge, raising significant questions regarding accountability and democratic legitimacy.

In brief, given that society will not exclude AI from its practices, we must recognise that these tools can make a real contribution. Indeed, the concept of e-participation can be interpreted as a profound transformation of the ways in which individuals take part in 'public affairs', taking the form of a broad, multi-level arena in which the principles of inclusion, equality and solidarity – already identified as the founding elements of participation (Ceri, 1996) – are redefined and rearticulated in the light of digital infrastructure. In such contexts, characterised by the presence of online communities, blogs, social media and digital platforms, the social actor acquires new forms of visibility and recognition within pluralistic environments, in which participation is no longer bound to physical spaces, but develops through connective and technologically mediated practices. A cultural shift is taking shape, resulting in the construction of a form of conscious and critical 'digital citizenship', understood as a fundamental prerequisite for effective AI governance. This perspective implies the recognition of new social needs in terms of education, which cannot be limited to the mere acquisition of technical skills, but must include forms of critical, ethical and reflective literacy regarding digital technologies. Only through the development of such skills will it be possible to promote truly inclusive and informed participation in decision-making processes that influence collective life, whilst simultaneously strengthening the democratic dimension.

In conclusion, e-participation, far from being a simple expansion of participatory spaces, represents a complex and ambivalent terrain in which opportunities for inclusion and risks of exclusion, democratic openness and new forms of algorithmic control are intertwined. The main challenge therefore lies in successfully combining technological innovation with social responsibility, keeping the relationship between the individual, technology, ethical considerations and society at the centre through a major collective effort that establishes clear guidelines at the regulatory level as well – a process already underway thanks to the Artificial Intelligence Act (2024).

REFERENCES

Abadi, M., Chu, A., Goodfellow, I., McMahan, H. B., Mironov, I., Talwar, K., & Zhang, L. (2016). Deep learning with differential privacy. Proceedings of the 2016 acm sigsac Conference on Computer and Communications Security. acm, Wien, pp. 308-318. DOI: 10.1145/2976749.2978318

Airoldi, M. (2022). *Machine Habitus. Toward a sociology of algorithms*. Polity Press.

Arnold, M., Bellamy, R. K., Hind, M., Houde, S., Mehta, S., Mojsilovic, A., & Nair, R. Natesan Ramamurthy, Baym, N. K. (2015). *Personal connections in the digital age* (2nd ed.). Polity Press.

Bellamy, R. K. E., Dey, K., & Hind, M., Hoffman, S. C., Houde, S., Kannan, K., Lohia, P., Martino, J., Mehta, S., Mojsilović, A., Nagar, S., Ramamurthy, K. N., Richards, J., Saha, D., Sattigeri, P., Singh, M., Varshney, K. R., & Zhang, Y. (2019). AI Fairness 360: An extensible toolkit for detecting and mitigating algorithmic bias. *IBM Journal of Research and Development*, 63(4/5), 4:1–4:15. https://doi.org/DOI: 10.1147/JRD.2019.2942287

Benanti, P., & Maffettone, S. (2024). *Noi e la macchina. Un'etica per l'era digitale*. Luiss University press.

Bennett, W. L., & Segerberg, A. (2012). The logic of connective action: Digital media and the personalization of contentious politics. *Information Communication and Society*, *15*(5), 739–768. DOI: 10.1080/1369118X.2012.670661

Bostrom, N. (2024). *Deep Utopia: Life and Meaning in a Solved World*. Ideapress Publishing.

Bovens, M., & Zouridis, S. (2002). From street-level to system-level bureaucracies. *Public Administration Review*, *62*(2), 174–184. DOI: 10.1111/0033-3352.00168

Ceri, P. (1996). *Politica e partecipazione*. Il Mulino.

Ceri, P. (2007). *Sociologia. I soggetti, le strutture, i contesti*. Laterza Editori.

Chomsky, N. (1980). *Rules and Representations*. Columbia University Press. DOI: 10.1017/S0140525X00001515

Coleman, S., & Shane, P. M. (Eds.). (2012). *Connecting democracy: Online consultation and the flow of political communication*. Cambridge MIT Press.

Dahlberg, L. (2011). Re-constructing digital democracy: An outline of four 'positions'. *New Media & Society*, *13*(6), 855–872. DOI: 10.1177/1461444810389569

European Parliament and Council of the European Union. (2024). *Regulation (EU) 2024/1689 laying down harmonised rules on artificial intelligence (Artificial Intelligence Act).* Official Journal of the European Union. https://eur-lex.europa.eu/eli/reg/2024/1689/oj

Gallino, L. (2007). *Tecnologia e democrazia.* Einaudi.

Gallino, L. (2014). *Dizinario di sociologia.* UTET.

Gillespie, T. (2014). The relevance of algorithms. In Gillespie, T. (Eds.), *Media technologies.* MIT Press. DOI: 10.7551/mitpress/9042.003.0013

Golder, S. A., & Macy, M. W. (2014). Digital Footprints: Opportunities and Challenges for Online Social Research. *Review of Sociology, 40,* 129–152.

Habermas, J. (1989). *The structural transformation of the public sphere* (Burger, T., Trans.). MIT Press. (Original work published 1962)

Habermas, J. (2006). Political communication in media society. *Communication Theory, 16*(4), 411–426. DOI: 10.1111/j.1468-2885.2006.00280.x

Hardman, P., Dell'Acqua, F., Ayoubi, C., Lifshitz-Assaf, H., Sadun, R., Mollick, E. r., Mollick, L., Han, Y., Goldman, J., Nair, H., Taub, S., & Lakhani, K. R. (2024). Structured prompting for educators: Experiment in hoz to get the best out of your favourite generative AI tools. Dr Philippa Hardman Substrack. Https://drphilippahardman.substack.com/p/strucutred-prompting-for-educators

Jenkins, H. (2007). Confronting the Challenges of Participatory Culture – Media Education for the 21st Century (Part Two). *Nordic Journal of Digital Literacy, 2*(2), 97–113. DOI: 10.18261/ISSN1891-943X-2007-02-04

Keppler, S., Sinchaisri, W. P., & Snyder, C. (2024). Backwards planning with generative AI: Case study evidence from US K-12 teachers. https://papers.ssrn.com/sol3/papers.cfm?abstract_id=4924786

Kissinger, H., Huttenlocher, D., & Schmidt, E. (2023). *L'era dell'intelligenza artificiale. Il futuro dell'identità umana.* Mondadori.

Kitchin, R. (2017). Thinking critically about and researching algorithms. *Information Communication and Society, 20*(1), 14–29. DOI: 10.1080/1369118X.2016.1154087

Kyriakidis, M., De Winter, J. C. F., Stanton, N., Bellet, T., Van Arem, B., Brookhuis, K., Martens, M. H., Bengler, K., Andersson, J., Merat, N., Reed, N., Flament, M., Hagenzieker, M., & Happee, R. (2019). A Human Factors Perspective on Automated Driving. *Theoretical Issues in Ergonomics Science, 20*(3), 223–249. DOI: 10.1080/1463922X.2017.1293187

Lastrico V. (2013), quando il forum sostituisce la fabbrica. Tentativi di costruzione identitaria nell'era della fine del lavoro. *Sociologia della comunicazine* XXIV, 46.

Lindner, R., Aichholzer, G., & Hennen, L. (Eds.). (2016). *Electronic democracy in Europe: Prospects and challenges of e-participation*. Springer. DOI: 10.1007/978-3-319-27419-5

Manti, F. (2014). *L'utopia della ciber agorà. Problematicità, limiti, possibilità della democrazia digitale. XLIX n. 211 online*. Einaudi Editore.

Markham, A., & Baym, N. (2009). *Internet Inquiry: Conversations about Method.* Sage., DOI: 10.4135/9781483329086

McCarthy, J., Minsky, M. L., Rochester, N., & Shannon, C. E. (1955). *A proposal for the Dartmouth summer research project on artificial intelligence*. Dartmouth College.

Medaglia, R. (2012). eParticipation research: Moving characterization forward (2006 2011). *Government Information Quarterly*, *29*(3), 346–360. DOI: 10.1016/j.giq.2012.02.010

Mittelstadt, B. D., Allo, P., Taddeo, M., Wachter, S., & Floridi, L. (2016). The ethics of algorithms: Mapping the debate. *Big Data & Society*, *3*(2), 1–21. DOI: 10.1177/2053951716679679

Molinari, B. (2025). From digital traces to artificial intelligence: New bourdaries from representativeness. *In The lab's quarterly*, 2025/ a. *XXVII*, (3), 193–212. DOI: 10.13131/unipi/x6c5-2t23

Mossberger, K., Tolbert, C. J., & McNeal, R. S. (2008). *Digital citizenship: The internet, society, and participation*. MIT Press.

OECD. (2020). *Innovative citizen participation and new democratic institutions: Catching the deliberative wave*. OECD Publishing.

OECD. (2021). *The OECD digital government policy framework*. OECD Publishing.

Pais, I. (2012). *La Rete che lavora: Mestieri e professioni nell'era digitale*. EGEA.

Preece, J. (2000). Online Communities: Designing Usability, Supporting Sociability. *Industrial Management & Data Systems, 100*(9), 459–460. DOI: 10.1108/imds.2000.100.9.459.3

Rediet, A., Barocas, S., Kleinberg, J., Levy, K., Raghavan, M., & Robinson, D. G. (2020). Roles for computing in social change. *Proceedings of the 2020 Conference on Fairness, Accountability, and Transparency.*

Sanjeev, A., & Barak, B. (2009). *Computational Complexity: A Modern Approach*. Cambridge University Press.

Selwyn, N. (2016). *Education and technology*. Bloomsbury.

Shirky, C. (2011). The Political Power of Social Media: Technology, the Public Sphere, and Political Change. *Foreign Affairs*, *90*(1), 28–41. https://www.jstor.org/stable/25800379

Spennemann, D. (2023). What has ChatGPT read? The origins of archaeological citations used by a generative artificial intelligence application, *arXiv*, https://doi.org//arXiv.2308.03301.DOI: 10.48550

Thompson, N. C., Greenewald, K., Lee, K., & Manso, G. F. (2020).The computational limits of deep learning. *ArXiv*, arXiv:2007.05558.

Thottoli, M. M. (2024). Leveraging information communication technology (ICT) and artificial intelligence (AI) to enhance auditing practices. *Accounting Research Journal*, *37*(2), 134–150. DOI: 10.1108/ARJ-09-2023-0269

Van Dijck, J., Poell, T., & de Waal, M. (2018).*The platform society: Public values in a connective world*. Oxford University Press. Oxford-Van Dijk, J. (2020). *The digital divide*. Polity Press. DOI: 10.1093/oso/9780190889760.001.0001

Weber, M. (1922). *Wirtschaft und Gessellschaft*. Tubinghen Mohr.

Xu, W. (2019). Toward Human-Centered AI: A Perspective from Human-Computer Interaction. I*NTERACTIONS*. *Interactions (New York, N.Y.)*, *2019*(4), 42–46. DOI: 10.1145/3328485

Zerilli, J., Knott, A., Maclaurin, J., & Gavaghan, C. (2019). Transparency in algorithmic and human decision-making: Is there a double standard? *Philosophy & Technology*, *32*(4), 661–683. DOI: 10.1007/s13347-018-0330-6

ENDNOTES

1 Given the complexity of the concept, it seems useful to recall, without any claim to exhaustiveness, some perspectives offered by classical sociology so that we may understand how the concept of social participation has evolved from its origins to the present day. The earliest forms of participation can be traced back to the reflections of Marx and Engels ([1848] 1993) on 'permanent associations', a concept also reiterated in Tocqueville's "*Democracy in America*", in which social participation is interpreted as the foundation of

democracy and civic cohesion. Durkheim also addressed this through his conceptualisation of the social contract ([1893] 1999), in which participation is implicitly invoked, insofar as society recognises its members no longer as objects, but as cooperators endowed with rights and subject to duties.

Simmel ([1908] 1950), in his conceptualisation of social circles, highlights how modern associations foster dynamics of cooperation capable of strengthening mutual bonds and nurturing the public spirit, framing social participation as a privileged space for the construction of sociality. Last but not least in terms of importance, Weber (1922) introduces a further dimension, emphasising the power dynamics that underpin participatory processes, thereby broadening the analysis beyond the cooperative dimension alone.

Chapter 7

Digital Data Infrastructures, Governance, and Social Services Evaluation:

Evidence From Italy and Norway

Marzia Cettina Severino
http://orcid.org/0009-0002-1710-8176
Sant'Anna School of Advanced Studies, Italy

Gloria Ziglioli
University of Agder, Norway

Francesca Pennucci
http://orcid.org/0000-0002-0580-1435
Sant'Anna School of Advanced Studies, Italy

ABSTRACT

The chapter addresses the following research question: how do digital data infrastructures shape the evaluative capacities of social services? Drawing on a comparative document analysis of data infrastructures in Italy and Norway, the chapter investigates how different approaches to data digitalisation can shape the governance, integration, and use of social services information systems. By foregrounding infrastructural design and governance functions, the analysis contributes to the debate on digital welfare governance, evaluative capacity, and the conditions under which administrative data infrastructures can enable more reflexive, evidence-informed, and adaptive social service systems. The chapter provides an empirically grounded

DOI: 10.4018/979-8-3373-8423-8.ch007

understanding of evaluation infrastructures as differentiated systems of data availability and use. The findings show how data infrastructures do not merely support evaluation but actively shape what becomes visible and evaluable in social services.

INTRODUCTION

The digital transformation of welfare systems is increasingly reshaping how public organisations govern, coordinate, and evaluate social services. Across Europe, governments are investing in digital technologies and administrative data systems to improve policy planning, service integration, accountability, and evidence-informed decision-making. While much of the existing debate on digital welfare has focused on algorithms, automated decision-making, and digital service delivery, less attention has been devoted to the underlying data infrastructures through which information is collected, organised, and made available for governance and evaluation purposes. This issue is particularly relevant in the field of social services, where governance is often characterised by fragmented responsibilities, multiple institutional actors, and complex service delivery arrangements. In such contexts, the capacity to evaluate services depends not only on methodological approaches or performance indicators, but also on the availability of information infrastructures capable of generating reliable, comparable, and actionable knowledge. Digital data infrastructures increasingly constitute the backbone of these processes, shaping what information becomes visible, how social needs and interventions are represented, and which dimensions of service provision can be monitored and evaluated. Adopting a socio-technical perspective, this chapter examines digital data infrastructures not merely as technological tools, but as governance architectures that influence knowledge production, organisational learning, and policy development. In particular, the chapter explores how different infrastructural configurations shape the evaluative capacities of social services and the balance between accountability-oriented and learning-oriented uses of data. To investigate these issues, the chapter compares two national cases characterised by different welfare traditions and digitalisation trajectories: Italy and Norway. Through an analysis of their respective social service information systems, the chapter examines how administrative data infrastructures contribute to making social services observable, measurable, and evaluable. The objective of the chapter is to provide both a conceptual and empirical contribution to the understanding of how digital data infrastructures shape the evaluability of social services and influence the production and use of evaluative knowledge within contemporary welfare systems.

The chapter is structured as follows. First, it provides a conceptual and institutional background situating digital data infrastructures within contemporary welfare governance, outlining the main features of the Italian and Norwegian welfare systems and their approaches to digitalisation. Second, it introduces the two empirical cases by describing the organisation of social services in Italy and Norway and the institutional architecture of their respective national social services information systems, SIUSS (and SIOSS) in Italy and the NAV-related administrative reporting systems (including KOSTRA) in Norway. Third, it examines the content, scope, and data production processes of these systems, focusing on what information is collected, by whom, at which governance levels, and for what purposes. The concluding sections comparatively discuss the two cases, highlighting how different digital data infrastructures shape evaluation practices and influence the balance between accountability-oriented and learning-oriented uses of data.

BACKGROUND

Welfare Digitalization, Digital Data Infrastructures, and the Evaluative Capacities of Social Services

Over the last decades, European welfare systems have undergone profound transformations driven by a policy agenda increasingly oriented towards digitalization. Digital technologies have become progressively embedded within welfare systems, reshaping the ways institutions collect information, identify needs, allocate resources, monitor interventions, and deliver services. Recent scholarship has interpreted these developments as part of the emergence of the "*digital welfare state*", highlighting how digitalization extends beyond the introduction of new technological tools and contributes to redefining the ways welfare systems organize access to benefits, coordinate the actors involved, and produce knowledge about social phenomena (Alston, 2019; van Toorn et al., 2024; Alexopoulou, 2024).

Attention to these transformations has grown significantly in recent years. The United Nations Special Rapporteur on extreme poverty and human rights warned of the risk that societies may "*stumble zombie-like into a digital welfare dystopia*" (Alston, 2019, p. 1), drawing attention to the social and political implications of digitalization, automation, and the datafication of social protection systems. At the same time, a growing body of research has examined the effects of digital transformation on welfare governance, focusing in particular on automated decision-making, algorithmic governance, surveillance, equity, and public-sector accountability (van Zoonen, 2020; Alexopoulou, 2024; van Toorn et al., 2024).

Much of this debate, however, has focused on the most visible digital technologies and their effects on decision-making processes. Comparatively less attention has been devoted to the infrastructures that make possible the production, organization, and circulation of the information on which such processes rely. Before an algorithm can be used to classify individuals, support administrative decisions, or automate procedures, systems must exist that are capable of collecting, organizing, and making available the data required for these operations. In this sense, digital data infrastructures constitute a fundamental component of the digital welfare state.

Rather than viewing them as merely technical tools for information management, the infrastructure literature suggests understanding them as constitutive components of organizational practices and governance processes. Star and Ruhleder (1996) define infrastructures as relational systems embedded within institutional routines and the everyday activities of organizations. Similarly, Kitchin (2014) argues that contemporary governance increasingly depends on interconnected systems for the collection, standardization, integration, and circulation of data. From this perspective, digital infrastructures are not simply technological supports for administrative action; rather, they constitute the architectures through which public organizations produce, organize, and use the knowledge required for their activities. This perspective raises a central issue for the analysis of public policy. The information available for governance does not emerge automatically from social reality; rather, it is the product of processes of classification, coding, and standardization that transform complex phenomena into information that can be used within organizations. Research on classification systems has shown that categories and standards are not merely descriptive tools but actively contribute to organizing knowledge by defining which aspects of reality can be recorded, compared, and mobilized in decision-making processes (Bowker & Star, 2000). Digital data infrastructures therefore participate in the construction of organizational and evaluative knowledge, shaping the ways in which needs, populations, interventions, and services are represented within welfare systems.

Indeed, digital administrative infrastructures shape the evaluative capacities of welfare systems, and social services particularly, in structuring the conditions under which performance, outcomes, and social impacts become measurable and actionable (Espeland & Stevens, 1998). Studies highlight persistent challenges related to data quality, fragmentation, and contextual interpretation (Dimas et al., 2023), but less frequently conceptualise administrative data infrastructures as evaluation architectures. Understanding these systems requires moving beyond technological narratives and examining their institutional logics, governance functions, and epistemic effects. Conceptualising evaluation as an infrastructural practice offers a productive analytical lens. Evaluation can be understood not merely as an accounting exercise or an episodic assessment activity, but as a learning process based on the transformation of data into actionable knowledge towards informing organisational learning, service redesign, and adaptive governance (Patton, 1997; Weiss, 1997). From this perspective, digital administrative data systems play a constitutive role in building availability of information and shaping what becomes evaluable, which indicators stabilise performance visibility, and how evidence circulates within governance arenas.

Digital data infrastructures should therefore not be understood as neutral repositories of information. They are designed, implemented, and continuously modified by organizations and institutional actors who determine what information is collected, how it is classified, which indicators are employed, and which relationships are made observable. The categories and standards embedded within information systems thus reflect specific organizational, institutional, and governance choices. Consequently, infrastructures contribute to defining which aspects of social reality become visible and measurable, which can be compared and evaluated, and which, by contrast, remain poorly represented or entirely excluded from processes of knowledge production (Bowker & Star, 2000).

The relevance of this issue becomes particularly evident in the field of evaluation. As Espeland and Stevens (1998) argue, the possibility of observing and comparing different phenomena depends on processes of quantification and commensuration that render them comparable through shared categories and metrics. Evaluation does not automatically derive from the availability of data; rather, it depends on the ways information is collected, organized, and made usable. In this sense, digital data infrastructures contribute to constructing the conditions that make evaluation possible, shaping which phenomena can be observed, which information can be mobilized, and which forms of knowledge can support decision-making processes. Historically, information systems in social services were developed primarily to support budgeting, resource allocation, and reporting requirements. Their main function was to document the use of public resources and monitor the implementation of specific interventions. Comparatively less attention was devoted to their potential role in supporting planning, evaluation, policy learning, and service improvement. As a result, evaluative knowledge has often remained fragmented, weakly comparable, and only partially embedded in decision-making processes (De Rosis et al., 2022; Nuti et al., 2017; Severino & De Rosis, 2026 under publication). Recent investments in digital data infrastructures promise to address some of these limitations by enabling greater standardization, interoperability, and longitudinal analysis across welfare systems. At the same time, they raise important questions regarding the forms of knowledge that can be produced through these systems and the ways in which such knowledge is mobilized within governance and evaluation processes. Digital data infrastructures can represent a crucial resource for strengthening the governance capacities of welfare systems. The availability of systematic and comparable information can facilitate coordination across levels of government, support benchmarking processes, improve knowledge of social needs, and provide more robust informational foundations for service evaluation and improvement.

From this perspective, digitalization should not be interpreted exclusively as a tool for control or administrative accountability, but also as a potential infrastructure for organizational learning and the development of more evidence-informed public policies (Weiss, 1997; Sanderson, 2002).

These issues are particularly relevant in the field of social services. In this chapter, we adopt a broad conception of social services as publicly organized and funded activities aimed at meeting essential human needs and promoting social inclusion, equality, and public value creation (Evers, 2005; Moore, 1995). Despite their importance, social services have historically been characterized by fragmented governance structures, decentralized responsibilities, and heterogeneous delivery models (Anttonen & Sipilä, 1996). Furthermore, many of the core dimensions of social intervention (including professional judgement, the construction of trust-based relationships, continuity of care, and the appropriateness of interventions) are difficult to translate into standardized administrative categories and, consequently, difficult to incorporate into monitoring and evaluation processes.

In this context, digital data infrastructures assume particular importance. Through the information they collect, organize, and make available, they contribute to defining which aspects of social intervention become objects of systematic observation and can be incorporated into evaluation processes. As Burton and van den Broek (2009) note, the introduction of information systems into social work can transform accountability relations, shifting them from forms primarily grounded in professional judgement towards more organizational and bureaucratic forms. At the same time, such systems can facilitate coordination, comparison across territorial contexts, the production of comparable knowledge, and improvements in service quality. Evidence-based approaches can support both professional and organizational improvement processes (Sackett, 1996). The issue, therefore, is not simply the availability of data, but the ways in which information infrastructures contribute to configuring the balance between accountability-oriented uses of information and learning-oriented forms of evaluation.

Although the debate on digital welfare has expanded rapidly in recent years, relatively little attention has been devoted to the role that digital data infrastructures play in shaping the evaluative capacities of social services. In particular, limited attention has been paid to how different infrastructural configurations influence the information available for evaluation, the forms of knowledge that can be produced, and the governance capacities that emerge from them.

Against this background, this chapter adopts an exploratory and comparative perspective to examine how different digital data infrastructures contribute to shaping the evaluative capacities of social services. Through a comparison between Italy and Norway, the analysis explores how different systems of data production and organization generate different conditions of evaluability and different ways of conceptualising the use of data for policy planning, service planning, accountability, and organizational learning. The objective is to understand how specific configurations of digital data infrastructures enable different forms of evaluation and different relationships between knowledge production, governance, and service improvement.

RESEARCH DESIGN AND METHODS

This chapter adopts an exploratory qualitative comparative design to examine how digital data infrastructures design shape the evaluative capacities of social services. Given the limited attention devoted to the relationship between digital data infrastructures and evaluability within social services, an exploratory approach is particularly appropriate for investigating how different infrastructural configurations make specific dimensions of social services observable and available for evaluation.

This study adopts a qualitative comparative design based on document analysis. Following Bowen (2009), document analysis is understood as a systematic procedure for reviewing, evaluating, and interpreting documents in order to generate empirical knowledge and develop analytical understanding. Rather than treating documents as neutral repositories of information, the analysis approaches them as institutional artefacts that both reflect and contribute to the organisation of social realities.

The analysis examines: (1) what information is collected through the infrastructures; (2) which dimensions of social services become observable and evaluable; and (3) how the resulting information can support accountability, planning, coordination, and organisational learning. The objective is to understand how different infrastructural configurations generate different conditions of evaluability within social services.

Study Setting: The Italian and Norwegian social service systems

The comparative design brings together two national cases, Italy and Norway, selected for their contrasting welfare regime configurations (Esping-Andersen, 1990) and their diverging trajectories of welfare digitalisation and administrative data consolidation.

The Italian social welfare system is commonly classified within the Mediterranean, Southern European, or familistic model (Esping-Andersen, 1990; Ferrera, 1996). Historically, it is characterised by a strong familistic orientation, where the family plays a central role in providing care and social protection, often compensating for limited public provision. Public intervention is typically residual and fragmented, operating according to subsidiarity principles, with significant reliance on informal support networks, typical of "countries with strong family ties" (Saraceno & Keck, 2010). The system is characterised by strong municipal autonomy, fragmented territorial governance, and historically weak national coordination in social services. Unlike more centralised or universalistic systems, Italian social services have long developed through heterogeneous local arrangements, multi-actor provision models, and differentiated administrative practices. As a result, access to and quality of services vary considerably across the country, contributing to uneven levels of social protection and reinforcing existing inequalities. Recently, there has been an attempt to align local objectives towards a national uniform approach to social service arrangements. Still, the impact of the reforms is limited and the heterogeneity persists.

Comparatively speaking, the Norwegian social welfare system is typically classified within the social democratic or Nordic model (Esping-Andersen, 1990). Historically, this is characterized by a "comprehensive, state-centred, and tax-financed" (Kettunen & Petersen, 2011: 2) social security system, driven by universalism, granting access to benefits and services based on residence (Anttonen et al., 2012). This has created and sustained high levels of equality, high employment rates, and a low-income inequality through decommodification mechanisms (SSB, 2025). The responsibility of planning and delivering health and social care services is decentralized at the local level (municipalities) where they are made available to all residents, regardless of age, financial, or social status (Sogstad et al., 2020). The most extensive organisational reform in the history of the Norwegian welfare state was introduced in 2006, establishing local Norwegian Labour and Welfare Service Centres, the Nav offices, aiming to make seamless and more integrated services (Røysum, 2013). Since then, Nav provides national insurance, employment and social security benefits, as well as social assistance.

Italy represents a case of recent investment in a unified national data infrastructure for social services - the *Sistema Informativo Unitario dei Servizi Sociali* (SIUSS) - established from 2017 with the aim of integrating information on social needs, benefits, and service provision. The systematic use of such a digitalized and centralized information system is expected to support integrated social service design, coordination, and evaluative practices within a highly decentralised welfare system. Norway, by contrast, relies on established digitalized administrative arrangements in which the local Norwegian Labour and Welfare Administration (NAV) offices use administrative information systems that routinely support social service delivery and governance. Such digitalized information systems enable the aggregation and reuse of administrative data for evaluative purposes across central and municipal levels.

Data Sources

For the Italian case, the analysis draws on legislation, ministerial decrees, technical documentation, operational guidelines, and reporting standards related to SIUSS, complemented by an in-depth examination of SIOSS. For the Norwegian case, the analysis draws on legislation regulating municipal reporting and social service evaluation, together with technical documentation related to KOSTRA and the administrative information systems supporting NAV.

The analysis focuses on the information collected, classified, and produced through these infrastructures, paying particular attention to the categories, indicators, reporting arrangements, and governance mechanisms embedded within them. More specifically, it seeks to identify which organisational, managerial, workforce, and service-related dimensions of social services become observable and evaluable through these systems and how the resulting information can be mobilised by policymakers and service managers for accountability, planning, coordination, and organizational learning purposes.

RESULTS

The Italian case: building evaluative capacity through digital data infrastructure

Italy provides a relevant context for analysing administrative data infrastructures as evaluation architectures. The *Sistema Informativo Unitario dei Servizi Sociali* (SIUSS), established by Legislative Decree No. 147/2017 (Art. 24) constitutes the national and unified infrastructure for the collection, integration, and management of data relating to social benefits, social needs, and the supply of social services in Italy. The development of SIUSS builds upon earlier efforts to establish national information systems in the field of social policies. Law No. 328/2000 had already envisaged the creation of a national Social Services Information System (SISS) to support knowledge, planning, and monitoring activities, while the Assistance Register (*Casellario dell'Assistenza*), established in 2010 and managed by INPS, created a national database on social benefits and beneficiaries. The founding legislation explicitly identifies knowledge production, policy planning, monitoring, evaluation, and the verification of *Livelli Essenziali delle Prestazioni Sociali* (LEPS) among the objectives of the system, thereby embedding evaluative functions within its institutional design. The introduction of the national anti-poverty scheme *Reddito di Inclusione* (REI) represented a major turning point in this trajectory. The implementation of the measure generated a growing need for integrated information on beneficiaries, multidimensional assessments, personalised intervention projects, and the interaction between economic support and social services.

The strategic objective of the SIUSS is to overcome the historical fragmentation of social data and to create a single, integrated and shared national information base supporting programming, monitoring, and evaluation of the welfare system. SIUSS consolidates previously separated information systems and unifies heterogeneous data sources. It integrates data on:

1. social benefits (means-tested and non-means-tested);
2. multidimensional assessments (e.g., disability, childhood, poverty);
3. personalised intervention projects (e.g., REI, RdC and related activation measures);
4. services delivered at local level (e.g., social secretariat, child protection, home care);
5. social workforce characteristics (profiles, qualifications, contracts).

Through this integration, SIUSS enables national-level monitoring who receives what, in which territories, through which services, and with which professional resources. The system is designed to ensure comprehensive knowledge of social needs and services delivered within the integrated social intervention framework, monitor compliance with essential levels of service provision, strengthen controls against undue benefit receipt, support integrated planning through interoperability with health, labour, and other relevant administrative systems, and produce statistical and research outputs.

Institutionally, SIUSS coordinates multiple actors. The National Social Security Institute (INPS) manages the component concerning benefits and social needs, while the Ministry of Labour and Social Policies (MLPS) manages the component concerning the supply of services. Municipalities, Territorial Social Districts (Ambiti Territoriali Sociali), and Regions are responsible for data transmission and validation.

Regarding the structural architecture, SIUSS is organised into two macro-components: The Information System on Social Benefits and Social Needs (managed by INPS); and the Information System on the Supply of Social Services (SIOSS, managed by MLPS). These components are functionally integrated but institutionally differentiated.

The first macro-component integrates and replaces the former *Casellario dell'Assistenza*. It consolidates multiple databases into a unified architecture designed to capture both monetary transfers and need assessments. It includes several structured databases:

1. Database of Means-Tested and Non-Means-Tested Benefits (PSA/PS)

Collects data on monetary benefits and in-kind support, including benefit typology, amount, duration, provider, ISEE value, and beneficiary identification data.

2. Database of Assessments and Personalised Projects (BDVPP)

Organised into thematic modules (disability and non-self-sufficiency; childhood and family; poverty and social exclusion), it collects indicators of vulnerability, multidimensional assessments, project characteristics, and socio-demographic information.

3. ISEE Information System (SII)

Links economic eligibility information to social benefit records.

The variables included cover beneficiary identification, benefit classification (according to national nomenclatures), duration and amount, responsible professionals and administrators, and data transmission modalities. This architecture allows individual-level traceability of benefit receipt across programmes and territories.

The second macro-component, regulated by Ministero del Lavoro e delle Politiche Sociali (2019) focuses on service provision and organisational capacity. Its unit of observation is the Territorial Social District (Ambito Territoriale Sociale).

SIOSS is articulated into two main databases:

1. Database of Activated Services (BDSA)

Collects data on service typology (according to the national nomenclature), management modality (direct, associated, contracted), access procedures, target groups, number of users, and thematic areas (e.g., family and minors; disability and non-self-sufficiency; poverty and social exclusion).

2. Database of Social Professions and Workforce (BDPOS)

Collects mandatory information on social workers and other professionals, including contractual typology, qualification, working hours, and employer.

This component enables the mapping of service supply and human resources across territories, linking structural capacity to demand and benefit data collected by INPS.

Municipalities, Regions, Territorial Social Districts, and INPS are required to transmit data to SIUSS, complete and validate reporting forms and ensure data accuracy (failure to transmit data may entail disciplinary and financial responsibility).

Despite its strategic relevance, implementation has faced several challenges: low municipal compliance in the initial years; operational difficulties (digital infrastructure, training, administrative capacity); perception of SIUSS as a bureaucratic reporting burden,; and limited interoperability with health, education, and regional information systems.

What Becomes Observable and Evaluable?

A first dimension made visible through SIUSS concerns social needs, benefit receipt, and intervention pathways. These components allow to connect information on social needs with information on benefits and interventions received by service users. Consequently, evaluability extends beyond the monitoring of individual programmes and can support a broader understanding of how social needs are identified, assessed, and addressed through social policies. The integration of these data enables policymakers and service managers to observe patterns of service utilisation, identify target populations, and monitor intervention pathways across different areas of social policy.

A second dimension concerns the availability and organisation of social services. This is particularly evident within the *Sistema Informativo dell'Offerta dei Servizi Sociali* (SIOSS), which collects information on the characteristics of social services operating across the national territory. SIOSS includes information on service typologies, target groups, organisational arrangements, and territorial distribution of services.

The inclusion of service supply information significantly expands evaluability by making organisational dimensions of social services systematically visible. Beyond documenting individual interventions, the infrastructure provides information on the availability of services across territories, enabling the assessment of service coverage, territorial disparities, and the alignment between social needs and available provision.

A third dimension concerns workforce resources. Through the Database on Social Services Professionals, SIUSS collects information on professional staff employed within social services. This component introduces a dimension that has traditionally remained difficult to monitor within social service information systems: the relationship between organisational capacity and service provision.

By making workforce resources visible, the infrastructure enables the evaluation of staffing levels, professional composition, and territorial distribution of social workers and other professionals. This broadens the scope of evaluability from services and users to include the organisational resources required for service delivery.

Unlike the Norwegian KOSTRA system, which is administered by a single national statistical authority, SIUSS operates through a multi-level and multi-actor governance arrangement. The Ministry of Labour and Social Policies coordinates the overall infrastructure and directly manages the Social Services Supply Information System (SIOSS), which collects information on service provision, organisational arrangements, and workforce resources through Territorial Social Districts (*Ambiti Territoriali Sociali*), Regions, and Autonomous Provinces. At the same time, information concerning social benefits, beneficiaries, multidimensional assessments, and personalised intervention projects is collected and managed by INPS, building upon the legacy of the Assistance Register (*Casellario dell'Assistenza*). Municipalities, Territorial Social Districts, Regions, and other public bodies contribute data to the system, while information flows are integrated within a common national framework coordinated by the Ministry. Evaluative capacity therefore relies not on a single data-producing organisation but on the ability to connect information generated and maintained across different administrative levels and institutional actors.

Recent reforms have further strengthened this evaluative function through the introduction of dedicated monitoring modules related to the *Livelli Essenziali delle Prestazioni Sociali* (LEPS). By collecting information on services and interventions that constitute nationally defined minimum standards, SIOSS increasingly supports not only the description of service provision but also the assessment of the implementation of essential social rights across territories.

Overall, SIUSS expands evaluability through the integration of information on social needs, benefits, interventions, services, and workforce resources. Its primary contribution lies in making relationships between these dimensions visible within a common informational architecture, thereby creating new opportunities for planning, coordination, and evaluation within a historically fragmented social services system.

Limits of Evaluability

Despite its potential, the Italian system implementation illustrates currently the challenges associated with building evaluative capacity through integrated digital data infrastructures. Several reports highlight persistent problems related to data completeness, uneven reporting practices across municipalities, interoperability between information systems, and differences in local administrative capacity.

These challenges affect the quality and comparability of the information available through the infrastructure and limit the extent to which data can be systematically mobilised for evaluation. In particular, variations in reporting practices across territories can produce gaps in coverage and reduce the reliability of comparisons.

Furthermore, the relational aspects of social services such as professional judgement, relational work, service quality, user experiences, and long-term intervention outcomes remain difficult to capture through the standardised administrative reporting system.

More broadly, the Italian case suggests that evaluative capacity depends not only on the existence of a well-structured, extensive, an integrated information infrastructure but also on the institutional, organisational, and professional conditions required to generate complete and reliable information. The main challenge therefore lies not simply in collecting data, but in ensuring that infrastructures are effectively populated, maintained, and used across different levels of governance.

The Norwegian Case: Building Evaluative Capacity through Standardisation and Comparability

In Norway, laws and regulations mainly regulate the mandatory reporting activities imposed on municipalities and county authorities. According to the *Local Government Act,* effective as of 2018, all municipalities and county authorities are obliged to provide the ministries (the state) with their annual information, through the electronic information system Municipality-State-Reporting (KOSTRA) (Section 16-1). Additionally, the Municipal Reporting Register (KOR) represents the legal framework and sets out the technical guidelines for reporting obligations across different areas that the state imposes on municipalities (Section 16-2).

KOSTRA was introduced in 1995, and since 2001 onwards all municipalities have been included into the system. The 2020 amendments to KOSTRA *Regulations* (2019) unified previous reporting rules into a single, comprehensive framework, with the aim of harmonizing and modernizing reporting requirements. The *KOSTRA Regulations* establishes a standardized reporting structure and lists the annual accounts to be submitted. They cover:

i. financial resources (called “artskontoene” in Norwegian, translated as generative accounts, including expenditures on personnel’s salaries, wages, expenses, purchases of goods and materials, and revenues from interests’ income, sales, and government grants etc.);
ii. the use of resources as well as services (called “funksjonskontoene” in Norwegian, translated as functional accounts, that state for which functions, policy area, and public services the expenditures and revenues are). The macro area included are political and administration, education, healthcare, culture and sport, transport, business and development, infrastructure, and social services. The macro-category social or welfare services includes functions related to social assistance, child welfare, labour-market and qualification measures, activation and services for elderly and people with disabilities, and housing support.

This information is submitted electronically once a year to Statistics Norway (SSB) (n.d.), which administers the KOSTRA system, processes and validates the data. Subsequently, SSB complies accounting and service data into key statistics that illustrates and assesses:

i. municipalities' priorities, shown through different amount of resources allocated for a particular service or an individual service areas;
ii. coverage rates, i.e. the share of the target population receiving the service;
iii. productivity, showing the costs or the amount of resources employed in relation to produce a unit of the service. However, the variations in the quality of the services are not taken into account;
iv. other service-related indicators which cannot be included in the previous headings

Within its area of expertise, each ministry determines what information about resource use and services must be reported. Through the integration of accounting and service data, KOSTRA enables national-level monitoring, generating management information about municipal activities which allows the state to compare how resources are used and to evaluate how municipalities prioritize service areas and the level of services provided to different target groups. It also aims to provide local decision-makers with relevant information for evaluating, planning, and managing municipal services.

In the area of social services, this reporting system concerns the municipal responsibilities carried out through the NAV. Although NAV is organized as a joint state-municipal administration, the municipal component of NAV reports both financial data on social assistance and other programmes, as well as service data such as the number of benefit recipients, duration of benefits, participation in activation and qualification programmes through KOSTRA.

What Becomes Observable and Evaluable?

A first dimension made visible through KOSTRA concerns the allocation of financial resources within municipal welfare services. The system collects detailed information on municipal expenditures through standardized accounting categories, allowing expenditures to be classified according to their nature and purpose.

This information makes resource allocation systematically observable and enables the evaluation of how municipalities prioritise different areas of welfare provision. Policymakers and administrators can therefore assess expenditure patterns, identify variations across municipalities, and monitor changes in resource allocation over time.

A second dimension concerns service provision and organisational activities. Through functional classifications, KOSTRA collects information on the services delivered by municipalities across a wide range of welfare sectors, including social services. These data are complemented by service statistics and indicators describing the volume, coverage, and characteristics of municipal activities.

The availability of standardised service information expands evaluability by making service provision comparable across municipalities. The infrastructure allows policymakers, administrators, and service managers to examine differences in service coverage, identify territorial variations, and assess how resources are translated into service provision.

A third dimension concerns organisational performance. KOSTRA combines financial, organisational, and service information to generate indicators that support the monitoring of productivity, efficiency, and service coverage. These indicators are widely used in municipal benchmarking processes and constitute an important informational basis for local and national governance.

Through these mechanisms, evaluability is oriented primarily towards the assessment of organisational performance through standardised comparison and benchmarking. The infrastructure supports the evaluation of how municipalities allocate resources, organise services, and perform relative to comparable local authorities.

Overall, KOSTRA expands evaluability through the systematic production of comparable information on resources, services, and organisational performance. Its primary contribution lies in making municipal activities visible and comparable across territories, thereby strengthening the informational foundations of monitoring, accountability, and performance assessment within the Norwegian welfare system.

Limits of Evaluability

Despite its extensive reporting capacity, the Norwegian infrastructure also presents important limitations. While KOSTRA provides comprehensive information on resources, expenditures, service provision, and organisational performance, it offers considerably less information on the qualitative dimensions of social services like as the Italian system. As a result, some of the most significant dimensions of social work practice remain only partially visible within the infrastructure.

This limitation reflects a broader tension within administrative data systems. The dimensions that are easiest to standardise and compare are often those related to resources, activities, and outputs, whereas the relational and processual dimensions of social intervention are considerably more difficult to translate into indicators and reporting categories.

The Norwegian case therefore illustrates both the strengths and limitations of evaluability through standardisation. While the infrastructure provides robust information for monitoring, benchmarking, and accountability, it is less well equipped to capture the qualitative and relational dimensions that are central to social work practice.

Comparison of digital data infrastructures, Different Evaluative Capacities

This chapter has examined how digital administrative data infrastructures shape the evaluation of social services, focusing on social services information systems in Italy and Norway. By comparing two welfare systems characterised by different institutional traditions and different trajectories of digitalisation and moving beyond approaches that primarily focus on algorithms, automated decision-making, or digital service delivery, the chapter explored data infrastructures through which information is collected, organised, and made available for evaluation within contemporary welfare systems.

In the Italian case, evaluability is primarily constructed through integration. The SIUSS infrastructure connects information on social needs, benefits, interventions, service provision, and workforce resources that have historically remained fragmented across administrative domains and governance levels. Through this integration, the infrastructure enables policymakers and service managers to observe relationships between needs, interventions, organisational resources, and service provision. The resulting evaluative capacity is therefore oriented towards understanding how different components of the social service system interact and how services respond to identified social needs.

In the Norwegian case, evaluability is primarily constructed through standardisation and comparability. KOSTRA generates information through common classifications, indicators, and reporting procedures that allow municipalities to be systematically compared. Rather than focusing on the relationships between needs and interventions, the infrastructure is designed to make resource allocation, service coverage, and organisational performance observable across territories. The resulting evaluative capacity is therefore oriented towards monitoring, benchmarking, and performance assessment.

The findings also reveal important commonalities. In both cases, digital data infrastructures make some dimensions of social services considerably more visible than others. As a result, what remains weakly represented within infrastructures often remains weakly represented within evaluation itself.

These findings contribute to ongoing debates on digital welfare governance by highlighting the importance of studying digital data infrastructures not simply as technical systems supporting information management, but as socio-technical architectures that shape knowledge production, organisational behaviour, and policy decision-making. In this sense, they can be understood both as the material foundations that enable the circulation of information within the network society (Castells, 1996) and as relational, practice-based systems embedded in organisational contexts (Star & Ruhleder, 1996).

Understanding how infrastructures define what becomes visible and measurable is essential for understanding how social services are governed, monitored, and improved. Critical scholarship in social work and public administration suggests that digitalisation should also be understood as both the outcome and the vehicle of a broader transformation in governance logics, in which measurement and reporting devices may reinforce forms of managerialism and bureaucratic control over professional practice (Burton & van den Broek, 2009). The adoption of information systems for planning and evaluation practices becomes one of the arenas in which this tension materialises. In fact, such systems can be designed and used either as infrastructures for a "reductionist" form of evaluation—centred on easily quantifiable outputs—or as enabling devices supporting learning, reflexivity, and service improvement. Burton and van den Broek (2009), illustrate this ambivalence empirically, showing how the introduction of information management systems in social work can transform accountability relations: from responsibilities grounded in professional values and situated judgement toward more organisational and bureaucratic forms of accountability, accompanied by increased documentation requirements and the risk of a "digital bureaucratisation" of practice.

However, introducing managerial mechanisms into the social services domains could be central to enhance the benchmarking and alignment between local practices, thus reducing geographical differentiation and heterogeneity, and enhancing the overall quality. The comparison between Italy and Norway shows that administrative data infrastructures shape the possibilities for evaluating social services, but also that the governance arrangements surrounding these infrastructures determine how data are actually used for monitoring, evaluation, learning, and the redesign of services and policies. More broadly, the two cases illustrate that evaluative capacity depends not only on the existence of digital systems, but on the organisational and institutional conditions under which data are produced, integrated, circulated, and used. In the Italian case, the establishment of the SIUSS represents an important institutional effort to overcome historically fragmented information flows and to build a unified national infrastructure for social policies. As designed, SIUSS does not only aim to capture social needs and benefits, but also the supply of services and the professional resources available across territories, including the presence of social workers and other social professions. In this respect, the Italian system has significant potential: it is meant to connect demand, service provision, and organisational capacity within a common informational architecture, and to support monitoring, planning, coordination, and statistical processing, including through the service-supply component (SIOSS). At the same time, the Italian case highlights that the evaluative capacity of such an infrastructure depends less on its formal design alone than on the effective completeness and regularity of data transmission. A crucial issue is that the most robust and systematic data flows concern monetary transfers and means-tested benefits, particularly those generated through central administrative systems such as INPS and linked to ISEE-based eligibility. By contrast, information on locally delivered services, organisational arrangements, and professional supply depends much more heavily on data uploaded by municipalities and territorial actors. The main critical issue, therefore, is not that SIUSS is poorly conceived as an information architecture, but that the local data flows on which part of its evaluative potential depends remain partial, uneven, and often incomplete. This asymmetry has direct implications for what becomes evaluable in practice. In the Italian case, the infrastructure performs relatively well in making visible the distribution of benefits, the territorial coverage of formal interventions, and some dimensions of organisational and workforce provision where data are available. However, it is much less effective in systematically capturing service processes and the qualitative dimensions of delivery. Information on user trajectories, continuity and intensity of support, integrated pathways of intervention, user experience, appropriateness of professional responses, and long-term outcomes (De Rosis et al., 2020; Severino & De Rosis, 2026 under publication) remains weakly developed or inconsistently recorded. In this sense, the problem is not simply one of data scarcity, but of selective visibility: some dimensions of welfare intervention become highly legible to the system, while others remain marginal or invisible. This point is particularly relevant if digital infrastructures are understood not only as repositories of information, but as architectures that shape action. As the Italian debate on SIUSS has also suggested, the issue is not only which data are collected, but how the system is designed to connect different databases, reduce fragmentation, support front-line work, and enable interoperable use across services and levels of government (Dimas et al., 2023). From this perspective, incomplete local reporting does not simply reduce data quality; it limits the possibility of transforming administrative records into a meaningful evaluative infrastructure capable of informing planning and service redesign.

The Norwegian case presents a different configuration. Here, administrative data infrastructures are embedded in a more integrated organisational setting, in which the circulation of data is more closely linked to service delivery, institutional coordination, and routine governance processes. Within NAV and related reporting arrangements, data are not only used for reporting upward but are more clearly integrated into organisational processes of reflection, self-assessment, and collective learning (Patton, 1997; Weis, 1997). Recent governance reforms, including the Trust Reform, reinforce this orientation by positioning evaluation not merely as compliance, but as part of a broader framework of professional reflection and continuous improvement (Tomei and Ziglioli, forthcoming).

FUTURE RESEARCH DIRECTIONS

Future research could extend this analysis by examining how information produced through digital data infrastructures is actually used within policy-making and organisational decision-making processes in the two countries and others. While this chapter has focused on the conditions of evaluability created by infrastructures, further research could investigate how evaluative information is interpreted, mobilised, and translated into organisational learning, policy change, and service improvement thanks to the digital infrastructure model. Ultimately, the chapter suggests that digital data infrastructures should be understood as infrastructures of evaluability. By shaping what can be observed, compared, and assessed, they contribute not only to the administration of social services but also to defining the very boundaries of what can be known and evaluated within contemporary welfare systems.

CONCLUSION

The comparison between the two cases therefore suggests that digital administrative infrastructures do not automatically produce evaluation capacity, nor do they automatically improve service quality. What they do is shape the boundaries of evaluability: they influence which aspects of social services can be observed, compared, monitored, and eventually problematised in policy and organisational terms. In Italy, the infrastructure has significantly expanded the possibility of observing needs, benefits, services, and workforce provision at the national level, but its effective use for evaluation is constrained by the uneven participation of local actors and by the weak visibility of service processes and quality. In Norway, by contrast, administrative data infrastructures are more strongly embedded in governance arrangements that enable them to support not only monitoring, but also learning-oriented evaluation. From the perspective of programming and policy redesign, this comparison is especially important. Administrative data infrastructures influence not only what policymakers know, but also what they are able to improve. Where data are concentrated on benefits, eligibility, expenditure, formal service provision, and workforce distribution, planning is more likely to focus on coverage, compliance, resource allocation, and geographical variation (Benedetto et al., 2024). These are all relevant dimensions. However, when information on service processes and quality remains weak or absent, programming is less able to address how interventions are delivered, how needs are interpreted, how professional discretion is exercised, and what kinds of outcomes services actually generate in people's lives (De Rosis,

2025; Severino & De Rosis, 2026 under publication; Pennucci et al., 2020; Coulter, 2006; Donabedian, 1988).

One of the main findings of the chapter is therefore that what remains outside the infrastructure often remains outside evaluation, and consequently outside policy attention. In the Italian case in particular, one of the most significant blind spots concerns service quality. While the infrastructure increasingly makes benefits, users, services, and parts of organisational and professional capacity visible, it still captures only to a very limited extent the relational, processual, and outcome-oriented dimensions through which quality in social services is actually produced. This is a crucial limitation if digital infrastructures are expected to support not only administrative control, but more reflexive, evidence-informed, and adaptive forms of governance. Overall, these findings suggest that the evaluative capacity of administrative data infrastructures depends less on technological sophistication alone than on their institutional embedding, on the completeness and interoperability of the relevant data flows, and on the governance logics within which they operate. Data systems can support monitoring, evaluation, learning, and the redesign of services and policies, but only insofar as they are able to render visible not only benefits and formal provision, but also organisational practices, professional resources, and the qualitative dimensions of service delivery. Strengthening these capacities remains one of the main challenges for building social service systems that are not only more data-rich, but also more equitable, reflexive, and responsive.

REFERENCES

Alexopoulou, S. (2024). Paradigm shift: Exploring the impact of digital technologies on the welfare state through a systematic literature review. *Social Policy & Administration*, *59*(1), 135–157. DOI: 10.1111/spol.13054

Alston, P. (2019). *Report of the Special Rapporteur on extreme poverty and human rights*. United Nations Human Rights Council.

Anttonen, A., Häikiö, L., Stefánsson, K., & Sipilä, J. (2012). Universalism and the challenge of diversity. In *Welfare state, universalism and diversity*. Edward Elgar Publishing. DOI: 10.4337/9781849805940.00006

Anttonen, A., & Sipilä, J. (1996). European Social Care Services: Is It Possible To Identify Models? *Journal of European Social Policy*, *6*(2), 87–100. DOI: 10.1177/095892879600600201

Benedetto, V., De Vita, E., & Nuti, S. (2024). Setting priorities in outpatient cardiovascular care to guarantee equitable access: The case of Tuscany region. *Research in Health Services & Regions*, *3*(1), 11. DOI: 10.1007/s43999-024-00047-9 PMID: 39177938

Bowen, G. A. (2009). Document Analysis as a Qualitative Research Method. *Qualitative Research Journal*, *9*(2), 27–40. DOI: 10.3316/QRJ0902027

Bowker, G. C., & Star, S. L. (2000). *Sorting things out: Classification and its consequences*. MIT press.

Burton, J., & van den Broek, D. (2009). Accountable and countable: Information management systems and the bureaucratization of social work. *British Journal of Social Work*, *39*(7), 1326–1342. DOI: 10.1093/bjsw/bcn027

Castells, M. (1996). *The rise of the network society*. Blackwell.

Coulter, A. (2006). Can patients assess the quality of health care?: Patients' surveys should ask about real experiences of medical care. *BMJ (Clinical Research Ed.)*, *333*(7557), 1–2. DOI: 10.1136/bmj.333.7557.1 PMID: 16809674

De Rosis, S. (2025). *Il ruolo degli utenti nella definizione, gestione e valutazione dei servizi. Focus sui servizi sanitari pubblici* (Vol. 10). Edizioni ETS.

De Rosis, S., Cerasuolo, D., & Nuti, S. (2020). Using patient-reported measures to drive change in healthcare: The experience of the digital, continuous and systematic PREMs observatory in Italy. *BMC Health Services Research*, *20*(1), 1–17. DOI: 10.1186/s12913-020-05099-4 PMID: 32299440

De Rosis, S., Ferrè, F., & Pennucci, F. (2022). Including patient reported measures in performance evaluation systems: Patient contribution in assessing and improving the healthcare systems. *The International Journal of Health Planning and Management, 37*(1), 144–165. DOI: 10.1002/hpm.3596 PMID: 36527717

DECRETO LEGISLATIVO 15 settembre 2017, n. 147, Disposizioni per l'introduzione di una misura nazionale di contrasto alla povertà (15 settembre 2017). https://www.normattiva.it/uri-res/N2Ls?urn:nir:stato:decreto.legislativo:2017-09-15;147!=vig

Dimas, G. L., Goldkind, L., & Konrad, R. (2023). Big ideas, small data: Opportunities and challenges for data science and the social services sector. *Big Data & Society, 10*(1), 20539517231171051. Advance online publication. DOI: 10.1177/20539517231171051

Donabedian, A. (1988). The quality of care: How can it be assessed? *Journal of the American Medical Association, 260*(12), 1743–1748. DOI: 10.1001/jama.1988.03410120089033 PMID: 3045356

Espeland, W. N., & Stevens, M. L. (1998). Commensuration as a Social Process. *Annual Review of Sociology, 24*(1), 313–343. https://www.jstor.org/stable/223484. DOI: 10.1146/annurev.soc.24.1.313

Esping-Andersen, G. (1990). The three worlds of welfare capitalism. *Polity.*

Evers, A. (2005). Mixed Welfare Systems and Hybrid Organizations: Changes in the Governance and Provision of Social Services. *International Journal of Public Administration, 28*(9–10), 737–748. DOI: 10.1081/PAD-200067318

Ferrera, M. (1996). The'Southern model'of welfare in social Europe. *Journal of European Social Policy, 6*(1), 17–37. DOI: 10.1177/095892879600600102

Forskrift om rapportering fra kommuner og fylkeskommuner mv. (KOSTRA-forskriften), FOR-2019-10-18-1412 (2019). https://lovdata.no/dokument/SF/forskrift/2019-10-18-1412

Kettunen, P., & Petersen, K. (Eds.). (2011). *Beyond welfare state models: Transnational historical perspectives on social policy*. Edward Elgar Publishing. DOI: 10.4337/9781849809603

Kitchin, R. (2014). The data revolution: Big data, open data, data infrastructures and their consequences. *Sage (Atlanta, Ga.)*. Advance online publication. DOI: 10.4135/9781473909472

Lov om kommuner og fylkeskommuner (kommuneloven) [Local Government Act], LOV-2018-06-22-83 § 24-9 (2018). https://lovdata.no/dokument/NLE/lov/2018-06-22-83/KAPITTEL_7-3#%C2%A724-9

Ministero del Lavoro e delle Politiche Sociali. (2019, 22 agosto). Decreto n. 103 del 22 agosto 2019 – Modalità attuative del Sistema informativo dell'offerta dei servizi sociali (SIOSS). https://www.lavoro.gov.it/documenti-e-norme/normative/Documents/2019/DM-103-del-22082019-SIOSS

Moore, M. H. (1995). *Creating Public Value: Strategic Management in Government*. Harvard University Press.

Nuti, S., De Rosis, S., Bonciani, M., & Murante, A. M. (2017). Rethinking Healthcare Performance Evaluation Systems towards the People-Centredness Approach: Their Pathways, their Experience, their Evaluation. *Healthcare Papers*, *17*(2), 56–64. DOI: 10.12927/hcpap.2017.25408 PMID: 29595446

Patton, M. Q. (1997). Utilization-focused evaluation: The new century text. *Sage (Atlanta, Ga.)*.

Pennucci, F., De Rosis, S., & Passino, C. (2020). Piloting a web-based systematic collection and reporting of patient-reported outcome measures and patient-reported experience measures in chronic heart failure. *BMJ Open*, *10*(10), e037754. DOI: 10.1136/bmjopen-2020-037754 PMID: 33020096

Røysum, A. (2013). The reform of the welfare services in Norway: One office–one way of thinking? *European Journal of Social Work*, *16*(5), 708–723. DOI: 10.1080/13691457.2012.722982

Sackett, D. L., Rosenberg, W. M., Gray, J. A., Haynes, R. B., & Richardson, W. S. (2007). Evidence based medicine: What it is and what it isn't. 1996. *Clinical Orthopaedics and Related Research*, (455), 3–5. DOI: 10.1136/bmj.312.7023.71 PMID: 17340682

Sanderson, I. (2002). Evaluation, policy learning and evidence-based policy making. *Public Administration*, *80*(1), 1–22. DOI: 10.1111/1467-9299.00292

Saraceno, C., & Keck, W. (2010). Can we identify intergenerational policy regimes in Europe? *European Societies*, *12*(5), 675–696. DOI: 10.1080/14616696.2010.483006

Sogstad, M., Hellesø, R., & Skinner, M. S. (2020). The development of a new care service landscape in Norway. *Health Services Insights*, *13*, 1178632920922221. DOI: 10.1177/1178632920922221 PMID: 32565676

Star, S. L., & Ruhleder, K. (1996). Steps Toward an Ecology of Infrastructure: Design and Access for Large Information Spaces. *Information Systems Research, 7*(1), 111–134. https://www.jstor.org/stable/23010792. DOI: 10.1287/isre.7.1.111

Statistisk sentralbyrå. (n.d.). Dokumentasjon av KOSTRA. https://www.ssb.no/offentlig-sektor/kostra/statistikk/kostra-kommune-stat-rapportering/om-kostra/dokumentasjon-av-kostra

Tomei, G., and Ziglioli, G. (forthcoming) Trust-enabled management, provision, and evaluation of public welfare services. Ambitions and questions from a paradigmatic Scandinavian experience. *Public Administration. An international quarterly*

van Toorn, G., Henman, P., & Soldatić, K. (2024). Introduction to the digital welfare state: Contestations, considerations and entanglements. *Journal of Sociology (Melbourne, Vic.), 60*(3), 507–522. DOI: 10.1177/14407833241260890

van Zoonen, L. (2020). Data governance and citizen participation in the digital welfare state. *Data & Policy, 2*, e10. DOI: 10.1017/dap.2020.10

Weiss, C. H. (1997). Theory-based evaluation: Past, present, and future. *New Directions for Evaluation, 1997*(76), 41–55. DOI: 10.1002/ev.1086

ADDITIONAL READING

Albano, R., Curzi, Y., & Radin, A. (2020). Social Work Assessment and Information Systems: A Critique of Managerialist Models and an Agenda for an Alternative Approach. In Addabbo, T., Ales, E., Curzi, Y., Fabbri, T., Rymkevich, O., & Senatori, I. (Eds.), *Performance Appraisal in Modern Employment Relations*. Palgrave Macmillan., DOI: 10.1007/978-3-030-26538-0_9

Espeland, W. N., & Sauder, M. (2007). Rankings and Reactivity: How Public Measures Recreate Social Worlds. *AJS; American Journal of Sociology, 113*(1), 1–40. DOI: 10.1086/517897

KEY TERMS AND DEFINITIONS

Digital data infrastructure: is understood not as mere technology-based networks, services, and assets that facilitate the flow of information and support various digital interactions and transactions; but as more complex socio-technical architectures that shape knowledge production, organisational behaviour, and policy decision-making.

Information systems: are understood not only as technical infrastructures, but mainly as enabling devices supporting learning, reflexivity, and service improvement through consistent and systematic data collection and elaboration.

Social services evaluation: is understood not merely as an accounting exercise or an episodic assessment activity, but as a learning process based on the transformation of data into actionable knowledge towards informing organisational learning, service redesign, and adaptive governance.

Chapter 8
High-Quality Social Data Science for Welfare Governance:
Online Probability Panels as Anchors for Digital Traces

Luciana Taddei
http://orcid.org/0009-0004-7280-6609
University "Magna Graecia" of Catanzaro, Italy

ABSTRACT

This chapter examines the integration of digital traces into welfare research from a methodological and epistemological perspective grounded in survey methodology. It argues that, although digitally generated data are analytically rich, they are insufficient for producing high-quality welfare evidence when detached from explicit research designs, as they lack defined reference populations, observable selection mechanisms, and contextual information. The chapter proposes Online Probability Panels as a methodological solution, conceptualised as research infrastructures that anchor digital traces within probability-based sampling and longitudinal designs. By linking digital data to inclusion probabilities, socio-demographic characteristics, and repeated observations, these infrastructures enable population inference, assessment of selection bias, and modelling of uncertainty. The chapter shows that high-quality data science for welfare governance depends on integrating digital traces within infrastructures that ensure interpretability, transparency, and methodological robustness.

DOI: 10.4018/979-8-3373-8423-8.ch008

INTRODUCTION

The digital transformation of welfare systems has profoundly reshaped both the production and the institutional use of social knowledge. Across policy domains such as income support, unemployment benefits, healthcare, housing, and social services, welfare institutions increasingly rely on data-intensive tools to design interventions, monitor outcomes, and allocate resources. This shift is commonly framed through the language of data science, understood as the growing integration of digital data, computational techniques, and analytical practices into policy-relevant research design and public governance.

In welfare contexts, however, the expansion of data science raises questions that extend well beyond technical capacity. Welfare systems operate at the intersection of social rights, institutional accountability, and distributive justice. Data used in this context cannot be treated as neutral inputs. They shape how problems are defined, how populations are classified, and how risks are assessed. For this reason, the central challenge of data-informed welfare is not data availability per se, but the production of evidence that is methodologically robust, socially interpretable, and institutionally legitimate.

This chapter addresses the following guiding question: how digital traces can be integrated into welfare research in ways that support population-representative, contextually grounded, and analytically robust evidence. More specifically, it examines whether and how research infrastructures—particularly Online Probability Panels—can provide the methodological conditions required to align data science practices with the epistemic and normative demands of welfare governance. While digital traces are widely used in welfare research, the conditions required to integrate them within population-based and inferentially robust designs remain insufficiently specified.

As highlighted by Ambrosio and colleagues (2026), the growing emphasis on big data has contributed to the widespread belief that contemporary societies can rely on digital information to analyse virtually any social, economic, or political phenomenon. In social research, this narrative has been reinforced by the diffusion of open data, encouraging the use of platform-derived data to study social dynamics at relatively low cost (Punziano et al., 2021; Trezza, 2023). Data generated by digital platforms have been widely adopted for their accessibility and their potential to capture large-scale behavioural patterns.

However, both methodological debates and empirical practices point to substantial limitations. Digital traces are typically not collected through known sampling procedures and lack clearly defined reference populations. They often provide limited contextual information and insufficient documentation of the processes through which data are generated. These features constrain their validity, comparability, and interpretability in welfare-oriented research. Moreover, digital traces are unevenly distributed across populations: they are fragmented across private actors and shaped by persistent digital divides, leading to the systematic underrepresentation of specific social groups.

Consequently, digital data cannot be treated as self-sufficient sources of welfare evidence, digital data cannot be treated as self-sufficient sources of welfare evidence. A growing body of literature stresses the need to combine them with other data sources—such as official surveys, probability-based panels, and research infrastructures—in order to allow population inference and meaningful interpretation (Aragona & De Rosa, 2018; Santini et al., 2020).

While existing research has critically examined both the opportunities and the limitations of digital traces, less attention has been paid to the conditions under which these data can be integrated into welfare research in a methodologically grounded way. In particular, current debates often identify problems of representativeness, interpretability, and uncertainty without specifying the research infrastructures required to address them.

This chapter contributes to this debate by conceptualising Online Probability Panels (OPPs) as anchoring infrastructures for welfare analysis. It argues that OPPs provide a concrete methodological framework through which digital traces can be linked to defined populations, longitudinal observation, contextual information, and transparent governance arrangements. In doing so, the chapter shifts the focus from the availability of digital data to the conditions under which such data can be transformed into welfare-relevant evidence.

Against this background, OPPs are examined as a key methodological infrastructure for data-informed welfare research. By combining probability-based recruitment, digital data collection, and longitudinal design, they offer a structured environment in which heterogeneous data sources—including digital traces—can be integrated and evaluated. Rather than opposing "traditional" survey data to digital data, OPPs enable their coexistence within a shared inferential and interpretative framework.

The chapter advances a specific conceptualisation of OPPs as anchoring infrastructures. Anchoring refers to the capacity of these panels to stabilise the meaning and quality of digital traces by embedding them within probability-based designs, sustained engagement with participants, and transparent governance procedures. Through this function, digital traces can be transformed from context-dependent signals into socially meaningful and policy-relevant evidence.

DATA SCIENCE AND WELFARE: METHODOLOGICAL OPPORTUNITIES AND EPISTEMIC CONSTRAINTS

The increasing prominence of data science in welfare systems reflects a broader transformation of how social problems are rendered measurable and governable. Predictive models, classification systems, and automated decision-support tools are now routinely employed to identify social risks, prioritise interventions, and evaluate policy outcomes. These developments are often justified in terms of efficiency, responsiveness, and evidence-based governance. At the same time, they introduce epistemic constraints that are particularly consequential in welfare contexts.

Welfare systems constitute a high-stakes domain for the production and use of data. Decisions informed by welfare data have immediate material consequences for individuals and households, affecting access to income support, services, and institutional protection. Errors in measurement, misclassification of social risks, or biased inference can therefore translate directly into social exclusion or unequal treatment.

From a methodological perspective, welfare research imposes particularly stringent demands. Data must facilitate population-level inference, capture social inequalities, and situate individual behaviours within institutional and structural contexts. In contrast to domains where prediction alone may be sufficient, welfare research requires data that can be explained, justified, and critically assessed. Interpretability is therefore not optional but a core epistemic requirement.

Data science approaches have gained traction in welfare research for several reasons. They allow the analysis of large and heterogeneous datasets, including unstructured and high-frequency information. They facilitate the identification of complex patterns and associations, and they support real-time or near-real-time monitoring aligned with contemporary policy demands.

Digital traces are particularly attractive in this regard. By capturing interactions with digital services, platforms, and devices, they appear to offer insight into behaviours that are difficult to observe through conventional methods. In policy discourse, this capacity is often framed as a solution to long-standing challenges such as measurement error, recall bias, and administrative fragmentation.

However, the methodological implications of this shift remain under-theorised. The expansion of analytical capacity is frequently conflated with improvements in knowledge quality. This obscures how data science methods inherit—and often amplify—the epistemic properties of the data on which they operate. Sophisticated algorithms cannot compensate for unclear populations, systematic exclusion, or limited contextual interpretability.

A central limitation of many digital data sources lies in their weak connection to well-defined populations. Digital traces are generated as by-products of socio-technical systems whose participation mechanisms are rarely transparent and often socially stratified. Access to digital services, platforms, and devices varies systematically by age, education, income, health status, and digital literacy—dimensions that are themselves central to welfare analysis.

This configuration gives rise to three interconnected methodological problems.

- First, selection processes are difficult to observe and quantify. Without a clear sampling frame or reference population, it becomes difficult to assess who is represented in digital data and who is systematically excluded. This constrains population inference and complicates the analysis of inequality.
- Second, interpretability is limited. Digital traces typically record actions or interactions but provide only partial information about motivations, constraints, and subjective meanings. In welfare contexts—where behaviour is shaped by institutional rules, conditionality, stigma, and strategic adaptation—the absence of contextual information significantly reduces explanatory capacity.
- Third, uncertainty is difficult to model and communicate. While computational models may produce precise estimates or predictions, the sources of error embedded in the data-generating process often remain opaque. This tension between apparent precision and substantive uncertainty poses a serious challenge for accountable welfare governance.

From this perspective, research design and data infrastructures become central (Taddei & Paolucci, 2026). Welfare research requires settings in which populations are clearly defined, selection processes can be examined, and heterogeneous sources can be related to one another in a transparent manner. The quality of data-intensive welfare research therefore depends less on the accumulation of ever more data and more on arrangements capable of aligning digital innovation with methodological rigour, contextual understanding, and institutional accountability.

These constraints indicate that digital traces cannot be treated as self-sufficient sources of welfare evidence. What is required, instead, are research infrastructures that embed digital data within clearly defined population frameworks. Such infrastructures also provide contextual information and render uncertainty explicit. Under this view, Online Probability Panels offer a particularly valuable methodological solution. By combining online data collection with probability-based recruitment and sustained engagement with participants, OPPs provide a robust foundation for integrating digital traces into welfare research without sacrificing inferential validity or analytical depth.

ONLINE PROBABILITY PANELS AS RESEARCH INFRASTRUCTURES FOR WELFARE ANALYSIS

The methodological limitations associated with digital traces in welfare research do not imply that such data should be excluded from analysis. Rather, they point to the need for research designs capable of embedding digital data within inferential frameworks that allow population-level generalisation, contextual interpretation, and transparent modelling of uncertainty. In this perspective, the central issue is not whether digital traces can be used in welfare research, but under which methodological conditions they can contribute to the production of robust and welfare-relevant evidence. OPPs represent one of the most promising responses to this challenge, insofar as their design addresses their design addresses the main inferential, contextual, and uncertainty-related limitations of digital trace data.

Online Probability Panels should be understood not merely as advantageous research settings, but as methodological solutions to three core epistemic challenges that characterise the use of digital traces in welfare research: (i) the problem of population inference, (ii) the problem of interpretability, and (iii) the problem of modelling uncertainty. Each of these challenges corresponds to a structural limitation of digital trace data and is addressed through specific features of OPP infrastructures.

First, with regard to population inference, digital traces typically lack a defined reference population and are generated through unknown and often highly selective participation mechanisms. As a consequence, it is difficult—if not impossible—to establish to whom observed patterns can be generalised. OPPs address this limitation through probability-based sampling and controlled recruitment procedures. By defining inclusion probabilities and a known target population, they make it possible to situate digital trace data within a statistically grounded inferential framework. Importantly, this does not eliminate selection processes, but renders them observable and measurable. Weighting, calibration, and nonresponse adjustment can then be systematically applied, allowing researchers to distinguish between behavioural patterns that are substantively meaningful and those that are artefacts of selection bias. In this sense, OPPs transform digital traces from population-ambiguous signals into data capable of supporting population-level claims under explicitly stated assumptions.

Second, with regard to interpretability, digital traces are structurally under-contextualised. They record behaviours, interactions, or transactions, but typically provide limited information about the social, institutional, and biographical conditions under which those behaviours occur. This creates a risk of over-interpreting behavioural regularities while overlooking the mechanisms that generate them. OPPs directly address this limitation through their capacity to collect rich, multidimensional, and longitudinal contextual data. By linking digital behaviours to socio-demographic characteristics, household conditions, labour market status, health, institutional experiences, and subjective perceptions, OPPs allow the interpretation of behavioural signals within structured social contexts. Crucially, this contextualisation is dynamic rather than static: repeated measurements allow researchers to analyse how meanings and behaviours evolve over time. As a result, the same digital trace may be interpreted differently depending on the trajectory in which it is embedded—for example, distinguishing between voluntary non-use of services and exclusion due to administrative or digital barriers. In this way, OPPs convert behavioural traces into sociologically meaningful evidence.

Third, with regard to the modelling of uncertainty, digital trace data are often characterised by a high degree of opacity. The processes through which data are generated, filtered, and recorded are frequently undocumented or only partially known, making it difficult to assess measurement error, coverage bias, or temporal instability. In many cases, uncertainty remains implicit and unquantified. OPPs provide a framework in which uncertainty can be explicitly modelled and evaluated. Their design makes it possible to identify multiple sources of error—including sampling error, nonresponse bias, measurement error, and attrition—and to incorporate them into analytical strategies. Moreover, the coexistence of multiple data sources within the same panel (survey responses, behavioural data, administrative records, sensor data) enables cross-validation and robustness checks. Discrepancies between data types can thus be analysed rather than ignored, turning inconsistency into an object of methodological inquiry. In this way, OPPs support a reflexive approach to data quality in which uncertainty is not suppressed but systematically examined and communicated.

Taken together, these features clarify the anchoring role of OPPs. Their function is not simply to host different types of data, but to stabilise the relationship between empirical traces, reference populations, and analytical meaning. They create the conditions under which digital traces—otherwise fragmented, selective, and weakly interpretable—can be embedded within a coherent inferential design. Viewed in this way, the contribution of OPPs is not additive (i.e., producing more data), but structural: they redefine the epistemic status of digital traces by integrating them into research designs that make inference, interpretation, and uncertainty explicit and accountable.

Figure 1. Online Probability Panels as Anchoring Infrastructures for Welfare Data Integration

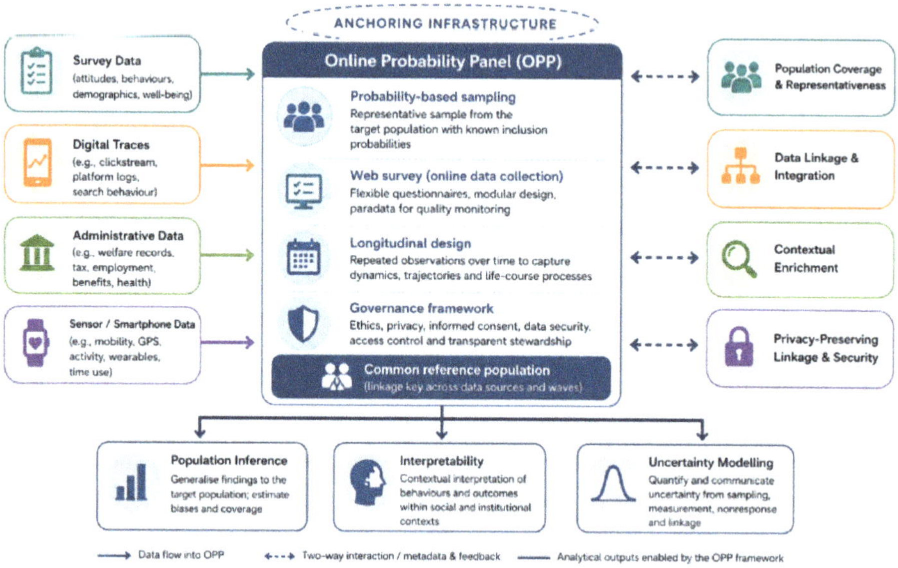

Source: generated by AI.

OPPs represent one of the most promising responses to these challenges. Rather than revisiting their limitations, the focus here shifts to how specific design features of OPPs make it possible to address them in practice.

OPPs combine three features that are seldom combined in contemporary data environments: probability-based sampling, digital data collection, and longitudinal panel design. This combination places them at the intersection of established survey methodology and methodological innovation in digital social research. As noted in the literature on online panel research, their distinctive value lies not simply in transferring traditional surveys to a web-based environment, but in integrating the logic of probabilistic inference with the flexibility, speed, and modularity of digital data collection (Callegaro et al., 2014; Blom et al., 2016). In welfare research, where evidence must remain socially interpretable and institutionally accountable, this combination is especially consequential.

From the standpoint of sampling theory, the defining feature of OPPs is their reliance on probability-based recruitment procedures. Unlike non-probability online samples or opportunistic platform data, OPPs are constructed through methods that allow researchers to define a reference population and to estimate selection probabilities. Recruitment may rely on population registers, address-based sampling, random digit dialling, or mixed-mode strategies, depending on national infrastructures and fieldwork conditions (Callegaro et al., 2014; Kocar & Kaczmirek, 2023). Methodologically, what matters is that inclusion does not depend solely on self-selection into a digital environment. This is particularly important in welfare research, where the analysis of inequality requires explicit attention to who is represented, who is excluded, and under which conditions.

In this sense, OPPs directly address one of the central weaknesses of digital traces: the absence of a clearly specified population framework. By anchoring data collection to a defined target population, they support the analysis of nonresponse, the application of weighting and calibration procedures, and the transparent assessment of error structures. These practices remain fundamental to the production of valid and generalisable knowledge in the social sciences (Couper, 2008; Cornesse & Blom, 2023). For welfare analysis, this inferential grounding is not merely technical. It is a precondition for evaluating policy effects, identifying social inequalities, and ensuring that evidence is not distorted by unobserved processes of selection and exclusion.

In parallel, OPPs should not be understood as a simple digital extension of conventional survey designs. Their online format allows for a high degree of adaptability in questionnaire design, fieldwork management, and data integration. Web-based administration makes it possible to implement complex routing, repeated short questionnaires, modular survey structures, multilingual instruments, and rapid fielding procedures, while also generating paradata that can be used to monitor response processes and improve data quality over time (Blom et al., 2016; ISTAT, 2017; Mauceri et al., 2020). This flexibility is especially valuable in welfare research, where rapidly changing institutional conditions often require timely and responsive data collection strategies.

A further strength of OPPs lies in their longitudinal design. Unlike cross-sectional surveys, panel studies are explicitly oriented towards the analysis of change, recognising that populations are dynamic and that social phenomena unfold over time (Lynn, 2012; Menard, 2002). By repeatedly observing the same individuals, OPPs allow researchers to investigate trajectories, transitions, and cumulative processes at the individual level, rather than relying exclusively on aggregate snapshots. This temporal dimension is particularly relevant for welfare research, where policy exposure, vulnerability, service use, and coping strategies evolve gradually and interact with life-course dynamics. In this respect, OPPs provide a methodological basis for moving beyond static descriptions towards more analytically robust accounts of social change (Ruspini, 2002).

The panel structure further extends this logic by enabling the systematic collection of contextual information over time. Welfare-relevant processes are shaped not only by observable behaviours, but also by household composition, employment conditions, health status, socio-economic resources, institutional experiences, and subjective perceptions. OPPs make it possible to measure these dimensions repeatedly and to relate them to digital behaviours, administrative interactions, or other forms of respondent-generated data. In doing so, they transform otherwise ambiguous behavioural signals into socially interpretable indicators. For example, patterns of online service use, non-use, or interruption can be analysed in relation to digital skills, administrative burden, income constraints, or experiences of stigma—factors that remain largely invisible in stand-alone digital trace data.

This integrative capacity is one of the main methodological advantages of OPPs (Callegaro et al., 2014; Scherpenzeel, 2011). OPPs function as infrastructures for heterogeneous data integration rather than as single-method instruments. Their value lies precisely in enabling different forms of data to coexist within a common inferential and interpretative framework. For welfare analysis, this means that digital traces can be incorporated without relinquishing the methodological standards required for population inference and contextual explanation.

Concurrently, the literature makes clear that OPPs are not free from methodological challenges. As in all longitudinal studies, attrition represents a major concern, especially when dropout is socially patterned rather than random. Over time, selective panel mortality may compromise representativeness and weaken inferential validity if not addressed through retention strategies, incentives, and refreshment samples (Maslovskaya & Lugtig, 2022). Repeated participation may also generate panel conditioning effects, whereby respondents alter their answers or behaviours as a consequence of continued involvement in the survey process (Menard, 2002). Moreover, although online administration offers clear advantages in terms of efficiency and flexibility, it can also introduce coverage problems where digital access and digital literacy remain socially unequal. For this reason, several OPPs have adopted mixed-mode recruitment procedures and, in some cases, provided devices or internet access to offline participants in order to reduce coverage bias and preserve representativeness (Scherpenzeel, 2009; Yeager et al., 2011).

These limitations do not weaken the case for OPPs. On the contrary, they illustrate why OPPs should be understood as infrastructures rather than merely as data collection tools. Building and maintaining an OPP requires continuous investment in recruitment, respondent engagement, technological support, sample refreshment, and methodological evaluation. The complexity of panel management is part of what gives OPPs their epistemic value: they make visible processes—coverage, nonresponse, attrition, measurement variation—that remain opaque in many other digital data environments. In welfare research, where evidence must remain accountable, contestable, and socially grounded, such visibility is a decisive advantage.

More broadly, OPPs are increasingly aligned with the principles of FAIR data and Open Science. Their modular structure allows core questionnaires to coexist with additional thematic modules, often proposed by external researchers or institutions, thereby widening access to robust data environments and democratising the production of social data. This feature is particularly relevant for welfare research, where the capacity to combine stable longitudinal measurement with flexible thematic innovation is essential for responding to emerging policy issues without sacrificing comparability over time.

For these reasons, OPPs can be conceptualised not simply as efficient online panels, but as epistemic and methodological infrastructures for high-quality data science in welfare research. They stabilise the relationship between data, populations, and interpretative frameworks. They make selection processes visible, support the modelling of uncertainty, and create the conditions under which digital traces can be interpreted in relation to socio-demographic, institutional, and subjective variables. Their contribution, therefore, lies not in generating more data as such, but in organising heterogeneous forms of data within a coherent and accountable design.

As welfare systems become increasingly digitalised, the challenge for social research is not to choose between surveys and digital traces, but to develop infrastructures capable of integrating them without sacrificing inferential validity, contextual depth, and transparency. Online Probability Panels offer a concrete response to this challenge. By anchoring digital data within probability-based, longitudinal, and ethically governed research designs, they provide one of the strongest available foundations for welfare analysis in the age of data-intensive governance.

As recent contributions have emphasised, probability-based online panels are increasingly used as platforms for methodological innovation in the integration of digital data into social research (Das, 2025). Rather than functioning solely as survey infrastructures, OPPs provide controlled environments in which new forms of data—such as behavioural experiments, linked administrative records, smartphone-based measures, wearable-device data, and other types of passive or donated digital traces—can be systematically incorporated within a probability-based and longitudinal design.

The following section illustrates how these innovations can be operationalised in practice, showing how OPPs allow the integration of heterogeneous data sources while preserving the inferential, interpretative, and epistemic standards required for welfare research.

INTEGRATING DIGITAL TRACES WITHIN ONLINE PROBABILITY PANELS

Having established the anchoring role of OPPs, this section focuses on how this integration can be operationalised in practice. Integration, in this context, should not be reduced to the aggregation of heterogeneous datasets. Rather, it refers to a research strategy in which different forms of data are generated, combined, and analysed within a shared probabilistic design that preserves a clearly defined reference population and a documented data-generating process.

When digital traces are incorporated without such a framework, their analytical richness is often accompanied by epistemic opacity. Within OPPs, by contrast, integration is governed by design: researchers can identify who contributes specific types of data, under which conditions, and with what implications for inference. This makes it possible to treat data integration not as a purely technical operation, but as a methodological process open to systematic evaluation (Callegaro et al., 2014; Couper, 2008). The following examples illustrate how this can be implemented in practice.

Behavioural Experiments and Controlled Environments

One of the most significant innovations concerns the integration of online behavioural experiments within probability-based panels. Traditionally, experimental research has faced a trade-off between internal and external validity: laboratory experiments provide high control but rely on small and socially selective samples, while online crowd-based experiments allow large-scale data collection but lack representativeness.

OPPs offer a way to overcome this trade-off by enabling the implementation of controlled experimental designs on large, diverse, and probability-based samples. Experimental data can be linked to rich background information collected within the panel and, importantly, embedded in a longitudinal design that allows the observation of pre- and post-treatment effects over time.

For welfare research, this integration is particularly relevant. It allows the analysis of behavioural responses to policy measures, decision-making under institutional constraints, and compliance with administrative rules in settings that are both analytically rigorous and socially grounded. For example, an experiment embedded in an OPP could test how different formats of welfare communication (e.g. simplified vs. bureaucratic language) affect benefit take-up or application completion rates across socio-economic groups. Experimental findings can thus be interpreted in relation to socio-demographic characteristics and life-course trajectories, rather than as isolated behavioural outcomes.

A concrete welfare-oriented example would be an experiment on the design of digital benefit communications. Panel members could be randomly assigned to different versions of an online message about an income-support scheme: one using standard bureaucratic language, one using simplified language, and one including additional information about eligibility and appeal rights. Because participants belong to a probability-based panel, researchers could examine whether message design affects comprehension, perceived eligibility, trust, and willingness to apply across different socio-economic groups. The same respondents could then be followed over time to assess whether initial responses translate into actual application behaviour, service use, or disengagement. In this case, the OPP would connect experimental control, population inference, and longitudinal observation within a single design.

Smartphone-Based and Sensor Data

A second area of innovation concerns the use of mobile technologies and sensor-based data collection. OPPs increasingly incorporate smartphone applications, GPS tracking, time-use diaries, and wearable devices, enabling the collection of high-frequency behavioural data that are difficult to capture through traditional surveys.

Smartphone sensors, for example, allow the measurement of mobility and activity patterns in real time (Struminskaya et al., 2021), while wearable devices provide continuous and objective indicators of behaviour, often revealing substantial discrepancies between self-reported and observed activity (Maher et al., 2017). These discrepancies are not merely measurement errors; they can themselves be analytically informative.

Within OPPs, the coexistence of survey data and sensor-based measures allows researchers to systematically compare different modes of observation. This makes it possible to identify recall bias, social desirability effects, and structural constraints shaping behaviour. In welfare contexts, such data can be used to relate behavioural patterns to access to services, living conditions, and local infrastructures, thereby linking individual behaviour to broader institutional and territorial contexts.

A concrete example concerns the study of physical activity and access to sports and health-related infrastructures. Wearable devices can record daily activity levels (e.g. steps, intensity of movement, sedentary time), while smartphone GPS data can capture actual mobility trajectories and the use of urban space. Within an OPP, these behavioural data can be combined with survey information on health status, income, education, time constraints, and perceived access to local facilities.

This integration allows researchers to move beyond aggregate indicators of "low physical activity" and to analyse how activity patterns are shaped by unequal access to infrastructures. For instance, individuals with similar health conditions may display very different activity levels depending on whether they live in areas with accessible sports facilities, safe walking environments, or public transport connections. GPS data can reveal whether individuals physically reach gyms, parks, or sports centres, while survey data can clarify whether non-use reflects economic barriers, lack of time, health limitations, or perceived exclusion.

The longitudinal dimension further strengthens this analysis. It makes it possible to observe how changes in local infrastructure—such as the opening of public sports facilities, urban regeneration policies, or subsidised access programmes—affect behaviour over time and across social groups. In this way, sensor-based data within OPPs do not simply measure activity levels; they allow the analysis of how health-related behaviours are embedded in spatial inequality, access to services, and welfare-relevant conditions.

Data Donation and Digital Trace Data

Another emerging approach is data donation, whereby respondents voluntarily provide access to personal digital data, such as usage histories, communication records, or patterns of media consumption. This model enables researchers to access digital trace data that are otherwise held by private platforms or remain inaccessible due to regulatory constraints.

Within OPPs, data donation is embedded in a framework of informed consent and respondent control, making participation processes transparent and analysable. Empirical evidence shows that willingness to donate data is socially patterned and influenced by factors such as trust, digital skills, and privacy concerns (Keusch et al., 2025; Toepoel et al., 2021).

This has important methodological implications. While data donation expands the scope of observable behaviours, it also introduces additional layers of selection that must be explicitly modelled. In welfare research, these participation dynamics are not only methodological challenges but also analytically meaningful indicators of institutional trust, perceived risk, and digital inequality.

A more concrete example concerns the voluntary donation of data from everyday digital platforms, particularly among younger populations. Panel participants could be invited to share their viewing histories from streaming services such as Netflix or their interaction data from social media platforms such as Instagram. These traces provide detailed information on content consumption, time use, and patterns of online engagement.

Within an OPP, these behavioural data can be analysed in combination with survey information on education, employment status, income, family background, and subjective well-being. This makes it possible to identify systematic associations between digital behaviours and underlying social conditions. For instance, specific patterns of media consumption—such as highly irregular usage, intensive late-night activity, or concentration on particular types of content—may be associated with educational disengagement, precarious employment, or social isolation when interpreted in relation to panel-based contextual variables.

From the standpoint of welfare analysis, the key advantage of this approach lies in its capacity to identify groups at risk that may not be easily detectable through traditional data sources. By combining behavioural traces with socio-demographic and longitudinal information, OPPs allow researchers to move from individual-level signals to structured profiles of vulnerability. These profiles can then inform the design of more targeted and differentiated welfare interventions.

For example, clusters of young individuals characterised by low employment stability, limited social participation, and specific patterns of online engagement could be identified as groups at higher risk of exclusion. This would support policymakers to tailor interventions—such as training programmes, outreach initiatives, or mental health help—not only based on demographic characteristics, but also on observed behavioural patterns and modes of engagement.

Importantly, the analytical value of data donation does not depend only on the content of the donated data, but also on the conditions under which donation occurs. Who agrees to share Netflix or Instagram data, who refuses, and under which conditions, becomes itself an object of analysis. Differences in participation may reflect varying levels of trust, digital literacy, or perceived vulnerability. Within a probability-based panel, these dynamics can be explicitly measured and incorporated into the analysis, allowing researchers to distinguish between behavioural patterns and participation biases.

Data Linkage and Enriched Infrastructures

OPPs also allow the linkage of panel data with administrative registers and external data sources. This allows researchers to combine subjective measures, behavioural data, and institutional records within a unified analytical framework.

Such integration significantly enhances analytical potential. Survey-based indicators of economic well-being, for example, can be compared with administrative income data, while behavioural patterns—such as service use or application timing—can be analysed in relation to policy eligibility and benefit receipt. This makes it possible to identify discrepancies between reported and recorded conditions, evaluate targeting mechanisms, and assess the real-world effects of policy design. More broadly, linked data infrastructures support benchmarking and the evaluation of predictive models, contributing to greater methodological transparency and cumulative knowledge production.

A practical example concerns the analysis of ageing, economic security, and well-being. OPP data can be linked to administrative pension records, providing detailed information on pension amounts, contribution histories, and benefit types. These data can then be combined with survey-based measures of family composition, living arrangements, health conditions, and subjective well-being, including life satisfaction.

This integration makes it possible to move beyond purely economic indicators of welfare and to examine how pension adequacy translates into actual living conditions. For instance, two individuals with similar pension incomes may report very different levels of life satisfaction depending on whether they live alone or within a supportive family network. Similarly, administrative data may indicate sufficient income levels, while survey responses reveal financial strain, unmet care needs, or social isolation.

From a policy perspective, this type of analysis provides more nuanced guidance for intervention. It allows policymakers to identify groups of older adults who are not necessarily poor in income terms but are nevertheless vulnerable due to weak family support, poor health, or limited access to services. This can inform the design of more targeted policies, such as community-based care programmes, social interventions, or adjustments to minimum pension schemes that take into account household context and living conditions.

Simultaneously, linkage can reveal gaps between formal eligibility and actual well-being. For example, individuals receiving pensions above eligibility thresholds for additional support may still experience low life satisfaction due to high care costs or lack of informal network. Identifying these mismatches can help refine targeting criteria and improve the alignment between administrative classifications and lived realities.

Methodologically, this approach also strengthens the validation of data. Administrative records provide precise information on income and benefits, while survey data capture subjective and contextual dimensions that are otherwise unobservable. Their combination allows researchers to assess the consistency of different measures and to interpret discrepancies as meaningful signals rather than errors.

Collectively, these innovations show how OPPs transform the integration of digital traces from a technical challenge into a question of research design. Rather than assuming that digital data are inherently superior or self-sufficient, OPPs create conditions in which different sources can be systematically compared, contextualised, and critically evaluated.

For welfare research, this has several implications. It enables the identification of selection biases, the interpretation of behavioural data in relation to social conditions, and allows the explicit modelling of uncertainty across data sources. More broadly, it promotes a reflexive approach to data quality, in which validity, inclusiveness, and interpretability are treated as empirical questions rather than as assumed properties of a given dataset.

By organising digital innovation within a probability-based and longitudinal framework, OPPs provide a foundation for integrating digital traces into welfare analysis without compromising the epistemic standards required for socially meaningful and institutionally accountable research.

Applied Example: Digital Welfare Access and Administrative Burden

To illustrate how Online Probability Panels operate as anchoring infrastructures in practice, consider the case of access to digital welfare services, such as online applications for income support or unemployment benefits. In many countries, welfare provision is increasingly mediated through digital platforms, where individuals are required to search for information, complete online forms, upload documentation, and interact with administrative systems. These processes generate large volumes of digital trace data, including platform access logs, clickstream data, and records of application completion or interruption.

When considered in isolation, such data provide only a partial and potentially distorted account of welfare access. For example, high rates of incomplete applications may be interpreted as low motivation or behavioural disengagement, while repeated access to online portals may be taken as evidence of active participation. However, without information on users' socio-economic conditions, digital skills, institutional experiences, and broader behavioural patterns, these interpretations remain highly ambiguous.

Within an Online Probability Panel, the same digital traces can be integrated into a structured and population-representative research design. Panel participants can be surveyed about income conditions, employment status, education, digital literacy, household composition, and prior interactions with welfare institutions. Notably, these data can be complemented with measures of attitudes, values, and perceptions—such as trust in institutions, perceived administrative burden, stigma associated with welfare receipt, or willingness to engage with digital services.

At the same time, behavioural data can be collected from multiple digital environments. Beyond administrative platforms, this may include donated data from social media profiles (e.g. patterns of information exposure or engagement), usage data from smartphones or wearable devices (e.g. daily routines, time constraints, mobility patterns), or other forms of digitally mediated behaviour. The integration of these heterogeneous sources within a probability-based panel makes it possible to relate observed behaviours to both socio-demographic characteristics and underlying orientations, in a way that is not achievable with stand-alone digital trace data.

This integration allows a fundamentally different type of analysis. Patterns of non-completion of welfare applications, for example, can be examined not only in relation to digital skills or access constraints, but also in relation to attitudes toward institutions, perceived complexity, or experiences of stigma. In parallel, broader behavioural patterns—such as irregular daily schedules captured through wearable data, or limited exposure to institutional information in social media environments—can help explain why some individuals struggle to complete administrative procedures.

From this perspective, OPPs make it possible to identify structured profiles of vulnerability that combine socio-demographic characteristics, behavioural patterns, and attitudinal dimensions. For instance, a group of individuals characterised by low digital skills, high perceived administrative burden, low institutional trust, and fragmented daily routines may be systematically more likely to interrupt or abandon welfare applications. Importantly, such profiles can be identified at the population level, rather than inferred from unrepresentative digital data.

The longitudinal dimension further strengthens this analysis. It allows researchers to observe whether these difficulties persist over time, are mitigated by policy changes (e.g. simplification of procedures, targeted communication), or lead to longer-term disengagement from the welfare system.

From a policy perspective, this approach provides actionable insights. It enables the design of more targeted interventions, such as simplified application procedures for specific groups, tailored communication strategies delivered through the digital environments they actually use, or support services addressing not only technical barriers but also trust and stigma. In this sense, digital traces are not used in isolation but are transformed—through their integration within OPPs—into structured evidence for identifying at-risk populations and guiding differentiated welfare policies.

From a methodological perspective, the contribution of OPPs in this scenario is threefold. First, probability-based sampling ensures that findings can be generalised to the relevant population, allowing policymakers to assess the extent and distribution of digital exclusion. Second, the integration of socio-demographic variables, attitudes, and multi-source behavioural data transforms digital traces into interpretable indicators of underlying social processes. Third, the panel structure makes it possible to model trajectories of access, failure, and adaptation over time, rather than relying on static snapshots.

In this way, OPPs do not simply add contextual variables to digital data. They reorganise the analytical framework within which such data are interpreted, enabling welfare-relevant evidence that is empirically robust, socially grounded, and directly applicable to policy design.

ETHICS, GOVERNANCE, AND TRUST AS METHODOLOGICAL CONDITIONS

In data-informed welfare research, ethics, governance, and trust are often treated as external constraints or afterthoughts on methodological innovation. From a methodological perspective, however, they constitute core conditions of data production. They shape who participates, under which terms data are shared, how linkage is authorised, and how findings are interpreted. This is particularly importantant in welfare research, where data practices intersect with vulnerable populations, asymmetries of power, and decisions with direct distributive consequences. Under these circumstances, ethical arrangements are not ancillary safeguards but integral components of data quality, legitimacy, and methodological robustness (Cerbara et al., 2026). This broader perspective aligns with work on open science and research integrity, which emphasises that transparency, accountability, and trust are deeply interconnected rather than separable domains (Fecher & Friesike, 2014; Haven et al., 2022).

This issue becomes especially salient when digital traces are incorporated into welfare research. Many digital data sources originate in environments where individuals have limited awareness of how data are generated, processed, or reused. In such contexts, the challenge extends beyond legal compliance to the epistemic fragility of data produced under conditions of opacity, weak consent, or perceived coercion. Research on survey participation has long shown that privacy concerns, perceptions of disclosure risk, and institutional trust influence willingness to participate and shape the composition of resulting datasets (Couper et al., 2008; Singer et al., 1993, 2003). In welfare settings, these dynamics are particularly consequential, as avoidance, selective participation, or strategic responses may reflect not only attitudes toward research, but also broader experiences of institutional vulnerability (Cerbara et al., 2026).

Within Online Probability Panels (OPPs), ethics and governance can instead be embedded directly within the research infrastructure. This represents one of their key methodological strengths. Probability-based panels such as LISS were developed not only to ensure inferential quality, but also to organise participation, consent, access, and data protection through stable and transparent procedures (Scherpenzeel, 2018; Centerdata, 2023a, 2023b). The methodological literature on probability-based internet panels has highlighted precisely this infrastructural dimension: panel quality depends not only on sampling and retention, but also on the reliability and credibility of the institutional arrangements that sustain repeated participation over time (Scherpenzeel, 2018; Cerbara et al., 2026).

In this perspective, informed consent should not be treated as a formal requirement appended to data collection, but as a substantive component of research design. In longitudinal infrastructures, consent is often layered, revisable, and specific to different forms of data use, especially when survey responses are linked to administrative records, geolocation data, or donated digital traces (Iphofen, 2017; European Commission, 2023). The comparative experiences of LISS, UKHLS, and SOEP are instructive in this regard. Across these infrastructures, ethical governance is operationalised through combinations of pseudonymisation or anonymisation procedures, tiered access systems, formal user agreements, ethics oversight, secure computing environments, and explicit rules governing record linkage and access to sensitive microdata (Centerdata, 2023a, 2023b; University of Essex, n.d.; DIW Berlin, 2025a, 2025b; Goebel et al., 2019; Cerbara et al., 2026). These arrangements not only protect confidentiality but also make the conditions of data production and reuse visible to both researchers and institutions.

This visibility has direct methodological value. When sampling procedures, weighting strategies, linkage rules, consent protocols, and access conditions are documented and open to review, the epistemic foundations of data production become transparent and subject to scrutiny. In welfare research, where data increasingly inform automated or semi-automated decision-making processes, such transparency is essential. It allows evidence to be explained, contested, and revised, rather than treated as an opaque technical output. In this sense, governance facilitates not only legal compliance but also reproducibility, accountability, and cumulative knowledge production (European Commission, 2023).

Trust plays a central role within this framework. Longitudinal infrastructures depend on sustained respondent engagement, which cannot be reduced to incentives or fieldwork efficiency alone. Participation is shaped by perceptions of legitimacy, fairness, and control (Couper et al., 2008). This is particularly evident in practices such as data donation, where participants are asked to share highly personal digital information. In such cases, patterns of consent, refusal, or selective participation are not merely nuisances to be corrected statistically; they provide insight into how individuals perceive data governance, institutional authority, and the social acceptability of digital research practices. Ethical governance within OPPs does not eliminate selection effects, but makes them visible and therefore analytically tractable (Cerbara et al., 2026).

The ethical dimension is equally central to open science and represents one of the defining strengths of OPPs. Open science is often associated with accessibility, interoperability, and reuse, but in longitudinal social research these objectives must be balanced against privacy protection, disclosure limitation, and differentiated access to sensitive data (Fecher & Friesike, 2014; Haven et al., 2022). The comparative European experience shows that this balance is achieved not through openness alone, but through governed openness: data are made as accessible as possible while remaining as restricted as necessary where disclosure risks persist (Cerbara et al., 2026). This principle is particularly important in panel studies, where repeated measurements and linked data sources may increase the risk of re-identification even when direct identifiers are removed (Fienberg & Willenborg, 1998; Doyle et al., 2001). Technical safeguards must therefore be combined with clear communication, institutional oversight, and privacy-by-design approaches from the earliest stages of infrastructure development (European Union, 2016; European Commission, 2023).

In this sense, ethics, governance, and trust are not external correctives to data-intensive welfare research, but part of its methodological core. They shape recruitment, retention, consent, linkage, and interpretation, and ultimately condition the possibility of producing evidence that is both analytically robust and socially legitimate. In welfare research, where data are inseparable from questions of rights, responsibility, and social protection, recognising this interdependence is essential.

By embedding ethical governance within probability-based and longitudinal designs, OPPs demonstrate that the quality of welfare data depends not only on technical integration, but also on the institutional and relational conditions under which evidence is produced, governed, and interpreted (Cerbara et al., 2026).

CONCLUSION: TOWARD HIGH-QUALITY SOCIAL DATA SCIENCE FOR WELFARE GOVERNANCE

The digital transformation of welfare systems has heightened expectations regarding the capacity of data and computational methods to improve policy design, monitoring, and delivery. Across domains such as income support, unemployment protection, health, housing, and social care, welfare institutions increasingly rely on digital infrastructures, algorithmic classifications, and large-scale data flows to identify needs, assess risks, and allocate resources. Within this broader transformation, digital traces have often been treated as particularly promising sources of evidence, as they appear to provide timely, granular, and behaviourally rich information about individuals and populations. Yet, as this chapter has argued, the analytical richness of digital traces does not automatically translate into robust, socially meaningful, or institutionally legitimate knowledge.

In welfare research, this distinction is especially important. Welfare data are never merely descriptive; they feed directly into decision-making processes that affect rights, access, eligibility, services, and redistribution. As a consequence, the quality of welfare evidence is not only a technical issue but also a normative one. Rigorous data science for welfare governance cannot be reduced to the speed, volume, or granularity of available data. Rather, it depends on the conditions under which data are produced, selected, linked, interpreted, and governed. When detached from explicit research designs, digital traces remain weakly grounded from both an inferential and contextual perspective. They often lack clearly defined reference populations, observable selection mechanisms, and the contextual information required to render behaviour sociologically meaningful and institutionally intelligible (Ambrosio et al., 2026; Taddei & Paolucci, 2026).

The central claim advanced throughout the chapter is that the integration of digital traces into welfare research is fundamentally an infrastructural question. What matters is not simply whether digital traces are available, but whether they are embedded within research environments capable of stabilising the relationship between data, populations, and interpretative frameworks. This is why the chapter conceptualises Online Probability Panels not merely as efficient digital survey tools, but as epistemic and methodological infrastructures. Their distinctive value lies in their capacity to anchor digital traces within probability-based sampling designs, longitudinal panel architectures, structured respondent engagement, and transparent systems of data governance. In doing so, they provide one of the most promising foundations currently available for reliable welfare evidence.

This argument aligns with recent work on longitudinal data infrastructures in Europe, which emphasises that high-quality social research depends on institutional arrangements combining methodological rigour, openness, long-term governance, and cumulative data production, rather than on isolated datasets alone (Primerano et al., 2026; Taddei & Paolucci, 2026a). Seen in this light, OPPs are important not only because they support digital data collection, but because they create the conditions under which heterogeneous data sources can be systematically integrated and evaluated. Survey responses, behavioural experiments, smartphone-based measures, wearable-device data, linked administrative records, and donated digital traces can all be related within a common probabilistic and longitudinal framework. This is not simply a technical enhancement; it is a methodological achievement that makes selection processes visible, facilitaes the modelling of uncertainty, and restores contextual depth to otherwise fragmented data.

A key contribution of the chapter has therefore been to move beyond dichotomous oppositions between "traditional" and "digital" data. The relevant question is not whether one source should replace another, but under which conditions different sources can be meaningfully combined. Within OPPs, the coexistence of multiple modes of data production enables comparisons between self-reports and behavioural measures, digital traces and administrative records, and longitudinal observations and short-term fluctuations. This supports a more reflexive understanding of data quality, in which validity, reliability, inclusiveness, and interpretability are treated as empirical and design-dependent issues rather than assumed properties of a dataset. In welfare research, where institutional processes, administrative burdens, stigma, vulnerability, and unequal access shape behaviour in profound ways, such a reflexive approach is indispensable.

The chapter has also shown that the value of OPPs lies not only in their inferential grounding, but in their capacity to facilitate contextual interpretation. One of the most significant weaknesses of stand-alone digital traces is that they typically record interactions or behavioural signals without providing sufficient information on motivations, constraints, life conditions, and institutional experiences. In contrast, OPPs make it possible to relate digital behaviours to socio-demographic characteristics, employment conditions, household composition, health status, subjective perceptions, and repeated observations over time. This longitudinal and contextual layering transforms otherwise ambiguous traces into evidence that can be interpreted within broader social trajectories and institutional environments. In welfare analysis, this distinction is crucial, as similar behavioural patterns may reflect very different realities: strategic adaptation to eligibility rules, exclusion from services, digital barriers, coping under scarcity, or genuine preference. Without such contextual anchoring, these possibilities remain methodologically indistinguishable.

A further major conclusion concerns the role of ethics, governance, and trust. One of the risks of contemporary data-intensive welfare systems is that ethical considerations are treated as external constraints on innovation rather than as constitutive elements of research quality. This chapter has argued against that view. In welfare research, ethics, governance, and trust shape participation, consent, data linkage, access conditions, and the legitimacy of knowledge production itself. Recent work on longitudinal data infrastructures and European panel studies confirms that robust consent procedures, controlled access, data protection safeguards, and transparent governance arrangements are not secondary additions, but central conditions for sustaining participation and preserving data integrity over time (Cerbara et al., 2026; Goebel et al., 2019; Haven et al., 2022). This is particularly relevant when digital traces are integrated through practices such as data donation or administrative linkage, where willingness to share information is itself socially patterned and analytically meaningful.

In this sense, OPPs demonstrate something broader than methodological efficiency. They show that ethical governance can be embedded within the research infrastructure itself. Voluntary participation, explicit recruitment procedures, layered consent, documented linkage rules, tiered access conditions, and institutional oversight do not simply reduce legal risk; they shape the epistemic conditions under which data become trustworthy. They make visible who participates, under which terms, and with what implications for representativeness and interpretation. In welfare contexts, where evidence must remain open to explanation, contestation, and revision, such visibility is essential. It is also one of the reasons why probability-based online panels are closely aligned with current discussions on open science, FAIR principles, and governed openness in social research infrastructures (Cerbara et al., 2026; Fecher & Friesike, 2014).

More broadly, the argument developed here suggests that the future of data-informed welfare research will depend less on the proliferation of digital data and more on sustained investment in infrastructures capable of governing their integration. As welfare systems increasingly operate through platforms, algorithms, and automated or semi-automated processes, the role of social research cannot be limited to passively adapting to digitalisation. It must instead actively contribute to shaping the conditions under which digital innovation becomes welfare-relevant evidence. This requires infrastructures that preserve interpretability, inclusiveness, transparency, and democratic accountability, while enabling methodological innovation and data integration. In this respect, the ongoing European debate on longitudinal data infrastructures and the development of national and comparative OPPs point in a promising direction for future welfare research (Taddei et al., 2026; Taddei & Paolucci, 2026a).

The broader implication is clear. High-quality data science for welfare governance is not simply a matter of better algorithms, faster processing, or larger datasets. It is the outcome of research designs and institutional arrangements that render digital data inferentially credible, socially meaningful, and publicly legitimate. Online Probability Panels provide a concrete model in this direction. They demonstrate how digital traces can be integrated into welfare research without sacrificing the methodological and normative standards on which trustworthy welfare knowledge depends. If welfare systems are to become more data-informed without becoming more opaque, unequal, or unaccountable, then the development of infrastructures of this kind is not optional. It is a central condition for the future of rigorous and publicly legitimate welfare research.

REFERENCES

Ambrosio, C., De Falco, C., & Taddei, L. (2026 forthcoming). *L'open science per il welfare: riflessioni sull'infrastruttura digitale FOSSR*. Welfare e Ergonomia, FrancoAngeli.

Aragona, B., & De Rosa, R. (2018). Policy making at the time of big data: Datascape, datasphere, data culture. *Sociologia Italiana, 11*, 173–185. DOI: 10.1485/AIS_2018/11_3434226

DIW Berlin. (2025a). *Data access – Conditions for downloading SOEP microdata.*

DIW Berlin. (2025b). *SOEP Research Data Center – Access to sensitive and regional data.*

Blom, A. G., Bosnjak, M., Cornilleau, A., Cousteaux, A.-S., Das, M., Douhou, S., & Krieger, U. (2016). A comparison of four probability-based online and mixed-mode panels in Europe. *Social Science Computer Review, 34*(1), 8–25. DOI: 10.1177/0894439315574825

Callegaro, M., Baker, R., Bethlehem, J., Göritz, A. S., Krosnick, J. A., & Lavrakas, P. J. (2014). *Online panel research: A data quality perspective.* Wiley. DOI: 10.1002/9781118763520

Centerdata. (2023a). *Privacy statement – LISS panel.* https://www.lissdata.nl/privacy

Centerdata. (2023b). *Ethics – LISS panel.* https://www.lissdata.nl/about-panel/ethics

Cerbara, L., Germani, D., & Santurro, M. (2026). Ethical implications in building longitudinal data infrastructures. In Taddei, L., & Paolucci, M. (Eds.), *Longitudinal data infrastructures in Europe: Tools for open science in social science research.* Springer. DOI: 10.1007/978-3-032-07005-0_4

Consiglio Nazionale delle Ricerche, Commissione per l'Etica e l'Integrità nella Ricerca. (2019). *Linee guida per l'integrità nella ricerca.*

Cornesse, C., & Blom, A. G. (2023). Response quality in nonprobability and probability-based online panels. *Sociological Methods & Research, 52*(2), 879–908. DOI: 10.1177/0049124120914940

Couper, M. P. (2008). *Designing effective web surveys.* Cambridge University Press. DOI: 10.1017/CBO9780511499371

Couper, M. P., Singer, E., Conrad, F. G., & Groves, R. M. (2008). Risk of disclosure, perceptions of risk, and concerns about privacy and confidentiality as factors in survey participation. *Journal of Official Statistics*, *24*(2), 255–275. PMID: 21603156

Das, M. (2025, May 5–6). Building on the LISS experience: Future challenges and opportunities for online probability-based panels [Conference presentation]. European Online Probability Panels (EOPPs), Milan, Italy.

Doyle, P., Lane, J., Theeuwes, J. J. M., & Zayatz, L. V. (Eds.). (2001). *Confidentiality, disclosure, and data access*. Elsevier.

European Commission. (2023). *Ethics and integrity in research*. Publications Office of the European Union.

European Union. (2016). Regulation (EU) 2016/679 (General Data Protection Regulation).

Fecher, B., & Friesike, S. (2014). Open science: One term, five schools of thought. In Bartling, S., & Friesike, S. (Eds.), *Opening science* (pp. 17–47). Springer. DOI: 10.1007/978-3-319-00026-8_2

Fienberg, S. E., & Willenborg, L. C. R. J. (Eds.). (1998). Disclosure limitation methods for protecting the confidentiality of statistical data. *Journal of Official Statistics*, *14*, 337–345.

Goebel, J., Grabka, M. M., Liebig, S., Kroh, M., Richter, D., Schröder, C., & Schupp, J. (2019). The German Socio-Economic Panel (SOEP). *Jahrbücher für Nationalökonomie und Statistik*, *239*(2), 345–360. DOI: 10.1515/jbnst-2018-0022

Haven, T., Gopalakrishna, G., Tijdink, J., van der Schot, D., & Bouter, L. (2022). Promoting trust in research and researchers: How open science and research integrity are intertwined. *BMC Research Notes*, *15*(1), 302. DOI: 10.1186/s13104-022-06169-y PMID: 36127719

Iphofen, R. (2017). *Ethical decision making in social research: A practical guide*. Palgrave Macmillan.

ISTAT. (2017). *L'effetto tecnica nelle indagini mixed-mode*. Istituto Nazionale di Statistica.

Keusch, F., Struminskaya, B., Mulder, J., & Jongerius, S. (2025). Data donation as a method to measure physical activity in older adults. *Journal of Medical Internet Research*, *27*, e69799. DOI: 10.2196/69799 PMID: 41004250

Kocar, S., & Kaczmirek, L. (2023). A meta-analysis of recruitment rates in probability-based online panels. *International Journal of Social Research Methodology, 27*(5), 589–604. DOI: 10.1080/13645579.2023.2242202

Lynn, P. (2012). *Longitudinal survey methods*. European Central Bank.

Maher, C., Ryan, J., Ambrosi, C., & Edney, S. (2017). Users' experiences of wearable activity trackers. *BMC Public Health, 17*(1), 880. DOI: 10.1186/s12889-017-4888-1 PMID: 29141607

Maslovskaya, O., & Lugtig, P. (2022). Representativeness in online panels. *Journal of the Royal Statistical Society. Series A, (Statistics in Society), 185*(3), 851–871. DOI: 10.1111/rssa.12801

Mauceri, S., Faggiano, M. P., & Di Censi, L. (2020). Survey 2.0. *Sociologia e Ricerca Sociale, 121*(121), 25–48. DOI: 10.3280/SR2020-121002

Menard, S. (2002). *Longitudinal research* (2nd ed.). SAGE. DOI: 10.4135/9781412984867

Primerano, I., Marchesini, N., Santelli, F., Taddei, L., & Cerbara, L. (2026). Secondary, longitudinal, and panel data in social science research. In Taddei, L., & Paolucci, M. (Eds.), *Longitudinal data infrastructures in Europe*. Springer. DOI: 10.1007/978-3-032-07005-0_2

Punziano, G., Marrazzo, F., & Acampa, S. (2021). Content analysis of CrowdTangle data. *Current Politics & Economics of Europe, 32*(4).

Ruspini, E. (2002). *An introduction to longitudinal research*. Routledge.

Santini, Z. I., Jose, P. E., Koyanagi, A., Meilstrup, C., Nielsen, L., Madsen, K. R., & Koushede, V. (2020). Formal social participation and health. *Social Science & Medicine, 251*, 112906. DOI: 10.1016/j.socscimed.2020.112906 PMID: 32151885

Scherpenzeel, A. (2009). *Start of the LISS panel*. CentERdata.

Scherpenzeel, A. (2011). Data collection in a probability-based internet panel. *Bulletin de Méthodologie Sociologique, 109*(1), 56–61. DOI: 10.1177/0759106310387713

Scherpenzeel, A. C. (2018). Longitudinal and probability-based internet panels. In *Social and behavioral research and the internet* (pp. 77–104). Routledge. DOI: 10.4324/9780203844922-4

Singer, E., Mathiowetz, N. A., & Couper, M. P. (1993). Privacy and census participation. *Public Opinion Quarterly, 57*(4), 465–482. DOI: 10.1086/269391

Singer, E., Van Hoewyk, J., & Neugebauer, R. (2003). Privacy and participation in the 2000 Census. *Public Opinion Quarterly*, *67*(3), 368–384. DOI: 10.1086/377465

Struminskaya, B., Lugtig, P., Toepoel, V., Schouten, B., Giesen, D., & Dolmans, R. (2021). Sharing smartphone sensor data. *Public Opinion Quarterly*, *85*(S1), 423–462. DOI: 10.1093/poq/nfab025 PMID: 34602867

Taddei, L., Biolcati Rinaldi, F., Biolcati Rinaldi, F., Heins, F., Marchesini, N., Paparusso, A., Pennacchiotti, C., Primerano, I., Piacentini, F., & Vezzoni, C. Santurro, M. (2026). The Italian way to an online probability panel. In L. Taddei & M. Paolucci (Eds.), *Longitudinal data infrastructures in Europe. Tools for Open Science in Social Science Research*. Springer.

Taddei, L., & Paolucci, M. (Eds.). (2026). *Longitudinal data infrastructures in Europe. Tools for Open Science in Social Science Research*. Springer. DOI: 10.1007/978-3-032-07005-0

Taddei, L., & Paolucci, M. (2026a). The rise of social science infrastructures in Europe and Italy. In Taddei, L., & Paolucci, M. (Eds.), *Longitudinal data infrastructures in Europe. Tools for Open Science in Social Science Research*. Springer. DOI: 10.1007/978-3-032-07005-0_5

Toepoel, V., Luiten, A., & Zandvliet, R. (2021). Response willingness and data donation. *Survey Practice*, *14*(1), 1–19. Advance online publication. DOI: 10.29115/SP-2021-0005

Trezza, D. (2023). To scrape or not to scrape. *Frontiers in Sociology*, *8*, 1145038. Advance online publication. DOI: 10.3389/fsoc.2023.1145038 PMID: 37006635

University of Essex. (n.d.). *Understanding Society: Ethics and data security*.

Yeager, D. S., Krosnick, J. A., Chang, L., Javitz, H. S., Levendusky, M. S., Simpser, A., & Wang, R. (2011). Comparing survey modes. *Public Opinion Quarterly*, *75*(4), 709–747. DOI: 10.1093/poq/nfr020

ADDITIONAL READING

Couper, M. P. (2017). New developments in survey data collection. In P. P. Biemer, E. de Leeuw, S. Eckman, B. Edwards, F. Kreuter, L. Lyberg, C. Tucker, & B. T. West (Eds.), *Total survey error in practice* (pp. 203–221). Wiley. DOI: 10.1146/annurev-soc-060116-053613

Groves, R. M. (2011). Three eras of survey research. *Public Opinion Quarterly, 75*(5), 861–871. DOI: 10.1093/poq/nfr057

Groves, R. M., Fowler, F. J., Couper, M. P., Lepkowski, J. M., Singer, E., & Tourangeau, R. (2018). Survey errors and survey costs. In *Survey methodology* (2nd ed., pp. 49–78). Wiley.

Japec, L., Kreuter, F., Berg, M., Biemer, P., Decker, P., Lampe, C., Lane, J., O'Neil, C., & Usher, A. (2015). Big data in survey research: AAPOR task force report. In P. P. Biemer, E. de Leeuw, S. Eckman, B. Edwards, F. Kreuter, L. Lyberg, C. Tucker, & B. T. West (Eds.), *Total survey error in practice* (pp. 165–191). Wiley.

Kitchin, R. (2014). Big data, new epistemologies and paradigm shifts. In *The data revolution: Big data, open data, data infrastructures and their consequences* (pp. 111–135). SAGE. DOI: 10.1177/2053951714528481

Knaflic, C. N., & Sakshaug, J. W. (2021). Integrating survey and digital trace data. In Wolf, C., Joye, D., Smith, T. W., & Fu, Y. (Eds.), *The SAGE handbook of survey methodology* (pp. 567–585). SAGE.

Kreuter, F. (2013). Improving surveys with auxiliary data. In Kreuter, F. (Ed.), *Improving surveys with paradata: Analytic uses of process information* (pp. 1–16). Wiley. DOI: 10.1002/9781118596869.ch1

Salganik, M. J. (2018). Foundational concepts for digital data. In *Bit by bit: Social research in the digital age* (pp. 11–40). Princeton University Press.

Tourangeau, R., Conrad, F. G., & Couper, M. P. (2013). *The science of web surveys*. Oxford University Press. DOI: 10.1093/acprof:oso/9780199747047.001.0001

KEY TERMS AND DEFINITIONS

Data Quality: A multidimensional and design-dependent concept referring to the validity, reliability, interpretability, and inclusiveness of data in relation to specific research objectives, populations, and institutional contexts, rather than an intrinsic property of the data themselves.

Data-Informed Welfare: An approach to welfare policy and research in which data support decision-making within structured research designs and institutional frameworks, remaining embedded in methodological judgement, contextual interpretation, and normative considerations related to rights, equity, and accountability.

Digital Traces: Data generated as by-products of interactions with digital systems, platforms, and devices, typically reflecting behaviours, transactions, or system logs rather than measurements produced within explicit research designs, and therefore characterised by limited contextual information and weak population anchoring.

Epistemic Anchoring: The process through which data are stabilised within explicit research designs, population frameworks, and governance arrangements, enabling their transformation from context-dependent signals into interpretable and welfare-relevant evidence.

Online Probability Panels (OPP): Research infrastructures based on probability sampling and longitudinal participation, designed to anchor heterogeneous data sources—including digital traces—within defined populations, enabling population inference, contextualisation, and transparent modelling of uncertainty.

Population Inference: The process of drawing conclusions about a defined population based on sample data, grounded in known inclusion probabilities, explicit sampling frames, and the possibility of assessing selection mechanisms and error structures.

Research Infrastructure: The organisational, technical, ethical, and methodological arrangements that structure how data are produced, integrated, governed, and interpreted, shaping the conditions under which knowledge becomes inferentially valid and socially legitimate.

Selection Bias: Systematic distortion arising when inclusion probabilities differ across individuals or groups and are not fully observed or controlled, affecting representativeness, comparability, and the validity of population inference.

Chapter 9
Reframing Data Governance in the Third Sector:
Digital Infrastructures, Epistemic Visibility, and Policy Futures in Welfare Systems

Giovanni A. Forte
http://orcid.org/0009-0009-7240-9095
University of Naples Federico II, Italy

Gabriella Punziano
http://orcid.org/0000-0001-8783-2712
University of Naples Federico II, Italy

Rosa Sorrentino
University of Naples Federico II, Italy

ABSTRACT

The Third Sector remains structurally underrepresented in data infrastructures and public policy knowledge frameworks. This chapter develops a theoretical reflection on the epistemic and governance challenges generated by fragmented, obsolete, and non-interoperable data concerning third-sector organizations. Drawing on sociological theory, digital governance scholarship, and debates on open data and algorithmic infrastructures, the chapter argues that data invisibility constitutes a structural form of policy marginalization. It proposes a conceptual framework for understanding third-sector data ecosystems. Building on theories of symbolic power, digital participation, and data governance, the chapter advances policy-oriented

DOI: 10.4018/979-8-3373-8423-8.ch009

propositions aimed at enhancing transparency, accountability, and evidence-based decision-making in welfare systems. The argument ultimately redefines digital transformation in the Third Sector as an epistemic and institutional reform necessary for future social resilience.

1. INTRODUCTION: DATA INVISIBILITY AS A STRUCTURAL POLICY PROBLEM

Across contemporary welfare regimes, the Third Sector occupies a structurally paradoxical position. On the one hand, it constitutes an indispensable pillar of social provision, increasingly embedded within hybrid welfare configurations that combine public intervention, market mechanisms, and civic action. On the other hand, it remains epistemically marginal within institutional data systems and policy analytics. The expansion of the Third Sector in Europe has been extensively documented, particularly in contexts marked by retrenchment or restructuring of the welfare state (Borzaga & Defourny, 2001; Salamon & Anheier, 1998). As welfare governance shifts toward pluralization and subsidiarity, third-sector entities (TSEs) have assumed central roles in health services, education, poverty relief, disability support, cultural production, environmental sustainability, and local development. Their importance became especially visible during the COVID-19 crisis, when they acted as rapid-response infrastructures capable of filling institutional gaps and reaching vulnerable populations often underserved by formal public systems (Borzaga, 2020; Punziano et al., 2023).

Yet visibility in practice does not translate into visibility in data. The paradox lies precisely in the mismatch between operational centrality and epistemic marginalization. The Third Sector is often underrepresented in official datasets, dispersed across fragmented regional registries, and poorly integrated into national statistical systems. As Lori and Zamaro (2019) have argued in the Italian context, available data on TSEs are frequently incomplete, outdated, and non-standardized, limiting their interpretability and policy relevance. This condition reflects what can be conceptualized as a structural invisibility: not the absence of activity, but the absence of coherent and interoperable representations within institutional knowledge frameworks. From a Bourdieusian perspective, such invisibility is not neutral. Data infrastructures function as sites of symbolic power, determining what is rendered legible, measurable, and therefore governable (Bourdieu, 1984). When organizations are weakly represented in administrative data, they risk exclusion from funding schemes, policy evaluation processes, and evidence-based planning.

The consequences of this epistemic gap are amplified in an era increasingly shaped by data-driven governance. Contemporary public policy relies heavily on predictive modeling, performance indicators, benchmarking systems, and algorithmic decision-support tools (Kitchin, 2014). Welfare systems are progressively embedded within digital infrastructures that privilege standardization, comparability, and machine-readability. When the Third Sector remains only partially mapped within such systems, governance tends to privilege actors that are more easily quantifiable—typically public administrations and formal enterprises—while undervaluing the relational, community-based, and often informal dimensions of third-sector activity. In this sense, data invisibility becomes a structural policy problem. It shapes resource allocation, constrains institutional recognition, and influences the strategic direction of welfare reform.

Addressing this issue requires more than technical modernization. Digital transformation in welfare systems must be accompanied by what may be termed an epistemic transformation: a reconfiguration of data governance frameworks capable of representing the organizational complexity, territorial embeddedness, and socio-economic impact of the Third Sector. Drawing on digital sociology (Marres, 2017), public policy analysis (Howlett et al., 2003), and debates on open data governance (Janssen et al., 2012), this chapter develops a theoretical argument that conceives third-sector data ecosystems as socio-technical assemblages. These assemblages intertwine institutional design, computational infrastructures, stakeholder participation, and normative choices about what counts as relevant knowledge. The challenge, therefore, is not simply to collect more data, but to construct dynamic, interoperable, and context-sensitive infrastructures capable of integrating heterogeneous sources and supporting evidence-based, equitable, and future-oriented welfare governance.

2. FROM REGISTRIES TO INFRASTRUCTURES: WHY EXISTING DATA SYSTEMS SYSTEMATICALLY UNDER-REPRESENT THE THIRD SECTOR

The persistent under-representation of Third Sector entities is often treated as a contingent problem of "missing information" that could be fixed by improving administrative procedures or expanding registries. Yet the issue is better understood as an infrastructural mismatch between what the Third Sector is-organizationally plural, territorially embedded, and dynamically adaptive-and what contemporary data systems are designed to capture: stable, standardized, and easily comparable units of governance. In other words, invisibility does not arise simply because data are absent; it emerges because institutional datasets are built around classificatory logics that privilege certain organizational forms and marginalize others. As science and technology studies have long argued, classification systems are not neutral containers of information but socio-technical devices that stabilize categories, define what counts as legitimate evidence, and distribute recognition and resources accordingly (Bowker & Star, 1999). When the Third Sector is forced into administrative categories that privilege legal form, formal registration, and compliance documentation, the resulting picture tends to flatten heterogeneity and obscure the very features that make the sector indispensable within welfare regimes: hybridity, multi-activity profiles, informal collaborations, volunteer intensity, and rapid reconfiguration under pressure.

This structural mismatch becomes particularly evident in data architectures that rely on self-registration as a prerequisite for visibility. Where the institutional gaze is mediated by registries, what appears is not the sector as such, but the subset of organizations that possess the time, competencies, and organizational stability required to comply with bureaucratic demands. This produces a cumulative advantage for more professionalized actors and a corresponding disadvantage for smaller, volunteer-based or resource-constrained organizations—precisely those that often operate closest to unmet social needs. The outcome is a stratified informational landscape that mirrors and may reinforce existing inequalities in organizational capacity, territorial resources, and access to policy channels. This is consistent with broader sociological accounts of how welfare governance increasingly operates through audit cultures, performance indicators, and evaluative infrastructures that reward legibility and penalize complexity (Power, 1997; Esping-Andersen, 1990). In such contexts, the Third Sector's contribution risks being simultaneously celebrated rhetorically and discounted analytically, because what cannot be rendered into standardized metrics becomes difficult to include in policy design, monitoring, and funding allocation.

The problem is intensified by the digital turn in welfare governance. As public administrations adopt data-driven decision-making, the informational ecosystem shifts from descriptive reporting toward predictive and automated forms of coordination. Here, invisibility becomes an algorithmic liability: if the Third Sector is missing, inconsistently encoded, or represented through impoverished variables, it will be weakly "seen" by analytic pipelines that increasingly guide priorities, risk assessments, and resource distribution. Scholarship on algorithmic governance shows that computational systems amplify the politics of prior data: they learn from what is recorded, reproduce the biases of existing classifications, and convert historical undercounting into future under-allocation (Eubanks, 2018; Kitchin, 2014; Pasquale, 2015). In this sense, the informational marginality of Third Sector entities is not merely a technical defect but a governance problem with distributive consequences. When welfare systems recalibrate around data infrastructures, the struggle over what is counted becomes a struggle over what is governable and, ultimately, what is supported. The policy challenge is therefore not only to "add more data," but to redesign the infrastructural imagination of welfare knowledge so that it can represent relational work, local embeddedness, and organizational change over time-dimensions that are central to Third Sector action but routinely excluded by registry-centric approaches.

3. DATA GOVERNANCE AS POLITICAL ARCHITECTURE: POWER, PARTICIPATION, AND THE DIGITAL WELFARE STATE

If data invisibility represents a structural governance problem, it is because data infrastructures themselves are political architectures. They do not simply store information; they organize fields of action, define epistemic hierarchies, and delimit the boundaries of policy imagination. In contemporary welfare systems, the shift toward digital governance has produced a reconfiguration of how knowledge is generated, circulated, and operationalized. As several scholars have argued, the move from bureaucratic documentation to data-driven governance entails a transformation in the very ontology of social problems: phenomena become actionable insofar as they are rendered into datasets, dashboards, and predictive variables (Kitchin, 2017; Ruppert et al., 2017). In this transformation, the Third Sector risks occupying a structurally subordinate position, not because it lacks relevance, but because its forms of action do not always conform to the logics of computational standardization.

Data governance must therefore be understood not merely as technical management but as a contested terrain where institutional priorities, epistemic values, and technological affordances intersect. Following Foucault's insight that knowledge and power are mutually constitutive, digital infrastructures can be seen as *dispositifs* that produce governable subjects and governable spaces (Foucault, 1975). In welfare systems, algorithmic tools increasingly participate in the allocation of resources, the evaluation of performance, and the anticipation of social risk. When Third Sector organizations are insufficiently represented within these infrastructures, their capacity to shape welfare agendas diminishes. What is not encoded cannot easily be compared; what cannot be compared struggles to compete for attention and funding. The politics of data thus translate into a politics of recognition.

At the same time, digital sociology reminds us that infrastructures are not closed systems but sites of negotiation and potential participation (Marres, 2017). The promise of open data and interoperable platforms lies in their capacity to democratize access to information and redistribute epistemic authority. However, openness alone does not guarantee equity. As Janssen et al. (2012) observe, open data initiatives frequently encounter barriers of usability, interoperability, and contextual interpretation. Without mechanisms for stakeholder engagement and co-construction, open data risks becoming a symbolic gesture rather than an effective governance tool. For the Third Sector, meaningful inclusion requires participatory data design, iterative validation of indicators, and recognition of the experiential knowledge held by practitioners and beneficiaries.

This raises a fundamental tension within digital welfare states. On one side stands the aspiration toward efficiency, automation, and scalability; on the other, the need for contextual sensitivity, relational accountability, and qualitative depth. Welfare governance increasingly oscillates between these poles. The integration of machine learning and automated reporting systems can enhance monitoring capacity and responsiveness. Yet, as scholars of algorithmic governance have cautioned, computational systems inherit and amplify the biases embedded in their training data (Beer, 2017; O'Neil, 2016). If Third Sector data are incomplete, outdated, or structurally skewed toward certain organizational types, automated systems risk reinforcing existing disparities rather than correcting them. In this sense, digital transformation without epistemic reform may inadvertently deepen inequality within welfare ecosystems.

A theoretically grounded approach to Third Sector data governance must therefore articulate three intertwined principles. First, infrastructures should be conceived as dynamic rather than static, capable of continuous updating and multi-source integration. Second, data architectures must incorporate both quantitative and qualitative dimensions, recognizing that organizational complexity cannot be reduced to administrative metrics. Third, governance frameworks should institutionalize participatory mechanisms that enable Third Sector actors to contribute to the definition of indicators and interpretative categories. Such an approach aligns with broader debates on data justice and democratic accountability in digital societies (Dencik et al., 2019). Ultimately, the transformation of welfare data systems is not merely a question of modernization; it is a question of whose knowledge counts, whose activities are rendered legible, and whose contributions are recognized as central to collective well-being.

4. FROM FRAGMENTATION TO INTEROPERABILITY: DESIGNING MULTI-SOURCE KNOWLEDGE ECOSYSTEMS FOR THE THIRD SECTOR

If the invisibility of the Third Sector stems from the structural inadequacy of existing registries and data architectures, the solution cannot lie in merely expanding administrative datasets. What is required is a reconfiguration of the epistemic model underpinning third-sector knowledge production. Fragmentation is not simply a technical issue of dispersed information; it reflects a deeper epistemological misalignment between the complexity of social organizations and the classificatory logics of bureaucratic systems. Moving from fragmentation to interoperability therefore demands both methodological innovation and institutional rethinking.

Methodologically, a multi-source data ecosystem must be conceived as an integrative framework capable of combining heterogeneous data streams-institutional, non-conventional, and computational-without collapsing their distinct epistemic qualities. Institutional data sources, such as national registries, statistical agencies, and ministerial databases, offer formal recognition and standardized metrics. However, they often capture only minimal administrative information. Non-conventional sources-organizational websites, digital platforms, media coverage, reports, and social media profiles-contain rich, dynamic, and context-sensitive information about organizational missions, partnerships, projects, and territorial embeddedness. The integration of these sources requires advanced methodological tools, including web scraping, API-based data harvesting, relational and non-relational database management, natural language processing, and machine learning classification models. Yet the technical capacity to aggregate data does not automatically generate meaningful knowledge. As Bowker and Star (1999) remind us, infrastructures embed classificatory choices that shape what can be known and compared. Therefore, interoperability must be accompanied by transparent indicator construction and explicit epistemic assumptions.

From an epistemic standpoint, multi-source integration represents a shift from static representation to dynamic modeling. Rather than treating third-sector entities as fixed units recorded at a given moment, data infrastructures should allow for longitudinal tracking, territorial comparison, and the detection of organizational transformation. Such dynamic systems can better capture phenomena such as rapid growth, decline, network reconfiguration, and innovation pathways. Importantly, this approach acknowledges that Third Sector organizations are not merely service providers but relational actors embedded in communities. Indicators should therefore include not only structural variables (legal form, workforce size, financial turnover) but also relational and contextual dimensions such as collaboration networks, beneficiary profiles, socio-territorial impact, and adaptive strategies in response to exogenous shocks. This multidimensionality reflects an epistemological commitment to representing complexity rather than reducing it to administrative minimalism.

At the same time, methodological sophistication must be matched by policy-oriented design principles. A multi-source knowledge ecosystem should be interoperable across governance levels-local, regional, and national-allowing policymakers to query data according to diverse analytical needs. For example, regional administrators may require granular territorial mapping to identify underserved areas, while national institutions may need aggregated indicators to monitor sector-wide trends. Interoperability thus becomes a policy instrument, enabling coordinated decision-making across scales. Moreover, the system should incorporate automated updating mechanisms to address the chronic problem of data obsolescence. Continuous integration through APIs and machine learning-assisted categorization can significantly reduce informational lag, ensuring that policy decisions are based on current realities rather than outdated records.

However, the epistemic legitimacy of such systems depends on participatory validation. Indicator construction and data interpretation must involve Third Sector stakeholders, including organizational leaders, practitioners, and beneficiaries. This participatory approach serves two purposes. First, it enhances data accuracy by incorporating experiential knowledge that may not be visible in formal documentation. Second, it democratizes the production of welfare knowledge, mitigating the risk that digital infrastructures reproduce top-down classifications disconnected from lived realities. In this sense, multi-source ecosystems should not be conceived solely as technological platforms but as governance arrangements that institutionalize dialogue between data producers, data subjects, and policymakers.

Policy proposals emerging from this framework can be articulated along several lines. First, welfare governance should invest in national interoperable platforms that integrate official registries with verified non-conventional sources, moving beyond static administrative databases. Second, indicator frameworks must be co-designed with sectoral actors to ensure contextual relevance and inclusiveness. Third, digital infrastructures should include open and queryable interfaces accessible to multiple user categories-researchers, policymakers, organizations, and citizens-thus fostering transparency and accountability. Fourth, sustainability plans must be embedded within institutional governance structures to guarantee long-term maintenance, continuous updating, and ethical oversight of data processes. Finally, the integration of AI-driven analytics should be guided by principles of transparency, bias mitigation, and human supervision, ensuring that algorithmic tools support rather than replace critical policy judgment.

In sum, the transition from fragmentation to interoperability is not simply a technical upgrade; it is an epistemic and political project. It entails reimagining the informational foundations of welfare governance in ways that recognize the Third Sector as a structurally central actor rather than a peripheral complement. By designing multi-source, dynamic, and participatory data ecosystems, policymakers can create the conditions for more equitable, evidence-based, and future-oriented welfare systems capable of responding to complex social challenges.

5. AI, ALGORITHMIC GOVERNANCE, AND THE FUTURE OF POLICY INTELLIGENCE IN WELFARE SYSTEMS

The integration of artificial intelligence into welfare governance marks a decisive shift in the epistemic architecture of public decision-making. AI-driven systems promise enhanced efficiency, predictive capacity, and real-time responsiveness. In principle, machine learning algorithms can identify patterns across vast and heterogeneous datasets, detect emerging social needs, and support evidence-based allocation of resources. Within the Third Sector ecosystem, such tools could enable the identification of underserved territories, the monitoring of organizational fragility, and the evaluation of socio-economic impact across regions. Yet this promise is inseparable from profound normative and ethical tensions.

AI does not operate in a vacuum; it is trained on existing data infrastructures and inherits their biases, omissions, and structural blind spots. As scholarship on algorithmic governance has demonstrated, automated systems often reproduce and amplify existing inequalities when they rely on incomplete or historically skewed datasets (Eubanks, 2018; O'Neil, 2016). If Third Sector entities are underrepresented in official data or captured through reductive variables, algorithmic models will not merely reflect that invisibility-they will operationalize it. Predictive systems may therefore prioritize actors that are more legible within standardized datasets, systematically marginalizing informal, volunteer-driven, or territorially embedded organizations whose contributions resist quantification. In this sense, AI can transform epistemic asymmetry into institutionalized policy bias.

The normative challenge lies in preventing what might be termed "automated marginalization." When welfare decisions are increasingly mediated by dashboards, scoring systems, and predictive indicators, governance risks becoming detached from the relational and qualitative dimensions that define much of Third Sector work. Care practices, community trust, social cohesion, and informal support networks are rarely reducible to discrete numerical variables. Yet algorithmic systems privilege precisely those dimensions that can be quantified and ranked. The danger is not simply technical error but a deeper epistemological narrowing: a redefinition of welfare value in terms of measurable outputs alone. As Pasquale (2015) has argued, opaque algorithmic systems can obscure the political choices embedded in computational design, rendering contestation more difficult and accountability less transparent.

At the same time, AI should not be rejected outright as incompatible with democratic welfare governance. Rather, its integration must be governed by explicit normative frameworks. Three principles are particularly crucial. First, transparency must extend beyond open access to include interpretability. Policymakers and stakeholders must be able to understand how models classify, predict, and rank entities. Black-box decision systems are incompatible with participatory governance in sectors that operate on principles of solidarity and public interest. Second, algorithmic oversight must include human supervision and deliberative review processes. AI should function as a decision-support system rather than a decision-maker, augmenting but not replacing institutional judgment. Third, continuous bias auditing is essential. Models should be periodically tested to assess whether they systematically disadvantage certain organizational forms, territories, or beneficiary groups.

Beyond risk mitigation, AI can also enable transformative policy intelligence if designed inclusively. For example, natural language processing tools can analyze qualitative reports, social media communication, and project documentation to extract thematic patterns that would otherwise remain dispersed. Machine learning can detect cross-regional similarities in innovation strategies, map collaboration networks, and identify emergent forms of social entrepreneurship. When integrated with participatory validation mechanisms, such tools can enhance rather than diminish epistemic plurality. The key lies in combining computational scale with contextual interpretation.

The future of welfare systems increasingly depends on the capacity to operate within complex, data-rich environments. Demographic shifts, climate-related vulnerabilities, migration flows, and public health crises generate rapidly evolving social needs. Traditional bureaucratic cycles often struggle to respond with adequate speed. AI-driven analytics offer the potential to shorten feedback loops between data collection and policy intervention. However, this acceleration must be accompanied by ethical safeguards and democratic anchoring. The central policy question is therefore not whether AI should be used, but under what governance conditions it can support equitable and accountable welfare transformation.

In the context of the Third Sector, AI-enabled policy intelligence should aim to correct invisibility rather than entrench it. This requires embedding representational justice within data infrastructures. Indicators must be designed to capture relational work and community impact. Data pipelines must incorporate multi-source integration to prevent informational monocultures. Stakeholder consultation should inform both model training and interpretative frameworks. Ultimately, AI in welfare governance should function as a tool for epistemic inclusion-expanding the range of visible actors and measurable contributions-rather than as a mechanism of technocratic closure.

The long-term implication is that digital transformation in welfare systems must be understood as a governance reform project rather than a technological upgrade. AI reshapes not only administrative efficiency but the epistemic conditions under which social value is recognized and redistributed. If properly governed, it can enhance transparency, coordination, and adaptive capacity. If uncritically implemented, it risks deepening existing asymmetries. The future of policy intelligence in the Third Sector will therefore depend on designing socio-technical systems that integrate computational power with democratic oversight, ethical reflexivity, and inclusive data practices.

6. POLICY PROPOSITIONS FOR THE FUTURE: TOWARD AN INCLUSIVE DATA ARCHITECTURE FOR THE THIRD SECTOR

If the previous sections have demonstrated that Third Sector invisibility is not an accidental gap but a structural feature of existing data regimes, then policy responses must address both infrastructural design and epistemic governance. The transformation required is not incremental but paradigmatic. It entails reconceptualizing Third Sector data not as auxiliary administrative information, but as a central component of welfare intelligence systems.

A first normative principle concerns the transition from static registries to dynamic, interoperable knowledge infrastructures. Administrative registers, while necessary for formal recognition, are insufficient as instruments of policy intelligence. Policymakers should invest in infrastructures capable of continuous updating through multi-source integration, combining official data, non-conventional digital traces, and validated qualitative insights. Interoperability must become a legal and technical requirement rather than a secondary feature. Without shared standards for data formatting, categorization, and exchange, regional fragmentation will persist, reproducing territorial inequalities in informational visibility. Harmonized frameworks should, however, remain adaptable to local specificities, ensuring that national comparability does not erase regional heterogeneity.

A second principle concerns the co-construction of indicators. Data infrastructures are never neutral; they embed classificatory decisions about what counts as relevant activity, impact, or value. Indicator design must therefore be participatory. Third Sector actors should not merely be data providers but epistemic contributors. Institutionalizing consultative mechanisms-through focus groups, deliberative panels, and iterative validation procedures-ensures that the metrics used to represent the sector reflect its organizational realities. Such participatory design strengthens legitimacy and enhances data accuracy by incorporating experiential knowledge that may otherwise remain unrecorded.

Third, digital infrastructures must be conceived as layered systems serving differentiated publics. Policymakers, researchers, sector organizations, and citizens require distinct levels of access and interpretative tools. Queryable platforms with customizable dashboards, interactive mapping systems, and automated reporting functions can support this plural usage. Importantly, access must be accompanied by interpretability. Data visualization and algorithmic outputs should be accompanied by methodological documentation and contextual explanation. Transparency is not achieved solely through openness but through intelligibility.

Fourth, the integration of AI and machine learning into Third Sector governance requires explicit normative safeguards. Algorithmic systems used for resource allocation, performance evaluation, or predictive modeling must operate under conditions of transparency, auditability, and human oversight. Independent bias assessments should be periodically conducted to evaluate whether certain organizational forms, territories, or beneficiary groups are systematically disadvantaged. Ethical review boards and regulatory frameworks should accompany algorithmic deployment within welfare governance, ensuring alignment with principles of equity, proportionality, and accountability.

Fifth, sustainability must be institutional rather than project-based. Data infrastructures risk deterioration if confined to temporary funding cycles. Long-term governance arrangements should assign clear responsibility for maintenance, updating, and technical evolution. Collaboration between national statistical agencies, ministries, research institutions, and Third Sector federations can provide the institutional anchoring required for continuity. Without such embedding, digital transformation remains episodic and fails to achieve systemic reform.

Finally, policy transformation must address the educational dimension. Building interoperable and inclusive data systems requires enhancing digital competencies within the Third Sector itself. Capacity-building programs aimed at improving data literacy, documentation practices, and digital governance awareness can reduce informational asymmetries and strengthen participatory engagement. In this way, data governance becomes not merely a top-down modernization strategy but a collective learning process.

Taken together, these propositions suggest that the future of Third Sector governance lies in constructing inclusive data architectures that integrate technological innovation with democratic accountability. The goal is not simply to render the sector visible, but to render it legible in ways that enhance equitable policy design, territorial cohesion, and social resilience.

7. CONCLUSION: RECONFIGURING WELFARE KNOWLEDGE FOR THE DIGITAL ERA

This chapter has argued that the invisibility of the Third Sector within welfare data infrastructures represents a structural governance challenge rather than a technical oversight. Drawing on sociological theories of symbolic power, digital sociology, and algorithmic governance, we have conceptualized data infrastructures as political architectures that shape what is recognized, funded, and governed. The

Third Sector's marginal position within these architectures reflects not its peripheral relevance but the inadequacy of existing classificatory systems to capture its hybrid, relational, and territorially embedded nature.

Methodologically, the chapter has advanced the case for multi-source, interoperable, and dynamic data ecosystems that combine institutional registries, non-conventional digital sources, and participatory validation processes. Such systems require both computational sophistication and epistemic reflexivity. Machine learning and AI tools offer unprecedented opportunities for real-time monitoring and predictive policy intelligence, yet they also risk amplifying existing informational biases if not embedded within ethical governance frameworks.

From a policy perspective, digital transformation in welfare systems must be understood as an epistemic reform. It entails redefining how knowledge about social actors is produced, validated, and operationalized. Inclusive data architectures can enhance transparency, enable more responsive policy design, and support equitable resource distribution. Conversely, failure to reform data governance risks entrenching asymmetries, privileging actors who are already administratively legible while marginalizing those whose contributions resist easy quantification.

The future of welfare governance thus depends on aligning technological innovation with democratic accountability. Building infrastructures that render the Third Sector visible, interpretable, and institutionally integrated is not merely a technical project but a normative commitment to pluralism, participation, and social justice. In an era characterized by complex crises and rapid transformation, the capacity to construct inclusive and adaptive knowledge systems may well determine the resilience of welfare regimes themselves.

REFERENCES

Beer, D. (2017). The social power of algorithms. *Information Communication and Society, 20*(1), 1–13. DOI: 10.1080/1369118X.2016.1216147

Borzaga, C. (2020). *La rilevanza economica la situazione e l'impatto della riforma.* [Lexical characteristics of Italian language]. Euricse Working Paper.

Borzaga, C., & Defourny, J. (Eds.). (2001). *The emergence of social enterprise* (1st ed.). Routledge. DOI: 10.4324/9780203164679

Bourdieu, P. (1984). *Distinction: A social critique of the judgement of taste*. Harvard University Press.

Bowker, G. C., & Star, S. L. (1999). *Sorting things out: Classification and its consequences*. MIT Press. DOI: 10.7551/mitpress/6352.001.0001

Dencik, L., Hintz, A., & Cable, J. (2019). Exploring data justice: Conceptions, applications and directions. *Information Communication and Society, 22*(7), 873–881. DOI: 10.1080/1369118X.2019.1606268

Esping-Andersen, G. (1990). *The three worlds of welfare capitalism*. Princeton University Press.

Eubanks, V. (2018). *Automating inequality: How high-tech tools profile, police, and punish the poor*. St. Martin's Press.

Foucault, M. (1975). *Discipline and punish: The birth of the prison*. Penguin Books.

Howlett, M., Ramesh, M., & Perl, A. (2003). *Studying public policy: Policy cycles and policy subsystems*. Oxford University Press.

Janssen, M., Charalabidis, Y., & Zuiderwijk, A. (2012). Benefits, Adoption Barriers and Myths of Open Data and Open Government. *Information Systems Management, 29*(4), 258–268. DOI: 10.1080/10580530.2012.716740

Kitchin, R. (2014). The data revolution: Big data, open data, data infrastructures and their consequences. *Sage (Atlanta, Ga.)*. Advance online publication. DOI: 10.4135/9781473909472

Kitchin, R. (2017). Thinking critically about and researching algorithms. *Information Communication and Society, 20*(1), 14–29. DOI: 10.1080/1369118X.2016.1154087

Lori, M., & Zamaro, N. (2019). Il profilo sfocato del Terzo settore italiano. [Lexical characteristics of Italian language]. *Politiche Sociali, 2*, 225–242.

Marres, N. (2017). *Digital sociology: The reinvention of social research*. Polity Press.

O'Neil, C. (2016). *Weapons of math destruction: How big data increases inequality and threatens democracy*. Crown Publisher.

Pasquale, F. (2015). *The black box society: The secret algorithms that control money and information*. Harvard University Press. DOI: 10.4159/harvard.9780674736061

Power, M. (1997). *The audit society: Rituals of verification*. Oxford University Press.

Punziano, G., Cicellin, M., Zito, E., Acampa, S., & Sorrentino, R. (2023). Role of the digital for the Third Sector in the Campania region (Italy): From the side of research to the side of the objects in the aftermath of the COVID-19 pandemic. *Italian Sociological Review*, *13*(2), 279–296.

Ruppert, E., Isin, E., & Bigo, D. (2017). Data politics. *Big Data & Society*, *4*(2), 1–7. DOI: 10.1177/2053951717717749

Salamon, L. M., & Anheier, H. K. (1998). Social origins of civil society: Explaining the nonprofit sector cross-nationally. *Voluntas*, *9*(3), 213–248. DOI: 10.1023/A:1022058200985

Chapter 10
Extreme Poverty, Digital Welfare, and Data Governance in Rome:
A Multilevel and Integrated Analysis of the Service Network for People Experiencing Homelessness

Sergio Mauceri
http://orcid.org/0000-0002-2229-8253
Sapienza University of Rome, Italy

Maria Paola Faggiano
http://orcid.org/0000-0002-6842-5406
Sapienza University of Rome, Italy

Luca Di Censi
http://orcid.org/0000-0002-7612-1701
Sapienza University of Rome, Italy

ABSTRACT

This chapter examines extreme poverty and homelessness in the metropolitan area of Rome through a multilevel and integrated research design. The analysis combines the secondary analysis of digitized administrative data, capture-recapture estimation, a web survey of services, Social Network Analysis, and qualitative case studies. After clarifying the definitional boundaries of homelessness through the ETHOS framework, the chapter discusses the role of Anthology as a digital welfare

DOI: 10.4018/979-8-3373-8423-8.ch010

infrastructure supporting case management, data governance, and organizational learning. Empirically, the study reconstructs the size and characteristics of the target population, maps the service system, identifies unmet needs and coordination patterns, and compares two organizational models. The findings support evidence-informed recommendations for strengthening multilevel governance, housing-oriented strategies, integrated interventions, and the quality and interoperability of administrative data.

1. INTRODUCTION

Extreme poverty represents one of the most severe and persistent forms of social exclusion in contemporary urban societies. It is most visibly embodied in homelessness, a condition in which low income, insecure housing, limited access to rights, fragile social ties, and socio-health vulnerabilities converge, severely limiting individuals' capacity to exercise agency and regain autonomy in the foreseeable future (Human Rights Council, 2012).

Homelessness is therefore understood here not as a discrete status or a purely economic condition, but as a multidimensional process of cumulative deprivation (Anand & Sen, 1997; Atkinson, 2003). Material scarcity, institutional disaffiliation, weakened social ties, and biographical ruptures interact over time, producing what earlier literature described as a 'career of impoverishment' and progressive detachment from work, family, services, and community networks (Berzano, 1987; Caritas Ambrosiana, 2008; Landuzzi & Pieretti, 2006).

In metropolitan contexts, these trajectories are intensified by housing market pressure, transient social relations, the density of informal survival economies, and the fragmentation of public and third-sector welfare provision. Rome is analytically significant because severe marginality unfolds within a complex service environment where emergency responses, case management, administrative data, and network coordination intersect.

The chapter contributes to the literature in three ways. First, it links the European Typology of Homelessness and Housing Exclusion (ETHOS) framework to a multilevel empirical reconstruction of severe housing exclusion. Second, it uses mixed methods to connect population estimates, service morphology, relational structures, and organizational models. Third, it examines digital welfare not only as an operational tool, but also as a governance infrastructure capable of rendering marginality legible while simultaneously generating selective forms of visibility and access bias.

Drawing on the results of a research project conducted by a research team at Sapienza University of Rome and led by Sergio Mauceri, the study focuses on the service network for people experiencing homelessness in metropolitan Rome. It pursues two closely interconnected objectives: reconstructing the size, characteristics, needs, and service trajectories of the target population; and assessing how digital infrastructures and data governance arrangements shape knowledge production, coordination, evaluation, and policy learning within urban welfare systems (Mauceri & Di Censi, 2024).

2. DEFINING THE POPULATION OF PEOPLE EXPERIENCING HOMELESSNESS

To address the complexity of extreme poverty, the research adopted the ETHOS typology, developed by the European Federation of National Organisations Working with the Homeless (FEANTSA, 2005). This framework makes it possible to distinguish among different forms of housing exclusion and to move beyond stereotypical representations of people experiencing homelessness.

The definition proposed by FEANTSA is structured around four overarching concepts – rooflessness, houselessness, living in insecure housing, and living in inadequate housing – all of which may be considered indicators of the absence of a stable dwelling. ETHOS therefore classifies homelessness according to individuals' living situations or housing conditions. These conceptual categories are further divided into 13 operational categories, which can be used for different policy purposes, including mapping problems and needs related to homelessness, as well as designing, monitoring, and evaluating relevant policies.

In line with this classification, the population includes individuals who: live in public spaces (on the streets, in shacks, abandoned cars, caravans, or warehouses); stay in night shelters and/or are forced to spend large portions of the day in public spaces; reside in hostels or temporary accommodation facilities; or live in housing units specifically designed for social support interventions (for single individuals, couples, or groups experiencing homelessness).

Alongside the diversification of needs within such a heterogeneous population, it is necessary to consider the possession of formal rights and support networks, bearing in mind that these forms of protection do not automatically translate into social inclusion. This is the case for many migrants who, despite holding regular employment and earning an income, struggle to secure rental housing and experience everyday forms of exclusion within local communities. Moreover, trajectories of social marginalization differ according to gender. They tend to be more numerous and severe among men, whereas women often benefit from stronger protection provided by family and social networks offering assistance and support (Mingione, 1996).

The relationship between gender and access to social services is complex and multifactorial, varying across contexts and types of services. However, a general tendency toward the overrepresentation of women among users of social services can be observed (Italian National Institute of Statistics [Istat], 2020).[1] These patterns are shaped by a range of factors, including social and cultural norms, economic opportunities, and living conditions. A contextualized analysis is therefore essential to understand the underlying causes of such differences.

The inadequacy of available resources – and the limited capacity to mobilize and enhance existing ones – represents an additional challenge. Policies aimed at addressing extreme poverty must therefore move beyond the mere provision of financial assistance and focus on activating individual and community capabilities, while also critically examining the social mechanisms that generate exclusion. Over time, people experiencing homelessness may become accustomed to exclusion and to being the object of prejudice (Gui, 1995). The longer individuals remain on the streets, the more difficult it becomes to engage them in forward-looking projects, as opposed to providing short-term and often ineffective forms of assistance such as almsgiving.

Working with individuals means fostering the possibility of rebuilding a future through sustained daily commitment (Archer, 2006; Cesareo, 2005). Although reception facilities remain insufficient in number, the attention and commitment shown by public institutions in addressing the issue represent an important step forward.

Interest, motivation, and resources are present and often overlapping. However, the importance of coordination among services directed at individuals is frequently underestimated, despite being essential to move beyond "stopgap measures" that risk reproducing cycles of dependency on emergency assistance (Accorinti et al., 1998).

This operational definition is analytically useful, but it also entails important limitations. ETHOS and service-based data render homelessness observable through categories, institutional contacts, and access points; they do not fully capture the lived experience, subjective meanings, and trajectories of people who remain outside formal services. The empirical analysis should therefore be read as a relational reconstruction of homelessness mediated through the welfare system, not as a comprehensive account of all forms of severe housing exclusion. This limitation reinforces the need for future research and evaluation designs that integrate administrative evidence with forms of service-user participation and voice.

3. DIGITAL WELFARE: THE ANTHOLOGY PLATFORM

The digitalization of local welfare, when conceived not merely as a tool for procedural streamlining, but as a cognitive and organizational infrastructure for case management, can enhance public administrations' capacity to interpret, govern, and respond to complex social phenomena such as severe housing exclusion. At the same time, digital welfare must also be understood as part of broader processes of datafication and platformization within social policy, in which administrative categories, data architectures, access rules, and interoperability standards actively shape how needs become visible and governable (Kitchin, 2014; van Dijck et al., 2018).

The literature further highlights the absence of fully stabilized and universally shared definitions, resulting in variability in measurement criteria and prevalence indicators. This variability directly affects both the intertemporal and interterritorial comparability of statistics and, more broadly, the construction of public policies (Fitzpatrick et al., 2021). In the European context, increasing pressure on housing markets, the contraction of affordable housing supply, and rising housing costs are associated with processes of socioeconomic polarization and emerging vulnerabilities that increasingly affect groups not traditionally positioned within "historical" forms of marginality (European Foundation for the Improvement of Living and Working Conditions [Eurofound], 2020; Fitzpatrick et al., 2021). The condition of the "working poor" and employment instability, particularly among young people and workers with discontinuous contracts, contribute to situations of housing insecurity and heighten the risk of downward mobility into housing exclusion, especially in large metropolitan contexts (Campedelli & Vesan, 2023; Eurofound, 2020).

Within this framework, the administrative recognition of homelessness intersects with service access practices and with symbolic and material barriers. Stigma, invisibility, and institutional disaffiliation may reduce the likelihood of contact with formal systems and, consequently, the "traceability" of the phenomenon (Berzano, 1992; Calvaruso & Scalise, 1987; Landuzzi & Pieretti, 2006; Pellegrino & Verzieri, 1991). Operationally, this implies that a significant share of potential demand remains latent, while observed demand is strongly conditioned by contingent factors (critical life events, climatic emergencies, bed availability, procedural changes, access regulations, and outreach capacity), with the risk that planning decisions may be based on partial or distorted data.

In this scenario, the introduction of digital welfare tools can help reduce information asymmetries, standardize data collection, increase transparency in eligibility criteria, and strengthen accountability, provided that such tools are accompanied by robust governance arrangements, shared rules, and processes of continuous evaluation and improvement (Organisation for Economic Co-operation and Development [OECD], 2019).

Recent debates in critical data studies, data justice, and digital welfare have shown that data infrastructures are not neutral systems. They classify needs, produce eligibility-relevant visibility, and redistribute organizational power among actors who differ in their ability to generate, access, and interpret data. The central issue is therefore not whether data are useful, but under which governance conditions they support social rights without expanding surveillance, discretionary exclusion, algorithmic opacity, or unequal treatment of people with more limited capacity to engage with formal systems (Alston, 2019; Dencik et al., 2019; Eubanks, 2018; Redden et al., 2020; Taylor, 2017).

Within this framework, the Anthology platform represents a particularly relevant example: a digital platform developed by Europe Consulting Onlus, awarded the Sodalitas Social Award in 2018 and adopted as a support tool for municipal welfare services and for the work of the Sala Operativa Sociale (Social Operations Room) (see Mauceri & Di Censi, 2024; Radicchi, 2024).[2] Functionally, Anthology was designed to integrate heterogeneous information drawn from operational sources (contacts, access records, interventions, referrals, outcomes) and to support both case management and aggregated analysis, enabling the linkage of individual-level data with information concerning services, professionals, locations, and timing of service use.

Such integration is crucial for systems addressing severe marginality, as the heterogeneity of actors involved (municipal services, third-sector organizations, accommodation facilities, street outreach units) and the fragmentation of individual trajectories tend to produce "siloed data" that are difficult to compare and rarely reusable for evidence-informed policy-making. In this sense, the platform is not merely an administrative repository, but a device capable of improving the quality of the information cycle: (i) standardized data collection; (ii) validation and consistency checks; (iii) descriptive and inferential analysis; (iv) feedback to decision-makers and practitioners; (v) recalibration of procedures and intervention models.

From a digital welfare perspective, the objective is not simply to record information, but to generate actionable knowledge, for example, identifying recurrent usage patterns, detecting early signals of chronicization, mapping points of network saturation, and pinpointing critical transitions between services (dropout, missed follow-up, interruptions in case management). This becomes particularly relevant in complex hubs such as the Polo Sociale Roma Termini (Roma Termini Social Hub), whose services comply with the International Organization for Standardization (ISO 9001/2015) quality-management standard, where process standardization can be reinforced by a digital infrastructure capable of rendering procedures, timelines, outputs, and, within measurable limits, outcomes traceable.

The governance challenge is therefore both technical and political. Data quality depends on registration practices, stable taxonomies, staff training, internal audits, and consistency checks; without these conditions, a digital infrastructure may produce opacity rather than transparency, especially when categories are applied unevenly across services or over time.

The integration of sensitive data also requires clear rules on minimization, purpose limitation, access control, traceability of operations, retention periods, and institutional accountability. These safeguards are essential to prevent mission creep and to ensure that information collected for care, coordination, or monitoring is not transformed into a mechanism of surveillance or exclusion.

Although Anthology is not presented here as an automated decision-making or predictive allocation system, it still shapes the conditions under which needs are recorded, compared, and acted upon. Administrative data can improve coordination and planning, but they may also reify categories, privilege more visible users, and penalize people whose trajectories are intermittent, distrustful of institutions, or only partially captured by service routines.[3]

Digital transformation is therefore meaningful only if embedded in a coherent evaluative and rights-oriented framework – one that links relevance, effectiveness, efficiency, impact, sustainability, and coherence (OECD, 2019) with transparency, contestability, proportionality, and stakeholder participation.

Anthology can thus be interpreted as an enabler of digital welfare insofar as it reduces knowledge fragmentation and supports evidence-building processes. Its effectiveness, however, depends on organizational maturity, data quality, governance rules, user-sensitive safeguards, and the capacity to translate data into responsible, explainable, and verifiable decisions (see Radicchi, 2024).

The empirical design that follows operationalizes this conceptual claim. Capture-recapture estimation, service monitoring, network analysis, and case studies are not separate technical blocks; together, they examine how a metropolitan welfare system observes homelessness, organizes responses, coordinates actors, and transforms digital traces into policy-relevant knowledge.

4. RESEARCH DESIGN

4.1. Research Objectives

The research design is grounded in the premise that homelessness must be studied simultaneously as a population phenomenon, a system of services, and a field of data-mediated governance. The study therefore combines demographic estimation, organizational monitoring, relational analysis, and qualitative interpretation within an integrated multilevel design.

The research project (Mauceri & Di Censi, 2024) focused on the overall system of services dedicated to people experiencing homelessness in Rome. It aimed to reconstruct the estimated size of the target population; the distribution and characteristics of services; the congruence between needs and service provision; patterns of cooperation among organizations; and distinctive intervention models.

The guiding research questions were: How many people experiencing homelessness are visible to the Roman service system? What services are available, and to which needs do they respond? Which needs remain insufficiently addressed? How are service providers connected to one another? Which organizational models help explain different ways of combining relational proximity, case management, and digital monitoring?

4.2. Research Context: The Metropolitan Area of Rome

As anticipated, the territorial scope of the study was deliberately limited to the capital city, given that Rome displays a particularly high incidence of people experiencing homelessness. According to the estimate produced by Istat for 2014, Rome accounted for 15.2% of the total population of people experiencing homelessness in Italy (7,709 individuals in absolute terms), compared to 16.9% (7,827 individuals) in 2011, ranking second only to Milan.[4]

A second reason concerns the contraction of service provision recorded in the same Istat survey on people experiencing homelessness. Unlike Milan, Rome experienced a reduction in the availability of soup kitchens and night shelters between 2011 and 2014, with the number of facilities decreasing from 61 to 45. Thus, despite a virtually unchanged potential user base, approximately one quarter of the services operating in the metropolitan area ceased their activities within a period of just four years.

It therefore became essential to investigate more closely the characteristics of the services delivered in relation to the needs of people experiencing homelessness within a metropolitan context characterized by high population density, fast-paced daily life, and the often transitory nature of social relationships – factors that may intensify conditions of exclusion and social marginalization.

4.3. Methodological Approach

The study adopted a mixed-methods design suited to a phenomenon whose measurement, interpretation, and governance cannot be reduced to a single source or technique (Amaturo & Punziano, 2016; Creswell & Plano Clark, 2011; Mauceri, 2019, 2024).

The quantitative component combined secondary analysis of digitized administrative data extracted from Anthology, capture-recapture estimation, and a structured web survey of services. The relational component used Social Network Analysis to reconstruct cooperative ties among organizations. The qualitative component relied on case studies to interpret intervention models and organizational practices in greater depth.

This articulation is not merely a matter of triangulation. It mirrors the multilevel structure of the phenomenon: individual trajectories are observed through administrative contacts; service responses are mediated through institutions and third-sector providers; and coordination emerges from networks of actors, rules, and information flows.

The project also adopted a multi-stakeholder configuration, involving the university research team, the Municipality of Rome through the Sala Operativa Sociale, the Italian Federation of Organizations for People Experiencing Homelessness (fio.PSD), third-sector organizations, and service managers. This configuration strengthened access to data and field knowledge, while also making the governance dimension of the research itself visible (Mauceri & Di Censi, 2024).

The study was situated within an evaluative perspective balancing accountability and learning (Martini & Sisti, 1999; Scriven, 1967). It did not assess service effectiveness in terms of individual outcomes – an objective that would have required direct involvement of service users and a different design – but identified strengths, gaps, and coordination issues in the responses implemented for people experiencing homelessness.

Accordingly, the recommendations developed in section 7 should be read as system-level implications derived from the combined analysis of population estimates, service provision, network structure, and organizational case studies.

4.4. Procedural Phases

4.4.1. Estimating the Population of People Experiencing Homelessness

Before undertaking a targeted analysis aimed at monitoring the operational modalities of service provision and reconstructing the network of services, it was deemed necessary to produce as accurate an estimate as possible of the population of people experiencing homelessness, understood as the potential beneficiaries of the interventions implemented in Rome (Di Censi, 2024).

The first phase of the research therefore involved organizing the digital data provided by the Sala Operativa Sociale (Social Operations Room) of the Municipality of Rome, extracted from the Anthology platform (see section 3), within which requests for access to the shelter system were recorded through reports submitted by mobile outreach units.

Using the capture-recapture method, and based on multiple reports submitted to the Sala Operativa Sociale (Social Operations Room), the size of the population of people experiencing homelessness was carefully estimated. The estimation was conducted from a diachronic perspective, reconstructing the numerical trend from 2014 to 2022, and introducing gender and citizenship as observable covariates (see section 5).

4.4.2. Service Census and Monitoring

Before conducting a targeted assessment aimed at monitoring the system of services provided to people experiencing homelessness, it was necessary to carry out a census in order to reconstruct an updated list of the various types of services operating in Rome.

The starting point was a list of services either formally contracted with the Municipality of Rome or delivering services in collaboration with the municipality, based on digitized data extracted from the Anthology platform (see section 3). This list was subsequently expanded through cooperation with several organizations that had previously mapped services dedicated to people experiencing homelessness in the capital, including the service maps developed by the Community of Sant'Egidio (2021) and Binario 95 (2021).

The services identified, comprising public services, soup kitchens, accommodation centers, parishes, and other third-sector organizations, amounted to a total of 115.

Email addresses of service managers were collected, and they were invited to participate in the second procedural phase of the project, which involved administering a structured web survey (Di Censi & Mauceri, 2024). The survey aimed to monitor operational modalities and assess indicators of adequacy in relation to the challenging task of responding to the wide range of needs expressed by people experiencing homelessness.[5]

Specifically, service managers were invited by email to complete an online questionnaire following their participation in an event held on May 19, 2022, organized in collaboration with fio.PSD. During this event, the research project was presented in order to encourage participation among organizations operating in Rome.

Overall, after several follow-up reminders, the questionnaire was completed by managers of just under half of the services (46 out of 115) between November 2022 and February 2023. Specific efforts were made, including through telephone contacts, to involve services considered crucial, namely those characterized by temporal stability, territorial coverage, and a large user base. Non-respondents were primarily parish-based services or organizations operating in a more informal or occasional manner.

Through the structured online questionnaire, participating service managers were asked to provide information regarding: the legal status of the managing organization; level of professionalization (number of professional staff and contractual arrangements); funding sources; services delivered; user flows in 2021; demographic characteristics of users; most recurrent needs; unmet needs; strategies or additional services required to address existing limitations; and, finally, evaluation practices adopted to monitor the effectiveness and impact of their activities.

Although the data refer only to a subset of services operating in the Roman territory, they typologically reflect the variety of available services and have generated significant findings with regard to monitoring the functioning of interventions (see section 6.2; Di Censi & Mauceri, 2024).

4.4.3. Reconstructing the Service Network

The subsequent procedural step consisted of conducting a Social Network Analysis (SNA) of the organizations working with people experiencing homelessness in the city of Rome (Deriu & Gallo, 2024). Network analysis provides valuable insights into patterns of collaboration among organizations and into potential gaps within the support network.[6]

The SNA was carried out through 28 telephone interviews with managers of organizations that agreed to participate (out of a total of 51 entities identified among public institutions, third-sector organizations, and parishes providing services to people experiencing homelessness). The interviews were conducted between November 2022 and February 2023.

A structured social network questionnaire was used to collect information on the types of services delivered, the duration of collaborations with other entities (alters), and the intensity of such collaborations. The overall network was subsequently reconstructed through the aggregation of the 28 ego-centered networks collected during the survey (see section 6.3).

4.4.4. Case Studies

In order to further explore typical service delivery strategies, qualitative case studies were conducted in April 2023 through in-depth interviews with service managers and focus groups with frontline staff. The case studies focused on two organizations operating in the city of Rome that differed significantly in their intervention methodologies and occupied central or otherwise prominent positions within the relational network reconstructed in the previous phase.[7]

The first case study examined the Diocesan Caritas of Rome (see Bruni & Schirmo, 2024), the first religiously affiliated nonprofit organization to provide services for people experiencing homelessness in the city. Over time, it has developed a diversified service provision in response to the increasing heterogeneity of needs.

The second case study focused on Europe Consulting (see Kopsaj & Radicchi, 2024), a more recent organization established approximately twenty years ago. Since its foundation, it has adopted an innovative and dynamic paradigm in both service delivery and organizational practices, relying on a fully digitized system for monitoring user flows and the characteristics of people experiencing homelessness.

The case studies completed the research cycle by enabling a focused analysis of best practices. Together with the other findings of the study, they contributed to initiating a process of reflection within the research team aimed at identifying guidelines to support services dedicated to people experiencing homelessness in consolidating intervention practices capable of responding more effectively to the diverse manifestations of extreme poverty (see section 7).

The integration of the different procedural phases comprising the research design allowed for a multilevel reading of extreme poverty, combining micro-individual, meso-relational, and macro-contextual levels of analysis (Mauceri, 2012, 2019). It also provided the empirical framework underpinning the reflection on the role of the Anthology platform as a digital welfare infrastructure.

5. ESTIMATING THE NUMBER OF PEOPLE EXPERIENCING HOMELESSNESS IN THE CITY OF ROME THROUGH THE CAPTURE-RECAPTURE METHOD

Estimating the size of the population experiencing homelessness constitutes both a technical and political prerequisite for service planning. Yet this task presents structural difficulties related to population mobility, fragmented institutional contacts, and the contested definitional boundaries of homelessness itself. In order to delimit the scope of observation, the approach adopted here relies on operational definitions consolidated at the European and statistical-administrative levels, with particular reference to the ETHOS Light classification and to the measurement framework developed at the European Union (EU) level (Edgar et al., 2007), as well as to the guidelines that have progressively informed the standardization of homelessness measurement.

At the national level, the analysis focuses on individuals who "do not have a dwelling or are in a situation of housing precariousness", including those sleeping rough or in makeshift shelters, those hosted in night shelters or temporary residential facilities, and those using soup kitchens and low-threshold services, in line with the operational definition adopted in official surveys (Istat, 2014, p. 9). This delimitation is necessary because it directly affects both dataset construction and the interpretation of estimates. A service-based estimate of observed contacts can approximate observed demand, but it does not automatically coincide with the entire population experiencing severe housing exclusion. It necessarily includes some components of the phenomenon while underrepresenting others.

In the present case, the main methodological challenge derives from the nature of the information source. The analysis is based on an administrative service archive: the database of the Social Operations Room of Roma Capitale, whose records are managed through the Anthology platform. Anthology provided the digital infrastructure through which contacts, interventions, and repeated reports concerning people experiencing homelessness within the municipal territory were recorded, organized, and made available for statistical processing. In the construction of the estimate, the platform was therefore not treated as a mere administrative repository, but as the operational information system that enabled the reconstruction of individual contact histories over time, the identification of repeated observations, and the deduplication procedures required to apply a single-source capture-recapture approach. Unlike classical capture-recapture designs, which are based on the cross-matching of multiple independent lists, this application relies on a single administrative source – the Anthology-based archive of the Social Operations Room – with repeated observations over time. An individual may appear more than once within a defined reference period, for example one year, and the distribution of the number of observed "captures" – one, two, three, and so forth – can be used to estimate the proportion of individuals who were never captured by the system, namely the unobserved zeros.

This approach is consistent with the literature on hidden populations, which supports the use of single-source models when information is available only through an administrative system and observation occurs through repeated counts (Mascioli & Rossi, 2006; Rossi, 1995, 2001). Operationally, the statistical unit is the identified individual, within the limits of identification and deduplication procedures, while the variable of interest is the count X, namely the number of times the individual was observed, contacted, or registered during the reference period.

Under the assumptions of a closed population – that is, the absence of substantial net inflows or outflows during the period under consideration – and homogeneous capture probabilities, X may be modeled using a Poisson distribution with parameter λ. However, since individuals with $X = 0$ are by definition not observed, the model effectively employed is a zero-truncated Poisson distribution, in which probabilities are conditional on the event $X > 0$. In intuitive terms, the model captures only individuals who have had at least one contact with the service system. Estimating the total population size N therefore requires indirectly reconstructing the number of individuals who had no recorded contact with services, by exploiting the shape of the recapture distribution among observed individuals.

The adopted procedure uses method-of-moments estimators and estimators based on ratios between the first frequency classes, for example between individuals observed only once and those observed twice. The equation linking these ratios to the parameter λ is solved numerically; in the original study, this was done using the secant method, in order to obtain a stable estimate of λ, and therefore of P(X = 0) and N. This step is crucial because, once λ has been estimated, the probability of non-capture, P(X = 0) = e^−λ, makes it possible to infer the overall population size, including both observed and unobserved individuals.

It is important, however, to stress that the assumption of homogeneous capture probabilities is rarely fully satisfied in social contexts. Some individuals have a higher probability of contact with the service system because of chronicity, proximity to service hubs, health-related needs, or greater institutional visibility. Others remain systematically less likely to be intercepted because of invisibility, stigma, self-exclusion, distrust of institutions, or territorial mobility. To address such heterogeneity, the literature proposes robust non-parametric estimators that partly correct for the underestimation produced by unequal catchability. Among these, the Chao estimator (Chao, 1987) and the Zelterman estimator (Zelterman, 1988) are frequently used because they rely on information from the first frequency classes and are less sensitive to long tails and extreme recapture patterns.

In this application, the estimate is therefore presented as a plausible range between a more parametric estimator, based on the zero-truncated Poisson model, and robust estimators, namely Chao and Zelterman. This strategy allows the analysis to incorporate, at least partially, the uncertainty generated by heterogeneity in capture probabilities.

From a data perspective, the analysis is based on the period 2014–2022 (Tables 1 and 2). For each year, the distribution of captures per individual was constructed, and the re-reporting rate – the proportion of individuals observed more than once during the reference period – was calculated. The results show a substantially stable re-reporting rate, ranging between 0.44 and 0.50, with an average of approximately 0.47. This indicates a substantial component of repeated contact with the service system, which may, from a policy perspective, be interpreted as a signal of chronicity, recurrence of need, or difficulty in achieving stable housing autonomy.

The total population estimates are relatively stable in the pre-pandemic period, although they show a downward trend between 2017 and 2019. According to the Chao estimator, the estimated population ranges from 14,784 individuals in 2016 to 11,954 in 2019. According to the Zelterman estimator, the corresponding range is between 16,871 in 2016 and 13,801 in 2019. The year 2020 shows a marked increase, with estimates rising to 19,377 according to Chao and 22,338 according to Zelterman. This increase should be interpreted cautiously, as it may reflect a combination of real changes in housing exclusion, pandemic-related disruptions, changes in urban mobility, operational reorganization of services, and modifications in access or registration routines. After a decline in 2021, the estimates increase again in 2022, reaching 15,645 according to Chao and 18,136 according to Zelterman.

*Table 1. Estimated size of the population of people experiencing homelessness in the Municipality of Rome based on the Chao estimator**

Year	$\hat{N}$	LB	UB	$\widehat{SE}$
2014	14,217	13,967	14,725	250
2015	14,390	13,829	14,999	298
2016	14,784	14,281	15,328	267
2017	12,870	12,425	13,354	237
2018	12,835	12,429	13,276	216
2019	11,954	11,544	12,400	218
2020	19,377	18,696	20,109	360
2021	14,135	13,642	14,671	262
2022	15,645	15,142	16,189	267

Source: Authors' elaboration based on Anthology administrative data, Social Operations Room of Roma Capitale.

* $\hat{N}$ represents the estimated total number of people experiencing homelessness during the period (observed + unobserved) obtained through the estimator; LB and UB denote the lower and upper bounds of the confidence interval, respectively; $\widehat{SE}$ is the estimated standard error.

*Table 2. Estimated size of the population of people experiencing homelessness in the Municipality of Rome based on the Zelterman estimator**

Year	$\hat{N}$	LB	UB	$\widehat{SE}$
2014	15,955	15,274	16,689	358
2015	16,703	15,888	17,596	435
2016	16,871	16,138	17,670	390
2017	14,767	14,104	15,495	355
2018	14,585	13,974	15,253	326
2019	13,801	13,175	14,491	335
2020	22,338	21,368	23,388	515
2021	16,773	16,002	17,616	411
2022	18,136	17,375	18,965	405

Source: Authors' elaboration based on Anthology administrative data, Social Operations Room of Roma Capitale.

* $\hat{N}$ represents the estimated total number of people experiencing homelessness during the period (observed + unobserved) obtained through the estimator; LB and UB denote the lower and upper bounds of the confidence interval, respectively; $\widehat{SE}$ is the estimated standard error.

In this perspective, integration with digital welfare tools such as Anthology can improve the reliability of estimates through more accurate deduplication, greater standardization of categories, and better quality of recorded data. It can also facilitate triangulation with other sources, including health records, temporary accommodation data, population registers, and local social service databases. Such triangulation is essential for strengthening the analysis and reducing dependence on a single administrative source.

Finally, it should be emphasized that service-based estimates necessarily capture the population "in relation to" the support system. For planning purposes, they must therefore be interpreted alongside indicators of accessibility, service capacity, dropout rates, effective case management, and the territorial and structural determinants of housing exclusion, including housing costs, in-work poverty, and family vulnerability. Only in this way can measurement avoid becoming self-referential to existing service provision and instead support a broader understanding of unmet need, institutional reach, and the structural conditions that produce homelessness.

6. RESEARCH FINDINGS ON THE SERVICE SYSTEM FOR PEOPLE EXPERIENCING HOMELESSNESS IN THE CITY OF ROME: WEB SURVEY, SOCIAL NETWORK ANALYSIS, AND CASE STUDIES

6.1. Introductory Remarks

This section presents the main empirical findings on the Roman service system, linking service organization, network coordination, and data governance. The aim is not only to describe available services, but to show how the system produces, circulates, and uses information about people experiencing homelessness.

The analysis proceeds along three complementary lines: the web survey reconstructs service provision, user profiles, and unmet needs; Social Network Analysis examines interorganizational collaboration and strategic nodes; the qualitative case studies interpret organizational models and innovation practices. Together, these strands clarify how emergency responses, case management, digital monitoring, and relational work interact in the metropolitan welfare system.

The findings portray a broad and collaborative system, but also reveal persistent fragmentation, uneven professional and digital capacities, and limited integration between low-threshold responses and long-term pathways. Digital welfare appears as a significant yet ambivalent resource: it can strengthen coordination and learning, but only if it is governed so as not to reproduce the visibility biases and asymmetries already present in the service system.

6.2. The Web Survey: Structure of Service Provision, User Profiles, and Unmet Needs

Within the outlined framework, the analysis of services represents a privileged vantage point from which to understand how the urban welfare system concretely responds to extreme poverty. The web survey conducted as part of the research served as a central tool for monitoring the system of services dedicated to people experiencing homelessness in the city of Rome. As noted above, the survey was completed by managers of 46 services out of the 115 identified across the metropolitan area. It made it possible to typologically reconstruct the main organizational characteristics of service provision, the profiles of users reached, and the needs to which the system responds effectively, as well as those that remain structurally unmet. In this sense, the web survey functioned as a bridge between the estimation of potential demand and the analysis of the concrete responses implemented by the service system.

The findings first and foremost provide a clear picture of the overall morphology of service provision. Within the sample of participating services, there is a marked prevalence of low-threshold interventions, such as soup kitchens, night shelters, and street outreach units, aimed at ensuring an immediate response to the primary needs of people experiencing homelessness. These services are fundamental for engaging the most marginalized situations and managing daily emergencies, and they constitute an indispensable component of urban welfare. By contrast, services oriented toward continuous case management, medium- to long-term support, and structured integration between social and health dimensions are numerically more limited. This configuration should not be interpreted as a shortcoming attributable to individual organizations, but rather as the outcome of a systemic arrangement that tends to privilege emergency responses over the construction of stable pathways out of homelessness.

This characteristic of service provision is reflected in the user profiles reached by the services. The data indicate a predominantly male population, with a significant presence of foreign nationals, in line with findings reported by other statistical and administrative sources (Italian Federation of Organizations for People Experiencing Homelessness [fio.PSD], 2017; Istat, 2014, 2022). Access to services frequently appears recurrent and marked by forms of repeated use, confirming the difficulty of interrupting exclusionary trajectories that tend to become chronic over time. Services often engage individuals who move within the system along discontinuous paths, characterized by repeated entries and exits, without necessarily achieving progressive advancement toward greater autonomy. In this respect, the web survey makes visible the tension between the system's capacity to guarantee immediate responses and its more limited impact on the long-term dynamics that sustain persistent vulnerability.

A particularly relevant contribution of the survey concerns the analysis of unmet needs. Among the service managers who participated in the study, the needs most frequently identified as difficult to address include housing hardship, understood not merely as the absence of shelter but as the lack of stable and personalized housing solutions, ongoing economic support, and socio-health integration, particularly with regard to mental health and substance use. These are areas in which the complexity of individual conditions would require strongly integrated interventions capable of overcoming the fragmentation between social services, health services, and labor market policies. The web survey findings show that such needs are neither residual nor marginal; rather, they represent structural nodes that consistently traverse the service system for people experiencing homelessness.

The persistent gap between the multidimensionality of expressed needs and responses organized primarily around sectoral services, often not integrated into unified support pathways, emerges as one of the most significant critical issues. Service responses are frequently constrained by limited resources, rigid institutional frameworks, and uneven distribution of competencies across the territory, making it difficult to construct personalized and continuous support trajectories. Within this framework, interventions tend to concentrate on managing urgency rather than progressively addressing the underlying conditions of exclusion, thereby indirectly contributing to the reproduction of chronicity.

Monitoring and evaluation practices are a critical interface between service provision and data governance. Although many organizations report monitoring activities, these often remain informal, weakly standardized, and oriented toward daily management rather than toward collective outcome learning. The uneven capacity to produce comparable data limits system-level coordination and weakens the possibility of using digital infrastructures as common evaluative resources.

Overall, the web survey shows a system with strong operational commitment and substantial capacity to address primary needs, but also a structural imbalance toward emergency responses. The main governance challenge is to transform fragmented service information into shared knowledge capable of supporting integrated pathways, medium-term planning, and accountability for outcomes.

6.3. The Network of Services for People Experiencing Homelessness: Structure, Relationships, and Coordination Dynamics

Social Network Analysis made it possible to complement the examination of service provision with a relational perspective aimed at understanding how the intervention system addressing people experiencing homelessness operates concretely as a network of interdependent actors. Unlike the web survey, which focused on organizational characteristics and services delivered by individual providers, Social Network Analysis (SNA) enables observation of the system as a whole, highlighting the structure of collaborative relationships, strategic nodes, and potential areas of marginality within the urban welfare system of Rome.

The findings first and foremost depict a broad and extensive network composed of over one hundred nodes, corresponding to entities and organizations that, in various capacities, operate in the field of combating extreme poverty in the metropolitan area of Rome. The overall density of collaborative ties indicates a widespread propensity for network-based work, representing a significant strength of the local service system. Connections among actors go beyond occasional interactions; rather, they form a structured web of relationships that reflects a shared awareness among practitioners of the impossibility of addressing the complexity of needs related to homelessness in isolation (see Figure 1).

Figure 1. Network graph of ego and alter nodes with eigenvector centrality measures

Source: Deriu & Gallo (2024), p. 135.

However, the presence of numerous relationships does not automatically correspond to a high level of integration or systemic coordination. The analysis of the network structure shows that breadth and density coexist with a marked heterogeneity in the positions occupied by different actors. The network does not appear horizontal, but rather internally differentiated, with some nodes occupying central roles and others positioned at the periphery or in marginal locations. In particular, certain long-established organizations and more structurally developed entities occupy highly central positions, functioning as key hubs for the circulation of information and the activation of collaborations among services.

Among these central nodes, the *Sala Operativa Sociale (Social Operations Room) of the Municipality of Rome* emerges as a particularly significant actor, configuring itself as a strategic reference point for coordinating interventions and managing access flows within the service system. Its position within the network reflects its institutional role in linking public and third-sector actors, as well as its function in mediating between demand and service provision. While the centrality of this node contributes to smoother relationships among services, it also highlights a concentration of coordination functions that may generate forms of relational dependency among less structured actors.

Alongside these central nodes, the analysis reveals the presence of a peripheral area within the network, primarily composed of smaller organizations, often characterized by high levels of organizational informality and limited resources. These actors tend to maintain more sporadic and less structured collaborative relationships, resulting in lower levels of integration within the main circuits of the system. Their peripheral position should not be interpreted as a lack of commitment or social relevance, but rather as the outcome of organizational and institutional inequalities that affect their capacity to participate fully in network-based collaboration.

The coexistence of stable, formalized collaborations and more episodic, informal ties constitutes a distinctive feature of the network of services for people experiencing homelessness in Rome. On the one hand, consolidated relationships foster greater continuity of interventions and facilitate coordination among complementary services. On the other hand, the presence of weak and intermittent ties signals the fragility of certain connections and the difficulty of systematically including all actors operating within the territory. In this respect, the network reflects the typical tensions of contemporary urban welfare, in which the plurality of actors simultaneously represents both a resource and a source of fragmentation.

The analysis of collaborative ties also shows that administrative and digital capacities affect actors' positions within the network. Organizations able to collect, manage, and exchange data tend to occupy more central positions, whereas smaller or less formalized entities face greater difficulties in entering coordination circuits.

Digital welfare therefore operates not only as a technical infrastructure, but also as a factor that may redistribute influence, visibility, and power within the service system.

This does not imply that digitalization inevitably increases hierarchy. Rather, the network can become a more inclusive governance infrastructure if digital tools are combined with shared protocols, training, interoperability, and support for peripheral actors. Without these conditions, the system risks depending excessively on a few central nodes and reinforcing asymmetries between well-equipped organizations and less resourced providers.

The Social Network Analysis thus links the empirical findings to the core argument of the chapter: coordination is relational and informational at the same time. The quality of welfare governance depends on the density of collaborative ties, the distribution of network centrality, and the capacity to transform data into collectively usable knowledge rather than into a resource concentrated in a few organizations.

6.4. Case Studies: Organizational Models, Intervention Practices, and Innovation in the Service System

Within the overall research design, the case studies represent an indispensable step for qualitatively deepening the research findings, enabling a more analytical reading of the dynamics that emerged from both the quantitative service analysis and the Social Network Analysis. By examining two organizations occupying strategic positions within the network of services for people experiencing homelessness in the city of Rome, it was possible to investigate more closely the organizational models adopted, the intervention practices developed, and the ways in which these organizations respond to the complexity of users' needs, identifying specific best practices.

The case studies were conducted through in-depth interviews with organizational managers and focus groups with frontline staff, generating rich qualitative material on intervention practices, organizational models, and strategies for addressing the needs of people experiencing homelessness. The selected cases – the *Diocesan Caritas of Rome* and the social cooperative *Europe Consulting Onlus* – were not chosen as representative of the entire system, but rather as salient expressions of two distinct and, in many respects, complementary approaches to addressing extreme poverty in the metropolitan context.

The first case study focuses on the Diocesan Caritas of Rome, one of the most historically significant actors within the landscape of services for people experiencing homelessness. Over time, Caritas has developed a multilevel intervention system that combines first-level reception services and responses to primary needs with more structured support pathways oriented toward social inclusion and the recovery of autonomy. This model is grounded in strong integration among material, relational, and socio-educational dimensions of intervention, enabling the organization to engage a heterogeneous population characterized by diverse trajectories of exclusion.

The in-depth interviews with managers and focus groups with staff highlight that one of the defining features of the Caritas approach lies in its interpretation of homelessness as the outcome of cumulative processes of marginalization rather than as a mere lack of material resources. This perspective translates into particular attention to building trust-based relationships with users and ensuring continuity of intervention, even when pathways are discontinuous or marked by setbacks. The organization's longstanding presence and territorial embeddedness further enable it to act as a coordinating hub among different services, strengthening network coordination and facilitating access to diversified resources for people experiencing homelessness.

The second case study examines Europe Consulting, a more recent organization established in a markedly different context from that in which Caritas developed, and characterized from its inception by a strong orientation toward organizational innovation and process digitalization. Unlike the model embodied by Caritas, Europe Consulting distinguishes itself through the adoption of fully digitalized monitoring and data management tools that allow for tracking user trajectories, analyzing service access flows, and systematically tailoring interventions. This approach facilitates the structured integration of information concerning needs, activated resources, and intervention outcomes, providing a solid knowledge base for the continuous adaptation of operational practices.

The qualitative analysis shows that the intensive use of data does not result in rigid standardization of interventions; rather, it enhances the capacity to modulate responses according to users' individual characteristics. The digitalization of processes makes it possible, at least in part, to overcome the informational fragmentation that often characterizes social work in complex urban contexts, fostering more grounded and informed case management. At the same time, this model requires specific competencies and significant organizational investment, which not all third-sector organizations are able to sustain.

The case also illustrates the ethical ambivalence of digital welfare. Digital monitoring can support continuity, personalization, and organizational learning, but it requires safeguards against over-standardization, excessive dependence on administrative categories, and unequal treatment of users whose needs are less easily captured in administrative data. For this reason, digital case management should be complemented by professional judgment, reflective supervision, and opportunities for user feedback.

The comparison between the two case studies highlights how different organizational models can coexist within the same service system, contributing in complementary ways to addressing the needs of people experiencing homelessness. On the one hand, the Diocesan Caritas of Rome embodies a "historical" model grounded in relational proximity and progressive adaptability, enabling it to engage situations of extreme marginality and ensure continuity even in the most fragile pathways. On the other hand, Europe Consulting represents an example of organizational innovation in which digitalization and systematic data use function as crucial tools for enhancing the effectiveness and personalization of interventions.

Both cases demonstrate that the capacity to respond to the complexity of extreme poverty does not depend on a single factor, but on the integration of organizational resources, professional competencies, and knowledge tools. In particular, the case studies confirm what emerged from the previous analyses: centrality within the service network is not merely a matter of size or institutional visibility, but is closely linked to the ability to act as hubs of coordination and innovation. In this sense, the examined organizations illustrate how certain actors come to function as reference models, influencing the practices and operational modalities of other actors within the system.

Taken together, the case studies show that effective responses to homelessness require the integration of relational proximity, organizational capacity, and responsible data use. Traditional forms of trust-building and innovative digital case management should not be treated as alternatives: the challenge is to combine them within governance arrangements that enhance continuity of care without reducing users to administrative traces.

The results therefore inform the policy discussion developed in the conclusion: improving homelessness governance in Rome requires not only more resources, but also stronger coordination, rights-oriented data governance, and a clearer connection between empirical evidence and strategic decision-making.

7. CONCLUSION AND RECOMMENDATIONS

The findings converge on four main results. First, capture-recapture estimates indicate a sizeable and fluctuating population made visible through the service system, with repeated contacts suggesting chronic or recurrent need. Second, the web survey reveals a service configuration strongly oriented toward low-threshold and emergency responses, while housing, economic support, and socio-health integration remain difficult to address. Third, Social Network Analysis shows a collaborative but internally asymmetrical network, where coordination depends heavily on strategic hubs. Fourth, the case studies demonstrate the complementary value of relational proximity and digital case management (Bruni et al., 2024).

Taken together, these results clarify the chapter's broader contribution beyond the Roman case. Rome exemplifies a wider European tension between the expansion of severe housing exclusion, the fragmentation of urban welfare systems, and the increasing reliance on digital infrastructures for coordination, monitoring, and evidence-informed policy. The case therefore contributes to broader debates on homelessness, datafication, platformization, and the governance of social rights in metropolitan contexts. Its relevance lies not only in the empirical reconstruction of a local service system, but also in the analytical possibility of observing how urban welfare systems produce, organize, and use knowledge about highly vulnerable populations.

A central implication of the analysis is that homelessness should not be governed only as an emergency condition, but as a dynamic process shaped by institutional contacts, interrupted trajectories, unmet needs, and unequal access to rights. From this perspective, the repeated use of services is not simply an indicator of individual vulnerability; it is also a signal of the limited capacity of the system to transform first contact into sustained support, housing stabilization, and social reintegration. This requires shifting the policy focus from episodic assistance to continuity of care, from service availability to service integration, and from administrative monitoring to accountable governance.

A first implication concerns prevention. Primary and secondary prevention should address the factors that precede entry into homelessness – rent arrears beyond tenants' control, evictions, hospital discharge without housing solutions, exit from total institutions, in-work poverty, family breakdown, migration-related vulnerability, and housing cost overburden – through rapid identification, early support, and coordinated social-housing responses. Prevention should not be conceived as a residual policy area, activated only before visible homelessness occurs, but as a structural component of urban welfare. This implies stronger connections between housing policy, income support, health services, employment measures, migration services, and local social work.

A second implication concerns the balance between emergency and long-term intervention. Outreach, soup kitchens, and shelters remain indispensable for engaging the most marginalized situations, but they should be systematically connected to case management, health and mental-health services, income support, and housing-led pathways. Otherwise, emergency responses risk stabilizing users' contact with the system without reducing chronicity. The point is not to oppose emergency and structural interventions, but to redesign their relationship: emergency services should function as gateways into integrated pathways rather than as the main organizational form through which homelessness is managed (Busch-Geertsema et al., 2010).

A third implication concerns housing. In the Roman context, night shelters and temporary accommodation should be rebalanced within a structural strategy aimed at long-term housing access and supported independent living, drawing on housing-led and Housing First evidence while ensuring adequate multidisciplinary support for people with complex needs (Padgett et al., 2016; Tsemberis, 2010; Tsemberis & Eisenberg, 2000; Tsemberis et al., 2004). Housing should be treated not only as an outcome of successful social intervention, but as a precondition for stabilizing health, rebuilding relational ties, restoring agency, and reducing repeated dependence on emergency services. This requires an institutional commitment to affordable housing, supported tenancy, mediation with landlords, and flexible accompaniment after housing placement.

A fourth implication concerns professional and organizational capacity. Continuity of care depends on sustainable caseloads, staff stability, supervision, interdisciplinary protocols, and evidence-oriented professional cultures. Strengthening these conditions is essential for transforming network collaboration into reliable support trajectories (Lamanna et al., 2018; Peters et al., 2022). The analysis suggests that collaboration cannot rely solely on informal ties, professional goodwill, or the strategic role of a few central actors. It requires stable governance arrangements, shared procedures, clear referral mechanisms, interoperable information systems, and institutional spaces where practitioners can jointly interpret complex cases and coordinate interventions.

A fifth implication concerns network governance. The Social Network Analysis shows that the Roman service system is not simply fragmented; it is organized around relational asymmetries that make some actors disproportionately important for coordination. This configuration can be productive when strategic hubs facilitate circulation of information, referrals, and organizational learning. However, it also creates vulnerability if coordination depends excessively on a limited number of actors or on informal relational capital. A more resilient welfare network should therefore combine hub-based coordination with distributed responsibilities, formalized collaboration agreements, and mechanisms that allow peripheral or smaller organizations to participate in decision-making and knowledge production.

Finally, the information infrastructure should be treated as a governed public good rather than as a purely administrative asset. This requires:

(a) improving data quality, deduplication, and consistency checks across services;
(b) defining shared taxonomies that are analytically useful without becoming rigid or stigmatizing classifications;
(c) institutionalizing process and outcome indicators that connect emergency access, continuity of care, housing trajectories, and unmet needs;
(d) integrating data sources and promoting interoperability while enforcing purpose limitation, minimization, access control, and traceability;
(e) using digital tools such as Anthology to sustain an institutional learning cycle consistent with evaluation criteria and capable of making policy effects verifiable (OECD, 2019);

(f) introducing periodic ethical and organizational audits to detect visibility bias, exclusionary effects, or unequal treatment generated by administrative routines;
(g) complementing administrative data with qualitative evidence and structured opportunities for service users to express needs, experiences, and perceived barriers to access.

This last point is particularly important. Administrative and service-based data are indispensable for planning, estimation, monitoring, and accountability, but they do not exhaust the social reality of homelessness. They capture individuals only when they become visible to services, and they risk underrepresenting those who are disconnected, distrustful, undocumented, mobile, or unable to comply with institutional access requirements. For this reason, digital welfare infrastructures should be accompanied by participatory and qualitative forms of knowledge production. The voices of service users are essential for understanding not only what services provide, but also how they are experienced, where barriers emerge, and which institutional practices may unintentionally reproduce exclusion.

The Roman case also points to a broader conceptual issue: data governance is not a neutral technical layer merely added to welfare systems, but one of the ways through which welfare systems define needs, classify subjects, allocate attention, and construct institutional priorities. Digital platforms can enhance coordination, transparency, and learning, but they can also narrow the field of visibility if categories are too rigid, if indicators privilege what is easily measurable, or if data are used without reflexive attention to power asymmetries. For this reason, the digitalization of homelessness services should be embedded within a rights-oriented framework that connects information management to substantive improvements in access, continuity, housing stability, and social recognition.

From a policy perspective, the challenge is therefore not simply to produce more data, but to produce better-governed data: data that are accurate, interoperable, ethically managed, analytically meaningful, and institutionally usable. Evidence-informed policy should not be reduced to administrative optimization. It should support collective learning, make unmet needs visible, reveal gaps in the service network, and help decision-makers evaluate whether interventions are reducing homelessness or merely managing its most visible manifestations.

In conclusion, an effective urban system for addressing homelessness requires an integrated strategy combining prevention, housing access, multidisciplinary case management, network coordination, and rights-oriented data governance. The Roman case shows that digital welfare can become a lever for institutional learning only when data are embedded in accountable organizational arrangements and connected to concrete improvements in access, continuity, and outcomes for people experiencing homelessness. The broader lesson is that digital infrastructures should be evaluated not only by their capacity to record and process information, but by their ability to support more equitable, coordinated, and transformative forms of urban welfare governance.

REFERENCES

Accorinti, M., Mirabile, M. L., Romano, M. C., & Sgritta, G. B. (1998). Profili di povertà estrema: Dieci anni di attività assistenziale della Caritas diocesana di Roma (Diocesan Caritas of Rome). *L'Assistenza Sociale*, *1*(January/March), 177–196.

Alston, P. (2019). *Digital welfare states and human rights: Report of the Special Rapporteur on extreme poverty and human rights* (A/74/493). United Nations General Assembly. https://digitallibrary.un.org/record/3834146

Amaturo, E., & Punziano, G. (2016). *I mixed methods nella ricerca sociale*. Carocci.

Anand, S., & Sen, A. (1997). Concepts of human development and poverty: A multidimensional perspective. In *Human development papers 1997: Poverty and human development* (pp. 1–20). United Nations Development Programme., https://digitallibrary.un.org/record/750303

Archer, M. (2006). *La conversazione interiore: Come nasce l'agire sociale*. Erickson.

Atkinson, A. B. (2003). Multidimensional deprivation: Contrasting social welfare and counting approaches. *The Journal of Economic Inequality*, *1*(1), 51–65. DOI: 10.1023/A:1023903525276

Berzano, L. (1987). Uomini senza territorio. *Sisifo*, *11*, 15–19.

Berzano, L. (1992). *Aree di devianza*. Il Segnalibro.

Binario 95. (2021, November 26). Roma: la mappatura dei servizi in città per le persone senza dimora. https://www.binario95.it/roma-mappatura-servizi-per-persone-senza-dimora-emergenza-covid-19/

Bruni, C., Cortese, C., Di Censi, L., & Mauceri, S. (2024). Un paradigma d'intervento in mutamento. In Mauceri, S., & Di Censi, L. (Eds.), *Povertà estreme. Un'analisi sul sistema dei servizi per le persone senza dimora a Roma* (pp. 232–242). FrancoAngeli.

Bruni, C., & Schirmo, E. (2024). Studio di caso: i servizi della Caritas diocesana di Roma. In Mauceri, S., & Di Censi, L. (Eds.), *Povertà estreme. Un'analisi sul sistema dei servizi per le persone senza dimora a Roma* (pp. 189–209). FrancoAngeli.

Busch-Geertsema, V., Edgar, B., O'Sullivan, E., & Pleace, N. (2010). *Homelessness and homeless policies in Europe: Lessons from research*. FEANTSA. https://ec.europa.eu/social/BlobServlet?docId=6442&langId=en

Calvaruso, C., & Scalise, M. M. (1987). *Essere barboni a Roma*. Labos.

Campedelli, M., & Vesan, P. (2023). Welfare digitalizzato, welfare digitale e i nuovi rischi sociali digitali: Un'introduzione. *Politiche Sociali / Social Policies, 10*(2), 169–192. https://doi.org/DOI: 10.7389/108019

Caritas Ambrosiana (Ed.). (2008). *Milano solidale: Temi e prospettive di intervento con gli ultimi*. Caritas Ambrosiana.

Cesareo, V. (Ed.). (2005). *Ricomporre la vita: Gli adulti giovani in Italia*. Carocci.

Chao, A. (1987). Estimating the population size for capture-recapture data with unequal catchability. *Biometrics, 43*(4), 783–791. DOI: 10.2307/2531532 PMID: 3427163

Comunità di Sant'Egidio. (2021). DOVE mangiare dormire lavarsi [Mobile app]. Google Play. https://play.google.com/store/apps/details?id=com.segidio.solidarieta

Creswell, J. W., & Plano Clark, V. L. (2011). *Designing and conducting mixed methods research* (2nd ed.). Sage.

Dencik, L., Hintz, A., Redden, J., & Treré, E. (2019). Exploring data justice: Conceptions, applications and directions. *Information Communication and Society, 22*(7), 873–881. DOI: 10.1080/1369118X.2019.1606268

Deriu, F., & Gallo, R. (2024). La rete degli attori territoriali operanti per la prevenzione e il contrasto della povertà estrema a Roma: efficacia e prospettive di miglioramento. In Mauceri, S., & Di Censi, L. (Eds.), *Povertà estreme. Un'analisi sul sistema dei servizi per le persone senza dimora a Roma* (pp. 137–160). FrancoAngeli.

Di Censi, L. (2024). La popolazione senza dimora nella città di Roma: una stima della numerosità. In Mauceri, S., & Di Censi, L. (Eds.), *Povertà estreme. Un'analisi sul sistema dei servizi per le persone senza dimora a Roma* (pp. 45–65). FrancoAngeli.

Di Censi, L., & Mauceri, S. (2024). I servizi per le persone senza dimora nell'area metropolitana: risposte istituzionali e informali. In Mauceri, S., & Di Censi, L. (Eds.), *Povertà estreme. Un'analisi sul sistema dei servizi per le persone senza dimora a Roma* (pp. 106–136). FrancoAngeli.

Edgar, B., Harrison, M., Watson, P., & Busch-Geertsema, V. (2007). *Measurement of homelessness at European Union level*. European Commission. https://ec.europa.eu/employment_social/social_inclusion/docs/2007/study_homelessness_en.pdf

Eubanks, V. (2018). *Automating inequality: How high-tech tools profile, police, and punish the poor*. St. Martin's Press.

European Foundation for the Improvement of Living and Working Conditions. (2020). *Living, working and COVID-19*. Publications Office of the European Union. https://assets.eurofound.europa.eu/f/279033/5e54520687/ef20059en.pdf

European Federation of National Organisations Working with the Homeless. (2005). ETHOS: European typology of homelessness and housing exclusion. https://www.feantsa.org/download/ethos2484215748748239888.pdf

Fitzpatrick, S., Watts, B., Pawson, H., Bramley, G., Wood, J., Stephens, M., & Blenkinsopp, J. (2021). *The homelessness monitor: England 2021*. Crisis. https://www.crisis.org.uk/media/244629/crisis-england-monitor-2021.pdf

Gui, L. (Ed.). (1995). *L'utente che non c'è: Emarginazione grave, persone senza dimora e servizi sociali*. FrancoAngeli.

Human Rights Council. (2012). *Guiding principles on extreme poverty and human rights (A/HRC/21/39)*. United Nations. https://www.ohchr.org/sites/default/files/Documents/HRBodies/HRCouncil/RegularSession/Session21/A-HRC-21-39_en.pdf

Italian Federation of Organizations for People Experiencing Homelessness. (2017). Homelessness in Italy: Policy, people and services.

Italian National Institute of Statistics. (2014). *La ricerca nazionale sulla condizione delle persone senza dimora in Italia. Anno 2013*. https://www.istat.it/it/files/2014/06/17915_Senza_dimora.pdf

Italian National Institute of Statistics. (2020). *La domanda e l'offerta di servizi sociali e socio-sanitari*.

Italian National Institute of Statistics. (2022). *Censimento della popolazione e delle abitazioni: Popolazione residente e dinamica demografica. Anno 2021*. https://www.istat.it/it/files/2022/12/CENSIMENTO-E-DINAMICA-DEMOGRAFICA-2021.pdf

Kitchin, R. (2014). *The data revolution: Big data, open data, data infrastructures and their consequences*. SAGE Publications.

Kopsaj, V., & Radicchi, A. (2024). Europe Consulting Onlus: un impegno tangibile per il benessere sociale e l'inclusione. In Mauceri, S., & Di Censi, L. (Eds.), *Povertà estreme. Un'analisi sul sistema dei servizi per le persone senza dimora a Roma* (pp. 210–231). FrancoAngeli.

Lamanna, D., Stergiopoulos, V., Durbin, J., O'Campo, P., Poremski, D., & Tepper, J. (2018). Promoting continuity of care for homeless adults with unmet health needs: The role of brief interventions. *Health & Social Care in the Community*, *26*(1), 56–64. DOI: 10.1111/hsc.12461 PMID: 28569397

Landuzzi, C., & Pieretti, G. (2006). *Servizio sociale e povertà estreme: Accompagnamento sociale e persone senza dimora*. FrancoAngeli.

Martini, A., & Sisti, C. (1999). *La valutazione come strumento di programmazione*. Città Studi Edizioni.

Mascioli, F., & Rossi, C. (2006). Il metodo della cattura-ricattura: Un esperimento didattico tra matematica e scienze naturali. *Induzioni*, *33*(2), 31–49.

Mauceri, S. (2012). Per una survey integrata e multilivello. Le lezioni dimenticate della Columbia School. *Sociologia e Ricerca Sociale*, *99*(99), 22–64. DOI: 10.3280/SR2012-099003

Mauceri, S. (2019). *Qualità nella quantità. La survey research nell'era dei Mixed Methods*. FrancoAngeli.

Mauceri, S. (2024). Il disegno di ricerca. In Mauceri, S., & Di Censi, L. (Eds.), *Povertà estreme. Un'analisi sul sistema dei servizi per le persone senza dimora a Roma* (pp. 37–44). FrancoAngeli.

Mauceri, S., & Di Censi, L. (Eds.). (2024). *Povertà estreme. Un'analisi sul sistema dei servizi per le persone senza dimora a Roma*. FrancoAngeli. https://series.francoangeli.it/index.php/oa/catalog/book/1151

Mingione, E. (Ed.). (1996). *Urban poverty and the underclass: A reader*. Blackwell. DOI: 10.1002/9780470712900

Organisation for Economic Co-operation and Development. (2019). Better criteria for better evaluation: Revised evaluation criteria definitions and principles for use. https://www.oecd.org/content/dam/oecd/en/publications/reports/2019/12/better-criteria-for-better-evaluation_f7a307eb/15a9c26b-en.pdf[REMOVED HYPERLINK FIELD]

Padgett, D. K., Henwood, B. F., & Tsemberis, S. J. (2016). *Housing first: Ending homelessness, transforming systems, and changing lives*. Oxford University Press.

Pellegrino, M., & Verzieri, V. (Eds.). (1991). *Né tetto né legge: L'emarginazione grave, le nuove povertà, i "senza fissa dimora"*. Edizioni Gruppo Abele.

Peters, L., Hobson, C. W., & Samuel, V. (2022). A systematic review and meta-synthesis of qualitative studies that investigate the emotional experiences of staff working in homeless settings. *Health & Social Care in the Community, 30*(1), 58–72. DOI: 10.1111/hsc.13502 PMID: 34255385

Radicchi, A. (2024). Appendice - Anthology: Help different. In S. Mauceri & L. Di Censi (Eds.), *Povertà estreme. Un'analisi sul sistema dei servizi per le persone senza dimora a Roma*. FrancoAngeli. https://series.francoangeli.it/index.php/oa/catalog/book/1151

Redden, J., Dencik, L., & Warne, H. (2020). Datafied child welfare services: Unpacking politics, economics and power. *Policy Studies, 41*(5), 507–526. DOI: 10.1080/01442872.2020.1724928

Rossi, C. (1995). Evaluating world drug policies: Towards a cost-effectiveness analysis of initiatives undertaken. *The International Journal on Drug Policy, 6*(4), 238–242.

Rossi, C. (2001). Using available data with dynamic models to estimate the extent of problem drug use. In *Modelling drug use: Methods to quantify and understand hidden processes* (EMCDDA Scientific Monograph Series No. 6, pp. 67–90). European Monitoring Centre for Drugs and Drug Addiction. https://www.euda.europa.eu/system/files/publications/922/Monograph6_159816.pdf

Scriven, M. (1967). The methodology of evaluation. In Tyler, R. W., Gagné, R. M., & Scriven, M. (Eds.), *Perspectives of curriculum evaluation* (pp. 39–83). American Educational Research Association.

Taylor, L. (2017). What is data justice? The case for connecting digital rights and freedoms globally. *Big Data & Society, 4*(2), 1–14. DOI: 10.1177/2053951717736335

Tsemberis, S. (2010). *Housing first: The Pathways model to end homelessness for people with mental illness and addiction*. Hazelden.

Tsemberis, S., & Eisenberg, R. F. (2000). Pathways to Housing: Supported housing for street-dwelling homeless individuals with psychiatric disabilities. *Psychiatric Services (Washington, D.C.), 51*(4), 487–493. DOI: 10.1176/appi.ps.51.4.487 PMID: 10737824

Tsemberis, S., Gulcur, L., & Nakae, M. (2004). Housing First, consumer choice, and harm reduction for homeless individuals with a dual diagnosis. *American Journal of Public Health, 94*(4), 651–656. DOI: 10.2105/AJPH.94.4.651 PMID: 15054020

van Dijck, J., Poell, T., & de Waal, M. (2018). *The platform society: Public values in a connective world*. Oxford University Press. DOI: 10.1093/oso/9780190889760.001.0001

Zelterman, D. (1988). Robust estimation in truncated discrete distributions with application to capture-recapture experiments. *Journal of Statistical Planning and Inference*, *18*(2), 225–237. DOI: 10.1016/0378-3758(88)90007-9

ENDNOTES

1 For example, women are more frequently beneficiaries of childcare services, basic social services, and socio-educational services. Men, by contrast, are more commonly represented among users of services for people experiencing homelessness, people who use drugs, and persons with disabilities.

2 The platform operates at multiple territorial levels. At the local level, Anthology is listed among the tools used to manage several services of the Department of Social Policies of the Municipality of Rome, supporting a broad network of facilities and service points (including Help Centers, night and day shelters, soup kitchens, and street outreach units) contracted with the administration; it also feeds the Osservatorio Cittadino sulle Marginalità (City Observatory on Marginality [OCM]), which gathers data from more than 150 contracted services. At the national level, on behalf of Ferrovie dello Stato Italiane (Italian State Railways) it supports the

3 Osservatorio Nazionale della Solidarietà nelle Stazioni Italiane (National Observatory on Solidarity in Italian Railway Stations [ONDS]), which analyses the activity of 20 Help Centers in the main Italian cities. Alongside these consolidated contexts, the network of services managed through Anthology is also described as being piloted in other municipal administrations beyond Rome.

4 The incidence in the Lombardy capital is 23.7%, representing a slight decrease compared to 27.5% in 2011. Palermo ranks third among Italian municipalities in terms of the number of people experiencing homelessness (5.7%, down from 8% in 2011), followed by Florence (3.9%), Turin (3.4%), Naples (3.1%, up from 1.9% in 2011), and Bologna (2%).

5 The data presented in section 6 derive from a re-elaboration of the empirical research findings published in Mauceri & Di Censi, 2024, to which reference is also made for a detailed description of the research design. See Di Censi and Mauceri (2024) for further insights into the findings related to the web survey.

6 A detailed discussion of the network structure, the metrics employed, and the data collection and analytical procedures is provided in Deriu and Gallo (2024).

7 See Bruni & Schirmo (2024) and Kopsaj & Radicchi (2024) for a detailed discussion of the selected organizational contexts, the research procedures, and the characteristics of the empirical material collected.

Chapter 11
Datafication and Digital Welfare:
Public Perceptions and the Legitimacy of Artificial Intelligence in Europe

Gianmaria Bottoni
http://orcid.org/0000-0002-1930-099X
University of Naples Federico II, Italy

Ferdinando Iazzetta
http://orcid.org/0000-0002-5641-8823
University of Naples Federico II, Italy

ABSTRACT

European welfare systems are undergoing a profound transformation driven by the integration of digital technologies, and artificial intelligence into public administration. This shift reflects processes of datafication, through which welfare increasingly operates as a sociotechnical system mediated by algorithms and digital platforms. While these innovations promise greater efficiency, predictive capacity, and resource optimization, they also raise concerns about opacity, surveillance, and inequality in access to social rights. The chapter examines an often-overlooked dimension of welfare digitalization: citizens' perceptions of artificial intelligence. Drawing on comparative data from Eurobarometer, it analyzes how attitudes toward AI vary across European countries. The findings reveal that public perceptions are structured around three main dimensions: technological optimism, concerns about automation-related job risks, and perceived digital skills. The results also highlight significant cross-national differences linked to institutional trust and socio-economic conditions.

DOI: 10.4018/979-8-3373-8423-8.ch011

1. INTRODUCTION: DATAFICATION, ARTIFICIAL INTELLIGENCE, AND THE SOCIOTECHNICAL TRANSFORMATION OF WELFARE

In recent years, European welfare systems have undergone a significant transformation driven by the increasing integration of digital technologies, data-driven infrastructures, and automated decision-making systems into public administration processes. This transformation is often interpreted as part of a broader process of datafication of society, through which social activities, institutional interactions, and collective needs are progressively translated into digital data that can be collected, analyzed, and used to inform public decision-making (Kitchin, 2017; Couldry & Mejias, 2019). At the same time, numerous studies have emphasized how the growing centrality of digital platforms is reshaping the functioning of public institutions, giving rise to what van Dijck, Poell, and de Waal (2018) describe as a platform society, in which digital infrastructures and algorithmic systems become structural components of contemporary governance. Within this context, welfare can no longer be interpreted exclusively as a redistributive system based on monetary transfers or social services; rather, it increasingly emerges as a sociotechnical infrastructure mediated by data, algorithms, and digital platforms. Artificial intelligence emerges in this context as one of the key tools through which public administrations seek to improve their capacity to predict, classify, and manage social needs. Data analytics systems, predictive models, and automated decision-making tools are increasingly employed to identify at-risk groups, monitor beneficiaries of social programs, and optimize the allocation of public resources (Margetts & Dorobantu, 2019). However, these transformations cannot be understood as merely technical innovations. As emphasized in the literature on critical data studies, processes of datafication involve a broader reconfiguration of the relationships between citizens, institutions, and digital infrastructures (Couldry & Mejias, 2019). Algorithms used in public contexts are not neutral tools. Rather, they incorporate classificatory categories, decision-making criteria, and normative assumptions that can profoundly influence access to social rights and public resources (Kitchin, 2017; Pasquale, 2015). In this sense, the introduction of algorithmic technologies into welfare policies may generate new opportunities for administrative efficiency and service personalization, while simultaneously producing new forms of institutional opacity, surveillance, and social inequality. In response to these developments, a growing body of literature has begun to examine the political and social implications of the digitalization of public policies. Recent studies have shown how the automation of welfare systems can contribute to redefining the boundaries of social citizenship, introducing new forms of classification and management of citizens based on data and algorithmic models (Eubanks, 2018; O'Neil, 2016). From this perspective, the digitalization of welfare increasingly appears as a field of tension between technological innovation, public governance, and social justice. Within this debate, the present chapter analyzes a dimension that has often been overlooked in discussions of welfare digitalization: citizens' perceptions and attitudes toward artificial intelligence and digital technologies. While much of the existing literature has focused on technical infrastructures, policy design, or the regulatory and ethical dimensions of algorithmic governance, less attention has been devoted to the ways in which these transformations are perceived, interpreted, and evaluated by citizens. Existing studies on public attitudes toward artificial intelligence have primarily examined issues such as technological trust, perceptions of automation, and the social acceptance of algorithmic systems (Araujo et al., 2020; Helberger, Araujo, & de Vreese, 2020; Zhang & Dafoe, 2019). By contrast, this chapter interprets public perceptions of AI as a constitutive dimension of the legitimacy of digital welfare and algorithmic governance. As studies on technological governance suggest, the sustainability of digital innovations within public institutions depends not only on technical efficiency, but also on the degree of trust, understanding, and social acceptance they are able to generate (Jasanoff, 2016; Shin, 2020; Starke & Lünich, 2020; Lee, 2018). In the context of welfare governance, this issue becomes particularly relevant because the use of algorithmic systems increasingly affects access to social rights, public resources, and administrative decision-making processes. From this perspective, the chapter examines European citizens' attitudes toward artificial intelligence using comparative data from Special Eurobarometer 101.4 – Artificial Intelligence and the Future of Work. The aim is not to assess the technical effectiveness of digital technologies in public policy, but rather to explore the structure of social perceptions of AI and to understand how these perceptions contribute to shaping the conditions under which digital welfare gains or loses legitimacy. The chapter is structured as follows. The next section examines the role of public perceptions and technological trust in processes of digital governance, discussing contributions from the literature on digital inequalities, the sociology of innovation, and studies of trust in technological institutions. The subsequent section then analyzes European citizens' attitudes toward artificial intelligence using comparative data from Special Eurobarometer 101.4 – Artificial Intelligence and the Future of Work. Finally, the concluding section discusses the implications of the findings for the broader debate on the digitalization of welfare and the governance of artificial intelligence in public institutions.

2. PUBLIC PERCEPTIONS, TECHNOLOGICAL TRUST, AND THE LEGITIMACY OF ALGORITHMIC GOVERNANCE

If the digitalization of welfare can be understood as a transformation of the administrative infrastructures of the state, it cannot be fully grasped without considering the dimension of public perceptions. Digital technologies, and artificial intelligence in particular, do not enter institutions as neutral tools nor as innovations that impose themselves automatically due to their technical efficiency. Rather, they are socially interpreted, debated, contested, and legitimized within specific cultural and institutional contexts. From this perspective, the adoption of AI in welfare systems depends not only on its operational performance but also on how citizens and social groups perceive its usefulness, risks, fairness, and controllability.

From this perspective, the diffusion of artificial intelligence within welfare systems raises not only technical or administrative questions, but also broader issues of institutional legitimacy. The implementation of algorithmic systems in public governance requires forms of social acceptance and public trust that cannot be taken for granted. In welfare contexts especially, where automated systems may affect access to rights, benefits, and public resources, citizens' perceptions become crucial in shaping the legitimacy of digital governance. Consequently, public attitudes toward AI should not be interpreted merely as opinions about technological innovation, but rather as indicators of the social conditions under which algorithmic welfare systems are perceived as fair, acceptable, and trustworthy. Studies in science and technology studies (STS) have long shown that technical innovations are inseparable from the social processes that make them acceptable, understandable, and governable (Jasanoff, 2004; Jasanoff, 2016; Winner, 1980; Bijker, Hughes, & Pinch, 1987). Similarly, more recent literature on artificial intelligence emphasizes that the key issue is not only *what algorithms do*, but also *how they are perceived, by whom*, and *under which social and normative conditions* (Lee, 2018; Araujo et al., 2020; Helberger, Araujo, & de Vreese, 2020; Shin, 2020; Shin, 2021). This shift in focus, from technical performance to the social legitimacy of AI, is particularly relevant in the context of public policy. When algorithmic systems are used to classify users, assess needs, allocate priorities, or support high-stakes decision-making, their acceptance cannot be taken for granted. Empirical research shows that citizens evaluate AI not only in terms of promised efficiency but also in relation to criteria such as fairness, accountability, explainability, privacy, and human oversight (Mittelstadt et al., 2016; Diakopoulos, 2016; Ananny & Crawford, 2018; Busuioc, 2020; Shin & Park, 2019; Starke & Lünich, 2020). In this sense, algorithmic governance emerges as a space of negotiation between innovation and normativity: it is not sufficient for a system to function; its operation must also be perceived as fair, understandable, and contestable.

It is precisely on this terrain that the literature on ethical AI and AI governance has increasingly focused, showing that principles such as fairness, transparency, accountability, privacy, safety, robustness, and human agency are not merely discursive embellishments but have become central conditions for the social and political acceptability of AI systems (Floridi et al., 2018; Jobin, Ienca, & Vayena, 2019; Hagendorff, 2020; European Commission, 2019; OECD, 2021; Berendt, 2019).

A key point for the purposes of this chapter is that these principles do not operate solely at the regulatory or institutional level; they also influence how citizens form their opinions about technology. The literature shows that public perceptions of AI tend to be structured around a tension between promise and threat. On the one hand, AI is associated with efficiency, speed, precision, innovation, service improvement, economic growth, and support for complex decision-making (Pew Research Center, 2018; Zhang & Dafoe, 2019; Cave, Coughlan, & Dihal, 2019; Merenkov, Campa, & Dronishinets, 2020). On the other hand, the same technology is perceived as a source of risks, including job displacement, surveillance, opacity, automated errors, discrimination, erosion of human autonomy, concentration of informational power, and reduced political accountability (O'Neil, 2016; Pasquale, 2015; Eubanks, 2018; Noble, 2018; Benjamin, 2019; Liang & Lee, 2017; Kieslich, Lünich, & Marcinkowski, 2021). The result is a configuration that can be interpreted as technological ambivalence: AI is neither simply embraced nor rejected but rather supported conditionally, within frameworks of selective trust and normative caution.

This ambivalence is also well documented in studies on trust in algorithms and the dynamics of algorithm appreciation and algorithm aversion. Some research shows that individuals may attribute greater neutrality and consistency to algorithmic systems compared to human decision-makers, especially in contexts where bias, favoritism, or corruption are suspected (Logg, Minson, & Moore, 2019; Miller, 2018; Köbis, Starke, & Rahwan, 2021). Other studies, however, demonstrate that trust can quickly decline when systems make errors, appear opaque, or limit human control (Dietvorst, Simmons, & Massey, 2015; Robinette, Howard, & Wagner, 2017; Salem et al., 2015).

Trust in algorithms is therefore neither unconditional nor stable. Rather, it depends on the context of use, the normative expectations surrounding the technology, and the possibility of attributing responsibility in cases of harm. In particular, several studies show that explainability, accountability, and fairness strengthen trust and satisfaction toward automated systems, although their relative effects may vary depending on the application domain and the type of decision involved (Shin & Park, 2019; Shin, 2020; Shin, Zhong, & Biocca, 2020; Kieslich, Starke, Došenović, Marcinkowski, & Lünich, 2020). These issues become even more significant in the field of welfare, where automation directly affects rights, access to public resources, and the administrative treatment of citizens. Unlike many other domains of AI application, welfare governance involves high-stakes decisions concerning eligibility, social benefits, and conditions of vulnerability. In such contexts, perceptions of procedural fairness and decision-making legitimacy become particularly crucial. Research on perceptions of fairness in algorithmic decision-making shows that individuals evaluate the use of algorithms differently depending on what is at stake, the policy domain, and the presence of human oversight (Grgić-Hlača, Redmiles, Gummadi, & Weller, 2018; Grgić-Hlača, Weller, & Redmiles, 2020; Wang, Harper, & Zhu, 2020; Starke et al., 2021). In some contexts, automation may be seen as more impartial than human decision-makers; in others, it may be perceived as overly rigid, incapable of grasping the complexity of individual circumstances, and therefore potentially unjust (Helberger et al., 2020; Marcinkowski et al., 2020; Acikgoz et al., 2020). For welfare policies, this represents a central issue. Algorithmic rationality may appear efficient, yet it risks coming into tension with social expectations of recognition, situational discretion, and sensitivity to the concrete circumstances of individuals. The legitimacy of digital welfare therefore also depends on the capacity of institutions to demonstrate that automation does not eliminate human mediation, public accountability, and the possibility of appeal.

Another important theoretical dimension concerns the relationship between perceptions of AI and institutional trust. The literature suggests that citizens do not evaluate technologies in the abstract but also in relation to the institutions that develop, implement, and regulate them. Trust in governments, public authorities, universities, technology companies, and international organizations significantly influences the acceptance of AI (Zhang & Dafoe, 2019; Liu & Priest, 2009; Starke & Lünich, 2020). Where institutional trust is stronger, technologies are more likely to be perceived as instruments of modernization and improvement of public action; where it is weaker, the same technologies may be interpreted as devices of control, surveillance, or political irresponsibility.

This dimension is particularly relevant in the European context, where welfare regimes, levels of public trust, and administrative cultures vary significantly across countries. In this framework, studying public perceptions of AI does not merely measure individual attitudes; it also provides insight into structural differences in the relationship between citizens, institutions, and sociotechnical innovation. The literature on digital inequalities adds another crucial layer to this discussion. Acceptance and understanding of AI are not evenly distributed across the population. Digital skills, educational attainment, familiarity with automated systems, labor market position, age, and access to informational resources all strongly influence how individuals interpret the opportunities and risks associated with technological change (van Dijk, 2020; Helsper, 2021; Ragnedda, 2018; Robinson et al., 2015). Individuals with greater digital capital are more likely to recognize the benefits of innovation, to trust their ability to interact with technological systems, and to develop more articulated expectations about the criteria that define a "good" AI. By contrast, groups with fewer digital resources may perceive AI as a distant, opaque, and difficult-to-control technology that potentially threatens their autonomy or security. Consequently, public perceptions of AI cannot be analyzed solely as cultural orientations; they must also be understood as expressions of the unequal distribution of cognitive, technological, and social resources. This point is particularly relevant for digital welfare: as access to services and rights increasingly occurs through digital interfaces, data infrastructures, and automated procedures, digital inequalities risk translating into inequalities of citizenship.

For this reason, an important strand of recent research emphasizes the need to involve citizens more directly in the design, implementation, and regulation of intelligent technologies. The concept of human-centered AI or human-centric AI does not simply refer to a generic attention to human needs; rather, it implies that systems should also be evaluated in light of the perceptions, expectations, and experiences of the individuals affected by them (Riedl, 2019; Lee, Kim, & Lizarondo, 2017; European Commission, 2019). From this perspective, the analysis of public opinion is not a marginal complement to technological governance but a substantive component of it. It helps to clarify which principles citizens consider most relevant, which trade-offs are perceived as acceptable, and which institutional configurations foster or undermine trust. The objective is not to automatically accommodate public preferences but to recognize that the construction of AI legitimacy requires a closer relationship between technical design, public regulation, and the social imaginaries through which technologies are interpreted (Srivastava, Heidari, & Krause, 2019; Webb et al., 2018). In summary, the theoretical debate converges around a fundamental insight: the governance of artificial intelligence – especially in public contexts – cannot be reduced to a matter of computational capacity or regulatory compliance. Rather, it concerns how societies define the conditions under which intelligent technologies can be used in ways that are legitimate, fair, and socially acceptable. Public perceptions of AI thus become a privileged lens through which to observe the tensions between innovation and control, efficiency and rights, promises of improvement and fears of exclusion. In this sense, studying European citizens' attitudes toward AI means interrogating not only the relationship between individuals and technology but also the social foundations upon which the legitimacy of contemporary digital welfare ultimately rests, or may begin to erode.

3. ATTITUDES TOWARD ARTIFICIAL INTELLIGENCE IN EUROPE

To empirically explore how European citizens interpret the diffusion of artificial intelligence and digital technologies, this section analyzes public attitudes toward these technologies using comparative data from Special Eurobarometer 101.4 – Artificial Intelligence and the Future of Work. This survey represents one of the most recent comparative studies conducted by the European Commission on citizens' perceptions of digital technologies and artificial intelligence. Fieldwork was carried out between 25 April and 22 May 2024 on representative samples of the adult population in the member states of the European Union. For decades, the Eurobarometer has been one of the principal instruments for the comparative analysis of European public opinion, providing standardized and comparable data on citizens' major social, economic, and political orientations. In the present study, the analysis adopts a macro-comparative perspective, using aggregated data available in the official comparative tables published by the European Commission. The unit of analysis is therefore the member state of the European Union (EU-27). Based on these comparative tables, an analytical matrix was constructed in which countries constitute the units of observation and indicators of attitudes toward artificial intelligence represent the variables. This structure makes it possible to observe macro-level patterns in European public perceptions by examining how opinions about artificial intelligence are configured at the national level and how they are distributed within the broader European comparative space. The objective is therefore not to explain individual differences among citizens but rather to identify recurring configurations of collective attitudes that characterize different national contexts. In this perspective, the aggregated percentages reported in the Eurobarometer tables are used as synthetic indicators of national public opinion (Table 1). The selection of variables was guided by three conceptual dimensions that are central to the sociological debate on artificial intelligence and the digital transformation of contemporary societies: technological optimism, perceptions of automation-related risks, and perceived digital skills. The first dimension refers to the extent to which citizens evaluate positively the impact of digital technologies and artificial intelligence on key areas of social and economic life. The second dimension concerns fears associated with automation, particularly regarding the possibility that robots and AI systems may replace human labor. The third dimension relates to individuals' confidence in their own ability to use digital tools in everyday life, in the workplace, and in learning contexts. Considering these three dimensions jointly makes it possible to observe the simultaneous presence of technological enthusiasm, social concern, and self-perceived digital competence. The variables used in the analysis derive from several questions included in the Eurobarometer questionnaire and were selected based on their theoretical relevance and the availability of comparable data across countries. In particular, the analysis includes indicators related to perceptions of the impact of artificial intelligence on society and the economy, evaluations of the use of robots and automated systems in workplaces, fears of job loss associated with automation, and individual perceptions of digital skills in different domains of everyday life.

Table 1. Indicators of Attitudes Toward Artificial Intelligence and Digital Skills (Eurobarometer 101.4)

Variable	*Eurobarometer Question Code*	*Indicator*	*Operationalization*	*Interpretation*
ai_positive_impact_society	QB1_2	Total Positive	Very positive + Fairly positive	% of respondents who believe digital technologies and AI have a positive impact on society
ai_positive_workplace	QB5	Total Positive	Very positive + Fairly positive	% of respondents with a positive perception of robots and AI in the workplace
ai_jobs_loss	QB6_1	Total Agree	Totally agree + Tend to agree	% who agree that robots and AI will destroy more jobs than they create
ai_steal_jobs	QB6_5	Total Agree	Totally agree + Tend to agree	% who agree that robots and AI take away people's jobs
ai_good_for_society	QB6_2	Total Agree	Totally agree + Tend to agree	% who agree that robots and AI are beneficial for society
digital_skills_daily	QB2_1	Total Agree	Totally agree + Tend to agree	% who feel sufficiently skilled in using digital technologies in daily life
digital_skills_job	QB2_2	Total Agree	Totally agree + Tend to agree	% who feel sufficiently skilled in using digital technologies for their job
digital_skills_future_job	QB2_3	Total Agree	Totally agree + Tend to agree	% who feel sufficiently skilled in using digital technologies for a future job
ai_positive_impact_economy	QB1_1	Total Positive	Very positive + Fairly positive	% who believe digital technologies and AI have a positive impact on the economy
digital_skills_learning	QB2_4	Total Agree	Totally agree + Tend to agree	% who feel sufficiently skilled to benefit from online learning opportunities

The percentages used in the analysis are derived from the comparative Eurobarometer tables and are constructed from two aggregated categories. For variables related to perceptions of the impact of technologies, the Total "Positive" category was used, which aggregates the responses *Very positive* and *Fairly positive* and represents the share of citizens who evaluate the impact of digital technologies or artificial intelligence positively across the different domains considered. For attitudinal variables, the Total "Agree" category was used instead, which aggregates the responses *Totally agree* and *Tend to agree* and measures the percentage of the population expressing agreement with statements concerning the effects of digital technologies and artificial intelligence. The percentages were used directly as quantitative indicators comparable across countries, since the data published by the European Commission are already weighted to ensure statistical representativeness at the national level. Non-response categories – *Don't know*, *It depends*, and *Not enough information* – were not included in the indicators used in the analysis, as they do not contribute to the measurement of positive attitudes or the level of agreement with the statements considered.

To identify the main dimensions structuring perceptions of artificial intelligence across European countries, a Principal Component Analysis (PCA) was applied. This multivariate analytical technique makes it possible to reduce the dimensionality of a set of correlated variables and to identify principal components that summarize the information contained in the data. The analysis was conducted using standardized variables and implemented through the Python programming environment and the scikit-learn library. The principal components were interpreted based on component loadings, that is, the relative contribution of each variable to the construction of each dimension. This approach allows the identification of recurring configurations in public attitudes toward artificial intelligence.

The analysis nonetheless presents several limitations. The use of aggregated data at the national level does not allow observation of within-country differences or variations across socio-demographic groups, nor does it permit the identification of individual-level causal relationships. Furthermore, the relatively limited number of units of analysis – corresponding to the countries of the European Union – suggests that the results should be interpreted primarily from an exploratory rather than inferential perspective. In this sense, the PCA should be understood mainly as a technique aimed at identifying latent configurations of attitudes toward artificial intelligence rather than causal mechanisms explaining their emergence. Moreover, although institutional trust is discussed theoretically as an important factor shaping perceptions of AI, it is not directly operationalized in the empirical analysis and therefore represents an important direction for future research. Despite these limitations, the adopted approach makes it possible to identify macro-level patterns in

European public perceptions and to provide a comparative perspective on the social configurations of attitudes toward artificial intelligence.

The results first reveal a strong relationship between indicators related to perceptions of the employment risks associated with automation. The variables measuring agreement with the statements that robots and artificial intelligence will destroy more jobs than they create and that AI will "take away people's jobs" show an extremely high correlation ($r = 0.94$), suggesting that both capture the same dimension, interpretable as a form of algorithmic anxiety related to transformations in the world of work.

A second pattern concerns the relationship between perceived digital skills and positive evaluations of artificial intelligence. Indicators of digital skills show relatively strong positive correlations with variables measuring favorable evaluations of the impact of digital technologies on society and work. In particular, the perception of possessing sufficient digital skills in everyday life is strongly correlated with the belief that robots and AI are beneficial for society ($r = 0.61$) and with a positive evaluation of the use of technologies in the workplace ($r = 0.52$). Similarly, the perception of being able to effectively use digital technologies for online learning is significantly correlated with positive evaluations of AI in the workplace ($r = 0.62$).

These results suggest that digital skills play a significant role in shaping attitudes toward emerging technologies. In line with the literature on digital inequalities (van Dijk, 2020; Helsper, 2021), digital capital represents not only a technical resource but also a cultural and cognitive factor that influences how individuals interpret and evaluate processes of technological innovation.

Finally, a negative relationship emerges between positive perceptions of artificial intelligence and fears of job loss. Contexts in which the use of digital technologies in the workplace is evaluated more positively tend to show lower levels of concern about the employment risks associated with automation. Overall, these findings suggest that attitudes toward artificial intelligence across European countries tend to organize around three main dimensions: trust in digital technologies, perceptions of automation-related employment risks, and perceived digital skills. This configuration anticipates the structure identified through the principal component analysis, which makes it possible to synthesize these dimensions within a more compact interpretative space.

Figure 1. Correlation Matrix of Attitudinal Indicators Toward Artificial Intelligence and Digital Skills in the EU-27

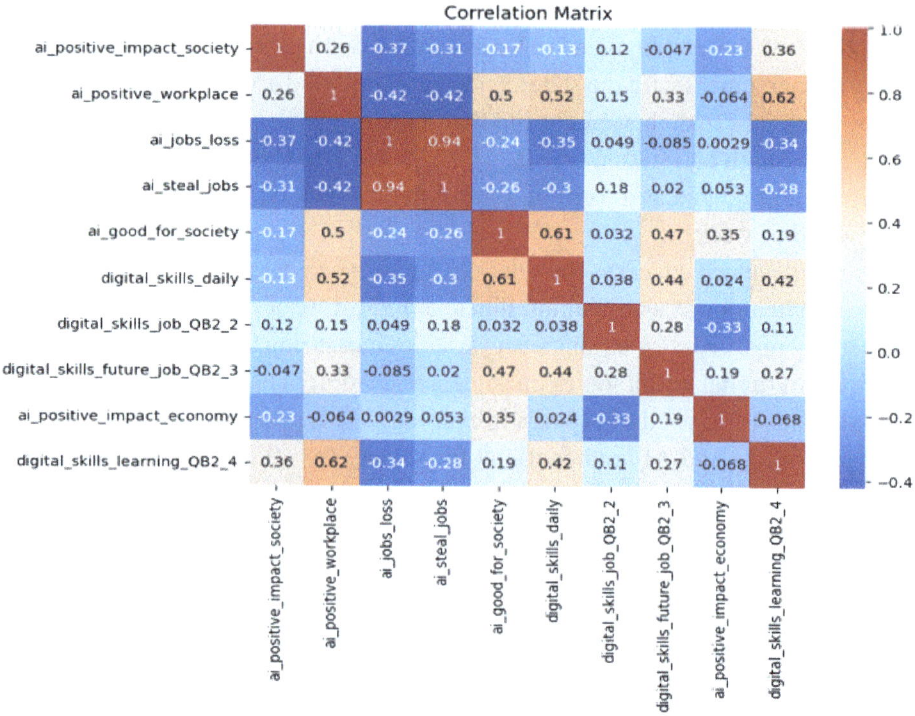

The Principal Component Analysis (PCA) made it possible to identify the main dimensions structuring European public opinions toward artificial intelligence. The results show that the first three components reproduce approximately 69% of the total variance in the data (eigenvalues of the first three components are 3.5, 2, and 1.6), suggesting the existence of a relatively coherent structure in attitudes toward AI across European countries (Table 2). More specifically, the analysis indicates that public perceptions of artificial intelligence tend to organize around three main dimensions: technological optimism, perceptions of the broader social impact of digital transformation, and perceived digital capital. Rather than representing isolated opinions about technology, these dimensions reflect broader tensions between expectations of innovation, fears associated with automation, and unequal levels of confidence in interacting with digital environments.

Table 2. Percentage of Variance replicated by the Principal Components

Component	*Variance Explained*
PC1	34.0%
PC2	19.5%
PC3	15.6%
PC4	8.6%
PC5	7.6%

In particular, the first component (Table 3), which reproduces approximately 34% of the total variance, contrasts positive evaluations of the impact of digital technologies and perceived digital skills with perceptions of the employment risks associated with automation. Variables such as positive perceptions of AI in the workplace, evaluations of the benefits of digital technologies for society, and confidence in one's own digital skills show high positive loadings, whereas indicators related to fears of job loss due to automation display negative loadings. This component can therefore be interpreted as a tension between technological optimism and automation anxiety. On the one hand, positive evaluations of AI reflect expectations of innovation, modernization, and the perceived capacity to benefit from digital transformation. On the other hand, concerns about job displacement express forms of insecurity associated with the increasing automation of labor.

The second component (Table 3), which explains about 19% of the variance, appears instead to capture broader normative evaluations of the social role of artificial intelligence. Variables related to perceptions of AI's impact on society and the economy contribute significantly to the definition of this dimension, suggesting more general orientations toward AI-driven social and economic transformation. Rather than reflecting a simple opposition between optimism and pessimism, this component captures how citizens interpret the broader societal implications of digital technologies.

Finally, the third component (Table 3) is strongly associated with indicators related to perceived digital skills, particularly the self-reported ability to use digital technologies in the workplace. This dimension can be interpreted as a form of digital capital, namely the set of skills, cognitive resources, and technological familiarity that enable individuals to interact effectively with digital environments. In line with the literature on digital inequalities (van Dijk, 2020; Helsper, 2021), these competencies represent a crucial factor shaping both the opportunities and the risks associated with digital transformation.

Table 3. Explained Variance of the Principal Components

	PC1	PC2	PC3	PC4	PC5	PC6	PC7	PC8	PC9	PC10
ai_positive_impact_society	0.163	0.488	0.168	0.474	0.249	-0.070	0.514	0.377	-0.072	0.055
ai_positive_workplace	0.444	-0.009	0.154	0.114	-0.252	-0.447	0.086	-0.509	-0.482	0.065
ai_jobs_loss	-0.400	-0.311	0.273	0.199	-0.296	-0.162	0.224	-0.025	0.052	-0.679
ai_steal_jobs	-0.377	-0.329	0.350	0.266	-0.176	-0.035	0.081	0.175	-0.120	0.688
ai_good_for_society	0.342	-0.419	-0.118	-0.112	0.102	-0.474	0.305	0.141	0.565	0.118
digital_skills_daily	0.392	-0.274	0.022	-0.280	-0.333	0.258	0.085	0.589	-0.383	-0.118
digital_skills_job_QB2_2	0.055	-0.021	0.646	-0.243	0.469	-0.276	-0.410	0.187	-0.077	-0.122
digital_skills_future_job_QB2_3	0.258	-0.393	0.258	0.142	0.376	0.597	0.243	-0.365	0.035	-0.037
ai_positive_impact_economy	0.020	-0.376	-0.447	0.526	0.335	-0.144	-0.348	0.169	-0.291	-0.120
digital_skills_learning_QB2_4	0.366	0.098	0.230	0.452	-0.401	0.153	-0.472	0.060	0.434	-0.023

Overall, the analysis suggests that attitudes toward artificial intelligence across European countries are not randomly distributed but tend to organize along three main dimensions: technological optimism, perceptions of the social impact of technologies, and perceived digital capital. This configuration reflects a broader tension between expectations of technological progress and concerns about the social consequences of automation, a dynamic that recent literature has often described as a form of "conditional acceptance" of digital technologies (Binns & Gallo, 2019; Floridi et al., 2018).

The representation of European countries in the space defined by the first two principal components also makes it possible to identify several macro-regional configurations in attitudes toward artificial intelligence. Northern European countries, such as Denmark, Sweden, and Finland, tend to be in the area characterized by higher levels of technological optimism and relatively positive evaluations of the impact of digital technologies. This position likely reflects the role of widespread digital skills, higher levels of institutional trust, and public policies oriented toward innovation that characterize these contexts (van Dijck et al., 2018).

By contrast, several countries in Southern and Eastern Europe tend to occupy positions associated with relatively higher levels of concern about the social consequences of automation and lower levels of confidence in the benefits of digital technologies. This configuration can be interpreted considering the different trajectories of economic development, labor market conditions, and digital inequalities that characterize different national contexts. As suggested by studies on the transformation of digital labor, perceptions of the risks associated with automation tend to be higher in contexts characterized by greater employment insecurity or lower levels of widespread digital skills. These differences suggest that the social legitimacy of AI-driven governance may vary significantly across European contexts, depending on levels of institutional trust, digital inclusion, and perceived economic security.

Overall, these results suggest that attitudes toward artificial intelligence do not simply reflect individual opinions about technology but are deeply embedded in the social and institutional structures that organize European societies. In this sense, the digitalization of welfare and the adoption of algorithmic systems in public policies cannot be understood solely as technical or administrative processes; rather, they should be interpreted as sociotechnical phenomena involving expectations, fears, and relations of trust between citizens and public institutions.

In line with perspectives from critical data studies (Couldry & Mejias, 2019; Kitchin, 2017), the diffusion of data-driven systems in social policies raises fundamental questions concerning the transparency, accountability, and democratic legitimacy of algorithmic decision-making. In this context, public perceptions of artificial intelligence assume a central role: they contribute to defining the conditions under which digital technologies become socially acceptable and, more broadly, the legitimacy of the emerging models of algorithmic governance within contemporary welfare systems.

Figure 2. Distribution of European Countries in the Space Defined by the First Two Principal Components of AI Attitudes

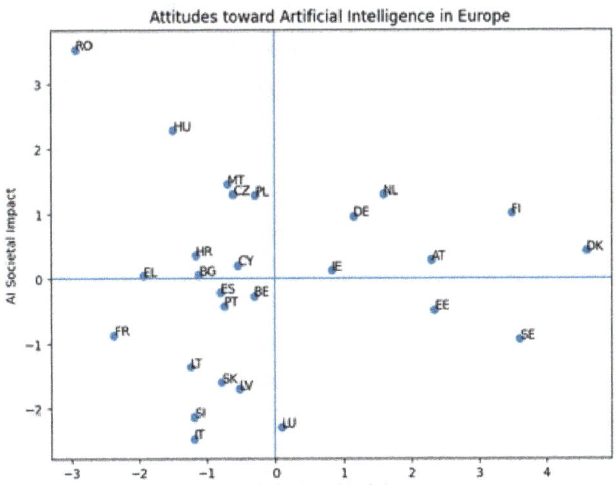

CONCLUSIONS: PUBLIC PERCEPTIONS AND THE LEGITIMACY OF DIGITAL WELFARE

The growing integration of data-driven systems and artificial intelligence tools into public policies is profoundly transforming the functioning of European welfare systems. As discussed in the previous sections, these processes do not merely involve the introduction of new administrative technologies but rather imply a broader sociotechnical reconfiguration of the relationships between citizens, data, and public institutions. In this context, digital welfare cannot be interpreted solely as a process of technological innovation or administrative modernization. Rather, its sustainability also depends on the social conditions of acceptance, trust, and legitimacy that accompany the adoption of algorithmic technologies within public institutions.

This chapter has addressed this issue by focusing on a dimension that often remains marginal in the debate on algorithmic governance: public perceptions of artificial intelligence. While a significant portion of the literature has focused on the technical, regulatory, or ethical aspects of AI, less attention has been devoted to the ways in which citizens interpret these transformations and to the implications that such perceptions may have for the legitimacy of digital policies. Through a comparative analysis of data from the Special Eurobarometer 101.4, this chapter has sought to partially address this gap by exploring the structure of attitudes toward artificial intelligence across European countries.

The results suggest that perceptions of AI are not randomly distributed across European populations but rather tend to organize around several recurring dimensions. In particular, the empirical analysis shows that attitudes toward digital technologies are structured around three main dimensions: technological optimism, perceptions of automation-related employment risks, and perceived digital capital. These dimensions reflect a structural tension between expectations of technological innovation and concerns about the social consequences of technological transformation, a dynamic that recent literature has often described as a form of conditional acceptance of digital technologies.

One of the most relevant findings concerns the role of perceived digital skills. The analysis shows that contexts characterized by higher levels of digital capital tend to express more positive evaluations of the impact of artificial intelligence on society and work, whereas lower levels of digital skills are associated with stronger perceptions of the risks of automation. This result confirms what the literature on digital inequalities has long suggested: the ability to understand, use, and interpret digital technologies represents a fundamental resource not only for accessing services but also for shaping opinions about technological change. In this sense, perceptions of AI partly reflect the unequal distribution of cognitive and technological resources within European societies.

A second important element concerns the institutional dimension of technological perceptions. The differences observed across countries suggest that attitudes toward artificial intelligence are closely intertwined with the social and institutional structures that characterize different national contexts. In countries characterized by higher levels of institutional trust, consolidated welfare systems, and widespread digital skills, AI tends to be more frequently perceived as a tool for innovation and improvement in public services. Conversely, in contexts characterized by greater economic insecurity or lower digital resources, the same technologies may be interpreted as potential sources of risk, control, or exclusion. These findings suggest that the digitalization of welfare cannot be fully understood solely through the analysis of technological infrastructures or policy strategies. The adoption of algorithmic systems in social policies is also a process of institutional legitimacy-building. Algorithms do not operate in a social vacuum: their acceptability depends on the level of trust in the institutions implementing them, the perceived fairness of decision-making processes, and the ability to maintain forms of public accountability and human oversight.

From this perspective, the chapter suggests that public perceptions of artificial intelligence constitute a crucial dimension of digital welfare governance. Understanding how citizens interpret the use of algorithmic systems within public institutions does not merely mean measuring individual opinions about technology; rather, it allows us to grasp the social foundations upon which the legitimacy of emerging data-driven models of public administration is built—or potentially contested.

These considerations also have implications for public policy debates. If the legitimacy of digital welfare partly depends on citizens' perceptions, then strategies for technological innovation should be accompanied by policies aimed at transparency, participation, and the development of digital skills. In particular, strengthening the digital capital of the population and improving the comprehensibility of automated decision-making processes may help reduce the informational asymmetries that often fuel distrust toward algorithmic technologies. Naturally, the analysis presented in this chapter has some limitations. The use of aggregated national-level data does not allow exploration of differences across socio-demographic groups nor deeper investigation of the individual-level factors influencing perceptions of AI. Moreover, the analysis focuses on a relatively limited set of indicators, which capture only part of the dimensions through which citizens evaluate digital technologies. Future research could therefore examine more closely the role of variables such as age, education, occupation, or direct exposure to automated systems, as well as more directly explore the relationship between technological perceptions and trust in public institutions.

Despite these limitations, the results suggest that the digital transformation of European welfare systems is not merely a question of technological capacity or administrative efficiency. Rather, it represents a deeply social and political process, in which the diffusion of algorithmic systems reshapes the ways in which citizens interact with the state. In this context, the legitimacy of digital welfare will increasingly depend on the ability of public institutions to integrate technological innovation with public accountability and social trust. Studying public perceptions of artificial intelligence thus becomes essential not only for understanding how technologies are adopted, but also for identifying the conditions under which they can become a stable and legitimate component of contemporary welfare institutions.

REFERENCES

Acikgoz, Y., Davison, K. H., Compagnone, M., & Laske, M. (2020). Justice perceptions of artificial intelligence in selection. *International Journal of Selection and Assessment, 28*(4), 399–416. DOI: 10.1111/ijsa.12306

Ananny, M., & Crawford, K. (2018). Seeing without knowing: Limitations of the transparency ideal and its application to algorithmic accountability. *New Media & Society, 20*(3), 973–989. DOI: 10.1177/1461444816676645

Araujo, T., Helberger, N., Kruikemeier, S., & de Vreese, C. H. (2020). In AI we trust? Perceptions about automated decision-making by artificial intelligence. *AI & Society, 35*(3), 611–623. DOI: 10.1007/s00146-019-00931-w

Benjamin, R. (2019). *Race After Technology: Abolitionist Tools for the New Jim Code*. Polity Press.

Berendt, B. (2019). AI for the common good?! Pitfalls, challenges, and ethics pen-testing. *Paladyn : Journal of Behavioral Robotics, 10*(1), 44–65. DOI: 10.1515/pjbr-2019-0004

Bijker, W. E., Hughes, T. P., & Pinch, T. (Eds.). (1987). *The social construction of technological systems*. MIT Press.

Binns, R., & Gallo, V. (2019). Trade-offs. Information Commissioner's Office blog.

Busuioc, M. (2020). Accountable artificial intelligence: Holding algorithms to account. *Public Administration Review, 80*(5), 825–836. DOI: 10.1111/puar.13293 PMID: 34690372

Cave, S., Coughlan, K., & Dihal, K. (2019). "Scary robots": Examining public responses to AI. *Proceedings of the 2019 AAAI/ACM Conference on AI, Ethics, and Society*. DOI: 10.1145/3306618.3314232

Couldry, N., & Mejias, U. A. (2019). *The Costs of Connection: How Data Is Colonizing Human Life and Appropriating It for Capitalism*. Stanford University Press.

Diakopoulos, N. (2016). Accountability in algorithmic decision making. *Communications of the ACM, 59*(2), 56–62. DOI: 10.1145/2844110

Dietvorst, B. J., Simmons, J. P., & Massey, C. (2015). Algorithm aversion. *Journal of Experimental Psychology. General, 144*(1), 114–126. DOI: 10.1037/xge0000033 PMID: 25401381

Eubanks, V. (2018). *Automating Inequality: How High-Tech Tools Profile, Police, and Punish the Poor*. St. Martin's Press.

European Commission. (2019). *Ethics guidelines for trustworthy AI*.

European Commission. (2021). *Proposal for a regulation laying down harmonised rules on artificial intelligence*. Artificial Intelligence Act.

Floridi, L., Cowls, J., Beltrametti, M., Chatila, R., Chazerand, P., Dignum, V., Luetge, C., Madelin, R., Pagallo, U., Rossi, F., Schafer, B., Valcke, P., & Vayena, E. (2018). AI4People—An ethical framework for a good AI society. *Minds and Machines*, *28*(4), 689–707. DOI: 10.1007/s11023-018-9482-5 PMID: 30930541

Grgić-Hlača, N., Redmiles, E. M., Gummadi, K. P., & Weller, A. (2018). Human perceptions of fairness in algorithmic decision making. In *Proceedings of the World Wide Web Conference* (pp. 903–912). DOI: 10.1145/3178876.3186138

Grgić-Hlača, N., Weller, A., & Redmiles, E. M. (2020). Dimensions of diversity in human perceptions of algorithmic fairness. *arXiv preprint arXiv:2005.00808*.

Hagendorff, T. (2020). The ethics of AI ethics: An evaluation of guidelines. *Minds and Machines*, *30*(1), 99–120. DOI: 10.1007/s11023-020-09517-8

Helberger, N., Araujo, T., & de Vreese, C. H. (2020). Who is the fairest of them all? Public attitudes and expectations regarding automated decision-making. *Computer Law & Security Review*, *39*, 105456. DOI: 10.1016/j.clsr.2020.105456

Helsper, E. J. (2021). *The digital disconnect*. Sage.

Jasanoff, S. (2004). *States of knowledge*. Routledge. DOI: 10.4324/9780203413845

Jasanoff, S. (2016). *The ethics of invention*. W. W. Norton.

Jasanoff, S. (2016). *The Ethics of Invention: Technology and the Human Future*. W.W. Norton.

Jobin, A., Ienca, M., & Vayena, E. (2019). The global landscape of AI ethics guidelines. *Nature Machine Intelligence*, *1*(9), 389–399. DOI: 10.1038/s42256-019-0088-2

Kieslich, K., Lünich, M., & Marcinkowski, F. (2021). The threats of artificial intelligence scale (TAI). *International Journal of Social Robotics*, *13*(7), 1563–1577. DOI: 10.1007/s12369-020-00734-w

Kieslich, K., Starke, C., Došenović, P., Marcinkowski, F., & Lünich, M. (2020). *Artificial intelligence and discrimination*. CAIS Factsheet.

Kitchin, R. (2017). Thinking critically about and researching algorithms. *Information Communication and Society, 20*(1), 14–29. DOI: 10.1080/1369118X.2016.1154087

Köbis, N., Starke, C., & Rahwan, I. (2021). Artificial intelligence as an anti-corruption tool (AI-ACT): Potentials and pitfalls for top-down and bottom-up approaches. *arXiv preprint arXiv:2102.11567.*

Lee, M. K. (2018). Understanding perception of algorithmic decisions: Fairness, trust, and emotion in response to algorithmic management. *Big Data & Society, 5*(1), 2053951718756684. DOI: 10.1177/2053951718756684

Lee, M. K., Kim, J. T., & Lizarondo, L. (2017). A human-centered approach to algorithmic services. In *Proceedings of the 2017 CHI Conference on Human Factors in Computing Systems* (pp. 3365–3376). DOI: 10.1145/3025453.3025884

Liang, Y., & Lee, S. A. (2017). Fear of autonomous robots and artificial intelligence. *International Journal of Social Robotics, 9*(3), 379–384. DOI: 10.1007/s12369-017-0401-3

Liu, H., & Priest, S. (2009). Understanding public support for stem cell research. *Public Understanding of Science, 18*(6), 704–718. DOI: 10.1177/0963662508097625

Logg, J. M., Minson, J. A., & Moore, D. A. (2019). Algorithm appreciation. *Organizational Behavior and Human Decision Processes, 151*, 90–103. DOI: 10.1016/j.obhdp.2018.12.005

Marcinkowski, F., Kieslich, K., Starke, C., & Lünich, M. (2020). Implications of AI (un-)fairness in higher education admissions. In *Proceedings of the 2020 Conference on Fairness, Accountability, and Transparency* (pp. 122–130). DOI: 10.1145/3351095.3372867

Margetts, H., & Dorobantu, C. (2019). Rethink government with AI. *Nature, 568*(7751), 163–165. DOI: 10.1038/d41586-019-01099-5 PMID: 30967667

Merenkov, A. V., Campa, R., & Dronishinets, N. P. (2020). Public opinion on artificial intelligence development. In *Culture* (pp. 565–574). Personality, Society in the Conditions of Digitalization.

Miller, A. P. (2018). Want less-biased decisions? Use algorithms. *Harvard Business Review.*

Mittelstadt, B. D., Allo, P., Taddeo, M., Wachter, S., & Floridi, L. (2016). The ethics of algorithms. *Big Data & Society, 3*(2), 2053951716679679. DOI: 10.1177/2053951716679679

Noble, S. U. (2018). *Algorithms of oppression*. NYU Press. DOI: 10.18574/nyu/9781479833641.001.0001

O'Neil, C. (2016). *Weapons of Math Destruction: How Big Data Increases Inequality and Threatens Democracy*. Crown.

OECD. (2021). *Recommendation of the Council on Artificial Intelligence*. OECD.

Pasquale, F. (2015). *The Black Box Society: The Secret Algorithms That Control Money and Information*. Harvard University Press. DOI: 10.4159/harvard.9780674736061

Pew Research Center. (2018). *Public attitudes toward computer algorithms*.

Ragnedda, M. (2018). *Conceptualizing digital capital*. Emerald. DOI: 10.1016/j.tele.2018.10.006

Riedl, M. O. (2019). Human-centered artificial intelligence and machine learning. *Human Behavior and Emerging Technologies, 1*(1), 33–36. DOI: 10.1002/hbe2.117

Robinette, P., Howard, A. M., & Wagner, A. R. (2017). Effect of robot performance on human–robot trust in time-critical situations. *IEEE Transactions on Human-Machine Systems, 47*(4), 425–436. DOI: 10.1109/THMS.2017.2648849

Robinson, L., Cotten, S. R., Ono, H., Quan-Haase, A., Mesch, G., Chen, W., Schulz, J., Hale, T. M., & Stern, M. J. (2015). Digital inequalities and why they matter. *Information Communication and Society, 18*(5), 569–582. DOI: 10.1080/1369118X.2015.1012532

Salem, M., Lakatos, G., Amirabdollahian, F., & Dautenhahn, K. (2015). Would you trust a (faulty) robot? In *Proceedings of the Tenth Annual ACM/IEEE International Conference on Human-Robot Interaction* (pp. 141–148). DOI: 10.1145/2696454.2696497

Shin, D. (2020). User perceptions of algorithmic decisions in the personalized AI system: Perceptual evaluation of fairness, accountability, transparency, and explainability. *Journal of Broadcasting & Electronic Media, 64*(4), 541–565. DOI: 10.1080/08838151.2020.1843357

Shin, D. (2021). The effects of explainability and causability on perception, trust, and acceptance. *International Journal of Human-Computer Studies, 146*, 102551. DOI: 10.1016/j.ijhcs.2020.102551

Shin, D., & Park, Y. J. (2019). Role of fairness, accountability, and transparency in algorithmic affordance. *Computers in Human Behavior, 98*, 277–284. DOI: 10.1016/j.chb.2019.04.019

Shin, D., Zhong, B., & Biocca, F. A. (2020). Beyond user experience: What constitutes algorithmic experiences? *International Journal of Information Management*, *52*, 102061. DOI: 10.1016/j.ijinfomgt.2019.102061

Srivastava, M., Heidari, H., & Krause, A. (2019). Mathematical notions vs. human perception of fairness. In *Proceedings of the 25th ACM SIGKDD International Conference on Knowledge Discovery & Data Mining* (pp. 2459–2468). DOI: 10.1145/3292500.3330664

Starke, C., Baleis, J., Keller, B., & Marcinkowski, F. (2021). Fairness perceptions of algorithmic decision-making: A systematic review of the empirical literature. *arXiv preprint arXiv:2103.12016.*

Starke, C., & Lünich, M. (2020). Artificial intelligence for political decision-making in the European Union: Effects on citizens' perceptions of input, throughput, and output legitimacy. *Data & Policy*, *2*, e16. DOI: 10.1017/dap.2020.19

van Dijck, J., Poell, T., & de Waal, M. (2018). *The Platform Society: Public Values in a Connective World.* Oxford University Press. DOI: 10.1093/oso/9780190889760.001.0001

van Dijk, J. (2020). *The digital divide*. Polity.

Wang, R., Harper, F. M., & Zhu, H. (2020). Factors influencing perceived fairness in algorithmic decision-making. In *Proceedings of the 2020 CHI Conference on Human Factors in Computing Systems* (pp. 1–14). DOI: 10.1145/3313831.3376813

Webb, H., Koene, A., & Patel, M.. (2018). Multi-stakeholder dialogue for policy recommendations on algorithmic fairness. In *Proceedings of the 9th International Conference on Social Media and Society* (pp. 395–399). DOI: 10.1145/3217804.3217952

Winner, L. (1980). Do artifacts have politics? *Daedalus*, *109*(1), 121–136.

Zhang, B., & Dafoe, A. (2019). *U.S. public opinion on the governance of artificial intelligence*. Oxford: Future of Humanity Institute

Compilation of References

Aarab, A., El Marzouki, A., Boubker, O., & El Moutaqi, B. (2025). Integrating AI in public governance: A systematic review. *Digital*, *5*(4), 59. Advance online publication. DOI: 10.3390/digital5040059

Abadi, M., Chu, A., Goodfellow, I., McMahan, H. B., Mironov, I., Talwar, K., & Zhang, L. (2016). Deep learning with differential privacy. Proceedings of the 2016 acm sigsac Conference on Computer and Communications Security. acm, Wien, pp. 308-318. DOI: 10.1145/2976749.2978318

Accorinti, M., Mirabile, M. L., Romano, M. C., & Sgritta, G. B. (1998). Profili di povertà estrema: Dieci anni di attività assistenziale della Caritas diocesana di Roma (Diocesan Caritas of Rome). *L'Assistenza Sociale*, *1*(January/March), 177–196.

Acikgoz, Y., Davison, K. H., Compagnone, M., & Laske, M. (2020). Justice perceptions of artificial intelligence in selection. *International Journal of Selection and Assessment*, *28*(4), 399–416. DOI: 10.1111/ijsa.12306

Ahn, M. J., & Chen, Y. C. (2022). Digital transformation toward AI-augmented public administration: The perception of government employees and the willingness to use AI in government. *Government Information Quarterly*, *39*(2), 101664. DOI: 10.1016/j.giq.2021.101664

Airoldi, M. (2022). *Machine Habitus. Toward a sociology of algorithms*. Polity Press.

Alexopoulou, S. (2025). Paradigm shift: Exploring the impact of digital technologies on the welfare state through a systematic literature review. *Social Policy & Administration*, *59*(1), 135–157. DOI: 10.1111/spol.13054

Allhutter, D., Alushi, A., Alcântara, R. C. D., Männiste, M., Pentzold, C., & Sosnowski, S. (2024). Public value in the making of automated and datafied welfare futures. *Internet Policy Review*, *13*(3). Advance online publication. DOI: 10.14763/2024.3.1803

Alston, P. (2019). *Digital welfare states and human rights: Report of the Special Rapporteur on extreme poverty and human rights* (A/74/493). United Nations General Assembly. https://digitallibrary.un.org/record/3834146

Alston, P. (2019). *Report of the Special Rapporteur on extreme poverty and human rights.* United Nations Human Rights Council.

Amato, F. (2025). *Assessing the Social Implications of Automated Decision Making Systems: A Case Study.* PhD Dissertation, University of Naples "Federico II".

Amato, F. (2026). Sistemi di Decisione Automatizzata. In Amaturo, E., Aragona, B., Acampa, S., & Amato, F. (Eds.), *Tecnologie emergenti e ricerca sociale. Prospettive teoriche e pratiche empiriche* (pp. 50–60). FrancoAngeli.

Amaturo, E., & Aragona, B. (2021). Critical optimism: A methodological posture to shape the future of digital social research. *Italian Sociological Review*, 11(4S), 167. DOI: 10.13136/isr.v11i4S.429

Amaturo, E., & Punziano, G. (2016). *I mixed methods nella ricerca sociale*. Carocci.

Ambrosio, C., De Falco, C., & Taddei, L. (2026 forthcoming). *L'open science per il welfare: riflessioni sull'infrastruttura digitale FOSSR.* Welfare e Ergonomia, FrancoAngeli.

Anand, S., & Sen, A. (1997). Concepts of human development and poverty: A multidimensional perspective. In *Human development papers 1997: Poverty and human development* (pp. 1–20). United Nations Development Programme., https://digitallibrary.un.org/record/750303

Ananny, M., & Crawford, K. (2018). Seeing without knowing: Limitations of the transparency ideal and its application to algorithmic accountability. *New Media & Society*, *20*(3), 973–989. DOI: 10.1177/1461444816676645

Andreassen, R., Kaun, A., & Nikunen, K. (2021). Fostering the data welfare state: A Nordic perspective on datafication. *Nordicom Review*, *42*(2), 207–223. DOI: 10.2478/nor-2021-0051

Anttonen, A., Häikiö, L., Stefánsson, K., & Sipilä, J. (2012). Universalism and the challenge of diversity. In *Welfare state, universalism and diversity*. Edward Elgar Publishing. DOI: 10.4337/9781849805940.00006

Anttonen, A., & Sipilä, J. (1996). European Social Care Services: Is It Possible To Identify Models? *Journal of European Social Policy*, *6*(2), 87–100. DOI: 10.1177/095892879600600201

Aragona, B., & De Rosa, R. (2018). Policy making at the time of big data: Datascape, datasphere, data culture. *Sociologia Italiana*, *11*, 173–185. DOI: 10.1485/AIS_2018/11_3434226

Araujo, T., Helberger, N., Kruikemeier, S., & de Vreese, C. H. (2020). In AI we trust? Perceptions about automated decision-making by artificial intelligence. *AI & Society*, *35*(3), 611–623. DOI: 10.1007/s00146-019-00931-w

Archer, M. (2006). *La conversazione interiore: Come nasce l'agire sociale*. Erickson.

Arkhipova, E. B., & Borodkina, O. (2021). The problems and contradictions of digital transformation of social services organizations in Russia. Sotsiologicheskie Issledovaniya, 4, 116–134. https://doi.org/DOI: 10.24412/2079-0910-2021-4-116-134

Arnold, M., Bellamy, R. K., Hind, M., Houde, S., Mehta, S., Mojsilovic, A., & Nair, R. Natesan Ramamurthy, Baym, N. K. (2015). *Personal connections in the digital age* (2nd ed.). Polity Press.

Ascoli, U., & Pavolini, E. (Eds.). (2015). *The Italian welfare state in a European perspective: A comparative analysis*. Policy Press., DOI: 10.1332/policypress/9781447316886.001.0001

Atkinson, P., & Coffey, A. (2004). Analysing documentary realities. In D. Silverman (Ed.), Qualitative research: Theory, method and practice (2nd ed., pp. 56–75). Sage.
Bateson, G., Jackson, D. D., Haley, J., & Weakland, J. (1956). Toward a theory of schizophrenia. *Behavioral science*, 1(4), 251-264

Atkinson, A. B. (2003). Multidimensional deprivation: Contrasting social welfare and counting approaches. *The Journal of Economic Inequality*, *1*(1), 51–65. DOI: 10.1023/A:1023903525276

Barocas, S., Hardt, M., & Narayanan, A. (2019). *Fairness and machine learning: Limitations and opportunities*. MIT Press.

Batool, A., Zowghi, D., & Bano, M. (2025). AI governance: A systematic literature review. *AI and Ethics*, *5*(3), 3265–3279. DOI: 10.1007/s43681-024-00653-w

Beer, D. (2017). The social power of algorithms. *Information Communication and Society*, *20*(1), 1–13. DOI: 10.1080/1369118X.2016.1216147

Bellamy, R. K. E., Dey, K., & Hind, M., Hoffman, S. C., Houde, S., Kannan, K., Lohia, P., Martino, J., Mehta, S., Mojsilović, A., Nagar, S., Ramamurthy, K. N., Richards, J., Saha, D., Sattigeri, P., Singh, M., Varshney, K. R., & Zhang, Y. (2019). AI Fairness 360: An extensible toolkit for detecting and mitigating algorithmic bias. *IBM Journal of Research and Development*, 63(4/5), 4:1–4:15. https://doi.org/DOI: 10.1147/JRD.2019.2942287

Benanti, P., & Maffettone, S. (2024). *Noi e la macchina. Un'etica per l'era digitale*. Luiss University press.

Benedetto, V., De Vita, E., & Nuti, S. (2024). Setting priorities in outpatient cardiovascular care to guarantee equitable access: The case of Tuscany region. *Research in Health Services & Regions*, *3*(1), 11. DOI: 10.1007/s43999-024-00047-9 PMID: 39177938

Benjamin, R. (2019). *Race After Technology: Abolitionist Tools for the New Jim Code*. Polity Press.

Bennett, W. L., & Segerberg, A. (2012). The logic of connective action: Digital media and the personalization of contentious politics. *Information Communication and Society*, *15*(5), 739–768. DOI: 10.1080/1369118X.2012.670661

Berendt, B. (2019). AI for the common good?! Pitfalls, challenges, and ethics pen-testing. *Paladyn : Journal of Behavioral Robotics*, *10*(1), 44–65. DOI: 10.1515/pjbr-2019-0004

Berzano, L. (1987). Uomini senza territorio. *Sisifo*, *11*, 15–19.

Berzano, L. (1992). *Aree di devianza*. Il Segnalibro.

Bielefeld, S. (2024). Digitalisation and the welfare state–how first nations people experienced digitalised social security under the Cashless Debit Card. *Journal of Sociology (Melbourne, Vic.)*, *60*(3), 599–617. DOI: 10.1177/14407833241232636

Bijker, W. E., Hughes, T. P., & Pinch, T. (Eds.). (1987). *The social construction of technological systems*. MIT Press.

Binario 95. (2021, November 26). Roma: la mappatura dei servizi in città per le persone senza dimora. https://www.binario95.it/roma-mappatura-servizi-per-persone-senza-dimora-emergenza-covid-19/

Binns, R., & Gallo, V. (2019). Trade-offs. Information Commissioner's Office blog.

Binns, R. (2018). Fairness in machine learning: Lessons from political philosophy. *Proceedings of the 2018 Conference on Fairness, Accountability, and Transparency*, 149–159. https://doi.org/DOI: 10.1145/3287560.3287598

Blom, A. G., Bosnjak, M., Cornilleau, A., Cousteaux, A.-S., Das, M., Douhou, S., & Krieger, U. (2016). A comparison of four probability-based online and mixed-mode panels in Europe. *Social Science Computer Review, 34*(1), 8–25. DOI: 10.1177/0894439315574825

Bonoli, G., & Natali, D. (Eds.). (2012). *The politics of the new welfare state.* Oxford University Press. DOI: 10.1093/acprof:oso/9780199645244.001.0001

Borzaga, C. (2020). *La rilevanza economica la situazione e l'impatto della riforma.* [Lexical characteristics of Italian language]. Euricse Working Paper.

Borzaga, C., & Defourny, J. (Eds.). (2001). *The emergence of social enterprise* (1st ed.). Routledge. DOI: 10.4324/9780203164679

Bostrom, N. (2024). *Deep Utopia: Life and Meaning in a Solved World.* Ideapress Publishing.

Bourdieu, P. (1984). *Distinction: A social critique of the judgement of taste.* Harvard University Press.

Bovens, M. (2007). Analysing and assessing accountability: A conceptual framework. *European Law Journal, 13*(4), 447–468. DOI: 10.1111/j.1468-0386.2007.00378.x

Bovens, M., & Zouridis, S. (2002). From street-level to system-level bureaucracies: How information and communication technology is transforming administrative discretion and constitutional control. *Public Administration Review, 62*(2), 174–184. DOI: 10.1111/0033-3352.00168

Bowen, G. A. (2009). Document analysis as a qualitative research method. *Qualitative Research Journal, 9*(2), 27–40. DOI: 10.3316/QRJ0902027

Bowker, G. C., & Star, S. L. (1999). *Sorting things out: Classification and its consequences.* MIT Press. DOI: 10.7551/mitpress/6352.001.0001

Bruni, C., Cortese, C., Di Censi, L., & Mauceri, S. (2024). Un paradigma d'intervento in mutamento. In Mauceri, S., & Di Censi, L. (Eds.), *Povertà estreme. Un'analisi sul sistema dei servizi per le persone senza dimora a Roma* (pp. 232–242). FrancoAngeli.

Bullock, J. B., & Chen, Y. C. (2024). The brave new world of AI: Implications for public sector agents, organisations, and governance. *Asia Pacific Journal of Public Administration, 46*(4), 321–325. DOI: 10.1080/23276665.2024.2356540

Burrell, J. (2016). How the machine "thinks": Understanding opacity in machine learning algorithms. *Big Data & Society, 3*(1), 2053951715622512. Advance online publication. DOI: 10.1177/2053951715622512

Burton, J., & van den Broek, D. (2009). Accountable and countable: Information management systems and the bureaucratization of social work. *British Journal of Social Work, 39*(7), 1326–1342. DOI: 10.1093/bjsw/bcn027

Busch-Geertsema, V., Edgar, B., O'Sullivan, E., & Pleace, N. (2010). *Homelessness and homeless policies in Europe: Lessons from research.* FEANTSA. https://ec.europa.eu/social/BlobServlet?docId=6442&langId=en

Busuioc, M. (2021). Accountable artificial intelligence: Holding algorithms to account. *Public Administration Review, 81*(5), 825–836. DOI: 10.1111/puar.13293 PMID: 34690372

Cabitza, F., Campagner, A., & Balsano, C. (2021). Humans in the loop: Investigating the integration of machine learning predictions into decision-making. *Artificial Intelligence in Medicine, 115*, 102055. DOI: 10.1016/j.artmed.2021.102055

Callegaro, M., Baker, R., Bethlehem, J., Göritz, A. S., Krosnick, J. A., & Lavrakas, P. J. (2014). *Online panel research: A data quality perspective.* Wiley. DOI: 10.1002/9781118763520

Calo, R. (2017). Artificial intelligence policy: A primer and roadmap. *SSRN, 51*(2), 399–436. DOI: 10.2139/ssrn.3015350

Calvaruso, C., & Scalise, M. M. (1987). *Essere barboni a Roma.* Labos.

Campedelli, M., & Vesan, P. (2023). Welfare digitalizzato, welfare digitale e i nuovi rischi sociali digitali: Un'introduzione. *Politiche Sociali / Social Policies, 10*(2), 169–192. https://doi.org/DOI: 10.7389/108019

Cannarsa, M. (2021). Ethics guidelines for trustworthy AI. *The Cambridge handbook of lawyering in the digital age, 30*, 97-283.

Caputo, N. (2026). Administrative Law's Fourth Settlement: AI and the Capability-Accountability Trap. *arXiv preprint arXiv:2602.09678.*

Caritas Ambrosiana (Ed.). (2008). *Milano solidale: Temi e prospettive di intervento con gli ultimi.* Caritas Ambrosiana.

Castells, M. (1996). *The rise of the network society.* Blackwell.

Castilla Barraza, J. G., & Romero-Rubio, S. A. (2024). The use of artificial intelligence in governance: A systematic review. In *International Conference on Advanced Research in Technologies, Information, Innovation and Sustainability* (pp. 110–125). Springer.

Cave, S., Coughlan, K., & Dihal, K. (2019). "Scary robots": Examining public responses to AI. *Proceedings of the 2019 AAAI/ACM Conference on AI, Ethics, and Society*. DOI: 10.1145/3306618.3314232

Centerdata. (2023a). *Privacy statement – LISS panel*. https://www.lissdata.nl/privacy

Centerdata. (2023b). *Ethics – LISS panel*. https://www.lissdata.nl/about-panel/ethics

Cerbara, L., Germani, D., & Santurro, M. (2026). Ethical implications in building longitudinal data infrastructures. In Taddei, L., & Paolucci, M. (Eds.), *Longitudinal data infrastructures in Europe: Tools for open science in social science research*. Springer. DOI: 10.1007/978-3-032-07005-0_4

Ceri, P. (1996). *Politica e partecipazione*. Il Mulino.

Ceri, P. (2007). *Sociologia. I soggetti, le strutture, i contesti*. Laterza Editori.

Cesareo, V. (Ed.). (2005). *Ricomporre la vita: Gli adulti giovani in Italia*. Carocci.

Chao, A. (1987). Estimating the population size for capture-recapture data with unequal catchability. *Biometrics*, *43*(4), 783–791. DOI: 10.2307/2531532 PMID: 3427163

Chomsky, N. (1980). *Rules and Representations*. Columbia University Press. DOI: 10.1017/S0140525X00001515

Choroszewicz, M., & Mäihäniemi, B. (2020). Developing a digital welfare state: Data protection and the use of automated decision-making in the public sector across six EU countries. *Global Perspectives*, *1*(1), 12910. Advance online publication. DOI: 10.1525/gp.2020.12910

Chouldechova, A., & Roth, A. (2020). A snapshot of the frontiers of fairness in machine learning. *Communications of the ACM*, *63*(5), 82–89. DOI: 10.1145/3376898

Citron, D. K., & Pasquale, F. (2014). The scored society: Due process for automated predictions. *Washington Law Review (Seattle, Wash.)*, *89*(1), 1–33.

Clarke, R., Michael, K., & Abbas, R. (2024). Robodebt: A socio-technical case study of public sector information systems failure. *AJIS. Australasian Journal of Information Systems*, *28*, 28. DOI: 10.3127/ajis.v28.4681

Coleman, S., & Shane, P. M. (Eds.). (2012). *Connecting democracy: Online consultation and the flow of political communication*. Cambridge MIT Press.

Comunità di Sant'Egidio. (2021). DOVE mangiare dormire lavarsi [Mobile app]. Google Play. https://play.google.com/store/apps/details?id=com.segidio.solidarieta

Considine, M., McGann, M., Ball, S., & Nguyen, P. (2022). Can robots understand welfare? Exploring machine bureaucracies in welfare-to-work. *Journal of Social Policy, 51*(3), 519–534. DOI: 10.1017/S0047279422000174

Consiglio Nazionale delle Ricerche, Commissione per l'Etica e l'Integrità nella Ricerca. (2019). *Linee guida per l'integrità nella ricerca.*

Cordella, A., & Tempini, N. (2015). E-government and organizational change: Re-appraising the role of ICT and bureaucracy in public service delivery. *Government Information Quarterly, 32*(3), 279–286. DOI: 10.1016/j.giq.2015.03.005

Cornesse, C., & Blom, A. G. (2023). Response quality in nonprobability and probability-based online panels. *Sociological Methods & Research, 52*(2), 879–908. DOI: 10.1177/0049124120914940

Couldry, N., & Mejias, U. A. (2019). *The Costs of Connection: How Data Is Colonizing Human Life and Appropriating It for Capitalism.* Stanford University Press.

Coulter, A. (2006). Can patients assess the quality of health care?: Patients' surveys should ask about real experiences of medical care. *BMJ (Clinical Research Ed.), 333*(7557), 1–2. DOI: 10.1136/bmj.333.7557.1 PMID: 16809674

Couper, M. P. (2008). *Designing effective web surveys.* Cambridge University Press. DOI: 10.1017/CBO9780511499371

Couper, M. P., Singer, E., Conrad, F. G., & Groves, R. M. (2008). Risk of disclosure, perceptions of risk, and concerns about privacy and confidentiality as factors in survey participation. *Journal of Official Statistics, 24*(2), 255–275. PMID: 21603156

Creswell, J. W., & Plano Clark, V. L. (2011). *Designing and conducting mixed methods research* (2nd ed.). Sage.

Crivellaro, C., Coles-Kemp, L., & Wood, K. (2020). "Computer says no": Exploring social justice in digital services. In *Hope under neoliberal austerity: Responses from civil society and civic action* (pp. 89–104). Policy Press., DOI: 10.1332/policypress/9781447356820.003.0007

Dahlberg, L. (2011). Re-constructing digital democracy: An outline of four 'positions'. *New Media & Society, 13*(6), 855–872. DOI: 10.1177/1461444810389569

Damen, W. W. (2025). Exposed to the elements: How European data protection law facilitates welfare dystopias and how to improve its level of protection. *European Journal of Social Security, 27*(2), 156–174. DOI: 10.1177/13882627251337402

Dandotiya, M., Goyal, N. K., Yadav, P., Sankhla, K., & Kumari, M. (2026). GENALYTICS: A Deep Dive Into Real-Time Insights via Generative AI. In *Generative AI-Powered Data Architectures* (pp. 105–134). IGI Global Scientific Publishing. https://doi.org/DOI: 10.4018/979-8-3373-5616-7.ch005

Das, M. (2025, May 5–6). Building on the LISS experience: Future challenges and opportunities for online probability-based panels [Conference presentation]. European Online Probability Panels (EOPPs), Milan, Italy.

de Almeida, P. G. R., & dos Santos, C. D.Junior. (2025). Artificial intelligence governance: Understanding how public organizations implement it. *Government Information Quarterly*, *42*(1), 102003. DOI: 10.1016/j.giq.2024.102003

De Rosis, S. (2025). *Il ruolo degli utenti nella definizione, gestione e valutazione dei servizi. Focus sui servizi sanitari pubblici* (Vol. 10). Edizioni ETS.

De Rosis, S., Cerasuolo, D., & Nuti, S. (2020). Using patient-reported measures to drive change in healthcare: The experience of the digital, continuous and systematic PREMs observatory in Italy. *BMC Health Services Research*, *20*(1), 1–17. DOI: 10.1186/s12913-020-05099-4 PMID: 32299440

De Rosis, S., Ferrè, F., & Pennucci, F. (2022). Including patient reported measures in performance evaluation systems: Patient contribution in assessing and improving the healthcare systems. *The International Journal of Health Planning and Management*, *37*(1), 144–165. DOI: 10.1002/hpm.3596 PMID: 36527717

DECRETO LEGISLATIVO 15 settembre 2017, n. 147, Disposizioni per l'introduzione di una misura nazionale di contrasto alla povertà (15 settembre 2017). https://www.normattiva.it/uri-res/N2Ls?urn:nir:stato:decreto.legislativo:2017-09-15;147!=vig

Decreto-legge 4 maggio 2023, n. 48. (2023). *Misure urgenti per l'inclusione sociale e l'accesso al mondo del lavoro*. Gazzetta Ufficiale della Repubblica Italiana.

Dencik, L., Hintz, A., & Cable, J. (2019). Exploring data justice: Conceptions, applications and directions. *Information Communication and Society*, *22*(7), 873–881. DOI: 10.1080/1369118X.2019.1606268

Desiere, S., Langenbucher, K., & Struyven, L. (2019). *Statistical profiling in public employment services: An international comparison*. OECD Social, Employment and Migration Working Papers.

Diakopoulos, N. (2016). Accountability in algorithmic decision making. *Communications of the ACM*, *59*(2), 56–62. DOI: 10.1145/2844110

Dietvorst, B. J., Simmons, J. P., & Massey, C. (2015). Algorithm aversion. *Journal of Experimental Psychology. General, 144*(1), 114–126. DOI: 10.1037/xge0000033 PMID: 25401381

Dignum, V. (2019). *Responsible artificial intelligence: How to develop and use AI in a responsible way* (Vol. 2156). Springer. DOI: 10.1007/978-3-030-30371-6

Dimas, G. L., Goldkind, L., & Konrad, R. (2023). Big ideas, small data: Opportunities and challenges for data science and the social services sector. *Big Data & Society, 10*(1), 20539517231171051. Advance online publication. DOI: 10.1177/20539517231171051

Dipartimento per la Trasformazione Digitale. (2022). *Piattaforma Digitale Nazionale Dati (PDND)*. Presidenza del Consiglio dei Ministri.

DIW Berlin. (2025a). *Data access – Conditions for downloading SOEP microdata.*

DIW Berlin. (2025b). *SOEP Research Data Center – Access to sensitive and regional data.*

Donabedian, A. (1988). The quality of care: How can it be assessed? *Journal of the American Medical Association, 260*(12), 1743–1748. DOI: 10.1001/jama.1988.03410120089033 PMID: 3045356

Dong, M., Bonnefon, J. F., & Rahwan, I. (2024). False consensus biases AI against vulnerable stakeholders. arXiv. /arXiv.2407.12143 (Preprint.)DOI: 10.2139/ssrn.4876227

Dong, M., Bonnefon, J. F., & Rahwan, I. (2025). Heterogeneous preferences and asymmetric insights for AI use among welfare claimants and non-claimants. *Nature Communications, 16*(1), 6973. Advance online publication. DOI: 10.1038/s41467-025-62440-3 PMID: 40730578

Doyle, P., Lane, J., Theeuwes, J. J. M., & Zayatz, L. V. (Eds.). (2001). *Confidentiality, disclosure, and data access*. Elsevier.

Dunleavy, P., & Margetts, H. Z. (2010). The second wave of digital era governance. *APSA 2010 Annual Meeting Paper.*

Dunleavy, P. (2006). *Digital era governance: IT corporations, the state, and e-government*. Oxford University Press. DOI: 10.1093/acprof:oso/9780199296194.001.0001

Dunleavy, P., Margetts, H., Bastow, S., & Tinkler, J. (2006). New public management is dead—Long live digital-era governance. *Journal of Public Administration: Research and Theory, 16*(3), 467–494. DOI: 10.1093/jopart/mui057

Edgar, B., Harrison, M., Watson, P., & Busch-Geertsema, V. (2007). *Measurement of homelessness at European Union level*. European Commission. https://ec.europa.eu/employment_social/social_inclusion/docs/2007/study_homelessness_en.pdf

Einhaus, M., & Klenk, T. (2024). Towards a platformised welfare state? *Der Moderne Staat*, *17*(1), 13–34. DOI: 10.3224/dms.v17i1.02

Ejim-Eze, E. (2025). The role of AI in effective social protection delivery: A focus on national cash transfer programs. In *AI and public sector transformation*. Springer., DOI: 10.1007/978-3-031-71678-2_9

Enqvist, L. (2024). Rule-based versus AI-driven benefits allocation: GDPR and AIA legal implications and challenges for automation in public social security administration. *Information & Communications Technology Law*, *33*(2), 222–246. DOI: 10.1080/13600834.2024.2349835

ePanstwo Foundation. (2019). *alGOVrithms: Are citizens governed by computer programmes?*

Espeland, W. N., & Stevens, M. L. (1998). Commensuration as a Social Process. *Annual Review of Sociology*, *24*(1), 313–343. https://www.jstor.org/stable/223484. DOI: 10.1146/annurev.soc.24.1.313

Esping-Andersen, G. (1990). The three worlds of welfare capitalism. *Polity*.

Esping-Andersen, G. (1990). *The three worlds of welfare capitalism*. Princeton University Press.

Eubanks, V. (2018). *Automating inequality: How high-tech tools profile, police, and punish the poor*. St. Martin's Press.

Eubanks, V. (2018). *Automating Inequality: How High-Tech Tools Profile, Police, and Punish the Poor*. St. Martin's Press.

European Commission High-Level Group on Artificial Intelligence. (2019). *Ethics guidelines for trustworthy artificial intelligence*. European Commission. https://digital-strategy.ec.europa.eu/en/library/ethics-guidelines-trustworthy-ai

European Commission. (2016). Regulation (EU) 2016/679 of the European Parliament and of the Council of 27 April 2016 on the protection of natural persons with regard to the processing of personal data and on the free movement of such data, and repealing Directive 95/46/EC (General Data Protection Regulation). *Official Journal of the European Union, L*, •••, 119.

European Commission. (2019). *Ethics guidelines for trustworthy AI*.

European Commission. (2021). *Italy's recovery and resilience plan*. European Commission.

European Commission. (2021). *Proposal for a regulation laying down harmonised rules on artificial intelligence*. Artificial Intelligence Act.

European Commission. (2023). *Ethics and integrity in research*. Publications Office of the European Union.

European Federation of National Organisations Working with the Homeless. (2005). ETHOS: European typology of homelessness and housing exclusion. https://www.feantsa.org/download/ethos2484215748748239888.pdf

European Foundation for the Improvement of Living and Working Conditions. (2020). *Living, working and COVID-19*. Publications Office of the European Union. https://assets.eurofound.europa.eu/f/279033/5e54520687/ef20059en.pdf

European Parliament and Council of the European Union. (2024). *Regulation (EU) 2024/1689 laying down harmonised rules on artificial intelligence (Artificial Intelligence Act)*. Official Journal of the European Union. https://eur-lex.europa.eu/eli/reg/2024/1689/oj

European Union. (2016). Regulation (EU) 2016/679 (General Data Protection Regulation).

European Union. (2024). *Regulation (EU) 2024/1689 laying down harmonised rules on artificial intelligence (AI Act)*.

Evers, A. (2005). Mixed Welfare Systems and Hybrid Organizations: Changes in the Governance and Provision of Social Services. *International Journal of Public Administration*, *28*(9–10), 737–748. DOI: 10.1081/PAD-200067318

Farooqi, A., Das, D., Tripathi, M., Dutta, R., Goyal, N. K., & Sheikh, M. F. (2026). Navigating Ethical Frontiers in AI-Driven Geriatric Care. In Stolakis, K., & Efthymiou, I. (Eds.), *AI for Geriatric Care in an Aging Society* (pp. 243–266). IGI Global Scientific Publishing., DOI: 10.4018/979-8-3373-5462-0.ch009

Fecher, B., & Friesike, S. (2014). Open science: One term, five schools of thought. In Bartling, S., & Friesike, S. (Eds.), *Opening science* (pp. 17–47). Springer. DOI: 10.1007/978-3-319-00026-8_2

Ferrera, M. (1996). The'Southern model'of welfare in social Europe. *Journal of European Social Policy*, *6*(1), 17–37. DOI: 10.1177/095892879600600102

Ferrera, M. (2005). *The boundaries of welfare: European integration and the new spatial politics of social protection*. Oxford University Press. DOI: 10.1093/0199284660.001.0001

Fienberg, S. E., & Willenborg, L. C. R. J. (Eds.). (1998). Disclosure limitation methods for protecting the confidentiality of statistical data. *Journal of Official Statistics*, *14*, 337–345.

Fitzpatrick, S., Watts, B., Pawson, H., Bramley, G., Wood, J., Stephens, M., & Blenkinsopp, J. (2021). *The homelessness monitor: England 2021*. Crisis. https://www.crisis.org.uk/media/244629/crisis-england-monitor-2021.pdf

Floridi, L., Cowls, J., Beltrametti, M., Chatila, R., Chazerand, P., Dignum, V., Luetge, C., Madelin, R., Pagallo, U., Rossi, F., Schafer, B., Valcke, P., & Vayena, E. (2018). AI4People—An ethical framework for a good AI society. *Minds and Machines*, *28*(4), 689–707. DOI: 10.1007/s11023-018-9482-5 PMID: 30930541

Forskrift om rapportering fra kommuner og fylkeskommuner mv. (KOSTRA-forskriften), FOR-2019-10-18-1412 (2019). https://lovdata.no/dokument/SF/forskrift/2019-10-18-1412

Foucault, M. (1975). *Discipline and punish: The birth of the prison*. Penguin Books.

Fountain, J. E. (2001). *Building the virtual state: Information technology and institutional change*. Brookings Institution Press.

Fourcade, M., & Healy, K. (2017). Seeing like a market. *Socio-economic Review*, *15*(1), 9–29.

Frey, C. B., & Osborne, M. A. (2013). *The future of employment: How susceptible are jobs to computerisation?* Oxford Martin School.

Friedman, B., & Nissenbaum, H. (1994). *Bias in computer systems*. Stanford University.

Gallagher, P., & Griffin, R. (2023). (In)accuracy in algorithmic profiling of the unemployed: An exploratory review of reporting standards. *Social Policy and Society*, 1–14.

Gallino, L. (2007). *Tecnologia e democrazia*. Einaudi.

Gallino, L. (2014). *Dizinario di sociologia*. UTET.

Gasser, U., & Schmitt, C. (2019). Professional norms in AI governance. In *Oxford handbook of ethics of AI*. Oxford University Press.

Gebru, T., Morgenstern, J., Vecchione, B., Vaughan, J. W., Wallach, H., Iii, H. D., & Crawford, K. (2021). Datasheets for datasets. *Communications of the ACM, 64*(12), 86–92. DOI: 10.1145/3458723

Germundsson, N., & Stranz, H. (2024). Automating social assistance: Exploring the use of robotic process automation in the Swedish personal social services. *International Journal of Social Welfare, 33*(3), 647–658. DOI: 10.1111/ijsw.12633

Gil-Garcia, J. R., Pardo, T. A., & Burke, G. B. (2010). Conceptualizing information integration in government. In Scholl, H. J. (Ed.), *E-government: Information, technology, and transformation* (pp. 179–202). M.E. Sharpe.

Gillespie, T. (2014). The relevance of algorithms. In Gillespie, T. (Eds.), *Media technologies*. MIT Press. DOI: 10.7551/mitpress/9042.003.0013

Goebel, J., Grabka, M. M., Liebig, S., Kroh, M., Richter, D., Schröder, C., & Schupp, J. (2019). The German Socio-Economic Panel (SOEP). *Jahrbücher für Nationalökonomie und Statistik, 239*(2), 345–360. DOI: 10.1515/jbnst-2018-0022

Golder, S. A., & Macy, M. W. (2014). Digital Footprints: Opportunities and Challenges for Online Social Research. *Review of Sociology, 40*, 129–152.

Goldsmith, S., & Yang, J. (2025). AI and the transformation of accountability and discretion in urban governance. *arXiv preprint arXiv:2502.13101.*

Government of Canada. (2019). *Algorithmic impact assessment*. Treasury Board of Canada Secretariat.

Government of Canada. (2019). Directive on automated decision-making. Treasury Board of Canada Secretariat. https://www.tbs-sct.canada.ca/pol/doc-eng.aspx?id=32592

Goyal, N. K., Gulati, K., Avasthi, A., Kapoor, S. K., Keswani, B., & Gupta, S. (2026). Securing the Imagination: Security and Privacy Challenges in Generative AI Systems. In Elbaghazaoui, B. (Eds.), *Generative AI-Powered Data Architectures* (pp. 239–266). IGI Global Scientific Publishing., DOI: 10.4018/979-8-3373-5616-7.ch010

Grgić-Hlača, N., Weller, A., & Redmiles, E. M. (2020). Dimensions of diversity in human perceptions of algorithmic fairness. *arXiv preprint arXiv:2005.00808.*

Grgić-Hlača, N., Redmiles, E. M., Gummadi, K. P., & Weller, A. (2018). Human perceptions of fairness in algorithmic decision making. In *Proceedings of the World Wide Web Conference* (pp. 903–912). DOI: 10.1145/3178876.3186138

Gui, L. (Ed.). (1995). *L'utente che non c'è: Emarginazione grave, persone senza dimora e servizi sociali*. FrancoAngeli.

Gurumoorthy, R., Rees, D., Miller, E. S., & Thomas, R. (2025). Data-driven AI in social care Wales: Identifying gaps and opportunities. *Proceedings of the European Conference on Innovation and Entrepreneurship*, 20(1), 285–294. https://doi.org/ DOI: 10.34190/ecie.20.1.4200

Habermas, J. (1989). *The structural transformation of the public sphere* (Burger, T., Trans.). MIT Press. (Original work published 1962)

Habermas, J. (2006). Political communication in media society. *Communication Theory*, *16*(4), 411–426. DOI: 10.1111/j.1468-2885.2006.00280.x

Hagendorff, T. (2020). The ethics of AI ethics: An evaluation of guidelines. *Minds and Machines*, *30*(1), 99–120. DOI: 10.1007/s11023-020-09517-8

Haitsma, L. M. (2025). Addressing discrimination in algorithmic profiling: Examining risk governance in Dutch public social security agencies. *European Journal of Social Security*, *27*(2), 191–212. DOI: 10.1177/13882627251351093

Hardman, P., Dell'Acqua, F., Ayoubi, C., Lifshitz-Assaf, H., Sadun, R., Mollick, E. r., Mollick, L., Han, Y., Goldman, J., Nair, H., Taub, S., & Lakhani, K. R. (2024). Structured prompting for educators: Experiment in hoz to get the best out of your favourite generative AI tools. Dr Philippa Hardman Substrack. Https://drphilippahardman.substack.com/p/strucutred-prompting-for-educators

Haven, T., Gopalakrishna, G., Tijdink, J., van der Schot, D., & Bouter, L. (2022). Promoting trust in research and researchers: How open science and research integrity are intertwined. *BMC Research Notes*, *15*(1), 302. DOI: 10.1186/s13104-022-06169-y PMID: 36127719

Helberger, N., Araujo, T., & de Vreese, C. H. (2020). Who is the fairest of them all? Public attitudes and expectations regarding automated decision-making. *Computer Law & Security Review*, *39*, 105456. DOI: 10.1016/j.clsr.2020.105456

Helsper, E. J. (2021). *The digital disconnect*. Sage.

Helsper, E. J. (2021). The digital disconnect: The social causes and consequences of digital inequalities. *Sage (Atlanta, Ga.)*. Advance online publication. DOI: 10.4135/9781526492982

Holstein, K., Wortman Vaughan, J., Daumé, H.III, Dudik, M., & Wallach, H. (2019). Improving fairness in machine learning systems: What do industry practitioners need? *Proceedings of the 2019 CHI Conference on Human Factors in Computing Systems*, 1–16. DOI: 10.1145/3290605.3300830

Howlett, M., Ramesh, M., & Perl, A. (2003). *Studying public policy: Policy cycles and policy subsystems*. Oxford University Press.

Human Rights Council. (2012). *Guiding principles on extreme poverty and human rights (A/HRC/21/39)*. United Nations. https://www.ohchr.org/sites/default/files/Documents/HRBodies/HRCouncil/RegularSession/Session21/A-HRC-21-39_en.pdf

Hwang, J. (2024). Navigating digital transformations: Innovation strategies in European social services. *Open Access Research Journal of Multidisciplinary Studies*, *8*(1), 189–203. DOI: 10.53022/oarjms.2024.8.1.0040

INPS. (2024a). *Arriva l'Intelligenza Artificiale per l'incrocio tra domanda e offerta di lavoro* [Comunicato stampa, 5 aprile 2024].

INPS. (2024b). *Messaggio n. 1384 del 08-04-2024. Linee guida per l'implementazione di sistemi di Intelligenza Artificiale – Direttiva n. 8.*

INPS. (2024c). *Bilancio di Sostenibilità 2023.*

INPS. (2024d). *Welfare as a Service (WaaS): Piattaforma dati per la cooperazione nel welfare territoriale.*

Iphofen, R. (2017). *Ethical decision making in social research: A practical guide*. Palgrave Macmillan.

ISTAT. (2017). *L'effetto tecnica nelle indagini mixed-mode*. Istituto Nazionale di Statistica.

Italian Federation of Organizations for People Experiencing Homelessness. (2017). Homelessness in Italy: Policy, people and services.

Italian National Institute of Statistics. (2014). *La ricerca nazionale sulla condizione delle persone senza dimora in Italia. Anno 2013*. https://www.istat.it/it/files/2014/06/17915_Senza_dimora.pdf

Italian National Institute of Statistics. (2020). *La domanda e l'offerta di servizi sociali e socio-sanitari*.

Italian National Institute of Statistics. (2022). *Censimento della popolazione e delle abitazioni: Popolazione residente e dinamica demografica. Anno 2021*. https://www.istat.it/it/files/2022/12/CENSIMENTO-E-DINAMICA-DEMOGRAFICA-2021.pdf

Janssen, M., Charalabidis, Y., & Zuiderwijk, A. (2012). Benefits, Adoption Barriers and Myths of Open Data and Open Government. *Information Systems Management*, *29*(4), 258–268. DOI: 10.1080/10580530.2012.716740

Janssen, M., & Estevez, E. (2013). Lean government and platform-based governance—Doing more with less. *Government Information Quarterly*, *30*, S1–S8. DOI: 10.1016/j.giq.2012.11.003

Janssen, M., & Van Der Voort, H. (2016). Adaptive governance: Towards a stable, accountable and responsive government. *Government Information Quarterly*, *33*(1), 1–5. DOI: 10.1016/j.giq.2016.02.003

Jasanoff, S. (2004). *States of knowledge*. Routledge. DOI: 10.4324/9780203413845

Jasanoff, S. (2016). *The ethics of invention*. W. W. Norton.

Jasanoff, S. (2016). *The Ethics of Invention: Technology and the Human Future*. W.W. Norton.

Jenkins, H. (2007). Confronting the Challenges of Participatory Culture – Media Education for the 21st Century (Part Two). *Nordic Journal of Digital Literacy*, *2*(2), 97–113. DOI: 10.18261/ISSN1891-943X-2007-02-04

Jobin, A., Ienca, M., & Vayena, E. (2019). *Global landscape of AI ethics guidelines*. AlgorithmWatch. DOI: 10.1038/s42256-019-0088-2

Johns, F. (2017). Data mining as global governance. In *Oxford Handbook of Law, Regulation and Technology*. Oxford University Press.

Joshi, D. (2024). AI governance in India–law, policy and political economy. *Communication Research and Practice*, *10*(3), 328–339. DOI: 10.1080/22041451.2024.2346428

Kanu, D. H. (2025). Digital public infrastructure: The building blocks for digital financial inclusion and taxation of the digital economy in Liberia. *SSRN*. DOI: 10.2139/ssrn.5738263

Kaun, A., Lomborg, S., Pentzold, C., Allhutter, D., & Sztandar-Sztanderska, K. (2023). Crosscurrents: Welfare. *Media Culture & Society*, *45*(5), 877–883. DOI: 10.1177/01634437231154777

Kawakami, A., Coston, A., Heidari, H., Holstein, K., & Zhu, H. (2024). Studying up public sector AI: How networks of power relations shape agency decisions around AI design and use. *Proceedings of the ACM on Human-Computer Interaction*, *8*(CSCW2), 1–24. DOI: 10.1145/3686989

Keppler, S., Sinchaisri, W. P., & Snyder, C. (2024). Backwards planning with generative AI: Case study evidence from US K-12 teachers. https://papers.ssrn.com/sol3/papers.cfm?abstract_id=4924786

Kersing, M., van Zoonen, L., Putters, K., & Oldenhof, L. (2022). The changing roles of frontline bureaucrats in the digital welfare state: The case of a data dashboard in Rotterdam's Work and Income department. *Data & Policy*, *4*, e24. DOI: 10.1017/dap.2022.16

Kettunen, P., & Petersen, K. (Eds.). (2011). *Beyond welfare state models: Transnational historical perspectives on social policy*. Edward Elgar Publishing. DOI: 10.4337/9781849809603

Keusch, F., Struminskaya, B., Mulder, J., & Jongerius, S. (2025). Data donation as a method to measure physical activity in older adults. *Journal of Medical Internet Research*, *27*, e69799. DOI: 10.2196/69799 PMID: 41004250

Khan, M. S., Umer, H., & Faruqe, F. (2024). Artificial intelligence for low-income countries. *Humanities & Social Sciences Communications*, *11*(1), 1–13. DOI: 10.1057/s41599-024-03947-w

Kieslich, K., Lünich, M., & Marcinkowski, F. (2021). The threats of artificial intelligence scale (TAI). *International Journal of Social Robotics*, *13*(7), 1563–1577. DOI: 10.1007/s12369-020-00734-w

Kieslich, K., Starke, C., Došenović, P., Marcinkowski, F., & Lünich, M. (2020). *Artificial intelligence and discrimination*. CAIS Factsheet.

Kissinger, H., Huttenlocher, D., & Schmidt, E. (2023). *L'era dell'intelligenza artificiale. Il futuro dell'identità umana*. Mondadori.

Kitchin, R. (2014). The data revolution: Big data, open data, data infrastructures and their consequences. *Sage (Atlanta, Ga.)*. Advance online publication. DOI: 10.4135/9781473909472

Kitchin, R. (2014). *The data revolution: Big data, open data, data infrastructures and their consequences*. SAGE Publications.

Kitchin, R. (2017). Thinking critically about and researching algorithms. *Information Communication and Society*, *20*(1), 14–29. DOI: 10.1080/1369118X.2016.1154087

Köbis, N., Starke, C., & Rahwan, I. (2021). Artificial intelligence as an anti-corruption tool (AI-ACT): Potentials and pitfalls for top-down and bottom-up approaches. *arXiv preprint arXiv:2102.11567.*

Kocar, S., & Kaczmirek, L. (2023). A meta-analysis of recruitment rates in probability-based online panels. *International Journal of Social Research Methodology*, *27*(5), 589–604. DOI: 10.1080/13645579.2023.2242202

Kroll, J. A. (2021, March). Outlining traceability: A principle for operationalizing accountability in computing systems. In *Proceedings of the 2021 ACM Conference on fairness, accountability, and transparency* (pp. 758-771). DOI: 10.1145/3442188.3445937

Kroll, J. A., Huey, J., Barocas, S., Felten, E. W., Reidenberg, J. R., Robinson, D. G., & Yu, H. (2017). Accountable algorithms. *University of Pennsylvania Law Review*, *165*(3), 633–705. DOI: 10.2139/ssrn.2765268

Kumari, M., & Goyal, N. K. (2026). Artificial Intelligence in the Cryptocurrency Ecosystem: Crime Mechanisms, Detection Strategies, and Legal Perspectives. In Lin, L. (Ed.), *Innovations in Cryptocrime and Financial Fraud* (pp. 245–282). IGI Global Scientific Publishing., DOI: 10.4018/979-8-3373-0675-9.ch007

Kumari, M., Khan, S. T., Gulati, K., Sharma, P., Goyal, N. K., & Sheikh, M. F. (2026). Procedural Content Generation Using Generative AI. In *Reshaping the Video Game Landscape With AI* (pp. 205–232). IGI Global Scientific Publishing., DOI: 10.4018/979-8-3373-4637-3.ch007

Kumari, M., Kumawat, R., Dutta, R., Khan, S. T., Goyal, N. K., & Sheikh, M. F. (2026). Wireless Communication and IoT Integration in Smart Clothing. In *Smart Wearables* (pp. 195–232). IGI Global Scientific Publishing., DOI: 10.4018/979-8-3373-4287-0.ch008

Kumari, M., Kumawat, R., Tripathi, M., Suganthi, K., Goyal, N. K., & Sheikh, M. F. (2026). Blockchain for Transparency and Traceability in Supply Chains. In Khan, M. (Eds.), *Maximizing Operational Efficiency* (pp. 35–64). IGI Global Scientific Publishing., DOI: 10.4018/979-8-3373-3109-6.ch002

Kuziemski, M., & Misuraca, G. (2020). AI governance in the public sector: Three tales from the frontiers of automated decision-making in democratic settings. *Telecommunications Policy*, *44*(6), 101976. DOI: 10.1016/j.telpol.2020.101976 PMID: 32313360

Kyriakidis, M., De Winter, J. C. F., Stanton, N., Bellet, T., Van Arem, B., Brookhuis, K., Martens, M. H., Bengler, K., Andersson, J., Merat, N., Reed, N., Flament, M., Hagenzieker, M., & Happee, R. (2019). A Human Factors Perspective on Automated Driving. *Theoretical Issues in Ergonomics Science*, *20*(3), 223–249. DOI: 10.1080/1463922X.2017.1293187

Laezza, V., Petrosino, A., & Luise, V. (2025). ChatGPT and the social appropriation of AI on Discord. *Fuori Luogo Journal of Sociology of Territory, Tourism. Technology*, *22*(1), 49–64. DOI: 10.6093/2723-9608/11111

Lamanna, D., Stergiopoulos, V., Durbin, J., O'Campo, P., Poremski, D., & Tepper, J. (2018). Promoting continuity of care for homeless adults with unmet health needs: The role of brief interventions. *Health & Social Care in the Community*, *26*(1), 56–64. DOI: 10.1111/hsc.12461 PMID: 28569397

Lancker, W. V. (2020). Automating the welfare state: Consequences and challenges for the organisation of solidarity. In *The digital welfare state* (pp. 149–168). Springer., DOI: 10.1007/978-3-030-44062-6_8

Landuzzi, C., & Pieretti, G. (2006). *Servizio sociale e povertà estreme: Accompagnamento sociale e persone senza dimora*. FrancoAngeli.

Lastrico V. (2013), quando il forum sostituisce la fabbrica. Tentativi di costruzione identitaria nell'era della fine del lavoro. *Sociologia della comunicazine* XXIV, 46.

Lee, M. K. (2018). Understanding perception of algorithmic decisions: Fairness, trust, and emotion in response to algorithmic management. *Big Data & Society*, *5*(1), 2053951718756684. DOI: 10.1177/2053951718756684

Lee, M. K., Kim, J. T., & Lizarondo, L. (2017). A human-centered approach to algorithmic services. In *Proceedings of the 2017 CHI Conference on Human Factors in Computing Systems* (pp. 3365–3376). DOI: 10.1145/3025453.3025884

Levy, K., Chasalow, K. E., & Riley, S. (2021). Algorithms and decision-making in the public sector. *Annual Review of Law and Social Science*, *17*(1), 309–334. DOI: 10.1146/annurev-lawsocsci-041221-023808

Liang, Y., & Lee, S. A. (2017). Fear of autonomous robots and artificial intelligence. *International Journal of Social Robotics*, *9*(3), 379–384. DOI: 10.1007/s12369-017-0401-3

Lindner, R., Aichholzer, G., & Hennen, L. (Eds.). (2016). *Electronic democracy in Europe: Prospects and challenges of e-participation*. Springer. DOI: 10.1007/978-3-319-27419-5

Lipsky, M. (1980). *Street-level bureaucracy: Dilemmas of the individual in public services*. Russell Sage Foundation.

Liu, H., & Priest, S. (2009). Understanding public support for stem cell research. *Public Understanding of Science*, *18*(6), 704–718. DOI: 10.1177/0963662508097625

Lodge, M., & Mennicken, A. (2017). Regulation of and by algorithm. *Regulation & Governance*.

Logg, J. M., Minson, J. A., & Moore, D. A. (2019). Algorithm appreciation. *Organizational Behavior and Human Decision Processes, 151*, 90–103. DOI: 10.1016/j.obhdp.2018.12.005

Lori, M., & Zamaro, N. (2019). Il profilo sfocato del Terzo settore italiano. [Lexical characteristics of Italian language]. *Politiche Sociali, 2*, 225–242.

Lov om kommuner og fylkeskommuner (kommuneloven) [Local Government Act], LOV-2018-06-22-83 § 24-9 (2018). https://lovdata.no/dokument/NLE/lov/2018-06-22-83/KAPITTEL_7-3#%C2%A724-9

Lu, S. (2020). Algorithmic opacity, private accountability, and corporate social disclosure in the age of artificial intelligence. *Vand. J. Ent. & Tech. L., 23*, 99.

Lynn, P. (2012). *Longitudinal survey methods*. European Central Bank.

Madan, R., & Ashok, M. (2023). AI adoption and diffusion in public administration: A systematic literature review and future research agenda. *Government Information Quarterly, 40*(1), 101774. DOI: 10.1016/j.giq.2022.101774

Maher, C., Ryan, J., Ambrosi, C., & Edney, S. (2017). Users' experiences of wearable activity trackers. *BMC Public Health, 17*(1), 880. DOI: 10.1186/s12889-017-4888-1 PMID: 29141607

Manti, F. (2014). *L'utopia della ciber agorà. Problematicità, limiti, possibilità della democrazia digitale. XLIX n. 211 online*. Einaudi Editore.

Marcinkowski, F., Kieslich, K., Starke, C., & Lünich, M. (2020). Implications of AI (un-)fairness in higher education admissions. In *Proceedings of the 2020 Conference on Fairness, Accountability, and Transparency* (pp. 122–130). DOI: 10.1145/3351095.3372867

Margetts, H., & Dunleavy, P. (2013). The second wave of digital-era governance: A quasi-paradigm for government on the Web. *Philosophical Transactions of the Royal Society A*, 371(1987).

Margetts, H., & Dorobantu, C. (2019). Rethink government with AI. *Nature, 568*(7751), 163–165. DOI: 10.1038/d41586-019-01099-5 PMID: 30967667

Markham, A., & Baym, N. (2009). *Internet Inquiry: Conversations about Method*. Sage., DOI: 10.4135/9781483329086

Marres, N. (2017). *Digital sociology: The reinvention of social research*. Polity Press.

Martini, A., & Sisti, C. (1999). *La valutazione come strumento di programmazione*. Città Studi Edizioni.

Mascioli, F., & Rossi, C. (2006). Il metodo della cattura-ricattura: Un esperimento didattico tra matematica e scienze naturali. *Induzioni*, *33*(2), 31–49.

Maslovskaya, O., & Lugtig, P. (2022). Representativeness in online panels. *Journal of the Royal Statistical Society. Series A, (Statistics in Society)*, *185*(3), 851–871. DOI: 10.1111/rssa.12801

Mauceri, S., & Di Censi, L. (Eds.). (2024). *Povertà estreme. Un'analisi sul sistema dei servizi per le persone senza dimora a Roma*. FrancoAngeli. https://series.francoangeli.it/index.php/oa/catalog/book/1151

Mauceri, S. (2012). Per una survey integrata e multilivello. Le lezioni dimenticate della Columbia School. *Sociologia e Ricerca Sociale*, *99*(99), 22–64. DOI: 10.3280/SR2012-099003

Mauceri, S. (2019). *Qualità nella quantità. La survey research nell'era dei Mixed Methods*. FrancoAngeli.

Mauceri, S., Faggiano, M. P., & Di Censi, L. (2020). Survey 2.0. *Sociologia e Ricerca Sociale*, *121*(121), 25–48. DOI: 10.3280/SR2020-121002

Mayer-Schönberger, V., & Cukier, K. (2013). *Big data: A revolution that will transform how we live, work, and think*. Houghton Mifflin Harcourt. Eubanks, V. (2018). *Automating inequality: How high-tech tools profile, police, and punish the poor*. Macmillan.

McCarthy, J., Minsky, M. L., Rochester, N., & Shannon, C. E. (1955). *A proposal for the Dartmouth summer research project on artificial intelligence*. Dartmouth College.

Medaglia, R. (2012). eParticipation research: Moving characterization forward (2006 2011). *Government Information Quarterly*, *29*(3), 346–360. DOI: 10.1016/j.giq.2012.02.010

Mehrabi, N., Morstatter, F., Saxena, N., Lerman, K., & Galstyan, A. (2019). A survey on bias and fairness in machine learning. *ACM Computing Surveys*, *54*(6), 1–35. DOI: 10.1145/3457607

Menard, S. (2002). *Longitudinal research* (2nd ed.). SAGE. DOI: 10.4135/9781412984867

Merenkov, A. V., Campa, R., & Dronishinets, N. P. (2020). Public opinion on artificial intelligence development. In *Culture* (pp. 565–574). Personality, Society in the Conditions of Digitalization.

Mergel, I., Dickinson, H., Stenvall, J., & Gasco, M. (2024). Implementing AI in the public sector. *Public Management Review*, 1–14.

Miller, A. P. (2018). Want less-biased decisions? Use algorithms. *Harvard Business Review*.

Mingione, E. (Ed.). (1996). *Urban poverty and the underclass: A reader*. Blackwell. DOI: 10.1002/9780470712900

Ministero del Lavoro e delle Politiche Sociali. (2019, 22 agosto). Decreto n. 103 del 22 agosto 2019 – Modalità attuative del Sistema informativo dell'offerta dei servizi sociali (SIOSS). https://www.lavoro.gov.it/documenti-e-norme/normative/Documents/2019/DM-103-del-22082019-SIOSS

Misuraca, G., Broster, D., & Centeno, C. (2012). Digital Europe 2030. *Government Information Quarterly*, *29*(S1), S121–S131. DOI: 10.1016/j.giq.2011.08.006

Misuraca, G., Medaglia, R., & Aquaro, V. (2021). Re-designing the UN e-government survey in light of the 2030 agenda for sustainable development: Towards a post-COVID digital society. In *Proceedings of the 14th International Conference on Theory and Practice of Electronic Governance* (pp. 198–202). DOI: 10.1145/3494193.3494221

Mittelstadt, B. D., Allo, P., Taddeo, M., Wachter, S., & Floridi, L. (2016). The ethics of algorithms: Mapping the debate. *Big Data & Society*, *3*(2), 1–21. DOI: 10.1177/2053951716679679

Molinari, B. (2025). From digital traces to artificial intelligence: New bourdaries from representativeness. *In The lab's quarterly*, 2025/ a. *XXVII*, (3), 193–212. DOI: 10.13131/unipi/x6c5-2t23

Moore, M. H. (1995). *Creating Public Value: Strategic Management in Government*. Harvard University Press.

Mossberger, K., Tolbert, C. J., & McNeal, R. S. (2008). *Digital citizenship: The internet, society, and participation*. MIT Press.

Noble, S. U. (2018). *Algorithms of oppression*. NYU Press. DOI: 10.18574/nyu/9781479833641.001.0001

Noveck, B. S. (2021). *Solving public problems: A practical guide to fix our government and change our world*. Yale University Press.

Nuti, S., De Rosis, S., Bonciani, M., & Murante, A. M. (2017). Rethinking Healthcare Performance Evaluation Systems towards the People-Centredness Approach: Their Pathways, their Experience, their Evaluation. *Healthcare Papers*, *17*(2), 56–64. DOI: 10.12927/hcpap.2017.25408 PMID: 29595446

Nuwasiima, M., Ahonon, M. P., & Kadiri, C. (2024). The role of artificial intelligence and machine learning in social work practice. *World Journal of Advanced Research and Reviews, 24*(1), 80–97. DOI: 10.30574/wjarr.2024.24.1.2998

O'Neil, C. (2016). *Weapons of Math Destruction: How Big Data Increases Inequality and Threatens Democracy*. Crown.

O'Neil, C. (2017). *Weapons of math destruction: How big data increases inequality and threatens democracy*. Crown.

OECD. (2019). *Artificial intelligence in society*. OECD Publishing.

OECD. (2019). *Oslo manual 2018: Guidelines for collecting, reporting and using data on innovation* (4th ed.). OECD Publishing.

OECD. (2020). *Digital Government Index: 2019 results*. OECD Publishing.

OECD. (2020). *Innovative citizen participation and new democratic institutions: Catching the deliberative wave*. OECD Publishing.

OECD. (2021). *Recommendation of the Council on Artificial Intelligence*. OECD.

OECD. (2021). *The OECD digital government policy framework*. OECD Publishing.

Organisation for Economic Co-operation and Development. (2019). Better criteria for better evaluation: Revised evaluation criteria definitions and principles for use. https://www.oecd.org/content/dam/oecd/en/publications/reports/2019/12/better-criteria-for-better-evaluation_f7a307eb/15a9c26b-en.pdf[REMOVED HYPERLINK FIELD]

Padgett, D. K., Henwood, B. F., & Tsemberis, S. J. (2016). *Housing first: Ending homelessness, transforming systems, and changing lives*. Oxford University Press.

Pais, I. (2012). *La Rete che lavora: Mestieri e professioni nell'era digitale*. EGEA.

Panda, M., Hossain, M. M., Puri, R., & Ahmad, A. (2025). Artificial intelligence in action: Shaping the future of the public sector. *Digital Policy. Regulation & Governance, 27*(6), 668–686.

Panoptykon Foundation. (2015). *Profiling the unemployed in Poland*.

Pasquale, F. (2015). *The black box society: The secret algorithms that control money and information*. Harvard University Press. DOI: 10.4159/harvard.9780674736061

Pasquale, F. (2019). *The second wave of algorithmic accountability*. Law and Political Economy.

Pasupuleti, M. (2025). Governance frameworks for ethical AI deployment in public sector services. [IJAIRI]. *International Journal of Academic and Industrial Research Innovations*, *5*(5), 561–573. DOI: 10.62311/nesx/rphcr17

Patton, M. Q. (1997). Utilization-focused evaluation: The new century text. *Sage (Atlanta, Ga.)*.

Patton, M. Q. (2002). *Qualitative research and evaluation methods* (3rd ed.). Sage.

Pellegrino, G., Söderberg, J., & Milan, S. (2019). Datafication from below: Epistemology, ambivalences, challenges. *Tecnoscienza – Italian Journal of Science &. Technology Studies*, *10*(1), 89–113.

Pellegrino, M., & Verzieri, V. (Eds.). (1991). *Né tetto né legge: L'emarginazione grave, le nuove povertà, i "senza fissa dimora"*. Edizioni Gruppo Abele.

Pennucci, F., De Rosis, S., & Passino, C. (2020). Piloting a web-based systematic collection and reporting of patient-reported outcome measures and patient-reported experience measures in chronic heart failure. *BMJ Open*, *10*(10), e037754. DOI: 10.1136/bmjopen-2020-037754 PMID: 33020096

Pertsas, G. (2025). Interoperability for welfare: Digitalization and state transformation in Greece. In *AI and welfare governance*. Springer., DOI: 10.4337/9781035338153.00011

Peters, L., Hobson, C. W., & Samuel, V. (2022). A systematic review and meta-synthesis of qualitative studies that investigate the emotional experiences of staff working in homeless settings. *Health & Social Care in the Community*, *30*(1), 58–72. DOI: 10.1111/hsc.13502 PMID: 34255385

Pew Research Center. (2018). *Public attitudes toward computer algorithms*.

Pew Research Center. (2018). *Public attitudes toward computer algorithms*. https://www.pewresearch.org/

Power, M. (1997). *The audit society: Rituals of verification*. Oxford University Press.

Preece, J. (2000). Online Communities: Designing Usability, Supporting Sociability. *Industrial Management & Data Systems*, *100*(9), 459–460. DOI: 10.1108/imds.2000.100.9.459.3

Presidenza del Consiglio dei Ministri. (2021). *Piano Nazionale di Ripresa e Resilienza*. PNRR.

Primerano, I., Marchesini, N., Santelli, F., Taddei, L., & Cerbara, L. (2026). Secondary, longitudinal, and panel data in social science research. In Taddei, L., & Paolucci, M. (Eds.), *Longitudinal data infrastructures in Europe*. Springer. DOI: 10.1007/978-3-032-07005-0_2

Prior, L. (2003). Using documents in social research. *Sage (Atlanta, Ga.)*.

Prior, L. (2008). Repositioning documents in social research. *Sociology*, *42*(5), 821–836. DOI: 10.1177/0038038508094564

Punziano, G., Marrazzo, F., & Acampa, S. (2021). Content analysis of CrowdTangle data. *Current Politics & Economics of Europe, 32*(4).

Punziano, G., Cicellin, M., Zito, E., Acampa, S., & Sorrentino, R. (2023). Role of the digital for the Third Sector in the Campania region (Italy): From the side of research to the side of the objects in the aftermath of the COVID-19 pandemic. *Italian Sociological Review*, *13*(2), 279–296.

Radicchi, A. (2024). Appendice - Anthology: Help different. In S. Mauceri & L. Di Censi (Eds.), *Povertà estreme. Un'analisi sul sistema dei servizi per le persone senza dimora a Roma*. FrancoAngeli. https://series.francoangeli.it/index.php/oa/catalog/book/1151

Radu, R. (2021). Steering the governance of artificial intelligence: National strategies in perspective. *Policy and Society*, *40*(2), 178–193. DOI: 10.1080/14494035.2021.1929728

Ragnedda, M. (2018). *Conceptualizing digital capital*. Emerald. DOI: 10.1016/j.tele.2018.10.006

Ranerup, A., & Svensson, L. (2023). Automated decision-making, discretion and public values: A case study of two municipalities and their case management of social assistance. *European Journal of Social Work*, *26*(5), 948–962. DOI: 10.1080/13691457.2023.2185875

Redden, J., Dencik, L., & Warne, H. (2020). Datafied child welfare services: Unpacking politics, economics and power. *Policy Studies*, *41*(5), 507–526. DOI: 10.1080/01442872.2020.1724928

Rediet, A., Barocas, S., Kleinberg, J., Levy, K., Raghavan, M., & Robinson, D. G. (2020). Roles for computing in social change. *Proceedings of the 2020 Conference on Fairness, Accountability, and Transparency*.

Riedl, M. O. (2019). Human-centered artificial intelligence and machine learning. *Human Behavior and Emerging Technologies*, *1*(1), 33–36. DOI: 10.1002/hbe2.117

Robinette, P., Howard, A. M., & Wagner, A. R. (2017). Effect of robot performance on human–robot trust in time-critical situations. *IEEE Transactions on Human-Machine Systems*, *47*(4), 425–436. DOI: 10.1109/THMS.2017.2648849

Robinson, L., Cotten, S. R., Ono, H., Quan-Haase, A., Mesch, G., Chen, W., Schulz, J., Hale, T. M., & Stern, M. J. (2015). Digital inequalities and why they matter. *Information Communication and Society*, *18*(5), 569–582. DOI: 10.1080/1369118X.2015.1012532

Røhnebæk, M. T., & Breit, E. (2022). 'Damned if you do and damned if you don't': A framework for examining double binds in public service organizations. *Public Management Review*, *24*(7), 1001–1023. DOI: 10.1080/14719037.2021.1882542

Rossi, C. (2001). Using available data with dynamic models to estimate the extent of problem drug use. In *Modelling drug use: Methods to quantify and understand hidden processes* (EMCDDA Scientific Monograph Series No. 6, pp. 67–90). European Monitoring Centre for Drugs and Drug Addiction. https://www.euda.europa.eu/system/files/publications/922/Monograph6_159816.pdf

Rossi, C. (1995). Evaluating world drug policies: Towards a cost-effectiveness analysis of initiatives undertaken. *The International Journal on Drug Policy*, *6*(4), 238–242.

Røysum, A. (2013). The reform of the welfare services in Norway: One office–one way of thinking? *European Journal of Social Work*, *16*(5), 708–723. DOI: 10.1080/13691457.2012.722982

Ruppert, E., Isin, E., & Bigo, D. (2017). Data politics. *Big Data & Society*, *4*(2), 1–7. DOI: 10.1177/2053951717717749

Ruspini, E. (2002). *An introduction to longitudinal research*. Routledge.

Russell, S., & Norvig, P. (2013). *Artificial intelligence: A modern approach* (3rd ed.). Pearson.

Sabater, A., López, B., Campdepadrós, R., & Sánchez, C. (2025). Participatory action research for AI in social services. In *AI and public sector innovation*. Springer., DOI: 10.1007/978-3-031-71678-2_4

Sacchi, S., & Scarano, G. (2024). Digital transformation of public employment services in the post-pandemic era: Evidence from Italy as a latecomer country. *The Australian Journal of Social Issues*. Advance online publication. DOI: 10.1002/ajs4.385

Sackett, D. L., Rosenberg, W. M., Gray, J. A., Haynes, R. B., & Richardson, W. S. (2007). Evidence based medicine: What it is and what it isn't. 1996. *Clinical Orthopaedics and Related Research*, (455), 3–5. DOI: 10.1136/bmj.312.7023.71 PMID: 17340682

Saikkonen, P., & Choroszewicz, M. (2025). Fostering socially and ecologically sustainable digitalisation of welfare states. *Social Inclusion (Lisboa)*, *13*, 10937. Advance online publication. DOI: 10.17645/si.10937

Salamon, L. M., & Anheier, H. K. (1998). Social origins of civil society: Explaining the nonprofit sector cross-nationally. *Voluntas*, *9*(3), 213–248. DOI: 10.1023/A:1022058200985

Salem, M., Lakatos, G., Amirabdollahian, F., & Dautenhahn, K. (2015). Would you trust a (faulty) robot? In *Proceedings of the Tenth Annual ACM/IEEE International Conference on Human-Robot Interaction* (pp. 141–148). DOI: 10.1145/2696454.2696497

Sanderson, I. (2002). Evaluation, policy learning and evidence-based policy making. *Public Administration*, *80*(1), 1–22. DOI: 10.1111/1467-9299.00292

Sanjeev, A., & Barak, B. (2009). *Computational Complexity: A Modern Approach*. Cambridge University Press.

Santini, Z. I., Jose, P. E., Koyanagi, A., Meilstrup, C., Nielsen, L., Madsen, K. R., & Koushede, V. (2020). Formal social participation and health. *Social Science & Medicine*, *251*, 112906. DOI: 10.1016/j.socscimed.2020.112906 PMID: 32151885

Saraceno, C., & Keck, W. (2010). Can we identify intergenerational policy regimes in Europe? *European Societies*, *12*(5), 675–696. DOI: 10.1080/14616696.2010.483006

Scherpenzeel, A. (2009). *Start of the LISS panel*. CentERdata.

Scherpenzeel, A. (2011). Data collection in a probability-based internet panel. *Bulletin de Méthodologie Sociologique*, *109*(1), 56–61. DOI: 10.1177/0759106310387713

Scherpenzeel, A. C. (2018). Longitudinal and probability-based internet panels. In *Social and behavioral research and the internet* (pp. 77–104). Routledge. DOI: 10.4324/9780203844922-4

Schou, J., & Pors, A. S. (2019). Digital by default? A qualitative study of exclusion in digitalised welfare. *Social Policy & Administration*, *53*(3), 464–477. DOI: 10.1111/spol.12470

Scriven, M. (1967). The methodology of evaluation. In Tyler, R. W., Gagné, R. M., & Scriven, M. (Eds.), *Perspectives of curriculum evaluation* (pp. 39–83). American Educational Research Association.

Seaver, N. (2017). Algorithms as culture: Some tactics for the ethnography of algorithmic systems. *Big Data & Society, 4*(2). Advance online publication. DOI: 10.1177/2053951717738104

Selwyn, N. (2016). *Education and technology*. Bloomsbury.

Sharma, P., Kumawat, R., Jain, G., Keswani, G., Goyal, N. K., & Sheikh, M. F. (2026). ML-Based IDS for Healthcare IoT. In *Resilient HIoT Systems* (pp. 185–214). IGI Global Scientific Publishing., DOI: 10.4018/979-8-3373-7610-3.ch007

Sheikh, M. F. A., Kapoor, S. K., Goyal, N. K., Tuba, E., & Rao, A. (2026). Enhancing Healthcare Security with Fog Computing and Blockchain Technology. In *Recent Advancements in Artificial Intelligence*. Springer., DOI: 10.1007/978-981-96-7760-3_38

Shin, D. (2020). User perceptions of algorithmic decisions in the personalized AI system: Perceptual evaluation of fairness, accountability, transparency, and explainability. *Journal of Broadcasting & Electronic Media, 64*(4), 541–565. DOI: 10.1080/08838151.2020.1843357

Shin, D. (2021). The effects of explainability and causability on perception, trust, and acceptance. *International Journal of Human-Computer Studies, 146*, 102551. DOI: 10.1016/j.ijhcs.2020.102551

Shin, D., & Park, Y. J. (2019). Role of fairness, accountability, and transparency in algorithmic affordance. *Computers in Human Behavior, 98*, 277–284. DOI: 10.1016/j.chb.2019.04.019

Shin, D., Zhong, B., & Biocca, F. A. (2020). Beyond user experience: What constitutes algorithmic experiences? *International Journal of Information Management, 52*, 102061. DOI: 10.1016/j.ijinfomgt.2019.102061

Shirky, C. (2011). The Political Power of Social Media: Technology, the Public Sphere, and Political Change. *Foreign Affairs, 90*(1), 28–41. https://www.jstor.org/stable/25800379

Shmueli, G., Bruce, P. C., Gedeck, P., & Patel, N. R. (2020). *Data mining for business analytics: Concepts, techniques, and applications in Python* (3rd ed.). Wiley.

Singer, E., Mathiowetz, N. A., & Couper, M. P. (1993). Privacy and census participation. *Public Opinion Quarterly, 57*(4), 465–482. DOI: 10.1086/269391

Singer, E., Van Hoewyk, J., & Neugebauer, R. (2003). Privacy and participation in the 2000 Census. *Public Opinion Quarterly*, *67*(3), 368–384. DOI: 10.1086/377465

Sogstad, M., Hellesø, R., & Skinner, M. S. (2020). The development of a new care service landscape in Norway. *Health Services Insights*, *13*, 1178632920922221. DOI: 10.1177/1178632920922221 PMID: 32565676

Spennemann, D. (2023). What has ChatGPT read? The origins of archaeological citations used by a generative artificial intelligence application, *arXiv*, https://doi.org//arXiv.2308.03301.DOI: 10.48550

Srivastava, M., Heidari, H., & Krause, A. (2019). Mathematical notions vs. human perception of fairness. In *Proceedings of the 25th ACM SIGKDD International Conference on Knowledge Discovery & Data Mining* (pp. 2459–2468). DOI: 10.1145/3292500.3330664

Starke, C., Baleis, J., Keller, B., & Marcinkowski, F. (2021). Fairness perceptions of algorithmic decision-making: A systematic review of the empirical literature. *arXiv preprint arXiv:2103.12016*.

Starke, C., & Lünich, M. (2020). Artificial intelligence for political decision-making in the European Union: Effects on citizens' perceptions of input, throughput, and output legitimacy. *Data & Policy*, *2*, e16. DOI: 10.1017/dap.2020.19

Star, S. L., & Ruhleder, K. (1996). Steps Toward an Ecology of Infrastructure: Design and Access for Large Information Spaces. *Information Systems Research*, *7*(1), 111–134. https://www.jstor.org/stable/23010792. DOI: 10.1287/isre.7.1.111

Statistisk sentralbyrå. (n.d.). Dokumentasjon av KOSTRA. https://www.ssb.no/offentlig-sektor/kostra/statistikk/kostra-kommune-stat-rapportering/om-kostra/dokumentasjon-av-kostra

Stranz, H., Germundsson, N., Hussénius, K., & Bergmark, Å. (2024). Automatisering av ekonomiskt bistånd. *Socialvetenskaplig Tidskrift*, *31*(1), 7–27. DOI: 10.3384/SVT.2024.31.1.4869

Struminskaya, B., Lugtig, P., Toepoel, V., Schouten, B., Giesen, D., & Dolmans, R. (2021). Sharing smartphone sensor data. *Public Opinion Quarterly*, *85*(S1), 423–462. DOI: 10.1093/poq/nfab025 PMID: 34602867

Sztandar-Sztanderska, K., & Mazur, J. (2025). Politics and algorithmic articulation of law: Tracing the discrepancies and backstage decision-making in the development of the profiling algorithm in Polish labour market policies. *International Journal of Law in Context*, *21*(4), 1–20. DOI: 10.1017/S1744552325100141

Taddei, L., Biolcati Rinaldi, F., Biolcati Rinaldi, F., Heins, F., Marchesini, N., Paparusso, A., Pennacchiotti, C., Primerano, I., Piacentini, F., & Vezzoni, C. Santurro, M. (2026). The Italian way to an online probability panel. In L. Taddei & M. Paolucci (Eds.), *Longitudinal data infrastructures in Europe. Tools for Open Science in Social Science Research*. Springer.

Taddei, L., & Paolucci, M. (Eds.). (2026). *Longitudinal data infrastructures in Europe. Tools for Open Science in Social Science Research*. Springer. DOI: 10.1007/978-3-032-07005-0

Taylor, L. (2017). What is data justice? The case for connecting digital rights and freedoms globally. *Big Data & Society*, *4*(2), 1–14. DOI: 10.1177/2053951717736335

Thompson, N. C., Greenewald, K., Lee, K., & Manso, G. F. (2020).The computational limits of deep learning. *ArXiv*, arXiv:2007.05558.

Thottoli, M. M. (2024). Leveraging information communication technology (ICT) and artificial intelligence (AI) to enhance auditing practices. *Accounting Research Journal*, *37*(2), 134–150. DOI: 10.1108/ARJ-09-2023-0269

Tiwari, S. P., Kostenko, O., & Yekhanurov, Y. (2025). *Understanding technology in the context of national development: Critical reflections*. SciFormat Publishing. DOI: 10.69635/978-1-0690482-3-3

Toepoel, V., Luiten, A., & Zandvliet, R. (2021). Response willingness and data donation. *Survey Practice*, *14*(1), 1–19. Advance online publication. DOI: 10.29115/SP-2021-0005

Tomei, G., and Ziglioli, G. (forthcoming) Trust-enabled management, provision, and evaluation of public welfare services. Ambitions and questions from a paradigmatic Scandinavian experience. *Public Administration. An international quarterly*

Trezza, D. (2023). To scrape or not to scrape. *Frontiers in Sociology*, *8*, 1145038. Advance online publication. DOI: 10.3389/fsoc.2023.1145038 PMID: 37006635

Tsemberis, S. (2010). *Housing first: The Pathways model to end homelessness for people with mental illness and addiction*. Hazelden.

Tsemberis, S., & Eisenberg, R. F. (2000). Pathways to Housing: Supported housing for street-dwelling homeless individuals with psychiatric disabilities. *Psychiatric Services (Washington, D.C.)*, *51*(4), 487–493. DOI: 10.1176/appi.ps.51.4.487 PMID: 10737824

Tsemberis, S., Gulcur, L., & Nakae, M. (2004). Housing First, consumer choice, and harm reduction for homeless individuals with a dual diagnosis. *American Journal of Public Health*, *94*(4), 651–656. DOI: 10.2105/AJPH.94.4.651 PMID: 15054020

United Nations Educational, Scientific and Cultural Organization. (2021). Recommendation on the ethics of artificial intelligence.

University of Essex. (n.d.). *Understanding Society: Ethics and data security*.

Van Dijck, J., Poell, T., & De Waal, M. (2018). *The platform society: Public values in a connective world*. Oxford University Press. DOI: 10.1093/oso/9780190889760.001.0001

van Dijk, J. (2020). *The digital divide*. Polity.

van Dijk, J. A. G. M. (2005). The deepening divide: Inequality in the information society. *Sage (Atlanta, Ga.)*. Advance online publication. DOI: 10.4135/9781452229812

van Toorn, G., & Carney, T. (2025). Decoding the algorithmic operations of Australia's National Disability Insurance Scheme. *The Australian Journal of Social Issues*, *60*(1), 21–39. DOI: 10.1002/ajs4.342

van Toorn, G., Henman, P., & Soldatić, K. (2024). Introduction to the digital welfare state: Contestations, considerations and entanglements. *Journal of Sociology (Melbourne, Vic.)*, *60*(3), 507–522. DOI: 10.1177/14407833241260890

Van Toorn, G., & Soldatić, K. (2024). Disablism, racism and the spectre of eugenics in digital welfare. *Journal of Sociology (Melbourne, Vic.)*, *60*(3), 523–539. DOI: 10.1177/14407833241244828

van Zoonen, L. (2020). Data governance and citizen participation in the digital welfare state. *Data & Policy*, *2*, e10. DOI: 10.1017/dap.2020.10

Veale, M., & Binns, R. (2017). Fairer machine learning in the real world: Mitigating discrimination without collecting sensitive data. *Big Data & Society*, *4*(2), 1–17. DOI: 10.1177/2053951717743530

Veale, M., & Brass, I. (2019). Administration by algorithm? In *Algorithmic Regulation*. Oxford University Press. DOI: 10.1093/oso/9780198838494.003.0006

Veale, M., Van Kleek, M., & Binns, R. (2018). Algorithmic fairness in high-stakes public decisions. In *Proceedings of the 2018 CHI Conference on Human Factors in Computing Systems*. DOI: 10.1145/3173574.3174014

Wachter, S., Mittelstadt, B., & Floridi, L. (2017). Why a right to explanation of automated decision-making does not exist in the General Data Protection Regulation. *International Data Privacy Law, 7*(2), 76–99. DOI: 10.1093/idpl/ipx005

Wang, R., Harper, F. M., & Zhu, H. (2020). Factors influencing perceived fairness in algorithmic decision-making. In *Proceedings of the 2020 CHI Conference on Human Factors in Computing Systems* (pp. 1–14). DOI: 10.1145/3313831.3376813

Watson, C., Crivellaro, C., Parnaby, A. W., & Kharrufa, A. (2024, May). Hostile Systems: A Taxonomy of Harms Articulated by Citizens Living with Socio-Economic Deprivation. In *Proceedings of the 2024 CHI Conference on Human Factors in Computing Systems* (pp. 1-17). DOI: 10.1145/3613904.3642562

Webb, H., Koene, A., & Patel, M.. (2018). Multi-stakeholder dialogue for policy recommendations on algorithmic fairness. In *Proceedings of the 9th International Conference on Social Media and Society* (pp. 395–399). DOI: 10.1145/3217804.3217952

Weber, M. (1922). *Wirtschaft und Gessellschaft.* Tubinghen Mohr.

Weiss, C. H. (1997). Theory-based evaluation: Past, present, and future. *New Directions for Evaluation, 1997*(76), 41–55. DOI: 10.1002/ev.1086

White House. (2016). *Artificial intelligence, automation, and the economy.* Executive Office of the President.

Winner, L. (1980). Do artifacts have politics? *Daedalus, 109*(1), 121–136.

Xu, W. (2019). Toward Human-Centered AI: A Perspective from Human-Computer Interaction. I*NTERACTIONS. Interactions (New York, N.Y.), 2019*(4), 42–46. DOI: 10.1145/3328485

Yanow, D. (2000). Conducting interpretive policy analysis. *Sage (Atlanta, Ga.).*

Yeager, D. S., Krosnick, J. A., Chang, L., Javitz, H. S., Levendusky, M. S., Simpser, A., & Wang, R. (2011). Comparing survey modes. *Public Opinion Quarterly, 75*(4), 709–747. DOI: 10.1093/poq/nfr020

Yeung, K. (2018). Algorithmic regulation: A critical interrogation. *Regulation & Governance, 12*(4), 505–523. DOI: 10.1111/rego.12158

Zajko, M. (2023). Automated government benefits and welfare surveillance. *Surveillance & Society, 21*(3), 246–258. Advance online publication. DOI: 10.24908/ss.v21i3.16107

Zakharova, I., Jarke, J., & Kaun, A. (2024). Tensions in digital welfare states: Three perspectives on care and control. *Journal of Sociology (Melbourne, Vic.)*, *60*(3), 540–559. DOI: 10.1177/14407833241238312

Zelterman, D. (1988). Robust estimation in truncated discrete distributions with application to capture-recapture experiments. *Journal of Statistical Planning and Inference*, *18*(2), 225–237. DOI: 10.1016/0378-3758(88)90007-9

Zenkl, T. (2025). The taming of sociodigital anticipations: AI in the digital welfare state. *Frontiers in Sociology*, *10*, 1556675. DOI: 10.3389/fsoc.2025.1556675 PMID: 40438260

Zerilli, J., Knott, A., Maclaurin, J., & Gavaghan, C. (2019). Transparency in algorithmic and human decision-making: Is there a double standard? *Philosophy & Technology*, *32*(4), 661–683. DOI: 10.1007/s13347-018-0330-6

Zhang, B., & Dafoe, A. (2019). *U.S. public opinion on the governance of artificial intelligence*. Oxford: Future of Humanity Institute

Zittrain, J. (2018). How to exercise the power you didn't ask for. *Harvard Business Review*.

Zuboff, S. (2015). Big other: Surveillance capitalism and the prospects of an information civilization. *Journal of Information Technology*, *30*(1), 75–89. DOI: 10.1057/jit.2015.5

Zuiderwijk, A., & Janssen, M. (2014). Open data policies, their implementation and impact: A framework for comparison. *Government Information Quarterly*, *31*(1), 17–29. DOI: 10.1016/j.giq.2013.04.003

About the Contributors

Gabriella Punziano, Ph.D. in Sociology and Social Research, is an Associate Professor of General Sociology at the Department of Social Sciences, University of Naples Federico II, Italy, where she teaches methodological courses on mixed and digital methods. Her research interests include: social research methodology; mixed and digital approaches; social policies and welfare regimes; analysis of public, institutional, and political communication phenomena; risk communication analysis on social and digital platforms; socioeconomic effects on the Third Sector; changes in individual behaviors; risk governance; science communication; the role of experts in the Covid-19 era; algorithmic feedbackloop in cultural consumption, digital literacy and awerness. Among her recent publications are: with Velotti, L. and Addeo, F. (2022), Covid 19: Government Policies and Human Social Behavior in Italy, CRC PRESS, Routledge, Taylor & Francis Group, UK; with Delli Paoli, A. (2022), Handbook of Research on Advanced Research Methodologies for a Digital Society, IGI Global, Hershey, Pennsylvania, USA; with De Falco, C.C. and Trezza, D. (2022), "Digital mixed content analysis perspective for the study of digital platform social data: an application on the analysis of the COVID-19 risk perception in the Italian Twittersphere," in Journal of Mixed Methods Research, Sage, 16(2); with Padricelli, G.M., Vettori, A. (2025). Algorithmic feedback loops in soft science disciplines. The Lab's Quarterly, 27(3); alone (2025). Adaptive Epistemology: Embracing Generative AI as a Paradigm Shift in Social Science. Societies, 15, 205.

Domenico Trezza holds a PhD in Social Sciences and Statistics from the University of Naples Federico II. He works in the field of monitoring and evaluating educational policies and methods and techniques for data analysis. He is currently assistant professor of Social Research Methodology in the Department of Social Sciences at Federico II and consultant for Ifel Campania for monitoring the Scuola Viva programme.

Giuseppe Luca De Luca Picione is an associate Professor of General Sociology at the University of Naples Federico II, he is a member of the Executive Board of the Italian University Network for Lifelong Learning and Scientific Director of the MIUR Research Centre on Adult Education in Campania. Rector's delegate to the Italian University Network for Lifelong Learning, he teaches Social Innovation and Lifelong Learning, Social Media Data Analysis, Sociology of Criminal Organisations and Security Policies, AI & Public, Social and Political Communication SociaLab.

***

Francesco Amato, PhD in Social Sciences and Statistics, is a research fellow at the University of Naples Federico II. His research interests focus on the methodological and epistemological aspects of digital social research.

Gianmaria Bottoni is a Researcher (RTT) at the University of Naples Federico II. His research focuses on social cohesion, quality of life, survey methodology, comparative studies, and quantitative methods.

Luca Di Censi, PhD, is Scientific Advisor at Human Foundation – Do & Think Tank for Social Innovation and collaborates in the teaching and research activities of the Department of Communication and Social Research at Sapienza University of Rome. He has participated in numerous research projects at both the national and European levels. Email: luca.dicensi@uniroma1.it

Lokeshwari D. V. is an Assistant Professor in the Department of Commerce and Management at Dayananda Sagar College of Arts, Science, and Commerce, Bengaluru, India, with more than seven years of experience in teaching and academic administration. She has taught across undergraduate and postgraduate programmes and has held key institutional roles, including AICTE Coordinator, Placement Officer, BBA Programme Coordinator, IQAC Committee Member, and PG Department In-Charge (M.Com.). She is an active researcher with publications in reputed journals, conference proceedings, books, and book chapters, and holds two patents. Her research focuses on financial literacy, sustainable finance, artificial intelligence in financial inclusion, behavioural finance, and educational technology. She also contributes to the scholarly community as a reviewer and invited speaker at academic and professional forums.

Maria Paola Faggiano, PhD in Social Science Methodology, is an Associate Professor of General Sociology at the Department of Communication and Social Research (CoRiS), Sapienza University of Rome, Italy. At the same department, she coordinates the Electoral Sociology Observatory "G. Statera" and serves as the scientific director of the Communication and Social Research Laboratory (CorisLab). She has published numerous contributions and articles in national and international journals on methodological and sociological topics. Email: mariapaola.faggiano@uniroma1.it

Giovanni Antonio Forte is an expert on the subject Metodologia e Tecniche per l'analisi della Comunicazione e dei Media Digitali, High Qualification Officer and Head of the municipal library of City of Casoria. Euro-Phd on Socio-economic and statistical studies, Univerisity of Rome, la Sapienza.

Basker G is a faculty member in the Department of Computer Science at KPR College of Arts, Science and Research. He is actively involved in teaching and academic development, with academic interests in computer science, emerging technologies, and practical computing applications. He is dedicated to mentoring students, contributing to curriculum development, and supporting institutional academic and research initiatives.

Senthilkumar G is a faculty member in the Department of Electronics at Sri Ramakrishna College of Arts and Science. He is actively involved in teaching and academic development, with a strong interest in electronics, emerging technologies, and student-centric learning. His professional focus includes curriculum enrichment, mentoring students, and contributing to institutional academic initiatives. Through his dedication to education and continuous learning, he strives to bridge theoretical concepts with practical applications in the field of electronics.

J. Viji Gripsy is an accomplished academician and researcher serving as the Head of the Department of Computer Science with Cognitive Systems at PSGR Krishnammal College for Women, Tamil Nadu. With over a decade of teaching and research experience, her expertise lies in mobile networks, wireless communication, and network security. She holds M.Sc., M.Phil., Ph.D., and Postdoctoral qualifications, and has contributed extensively to academia through numerous journal publications, book chapters, and research projects. Dr. Viji Gripsy has also received multiple recognitions, including Best Faculty Awards, and actively participates in curriculum development, academic boards, and professional engagements, reflecting her commitment to advancing research, innovation, and quality education.

Ferdinando Iazzetta, PhD, is a sociologist and holds a PhD in European History from Sapienza University of Rome. He currently collaborates with the University of Naples Federico II and the University of Rome "Foro Italico" on national research projects exploring the relationships between health, nutrition, social behaviours, and digital transformations. His research interests focus on the sociology of health and lifestyles, social inequalities, sustainability, and well-being, with particular attention to the cultural and territorial dimensions of health. He also works on science and political communication, with a specific interest in public participation and representation in contemporary digital environments.

Vincenzo Laezza, Ph.D. candidate in Social and Statistical Sciences at the University of Naples Federico II. His research focuses on generative AI at the intersection of platform studies, political economy of technology and computational social science.

L. Sheeba Lakshamana is an accomplished faculty member in the Department of BCA at PSGR Krishnammal College for Women, with significant contributions to teaching, research, and academic development. Her research interests span areas such as computer networks, network security, intrusion detection systems, machine learning applications, IoT, and emerging trends in computing. She has published numerous research articles in reputed journals and conference proceedings and has also authored books and academic manuals on programming and data analysis tools. She is actively involved in curriculum enrichment, student mentoring, and professional development activities, and is committed to promoting research-driven and application-oriented learning.

PraneeshM. is an academician in the Department of Computer Science with Data Analytics at Sri Ramakrishna College of Arts and Science. He is actively involved in teaching, research, and mentoring students in areas such as data analytics, machine learning, and emerging computing technologies. With a strong commitment to academic excellence, he contributes to curriculum development and promotes innovative learning practices. His research interests include data-driven decision-making, artificial intelligence, and real-world analytics applications, and he has participated in various academic initiatives, workshops, and collaborative projects aimed at enhancing students' technical and analytical skills.

Sergio Mauceri, PhD, is Full Professor of General Sociology in the Department of Communication and Social Research at Sapienza University of Rome, where he teaches Social Research Methodology and Research Strategies for Innovative Organizations, and serves as Director of the inter-university second-level Master's programme in Methodology and Advanced Techniques of Social Research (Me-TARS). He has published numerous contributions and articles in national and international journals on methodological and sociological topics. Email: sergio.mauceri@uniroma1.it

Kamalam KS is a dedicated Assistant Professor in the Department of Computer Applications at PSGR Krishnammal College for Women, Coimbatore. With a strong academic background and a passion for teaching, she has made significant contributions to the field of computer science through research, publications, and academic guidance. Her areas of interest include data analytics, machine learning, and cloud computing. Dr. Kamalam is known for her commitment to student-centered learning and active participation in departmental activities, workshops, and curriculum development. Her blend of academic rigor and practical insight continues to inspire and empower young women in the tech domain.

Luciana Taddei is a methodologist specializing in advanced social research. She earned her degree from the University of Rome "La Sapienza" and completed her PhD through a joint program between the University of Genoa and the Universidad Nacional de Tres de Febrero (UNTREF) in Buenos Aires. She teaches at the University "Magna Græcia" of Catanzaro and the University of Calabria. Her work focuses on survey and mixed methods, digital data integration, longitudinal studies, and social science research infrastructures, with particular attention to Open Science and a thematic interest in well-being and sports research. At the National Research Council (CNR-IRPPS), she contributed to the FOSSR project, helping to develop the first Italian Online Probability Panel. She has authored over 50 scientific publications and co-edited, with Marco Paolucci, Longitudinal Data Infrastructures in Europe (Springer, 2026). Since 2026, she has been a researcher at the Italian National Institute of Statistics (Istat).

Index

A

C

D

E

G

I

L

P

R

S

T

W

www.ingramcontent.com/pod-product-compliance
Lightning Source LLC
LaVergne TN
LVHW080902300926
849162LV00003B/522